Group
Counseling

Group
Counseling
Third Edition

Merle M. Ohlsen, *Ph.D*
Indiana State University
and University of Illinois

Arthur M. Horne, *Ph.D*
Indiana State University

Charles F. Lawe, *Ph.D.*
Emory University

With a foreword by G. M. Gazda, The University of Georgia

HOLT, RINEHART AND WINSTON, INC.

New York   Chicago   San Francisco   Philadelphia
Montreal   Toronto   London   Sydney   Tokyo

DEDICATION

We dedicate this book to the faculty, staff, students, and alumni of the Department of Counseling of Indiana State University, and to the memory of Carl Rogers, a person who touched our lives and contributed to the betterment of humanity.

The following publishers have granted permission to quote from their publications on the pages listed.
Pp. 109, 128 reprinted with permission from F. H. Kanfer and A. P. Goldstein, *Helping People Change*, copyright 1986, Pergamon Books Ltd.
Pp. 198, 200, 201 from *On Death and Dying* by Elisabeth Kübler-Ross. Reprinted by permission of Macmillan Publishing Company.
Pp. 108, 149, 161, 162, 171-173 from *The Theory and Practice of Group Psychotherapy* by Irvin D. Yalom. Copyright ©1970, 1975, 1985 by Basic Books, Inc. Reprinted by permission of Basic Books, Inc., Publishers.

Printed in the United States of America

8901   118   98765432

Library of Congress Cataloging-in-Publication Data

Ohlsen, Merle M.
   Group Counseling

   Bibliography: p
   Includes indexes.
   1. Group counseling.   I. Horne, Arthur M., 1942–
II. Lawe, Charles F.   III. Title.   [DNLM: 1. Counseling
2. Psychotherapy, Group.   WM 430 032g]
   BF637.C6048   1988   158'.3   87-17599

ISBN 0-03-008464-4

Holt, Rinehart and Winston, Inc.
The Dryden Press
Saunders College Publishing

FOREWORD

It is a rare privilege to write the foreword to a major publication of my former Major Professor, Merle M. Ohlsen.

The third edition of *Group Counseling* by Merle M. Ohlsen and his co-authors, Arthur M. Horne and Charles F. Lawe, represents a significant modification and enlargement of the second edition. This edition contains seventeen chapters versus fourteen in the second edition. In fact there are six new chapters with three of the chapters in the second edition being incorporated in other chapters. Of the six new chapters, four represent additions that I believe fully complete coverage of the group counseling field and fill voids in the second edition.

I am particularly pleased to see the additions of the following chapters: Theories of Treatment, Counseling Adults in Groups, Working with Structured Groups, and Professional Preparation and Ethical Guidelines. With the addition of these chapters, *Group Counseling* becomes one of the most comprehensive texts available.

Ohlsen's enthusiasm for group counseling continues to show throughout this text. I say, "continues to show," because Ohlsen's enthusiasm for his profession and especially group counseling has motivated me and countless other students to become counselors and educators of counselors, and especially group counselors. In addition to Ohlsen's enthusiasm for whatever he does, he also believes in comprehensively studying and documenting his work. Ohlsen and his co-authors have pooled their talents to provide the field with a very scholarly publication.

What can one expect from *Group Counseling* (third edition)? The authors take an eclectic position that is based on a multi-intervention model. Their position is that to effect change in individuals with a variety of problems requires a variety of interventions from a variety of theoretical models with their differing intervention strategies. The background for interventions is built on a comprehensive discussion of group dynamics and group processes. Methods for selecting and orienting group counselors are presented in detail. Cases are included throughout the text to illustrate the point being made or the position taken. Special procedures for children, adolescents, and adults are described and documented. The text closes appropriately with chapters on appraisals of group counseling and professional preparation and ethical guidelines.

Although the text addresses the application of group counseling to all age groups in various settings, the thrust appears to be on adolescents and young adults in educational settings. For this reason, it is especially valuable for training school counselors but is certainly not limited to this group, as exemplified by the chapters on Counseling Adults in Groups, Working with Structured Groups, and a chapter segment on marriage and family therapy.

Whether or not one agrees (and I do) with the eclectic position taken by the authors of *Group Counseling*, it is such a comprehensive and thoroughly documented text any serious student should study it. I am especially pleased to endorse this scholarly contribution to the speciality field of group counseling.

G. M. Gazda, Ed.D.

PREFACE

Group Counseling was first published in 1970. The first edition represented the current state of the art of group counseling, as well as a description of the group counseling model practiced by Merle Ohlsen. The book gained very good acceptance in colleges, universities, training centers, and human service sites both in the United States and abroad. In 1977 the second edition of the text was published, representing an updating of group counseling from the literature and practice as well as a description of the evolving practice of Merle Ohlsen. The second edition also served as a primary text for group counseling courses and for practica in group counseling.

For this, the third edition, the publisher conducted a survey of professionals who regularly use *Group Counseling* to elicit their recommendations for change. They provided the authors with very helpful suggestions which were incorporated into this edition.

Whereas the earlier editions were designed for counselors who treat primarily reasonably healthy clients, this edition introduces case materials to illustrate how the approach also can be used to treat clients who require remediation as well as developmental counseling. In other words, the book is designed for graduate students in psychology as well as counselor education.

Like its predecessors this edition stresses teaching clients to recognize their pain, to discuss it openly in their counseling group, to define precise goals, to develop the self-confidence and skills required to implement their desired new behavior, and to seek significant others' reinforcement of these new behaviors. Clients learn to take responsibility for themselves, to help others, and to solicit and provide quality support.

The book presents the writers' model of working with groups. They have developed the book as though they are working directly with their students, for they have found their clearest, most effective writing occurs when they have specific students in mind and address their points to them. Feedback on previous editions has indicated that the writing style, the clarity of presentations, and the examples have been particular strengths of those editions; they have attempted to maintain those strengths.

This book begins with a discussion of the helping process from a group perspective. It is assumed students will have completed at least a basic counseling techniques course and mastered basic counseling skills. The focus of Chapter 1, then, is upon the process of helping clients in a group—the chapter presents an overview of the model we use.

Chapters 2, 3, and 4 introduce the student to group theory from the perspective of group applications of major counseling and psychotherapy approaches, as well as group processes, such as leadership style, group stages, and skill development techniques. Chapter 4 reviews the therapeutic forces of groups and describes how the model incorporates aspects of several theories and processes.

Chapter 5 describes the client problem classification that has been developed to help clients cope with these problems. Chapter 6 illustrates how the authors use the problem classification to develop precise goals specific to the individuals who will be participating in group counseling. They believe that goals must be tailored to the individual client's needs.

The above chapters have identified major theories of counseling and psychotherapy, described the models which they use, discussed client selection and goals development: all components leading up to and beginning a group. The next chapters describe particular aspects of groups once they have begun. Chapter 7 explains resistance and how to handle it within a group setting; Chapter 8 deals with transference and countertransference. The next three chapters discuss the problems of treating certain clients in groups; the emotionally debilitated (Chapter 9); the other-controlled (10), and the reluctant (11). Chapter 12 describes specific alterations to be made when counseling children in groups, while Chapter 13 does the same with adolescents and Chapter 14 with adults.

Chapter 15 addresses the alterations needed to work with skill-specific groups, such as weight management, stress control, and stop-smoking.

Chapter 16 addresses professional issues within the group counseling framework, and defines the ethical guidelines from which group counselors must operate.

Chapter 17 deals with appraisal in group counseling from two perspectives; (1) how a practitioner will develop a process of assessing his or her effectiveness as a group leader; (2) how effective group counseling is based upon research in the field as well as directions research should be going to enable group counseling to become a more firmly established method within the counselor's skill repertoire. Following Chapter 17 an appendix presents ASGW/AACD ethical guidelines.

This book is designed to encourage counselor educators and psychologists to select students for admission to preparation in group counseling with great care, nurture their development during graduate education, and persuade them to continue their personal as well as professional growth following completion of their graduate program. Peer supervision on the job is encouraged to further such continuing growth; so is research. Both motivate counselors to appraise the worth of various approaches for whom under what circumstances and to seek out new ways of helping their clients.

A. M. HORNE

CONTENTS

Chapter 3
PROCEDURES FOR GROUP COUNSELING   80

Chapter 4
THERAPEUTIC FORCES IN A COUNSELING GROUP   107

Chapter 5
LABELING CLIENTS' PROBLEMS   127

Chapter 6
CLIENT'S COUNSELING GOALS   144

Chapter 7
RESISTANCE   161

Chapter 8
TRANSFERENCE AND COUNTERTRANSFERENCE   179

Chapter 17
PROFESSIONAL PREPARATION AND ETHICAL
GUIDELINES   378

1

GROUP COUNSELING: A HELPING PROCESS

Counseling is an accepting, trusting, and safe relationship in which clients learn to discuss openly what worries and concerns them; to define precise goals for change; to acquire essential skills for effecting change; and to develop the courage and self-confidence to implement desired new behaviors. Counseling may take a variety of forms and characteristics, including:

- individual or group
- open topics or clearly specified areas of concern
- settings within schools, clinics, homes, or other

This book is about group counseling, a special form of counseling. The model presented in this book is appropriate for working with a variety of ages; in a broad range of settings; dealing with the numerous problem areas that counselees experience; and with a variety of techniques and methods available. The group-counseling approach has evolved into a therapeutic intervention process that has many advantages for the counselees who are served, as well as for the institution or agency in which the services are delivered.

WHY GROUP COUNSELING?

Group counseling is a helping process that provides the opportunity for counselees to identify goals of change; to develop skills necessary to achieve those goals; and to practice those skills within a safe, structured setting. As counselees successfully implement their desired new behaviors, they report their successes to fellow clients. When they fail, they feel sufficiently secure within their group to review frankly what has happened, soliciting feedback from the other group members and deciding whether to try a new solution or to figure out how to make the unsuccessful one work. Parents, teachers, and friends may not notice the change that counselees have made and may, therefore, fail to provide

1

support and encouragement; whereas the group members will be able to provide the support and encouragement counselees need to maintain their growth.

Counselees also learn to assist their fellow counselees while accepting assistance in return; to develop the courage to act while they are exploring alternate solutions and learning new interpersonal skills; and to accept and give frank, yet considerate, feedback to fellow counselees. When group members discover they can trust their counselor and fellow group members, they are more likely to give up façades, talk openly about themselves and their problems, learn to accept themselves, dare to implement desired new behaviors, and encourage others to take such risks, too. During this process, the counselor supplements what she has tried to communicate to her prospective clients in describing group counseling and the process of selecting clients for the group; clarifies what counselees may expect from her and from each other; teaches them to be helpers as well as helpees while reinforcing client modeling for both these behaviors; and conveys her commitment to help them change. As the therapeutic potency of the counseling group increases, the counselees' personal respect for each other grows; and, consequently, they learn to tolerate individual differences and to accept different solutions to similar problems. They also learn to accept responsibility for their own growth and for helping their counselor develop and maintain a therapeutic climate.

Many counselees find it easier to discuss their problems openly in group counseling than in individual counseling. When counselees observe others discussing their problems openly, sense others' acceptance of those who can talk openly, and realize the extent to which their peers can understand and help each other, they are encouraged to discuss their problems also. They value the feedback of group members. They are even more encouraged when they notice their behavior changes. On the other hand, they note that members can put pressure on those who talk but fail to act. Nevertheless, reluctant clients do not seem to react as negatively in the group setting as they do when teachers, parents, spouses, employers, or others exert pressure to behave more appropriately. Perhaps it is because fellow counselees seem to push their members toward their own goals rather than others' goals for them.

Some readers may conclude that counseling groups develop into ongoing, continuing relationships. While some authors, such as Bach (1954) and Mowrer (1973) encourage continuing relationships, membership in a counseling group should be looked upon as a temporary relationship. Counseling groups are formed to assist counselees in learning to resolve their problems (including the inability to develop and maintain meaningful relationships with significant others) and, where desirable, to select and develop new relationships. While they learn to care for fellow group members, successful counselees recognize that fellow clients cannot and should not be substituted for their significant others outside of counseling. When they fail to develop meaningful relationships outside of counseling, counselees tend to seek group treatment periodically, in order to re-experience closeness and intimacy. They must, instead, use their time in counseling to learn more adaptive ways of coping with the forces within their real world.

Lieberman, Yalom, and Miles (1973) found that those who profited most from their group experiences perceived their group therapy relationships as temporary, and applied what they learned within their treatment groups outside. These authors present therapy groups as social oases where people can drop the façade of competence demanded by a fast-moving, competitive society and discuss their doubts, fears, and disappointments (Lieberman et al., 1973). Their most-successful clients learned to be more trusting, open, honest; to give and accept forthright feedback; to recognize the curvilinear nature of openness (when and with whom too much or too little openness jeopardizes human relationships); and to apply a humanistic view of people more consistently in order to encourage personal development. Though models discovered in their treatment groups (including the leader) had a great impact upon them, clients tended to become more inner-directed; perhaps they developed more confidence in their own judgments and used models selectively.

A MODEL FOR UNDERSTANDING COUNSELEES

Prior to discussing group counseling as a model for helping people change, it is important to understand how and why people are as they are. Many theories exist that explain human development, personality development, and dysfunctional behavior. A number of theories of counseling have evolved over the years to assist counselors in forming a framework for understanding clients' behavior and for providing a means to effect change in their clients' lives. Based upon our study and use of these various theories, the model presented here represents our explanation of how counselees become as they are.

Learning as Living

The lives we live take the form and shape they do through the sundry learning experiences we have from birth through death. The learning process is influenced by many factors, including the genetic inheritance we bring with us and the environmental circumstances of our families; but our learning process determines how we will live with the circumstances of our heredity and environment.

Learning occurs in response to social circumstances. All people are born with social interests, a desire for and a valuing of social contact, though some seem to find social interaction more satisfying than others. It is through social interactions that we learn our skills of living, our values and beliefs, and our sense of self.

Modeling

One form of social learning is modeling. By observing the behaviors of others, models, we develop skills and attitudes. Modeling may be direct, as in the way children observe their parents and begin to develop patterns of behavior modeled after parental interactions (mommies do X, daddies do Y; mommies cry, daddies don't). The work of social learning theorists such as Bandura (1977) indicates that observing people is a very powerful learning mechanism. Vicarious learning through observing models indirectly may be just as powerful. Examples we see on television, in films, or read about in books are able to influence our beliefs and attitudes shaping the way we behave and interact. This is clearly evidenced by the high value placed on advertising in our society. Advertising assumes that, through the modeling of some behavior sponsors wish increased, consumers will in fact follow through in their behavior.

Reinforcement

Modeling works effectively as a learning process because people wish to increase the positive aspects of their lives and reduce the negative. By observing others, models, we are able to see ways in which they handle situations; and by engaging in similar actions, we may be able to be as successful as the models themselves in performing acts we wish to be able to do, or to gain the reinforcers the models have received. When the child mimics a parent and then gets an approving tousle of the head, the mimicking behavior tends to become an established pattern of behavior for it has produced positive results. Similarly, if a child mimics a parent's actions and is ignored or rebuffed, the child is likely to decide to avoid that pattern of behavior in the future since it does not yield positive payoffs. That does not mean the behavioral repertoire has not become a part of the child's behavioral potential, but rather that the child has decided that engaging in that behavior is not rewarding currently. All of us know how to engage in behaviors that we choose not to use (burglary, murder, going over Niagara Falls). While we may have the skill, we do not have the values—the belief that the behavior would yield positive results for us—and so we choose not to follow through behaviorally with what we know.

Social Exchange

Akin to reinforcement is social exchange theory. The assumption in operation in social exchange theory is that people engage in social interactions because of the anticipation of reciprocal payoffs. That is, people interact—work and live together—with the expectation that there will be a payoff for the interaction. The payoff may take many forms:

- financial, as in our work relationships

- intimacy, as in our marital or friendship groups
- prestige, as in the pride we take in our accomplishments
- sex, as in particularly satisfying experiences
- fun, as in certain activities or with preferred individuals
- security, as in avoiding pain rather than taking risks

While the payoff may not be obvious to the observer, people do not remain in social relationships without some expectation of benefit. From a counseling perspective, our task frequently is to identify what the benefit, or anticipated benefit, is and to help clients identify whether their expectations are being fulfilled or whether alternative payoffs might be more appropriate.

Relationships are said to be reciprocal when both people in the relationship give and receive. When the relationship becomes unbalanced, when one gives and the other receives, then the system is unlikely to continue without some compensating arrangements. For example, the relationship may be unbalanced for some time: as when one spouse works to put the other through school, but anticipates that equality of opportunity will occur upon graduation so that both will benefit from the experience. But when reciprocity is not a part of the relationship, either it ends or an unhealthy interaction develops: as in the case of spouse abuse, where one spouse is abused and wants out of the marriage but sees no options financially or socially. One function of counseling is to help people identify and open up their options for living.

The Process of Change

In order to help counselees effect the changes in the lives they wish to have, it is important to understand and work with them on the following: behavior, affect, cognitions, environment, history, and biology. (In Chapter 5 we identify ways of labeling counselees' problems which will incorporate these.)

Behavior

People do things. The things they do we call their behavior. Some behavior is very effective in helping us function in our daily lives while other behavior is, at best, irrelevant and, at worst, very destructive. Most people enter counseling because of what they are doing (excesses in behavior, such as temper tantrums, excessive drinking or eating) or are not doing (deficiencies in behavior, such as sexual inadequacy, poor study habits, inadequate social-interaction ability). A goal of counseling is to help counselees identify goals for behavior change and establish a program for bringing about the desired changes. It is important to be clear about the behavior to be addressed, for this is a measurable variable: we can identify a base level of functioning upon entry and then identify how much change has occurred at the end of counseling. A clear understanding of what people *do* is essential to effective counseling.

Affect

The second major reason people enter counseling is because they do not feel happy or fulfilled in their lives. Affect refers to how people feel emotionally. Affect can also be seen in excesses (too much anger, too much sadness) and in deficits (feelings of inadequacy, not being loved). While some approaches to counseling do not attend to affect because the emphasis is on behavior change, counselees are very unlikely to change until they feel they are understood and that their emotional state is appreciated by the counselor.

Cognitions

People think. They have beliefs and attitudes. These characteristics, referred to as cognitions, are as important in understanding counselees as is behavior and affect. Understanding the phenomenological field of the counselee, the way that person perceives the world, is crucial in understanding the behavior and feelings the person manifests; for it is through an awareness of their perceptions that their behavior begins to have meaning.

Two people are likely to respond to an identical situation in different behavioral and affective ways. This is because they perceive the situation differently. Some people at an oceanside picnic may be in awe of the sun setting, while others may be distressed because their light is being lost. Both groups see the same sunset, but respond differently, based upon their cognitive interpretation of the situation. A number of writers have described the importance of understanding cognitions, including Ellis (1984), Beck (1976), and Meichenbaum (1977). A simplified version of the relationship of behavior and affect cognitions is as follows:

- A situation occurs.
- The person thinks about the situation.
- Based upon what the person thinks, feelings develop.
- The person behaves consistently with the feelings.
- Based upon the behavior, consequences occur.

With the example of the sunset, a person may be aware the sun is setting and begin thinking about the beauty of nature and how fortunate one is to be able to observe and participate in the experience. He is then likely to have comfortable, relaxed feelings, and will behave in a warm and friendly manner with those around, who are then likely to respond in a reciprocal manner. The person, however, who perceives the sun going down as a loss of light may begin thinking how much more difficult that may make matters in preparing the food. This perception can lead to anger, and angry people generally behave in angry ways. As the person becomes angry, the behavior may be seen in a negative way, or in a fearful way, by others who will then provide consequences. The same stimulus, a sunset, results in two very different consequences because of the different perceptions and thought processes of the people involved.

Environment

Behavior, feelings, and thoughts do not occur in isolation; and the environment takes many different forms. The difficulties counselees experience may be general, occurring in all environments (such as fear of people, lack of social skills with all people), or may be situation specific (such as difficulty getting along at work or at school, fear of flying). It is important to understand the environmental context of people's behavior in order to understand what maintains the inappropriate way they handle situations. Many theorists refer to the environment as a system and identify multiple systems that people may be a part of, including:

- *Family.* Within the family system, the person may be a member of a couples system (husband); a parent system (son to his parents, father to his son); a sibling system (brother to his brothers and sisters); and any combination of other subsystems that may develop.
- *Work.* Within work systems there are a number of different subsystems based upon the line and staff functions, the hierarchical nature of the organization, and the purpose of the business.
- *School.* Again, within each major system, subsystems develop.

To be effective, counselors must understand systems and the functional nature of relationships within systems. While behavior may be inappropriate and even severely dysfunctional, if it has continued for some time, then it serves a purpose within the system and helps to maintain the system. Behavior change is unlikely within a system without attention to the aspects of the system which maintain the behavior. Therefore, counselors will attend to the impact of the individual on the environment, but also the impact of the environment on the individual. One does not change without the other: there is a reciprocity that maintains each. Behavior influences the environment, and the environment influences the behavior, in a reciprocal manner.

History

History does not cause people to behave the way they do. Rather, people behave today the way they do because of how they have learned to behave in the past, the beliefs and attitudes they developed previously, and the way they interacted with the environment, the system, as they became who they now are. Some theorists ignore the role of history on the individual, stating that history is not important. The background of the individual is important to the extent that it helps us understand how the person came to be as he is today, or what maintains that person in dysfunctional patterns.

History may be defined as an element of cognition: that history is only important to the extent that it influences the beliefs and perceptions of the person today. This leads us to helping the counselee identify what is of importance in the past, how that has influenced him to be what he is today behaviorally and affectively, and can suggest ways of intervening. Examples may include:

Family Constellation.   The work of the Adlerian movement to help identify the importance of one's lifestyle through the family constellation has contributed substantially to our understanding of how people perceive themselves in relation to their family of origin and their current family. One's position in the family of origin may play a determining role in how a person perceives himself in his current life. Ignoring family background would miss this important information (Ansbacher, 1972).

Unfinished Business.   People oftentimes have unfinished business with people from their past. Understanding the context of this, the meaning it has for counselees, has to be addressed rather than ignored, for the historical context of the situation determines how the person behaves and feels today.

Irrational Beliefs.   Many of the irrational beliefs people have were learned in a historical context that must be recognized and addressed. While behavioral skills learning may teach new ways of handling situations, if the beliefs related to the skills do not change also, then the skills will not be maintained. And if the beliefs are not tied to the historical context in which they were learned, they will not be as readily changed. An example of this shows a person with a signature phobia: he couldn't sign his name in public. The phobia was traced to the irrational belief of having to be perfect, to always be a positive reflection on his politically prominent family. This was put into historical context of the father always being critical and demanding perfection in everything of a public nature. The historical context, combined with addressing the irrational belief, followed with assertiveness training and desensitization, led to effective change. Previous attempts by desensitization alone had been ineffective.

Understanding history does not mean that a counselor has to spend extensive time on history taking. Rather, it means that as the counselor works, attention will be paid to the historical context in which behavior, feelings, and beliefs have developed, as well as the environmental system that maintains the inappropriate/dysfunctional pattern today.

Biology

Counselors cannot change biology, heredity. People are born with certain characteristics that are beyond control to change: sex, race, physical handicaps, intellectual level, illnesses. However, it is important to understand the role that heredity and biology play in determining how the person lives today. While sex does not cause people to have a particular personality pattern, for example, it does impact how the person will be seen in and will see the world. While it is important for counselors to have a firm understanding of how individuals see themselves in the context of their biological heritage, it is also important that they have a firm grounding in human development, multicultural counseling, and the impact of handicaps upon the personality development of individuals. While we work with people as they are biologically, we must be aware of the impact of their biology on their development.

People want to be understood; and counselors who ignore the biological contributions to current behavior are not showing respect for clients. The affirmation of understanding does not have to be extensive, but it must be made. In a family therapy project we have conducted for parents with attention-deficit disorder children, it has been very important to acknowledge the contribution of biology to the current behavior of the children before attempting to move to skill development. It has become very important to say:

> Since Billy is an attention-deficit disorder child, you have had a lot of turmoil in your lives. This has caused stress throughout the family, with all of you suffering, including Billy, because he has this problem. What we want to do with you is help you learn more effective ways of dealing with Billy's behavior, ways of handling him differently than you now are able to do. In the process, each of you will change because as the household becomes less aversive, you will be able to relate to each other more positively. And that, while not erasing Billy's attention-deficit disorder, will help him to be more effective at home and school.

In sum, the six areas of understanding counselees are not exclusive in any way. Rather, they all function together to help us develop an understanding, a picture, of the person behaviorally, internally (affect, cognitions), externally (environment), and experientially (history, biology). Alfred Adler called his therapy *individual psychology* because he wanted to understand and work with the total individual, not with a part. Frederick Perls called his form of treatment *Gestalt therapy* because he wanted to study the total gestalt, the total person. And Arnold Lazarus, even more recently, identified the importance of working with all aspects of a person when he described his multi-model approach to therapy. The model we are presenting advocates the same, to work with the total person. To do so requires an understanding of how the areas function together to create the person who presents himself as a counselee to us.

COUNSELING IN A GROUP CONTEXT

Helping people change can take many forms. Group counseling is particularly effective as a form of intervention for many people, particularly in light of the process of helping people change, as described above. Since behavior is learned in a social context, changing within a social context is very natural. The group provides many opportunities, consistent with the model presented, for helping change occur.

Group Counseling versus Individual Counseling

The Nature of Learning.   People learn in a social context. While individual counseling allows for learning to occur, it is likely to be quicker and more powerful in a group setting; for in the group, an individual has peers who are more likely to confront him in a setting where helping behavior is expected. A person is less likely to learn effective social skills, assertiveness behavior, and similar social abilities in a one-to-one relationship than in a group context. Also, the best of counselors will miss some important material being presented, but in a group setting there are many more sets of ears listening for the therapeutic material being presented. Any particular bias of the counselor will be clearer in a group context in which other people are participants.

Social Support.   While individual counseling can provide a supportive relationship, the group membership can provide a far broader level of support. The support in individual work is from one person, and that person is in an authority role. Whereas in the group, the members can provide a larger base of encouragement and validation, while still allowing the authoritative endorsement of the counselor.

New Behaviors.   In individual counseling responsibility of developing ideas and suggestions for change reside in the counselor and client. In the group, the membership becomes a valuable resource in developing suggestions for change and procedures for bringing about the changes. In the groups, described previously, for parents of attention-deficit disorder children, the parents have been able to generate considerably more ideas for management and change processes than have the counselors.

Therapy Skills.   While the purpose of group counseling is to provide assistance to counselees in need of help, group counseling also emphasizes the therapeutic nature of helping. All counselees are expected to learn and use skills of listening, problem solving, and ways of identifying the effectiveness of the group work. People help each other. In the process they learn helping skills for themselves to use with their significant life partners and acquaintances, and they learn to apply those skills to solving their own problems. Clients are recognized for their contributions and develop leadership skills and abilities as contributors to their social group.

Peer Confrontation. While counselees sometimes challenge or resist input from the counselor, it is more difficult to ignore input from group members. The other members of a group are peers in status, all are clients in a group setting. While counselor comments may be discounted as being authoritarian, establishment/institution oriented, or old-fashioned, peer comments cannot as easily be dismissed. It is our experience that counselees are more likely to accept feedback, both negative and positive, from peers within a group than from individual counselors.

A Variety of Roles. In individual counseling all roles to be examined are left to the abilities of the counselor and counselee. In the group setting there are more people, and they can serve as models, coaches, role players, and peers. The potential for role playing and for developing modeling experiences becomes greatly expanded.

Group Norms Develop. In a group setting norms for appropriate behavior develop and people tend to conform to those norms. Those who do not conform are confronted by the group and the confrontation itself can become a therapeutic matter to be addressed by the group. Thus, they learn from peers the consequences of rejecting group norms, how to participate in changing the norms, and what is to be gained by conforming. Most members require agreement on norms pertaining to confidentiality, self-disclosure, peer support, encouraging problem solving, helping define alternatives for change and growth, and adhering to group-established rules, such as confidentiality. Norms can develop that are counter-productive, such as being competitive, not completing assignments, being critical. It is the counselor's responsibility to be aware of the nontherapeutic norms developing and present these as a group issue to be dealt with as a counseling issue for all.

Counselor Bias. All counselors bring their values to counseling. There are few checks and balances in individual counseling for the values of the counselor. On the other hand, in a group setting, the counselor's values, beliefs, perceptions, and goals are more public and do face the scrutiny of a visible audience rather than the evaluation of a single individual.

Less Costly. While cost should be the least important factor, still counselors may impact a significantly larger number of people in a shorter period of time in a group setting than is possible in individual work. In institutional settings where counselor time and facilities are limited, such as schools, community mental-health centers, and university counseling centers, counseling groups provide for an economical delivery of services.

GROUP COUNSELING: SPECIFIC FEATURES

There are numerous models for helping people in groups, ranging from teaching a class to intensive long-term group psychotherapy. There are highly structured skill-oriented groups, such as weight-loss programs, and very unstructured open-ended offerings such as sensitivity or growth groups. The following queries present some specific features of the model of group counseling that we teach.

1. *Where does group counseling fall on the continuum of the learning or educational model versus the medical treatment model?* As was indicated in the above discussion of how people become as they are, we base our work upon the learning model. We believe that people learn to be as they are through interactions with family, school, work, and other social settings. Therefore, rather than treat the person who seeks help as a patient with an illness, we choose to work with people who seek assistance when they recognize that their learned behaviors are not enabling them to function satisfactorily or that they are confronted with developmental tasks with which they have not learned to cope. While most people coming for help are not able to state clearly what assistance they need, we have found that the problems people bring to counseling are concerns that can be addressed through the broad learning approach described.

2. *How does counseling differ from psychotherapy?* Psychotherapy is a process designed to bring about personality restructuring and to deal with persons who are so severely emotionally disturbed as to be unable to function effectively in society. It is a long-term relationship that requires intensive sessions in both number and emotional level of involvement. Group counseling is a process designed to help people who are not living their lives as effectively as they could; who have learned debilitating, or even damaging, ways of interacting with themselves and others; and who have not developed the skills to handle life-adjustment problems.

Group work may be seen as a continuum:

educational/ growth-oriented groups	group counseling	group psychotherapy

Educational/Growth-Oriented Groups

On this end of the continuum we find persons whose lives are reasonably well-adjusted. They are making it quite satisfactorily from day to day. However, they want their lives to be fuller and have more meaning. They seek experiences that will allow them to continue growing and become what their potential will allow. Examples of these groups include:

Marital Enrichment.   Persons whose marriages are satisfactory and who would like to enrich the marriage, make it better than it currently is, often join marital enrichment groups. Marital enrichment is not to treat a troubled marriage, but to help an already effective one become even more enriched. These may be for a weekend, part of an ongoing series, or offered as a retreat for part of a summer vacation.

Encounter Groups.   Persons who are living satisfactorily but would like the assistance of a group experience to help them understand themselves better, to become aware of themselves more fully than is possible through individual introspection. Encounter groups are not designed to cure problems, but to help participants encounter, become aware of, themselves and others on a deeper level.

Skills Groups.   Many skills groups have been developed to help persons who are living life very effectively but would like to develop additional skills. This may involve social skills, such as may be found in some assertiveness training groups, occupational exploration groups as may be offered to adolescents who would like additional assistance in career exploration and development, and programs for talented and gifted children.

Group Counseling

More toward the middle of the group continuum is group counseling. In these groups would be persons who are making it from day to day in their living, who are able to maintain themselves, but who are not doing it as effectively as the persons described above. Instead, there are definite problems or concerns these people have developed that prevent them from being as happy or as effective as they would like to be. Their problems may be broken down into the following areas:

- completing unfinished business
- inaccurate or inadequate information about one's self or one's problem situation
- self-defeating beliefs and/or behaviors
- problems in managing crises
- problems in mastering developmental tasks
- problems in managing passages

These problem areas will be described in detail in Chapter 5. As can be seen, they are topics that average people can be expected to encounter; so dealing with them is seen as a normal task, not an illness in which a sick person has to be treated. These persons require remedial treatment, but they can survive without it.

Group Psychotherapy

Group psychotherapy is not a process designed for most people. It is a process specifically developed to treat persons who are in need of or desire a personality restructuring, who are so debilitated as to not be able to function effectively in their day-to-day lives. Group psychotherapy is characterized by being long-term in nature; relies upon elaborate diagnosis in order to diagnose and classify the problem; places considerable emphasis on the history of the person that led to the current emotional disturbance; and is not seen as a process in which average people would engage (Alexander & French, 1946).

3. *To what extent do counselors help counselees understand why they behave and feel as they do?* A question often asked by people who enter counseling is "Why am I like this?" A reply to that question is "Why shouldn't you be like this?" All of an individual's history has led up to that person being as he is; and people know their history. Therefore, an emphasis is placed on helping the person define the current state of concern, establish goals to remedy the concern, and then implement a program to bring about the successful change he wishes to make. Rather than encourage counselees to try to understand why they feel and behave as they do, search for insight, the counselor helps them discuss openly how they feel, helps them learn to accept themselves and recognize and use their potentialities to effect change.

The question of whether insight precedes or follows change is one that has not yet been fully answered, and probably does not need to be answered. What is known is that change can occur without insight, and insight can occur without change. In order to accomplish effective and lasting change, though, it seems that both are to some extent necessary. However, the counselee may not need to have an understanding, an insight, which addresses the historical context. For example, in conducting assertiveness groups of nuns, we found change could occur in a short-term group-counseling format. The change did not maintain at a six-month follow-up, however. Upon investigating reasons for the erosion of skills, it was learned that while the sisters knew the behaviors, they had not accepted that they had a right to engage in the behaviors. After adding a cognitive retraining component developed from the rational-emotive therapy approach, the behavioral changes were effectively maintained for a one-year follow-up. It was important that the participants not only understand how to engage in the behavior, but also have a cognitive restructuring that supports the behavior.

4. *How long does group counseling take?* Many group counselors have demonstrated that clients can be helped in ten to twelve weekly sessions of approximately 90 minutes. Younger clients tend to profit from shorter sessions scheduled two or more times a week. The time-limited approach of group counseling differs from other models, such as encounter groups which may be open-ended in number of sessions, or marathon groups which may go for three

days with few or no breaks. Marital enrichment groups often are very short, a day in length, or open-ended, going for years with members joining and leaving as their interests dictate. On the other end, group psychotherapy has, at times, gone on for years, and certainly goes on longer than the ten to twelve sessions usually experienced by counseling groups.

It should be noted that short-term treatment has been found to be effective for bringing about lasting change (Adler, 1972; Barten, 1971; Bellack & Small, 1965; Buda, 1972; Oxley, 1973; Rhodes, 1973; Schafer, 1973; Wolberg, 1965). Carney (1971) found that, in general, length of therapy does not influence results. In analyses based on 475 controlled studies of psychotherapy, one conclusion of Smith, Glass, and Miller (1980) was:

> Differences in how psychotherapy is conducted (whether in groups or individually, by experienced or novice therapists, for long or short periods of time, and the like) make very little difference in how beneficial it is (pp. 183–89).

And Strupp and Binder (1984, p.3) have indicated that "short-term psychotherapy is increasingly being called the wave of the future. . . ." They identify several reasons for the trend toward shorter treatment, including: usually outpatient therapy generally does not run more than 20 sessions; persons and businesses that finance therapy have become increasingly concerned about the costs of treatment; a failure to demonstrate that long-term treatment is more effective than short-term involvement.

5. *To what extent do counselors who apply the methods presented in this book try to convey expectations to prospective clients?* While some group approaches provide minimal structuring, group counselors attempt to convey precisely what will be expected of group members, including: what choices they have in structuring their relationships; what they can expect of their counselor; and how counselees like themselves have been helped. This is done to provide them with the essential data which they must have in order to decide for themselves whether or not to participate; to prepare them to accept their responsibility for developing a therapeutic climate; and to ensure "truth in packaging."

6. *How much responsibility should a counselor give to counselees?* Persons who enter group counseling do so for a reason: they want to make changes in their lives. Some models of therapy take the position that people do not want to change; that, in fact, they enter treatment to be declared "sick" or "unchangeable." Counselors who endorse the group-counseling model presented here have a great deal of confidence in the group members' ability to learn to be clients and helpers, for being therapeutic with others and with themselves. It is expected that group members are responsible and want change, so opportunities for them to experience positive change are provided. If the counselor discovers clients who

cannot or do not accept responsibility, then the counselor teaches them how to do so, providing the encouragement and structure necessary for the counselees' success in taking such responsibility. Group counselors work to develop independence, not dependence.

7. *To what extent does the counselor expect group members to define goals for change and to define criteria to assess their own therapeutic progress?* Developing specific goals and criteria are basic to the approach described in this book. The process serves several purposes:

- There must be a direction to counseling. Group counseling is not a process of several people getting together for a social engagement. Developing specific goals leads to identifying effective methods of achieving those goals. The goals and criteria established are like road maps to follow making certain that people do in fact reach the destination they have indicated they want.
- Specificity in goals and criteria help counselees develop enthusiasm. They are encouraged by being able to clearly identify what they want, having steps to achieve what they want, and given a way of assessing when they have achieved what they want.

It is important to be certain that the goals established are in fact the counselees', not the counselor's.

8. *Are clients merely encouraged to adjust to their environment?* Adjustment or adapting to the circumstances of their lives, their environment, is at times a goal of counseling for frequently counselees do need assistance in learning to live and cope with their environmental circumstances. Helping people deal with grieving, or helping rebellious students learn to work within the system are examples of helping counselees learn to adapt to their environment.

While counselors will help counselees with this issue, it is important to be aware of the professional and ethical responsibility of identifying why the problem exists and to help change the system which has produced the problem if that is appropriate. In working with children, for example, it is important to understand the behavior within the context of the situation. The child who misbehaves in school because of boredom is quite different from one who is academically retarded, but in both cases changing the system may be even more important than working directly with the child.

9. *How are clients selected for group counseling?* In group work, there is great divergence on the selection process. Some group leaders, particularly those oriented toward encounter or growth groups, choose to do very little initial screening of participants. Their assumption is that it is the responsibility of the participants to select the activity that is most appropriate for them. On the other end of the continuum, analytically oriented therapists are likely to require extensive intake evaluations, often including psychological assessment, intensive interviews, and complete case histories.

Group-counseling leaders are in the middle of the two extremes. They are likely to ask questions such as:

- What assistance does the counselee want and require?
- Is the counselee the type of person who tends to be helped or hurt by the technique for which I am selecting members?
- How do I feel toward the counselee?

Counselees are selected based upon their understanding of the purpose of the group; what the group leader and group member expectations will be; their ability to clearly express their goals or intended work; and a commitment to work both for themselves and for their fellow group members. Clients are selected who demonstrate an ability to be responsible for working to achieve their goals and the goals of the group. Group counseling is usually offered to reasonably healthy persons who are allowed to decide whether or not they want to participate. Selection and clients' participation in the process are discussed later.

10. *How is resistance perceived by those who use this model of group counseling?* Resistance is discussed in some detail in Chapter 7. For now, it is important to clarify how group counseling differs from other group approaches regarding resistance. Encounter group leaders use feedback to confront resisting members with their unproductive behavior. Likewise, analytically oriented therapists frequently use interpretations to explain to resisting clients why they are behaving as they are.

Group counselors see resistance as a normal reaction arising for any of several reasons. First, clients contract for assistance and desire help making changes in their lives. During the process of being helped, however, they often begin to question whether the desired changes are worth the pain and discomfort required to achieve the goals. Often they wonder whether, even with all the work involved, the goals can be accomplished. Second, even though the roots of resistance are within the client, counselors at times may enhance it by their own inappropriate behaviors or by countertransference reactions. It is the responsibility of the counselor to attempt to address these issues both with the client(s) involved and with a trusted colleague through peer supervision. Third, what is commonly seen as resistance by many counselors may be more accurately described as selecting the wrong goals to work on. At times counselees identify goals they want to achieve, but after beginning the process clarify their expectations and change. Counselors must be alert for this occurrence.

Finally, resistance is attributed to counselees when lack of understanding may be more appropriate. When counselors make assignments and give homework to counselees, it is the counselor's responsibility to ascertain the level of understanding the client has. Failure to understand the assignment may be an indication of a counselee who wants to work on concerns but does not know how. Counselors may assign clients a task that seems reasonable and with which the clients agree; but later a client may find out he does not know the steps to follow in order to accomplish that task. Counselors need to engage in a problem-solving approach when this occurs: What went wrong? Let's figure out why. Let's decide whether a new plan needs to be developed or whether the old plan needs to be revised or explained better.

11. *How is the transference phenomenon dealt with by counselors who use this treatment model?* Most client-centered counselors and encounter-group leaders do not perceive transference to be important in their treatment. Most analysts, on the other hand, look upon the development of transference, the opening up of these feelings to interpretation, and the patient's learning to reevaluate and to come to terms with the feelings as central to the treatment process.

When a client experiences a transference reaction he assigns another group member the *role* of a significant other, with whom he has some unfinished business, and treats this person (the transference object) *as though* she were the significant other. When this occurs in the group, the counselor helps the client express feelings toward the transference object and resolve any problems that may result from it. If the transference object appears to be confused, the counselor helps her discuss how it feels to be treated inappropriately and encourages her to convey how she wants to be accepted, or rejected, for who she really is rather than for what someone inappropriately perceives her to be. The counselor also helps the original counselee in the interaction then to explore with whom it is outside the group that he has the original problems, and to decide what unfinished business must be worked through with that significant other, and to implement the new behavior.

12. *Who determines when a counselee terminates?* During the initial interview the counselor and counselee determine specific goals to be accomplished and define criteria they may use to assess progress. Goals and criteria are then shared among the group members. Most counselors terminate the relationship when-ever a majority of the members decide either that they have achieved their goals or they have accomplished all they can at the present time.

Prior to beginning the group many counselors establish the number of sessions they will meet. If members complete their goals prior to the ending of the group, they are allowed to drop out; but most choose to remain in the group in order to help their fellow group members and to continue learning from the experiences of others.

Closing experiences, rituals, are used to give members an opportunity to say their goodbyes, to appraise their progress, to identify any unfinished business on which they will continue to work on their own, and to plan their follow-up session and/or report.

SETTING UP FOR SUCCESS

Practicing and prospective counselors often like to know precisely how they should go about helping their counselees. While all counselors vary in their approach to helping and there are individual differences among all helpers, the components described in this section have been found to be useful to group counselors.

Before going into the components, it is important to understand a basic underlying theme of the model: setting up for success. Just as in any endeavor, there are differences in the effectiveness of group counselors. One reason for this difference is that some counselors prepare themselves very carefully to experience success with their groups while others do not. You are encouraged to set yourself up for success rather than failure or mediocrity. The following components describe how you might do this.

Counselor Skills

Goldstein and Myers' Model

Goldstein and Myers (1986) have identified components of interviewing which lead to an effective, therapeutic, outcome. The first element is attractiveness of the counselor. If counselors are seen as attractive in terms of similarity, competence, and relationship skills, then clients are likely to be open and communicative with them. Those counselors who are not seen as attractive are rejected by clients. Counselor attractiveness can be enhanced by a number of methods. Goldstein and Myers have described several:

Client Structuring.   Structuring may involve directly telling the client that the client will like the counselor ("You are quite fortunate to be assigned to Ms _____, who is one of the most helpful counselors on our staff—you're sure to like working with her."). Structuring also can involve describing the counselor's positive qualities ("Ms _____ is one of our most eminent therapists."); or can provide information about expectations for treatment ("Ms _____ will expect you to make rapid positive changes in your anxiety concerns. She'll ask you to provide specific examples of your problem situations and keep a record of difficulties you experience."). Egan (1985), Lawe, Horne, and Taylor (1983), Hilkey, Wilhelm, and Horne (1982), and Hughes (1983) describe additional examples of structuring in counseling settings.

Client Imitation.   Imitation involves having clients be exposed to models. This may occur through audio or videotapes in which the client observes other clients presenting their concerns and receiving assistance. Basically, this model teaches clients how to prepare to be clients and demonstrates to them what counseling is like. Model-reinforcement counseling, described by Horne and Matson (1976) demonstrates a group-counseling model in which students experiencing speech anxiety listened to audio tapes of models presenting their concerns and having their problems be effectively addressed in ensuing sessions. Murphy, Jessell, and Horne (1988) have described a similar process for counselors-in-training using videotaped models for anxiety reduction.

Client Conformity. In experimental research on conformity, an individual will often find the group leader more attractive than previously had been true if the majority of the group identifies the leader in positive terms. This is also true if one very vocal leader in the group expresses positive expectations and evaluations about the leader. In an open group format for aggressive teenagers, it was found that new students who initially entered the group very defensively would change quickly if the other group members described their group experiences in very positive terms.

In addition to the processes that Goldstein and Myers describe for establishing attractiveness on the part of the client, they also identify several counselor characteristics that particularly contribute to effective relationship development:

Helper Expertness. When the helper is identified as an expert in her field, clients are more likely to have positive expectations from their experiences. In a series of research studies undertaken to demonstrate this effect (Schmidt & Strong, 1970; Corrigan et al., 1980), it was found that counselors introduced as students, trainees, beginners, or generalists were much less likely to evoke positive expectations than were those identified with high-status descriptions and labels. Cahill, Jessell, and Horne (1979) found this to be true for prisoners in group counseling when the issues revolved around psychological treatment, legal questions, or topics external to the prison setting. Paraprofessionals were identified as more helpful for problems related to life within the prison itself and inmate/inmate conflicts, for it was believed paraprofessionals would have more knowledge (and therefore status) within that particular setting.

Helper Credibility. This includes status or expertness, as described above, but also reliability of the counselor for accurate information and trustworthiness within the community involved. Also, counselors are considered more credible if the client perceives that the counselor is interested in helping the client achieve his or her own goals as compared to meeting the agenda of the counselor.

Helper Empathy. The ability to understand the client's words and feelings and to communicate that understanding back to the client in such a way that the client feels fully understood is a basic element in the helping process. Empathy has been a central topic of investigation in counseling since the 1940s, and enough is known about defining, measuring, and teaching empathy to indicate that it is a key ingredient to effective interviewing. People who do not feel understood do not share their pain. While empathy is not sufficient for helping clients change, it is a necessary basic component.

Helper Warmth.   Clients who experience a judgmental or evaluative counselor are unlikely to open up and share. On the other hand, clients who encounter a counselor who is warm, gentle, and accepting are likely to share their deepest concerns. In a study conducted by Goldstein (1971), he found that when the liking of one individual (A) was increased through structuring, relationship enhancement, or some other process, the liking of the other individual (B) was also increased, though they had applied no procedures to increase the liking of B. This has been our experience in group counseling: the demonstration of a warm, accepting relationship within a group setting by the counselor leads to modeling by group members.

Helper Self-disclosure.   Work by Jourard (1964) has demonstrated the basic importance of *effective*, helper self-disclosure, and research by Sermat and Smith (1973), Simonson and Apter (1969), and Simonson and Bahr (1974) has shown that self-disclosure on the part of counselors is reciprocated by client self-disclosure and increased confidence in the counseling process. Self-disclosure on the part of the client related to problems and needs does not need to be matched by counselor disclosure of a personal problem—that is, ineffective self-disclosure—but does need to be responded to by the offering of therapeutic conditions and revealing the counselor's position regarding the client, counseling process, and related items.

Goldstein and Myers indicate that the relationship enhancers described above lead to relationship components of *liking, respect,* and *trust* of the counselor by the client. The relationship consequences are *communication, openness,* and *persuasibility.* This in turn leads to an outcome of *client change.*

Ivey's Model

A more-elaborate presentation of a therapeutic model has been presented by Ivey (1983) in his *microskills hierarchy.* He presents his model as a pyramid diagram. Going from the base of the pyramid to the peak are the following levels of relationship skills:

Attending Behavior.   At the basic level is nonverbal attending, including eye contact, proximics (personal space and interpersonal distance), vocal qualities, and ability to follow verbalizations.

Client Observation Skills.   Being aware of client behavior and understanding the client—how he thinks and behaves in relation to other people—involves having the counselor be able to observe and be aware of client verbal and nonverbal behavior. It also involves being aware of the consistency of client statements and identifying inconsistencies.

Open and Closed Questions.   Closed questions provide specific responses from clients, but put the responsibility of the session with the counselor ("Did you have an argument with your parents?" "Was the argument about your grades?"). Open questions provide more opportunity for the client to provide direction ("Tell me what the concerns are about how you are getting along with your parents." "Can you describe some of the situations where you and your parents are at odds with one another?").

Encourage, Paraphrase, and Summarization.   Counselor responses that include these characteristics demonstrate basic listening skills and enhance the quality of the relationship. These skills clearly demonstrate to the client that he or she has been heard clearly and that the phenomenological field of the client—how the client sees the world—is understood.

Reflection of Feeling.   When a counselor identifies what the client is feeling emotionally and responds to the client in a manner that reflects that understanding, the client feels understood and appreciated. ("When your dad gets onto you about your grades, you feel angry that he doesn't have confidence in you . . . and guilty, too, it seems, that you have let him down.")

Reflection of Meaning.   The counselor who attends to the statements of clients will hear the meaning the statements have for the client. Different people have differing perceptions of situations, though the situations may seem similar. It is the differing perceptions, the beliefs and attitudes that clients have about the situation, that give them special meaning to the client. It is important for the counselor to be able to hear these meanings and to respond to the client in such a way that the client develops a better understanding also of what is important to him.

Focusing.   This skill involves being able to direct the client to discuss in more detail and more depth particular issues. This skill is what allows the counselor to be a director of traffic flow, to direct where the interview will go. While this is an important skill, it should not impede the client in self-exploration, but rather should be used after problem areas have been defined, or when the session needs specific direction, as in termination as the session time ends.

Influencing Skills.   Once problems have been identified, it is appropriate for counselors to provide direction, offer instruction, information, explanations, feedback, and in other ways provide the structure for influencing the counseling process.

Confrontation.   Confrontation is a fairly sophisticated skill in that the counselor must be able to confront the client with discrepancies and incongruent statements, while still demonstrating a supportive and understanding relationship.

Skill Sequencing.   This involves knowing when which skill is appropriate and called for, and being able to identify what stage of the counseling interview one is in and what the necessary skills are for that stage. Ivey defines the stages of an interview:

1. rapport/structuring
2. defining the problem
3. defining a goal
4. explorations of alternatives and confronting
5. generalization to daily life

Skill Integration.   The peak of the pyramid, as described by Ivey, is the integration of skills into the theoretical model(s) of the counselor; understanding what skills are called for in differing situations; and knowing what cultural limitations there are for the various skills.

Egan's Model

Another framework for viewing the counseling relationship is presented by Egan (1985). He suggests a three-stage model: Stage I is problem exploration and clarification; Stage II is the development of new perspectives and setting of goals; and Stage III is an action stage. In a group-counseling format, the first part of Stage I will be met during the intake interview where expectations of counseling are reviewed and the relationship is begun. The stage will also continue during the initial group meetings as the counselor works within the group setting to help clients present their concerns and clarify their problems within the group structure. Also during the intake interview, Stage II will begin. During the initial session, the counselor will help clients try to establish clear goals and to see their problems in a positive, more optimistic manner than they previously have been able to see them. In Stage III the counselor and the group members will use the group processes to put their goals into action. Role play, behavioral rehearsal, and specific skills training exercises, followed by homework, are used to help clients achieve their goals.

ELEMENTS IN THE GROUP HELPING PROCESS

The counseling skills described above are used throughout the relationship that is developed. There are other elements in the group-counseling process that facilitate effective work with counselees. While all counselors will use the elements in different ways, depending upon their own approach to counseling, the clients involved, and the nature of the group, the following elements have been found to be very helpful for understanding the process of beginning and maintaining the counseling group.

Developing the Relationship

The extent of a client's recognized need for assistance, the understanding of the helping process, the counselor's reputation as a helper, and the counselor's initial responses to the client can all contribute to or interfere with building a counseling relationship. The counselor begins developing a counseling relationship at the first contact. It may be a casual meeting; a discussion that follows a formal description of the treatment process of prospective clients; or endorsement by a former client who profited from counseling. Wherever or however clients meet the counselor, they should find in that person the personal qualities that enable them to accept and trust the counselor. They must believe that confidences can be kept; that the counselor can listen and not be shocked; that there will be the opportunity for the clients to work out their own solutions without the counselor exhibiting doubts about their ability to solve those problems—by giving advice or some such protective tactic.

During the process of developing the relationship, counselors attempt to convey to prospective clients who they are; what they do to help clients; what they expect of clients in a group; what participants can expect from the group counselor; and how group counseling is likely to help them. The counselor listens to each person, providing individual attention and expresses care and an interest in helping—all without becoming unwholesomely involved with the client. The counselor helps clients realize that they can talk about anything or anybody with the expectation that confidences will be kept. The counselor detects how clients feel and is able to reflect and help them discuss these feelings. When, for example, an adolescent wonders whether he can discuss his feelings of anger toward his mother, whom he also loves very much, the counselor enhances the relationship by reflecting how deeply she feels for and with the client on this issue; by helping him discuss the deep desire to improve the relationship with his mother; and by noting fellow clients' compassion for him as he struggles with the problem.

Beginning the First Individual Conference

While the subject of the book is group counseling, we find that individual sessions facilitate the group process. The first meeting for persons interested in participating in a group is usually the intake interview (which will be described more fully later in the chapter). Most often during the intake interview or in a subsequent individual session, the client speaks first— especially when he seeks counseling after having heard the counselor describe the process and what is expected from him. During the individual session the counselor attempts to determine whether the client knows what is expected of group participants and specifically what the client would like to work on in the group.

The client's readiness to discuss some difficult topics is enhanced by helping him explain to the counselor what concerns or topics are threatening or embarrassing to discuss. Shyness, lack of trust, and doubts about being able to be helped may lead to the person having difficulty sharing either with the counselor or with the entire group. Detecting what the client is experiencing, reflecting accurately what is felt, and encouraging an open discussion enhances openness. As openness occurs between the client and the counselor, the client takes greater responsibility for talking about whatever is worrisome or upsetting; works at developing specific goals for change; and takes responsibility for learning new and more appropriate behaviors.

Developing specific goals for all clients, but especially for adolescents, leads to more open discussion and enhances the counseling relationship. Adolescents are engaged in a process of individuation, developing their separate identities, and thus are very wary of therapy that stresses basic personality change (Holmes, 1964). Adolescents can accept their need for learning new skills more easily than they can agree to therapy or counseling in which the goal is personality change or which addresses intensive work on identity. Most clients react positively to a helping relationship for which they volunteer and in which they are expected to accept responsibility for learning their own desired new behaviors.

Detecting a Client's Feelings

During the counseling process, the counselor must demonstrate caring and understanding of the situation of each client. The counselor, in order to do this, must be able to accurately understand what the client is feeling, to perceive what the client is experiencing as the client lives the situations of his life. The counselor must be able to understand what it is like to be in the circumstances of the client, to know precisely how the client is hurting, what the client would like to do about the problem, or what skills the client would need to develop to handle the problem. The sources of data the counselor has available are observations of how the client is struggling to express himself on certain topics, the way approach–avoidance behavior is demonstrated, speech patterns used, and the nonverbal cues provided, including facial expressions and bodily movements. The use of emotionally laden words and the pattern of describing one's life provide the counselor attuned to empathic listening with clues as to the difficulties the client is experiencing.

Different clients may use similar behavior to express very different emotions: what for some would convey hostility for others would convey affection—for example, tease or make sarcastic remarks when they really want to convey affection, and vice versa. When some clients feel hostile they attack, others act bored or indifferent or defensive. In any case, counselors must recognize that in order to understand clients' behavior; they must take cognizance of everything learned about a particular client. Each client has an individual lifestyle and consequently a unique way of revealing true inner feelings. Thus, counselors realize that a client may even wish to convey something very different from what the words communicate. The client may mask real feelings out of shame for either the feelings or for what he has done. Also, clients mask feelings when they are uncertain about the ability to trust the counselor or fellow clients.

In addition to uncovering essential data for an accurate reflection, the counselor's effort to detect the client's genuine feelings conveys caring; it also conveys the counselor's respect for the client and the desire to help the client accept responsibility for his own personal growth. Though external sources such as case histories and intensive interviews with significant others (teachers, spouse, parents, employers, and so on) can provide useful data to enrich the understanding of a client, the counselor tends to be most productive when encouraging clients to accept primary responsibility for revealing the relevant data that will be required to help them implement desired new behaviors.

Reflecting a Client's Feelings

From what was presented in the previous section, it is evident that today's therapies call for less use of interpretation and more use of reflection than was true previously. In order to use either method, a counselor must understand the client's behaviors, feelings, thoughts, environment, history, and be able to communicate these understandings accurately to the client.

There are two primary distinctions that differentiate interpretation and reflection: the extent to which the counselor (1) assumes the expert role and (2) assumes responsibility for the client. When a counselor interprets a client's behavior, the counselor is assuming the role of the expert: "Because your teacher embarrassed you, and you didn't know what else to do at the time, you talked back and then got kicked out of class." This "expert" role encourages the client to feel increasingly dependent and to expect advice from the counselor. Furthermore, most clients, and especially adolescents, tend to perceive interpretation as attack (Dougherty, 1974; Helner, 1972; Katz et al., 1959). Helner's fourth- and tenth-grade students preferred advice giving and probing to both reflection and interpretation. Dougherty's fourth- and tenth-graders also preferred advice giving to both Adlerian interpretation and traditional analytic interpretation.

Taylor's (1974) tenth-grade subjects reacted with approach to all four of the techniques he studied, but they reacted differently to the techniques. Their order of preference for response style was content probing, affect probing, reflection, and advice giving. There are at least three possible explanations for why Taylor's adolescent subjects may have reacted less favorably to reflection than to probing: (1) Reflection is not a response with which they have had much experience; (2) They recognize and react somewhat fearfully to the underlying responsibility associated with reflections; (3) The reflections with which Taylor's subjects were confronted may have been somewhat too deep for them in that experimental setting.

In group counseling if the counselor notices a member becoming uneasy or uncomfortable in response to the counselor's use of reflections, that does not mean that reflections should be stopped. Rather, the counselor should try to detect and reflect the client's underlying feelings, explain the purpose of reflective statements, and what the reflection reveals about the counselor's or fellow clients' feelings and understanding about the client. For example:

> Perhaps that made you feel a little uncomfortable or made you wonder what I was trying to do. That kind of a helping response is called a *reflection*. When I use it I am trying to understand you and to make it safe for you to talk about what is bothering you. In other words, it is meant to be an encouraging response; you will discover that you and the other group members can learn quickly to use it to help each other, too. When any of us use it here, we are saying we care about you, we want to help you, and we believe you have what it takes to solve this problem.

If the counselor's response to the boy who was criticized in front of the other students had been a reflection, the counselor would not have tried to explain why the boy felt and behaved as he did. Instead, the counselor would have tried to detect and mirror back the content of the expression and the feelings associated with the content. This could have moved the boy toward some action, using a reflection such as:

> Your teacher embarrassed you. As you think about it now perhaps you would like to discuss how you could resolve the conflict with your teacher, and even role play how you could go about talking with the teacher about the conflict.

Thus, the counselor reacts more as an equal who is trying to sense what the client is experiencing, to communicate with the client in order to help him discuss his feelings openly, to identify desired new behaviors, and to implement them. Such a reflection tends to be most productive when its focus is a little deeper and a little ahead of where the client is.

Relating Discussion of Feelings to Behavioral Goals

As the counselor listens to counselees in the group discuss what worries and upsets them, the counselor tries to decide when clients have talked sufficiently and obtained adequate feedback from the counselor and other group members to be ready to define specific goals. If clients feel pressured to define goals before they have talked about their feelings, they may conclude that fellow clients either do not care or that they have not obtained enough data to be helpful. When, therefore, the counselor wonders whether a client is ready to define specific goals for behavioral change, a reflection can be made which checks out where the client is:

> I think we understand how you feel about _____ ; perhaps you are ready to discuss what you would like to do differently with _____ in order to improve the situation for you.

The counselor may also incorporate in a reflection a desired new behavior, as the counselor did in the previous section. Early in the life of a group, a counselor may use the clients' own case materials to teach them to expect and to facilitate the definition and implementation of behavioral goals. The counselor also helps the group members understand why it is better for one of them rather than for the counselor to ask:

- What can or do you want to do about this situation now?
- What are your long-term goals and with what can you begin today?

For example, in a marriage-counseling group in which both spouses were present, a male client had talked several times about how deeply he loved his wife and yet at the same time how much he seemed to want to hurt her, but had never exhibited any inclination to change his behavior. After one such speech about his wife another male client frowned, paused a moment, and then responded:

> I can see how you are hurting, but all you do is talk about hurting. I cannot seem to grasp what you want to do about it. I cannot tell whether you want to continue to live in misery, split, or change your behavior. In any case, you must learn to behave differently or you will repeat the same mistakes with some other woman. What new skills, ways of behaving, must you learn to develop a good life with your wife, or with some other person?

Sometimes a client is ready to move from discussion of feelings to discussion of goals, but does not know how to do it. On such an occasion a counselor may say:

> It sounds like you believe that you have the interests, abilities, and aptitudes to be an electrician. I am wondering whether you would like for us to help you talk about what you must do to become an electrician or help you figure out how to tell your parents that you don't want to go to college?

On the other hand it may be better to say nothing. The client may be pleased to discover that the counselor and fellow clients can listen patiently while he or she wrestles with conflicting feelings and motivations. The client may be even more pleased to discover that other clients are simultaneously struggling with similar problems, that they will own up to their problems, and that the conflicts, issues, and problems can be discussed openly in the group.

Sometimes, however, a counselor may allow clients to wallow needlessly in painful material. Such a counselor may permit clients to achieve catharsis to the point where they lose much of their motivation to change. Sometimes clarification is required. When, for example, a junior-high-school boy indicated in the intake interview that his primary goal was to learn to get along with classmates, the counselor asked, "With whom would you like to learn to do that?" The boy's response to that question was a long one, including the names of two boys and one girl with whom he would like to develop a close friendship. A further clarification response opened up the topic even more and identified the need to practice relationship building and social-skills maintenance abilities. Consequently, the counselor responded as follows:

> That helps. Now I know with whom you would like to develop special friendships. You also would like to learn how to tell them how you feel toward them, to check out whether or not they think they could like you, and for those who also think they could develop good friendships with you, to figure out how to encourage the growth of that friendship. Perhaps that is a skill that we could practice in the group.

If this was the first time role playing had been introduced the counselor would have described it and explained briefly how it is used in group counseling. Discussions such as the one presented here from the counselor to the client open the way for other counselor responses that help clients formulate criteria for appraising their own growth:

> How will you know when you have learned to do that? How will you behave differently? How will your family and friends perceive you differently? Precisely how will you feel differently about yourself?

Thus, even prospective clients learn in the intake interview how to formulate precise goals and to appraise their achievement of such goals. De Esch (1974) concludes that clients' experiences in formulating behavioral goals and criteria for appraising their own growth may account for the fact that his control subjects achieved almost as much growth as his experimental subjects did.

A client's criteria for appraising growth also can be used by the counselor to determine whether a client is being helped by a treatment, can be helped at this time, should be treated by some other method, or should be referred to someone else for treatment (or whether one of the client's significant others should be treated instead of, or with, the client).

Helping Clients Define Mini-Goals

Once clients have defined their goals, most profit from breaking up their goals into mini-goals, or at least from deciding with what they feel most confident to begin implementing desired new behaviors. Some like to break their long-term goals into steps and put those steps into a hierarchical order. The way the counselor helped the junior-high-school boy who requested assistance in learning to relate differently with classmates illustrates how a counselor uses reflections and clarification responses to help a client do two things simultaneously: define a more-precise goal with specific target persons; and break the larger goal into mini-goals that can be tackled one at a time.

Teaching Clients Good Client and Helper Behaviors

Basically, a part of group structuring is the teaching of new skills for behavior change; and this is begun when the counselor first tells a prospective client about group counseling, answers any questions about the process, and announces what will be expected from the client. The better a client understands what is expected before beginning the group, the more eager the client is to learn to function effectively as a client and as a helper of others in the group. Nevertheless, most clients at one time or another will exhibit some uncertainty about how to act. When this occurs the counselor tries to detect and reflect what the clients want to know, encourages a fellow client to explain what is expected and, better still, demonstrate it.

The counselor also should watch from the beginning for specific instances in which clients have functioned especially well as helpers, as well as clients, and should point these helping skills out to the rest of the group. When, for example, a counselor observed that Jim had detected how Kathy was feeling and had made it safe for her to share her feelings, this was called to the attention of the group. A counselor can also replay recordings of counseling sessions in order to point out good examples of group members' performances in both roles. Such counselor behavior tends to reinforce a member's desired behavior and encourage others to use that person as a model. Hilkey's (1975) results suggest that even poor treatment risks (incarcerated criminals) treated in groups in which they were taught client and helper roles through use of fellow prisoner models on video recordings profited more from group counseling in the first few sessions than did similar clients who were counseled by the same counselors but without being systematically taught these two roles.

Teaching Clients Interpersonal Skills

Films and video recordings can be used to teach clients the interpersonal skills necessary to learn new ways of interacting. Most counselors tend to prefer the use of role playing to teach these skills. In a role-playing situation it is possible for the client to provide a description of the situation, other persons involved, the emotional reaction to the situation, and to involve the other group members in the struggle of identifying appropriate people from the group to participate in the role playing. This helps both the group member and the other members understand the situation, and this assists other clients of the group in providing helpful feedback.

Teaching Clients to Communicate Their Goals to Significant Others

Usually clients want to practice in their counseling groups what they want to say to their families, friends, or co-workers. Sometimes they wish to write what they want to convey and get feedback on the letter before they mail it. It is helpful to select actors for role playing, to role play the scene, and to solicit feedback from fellow clients before attempting either oral or written communication with significant others. In any case, they require and appreciate assistance in formulating and in communicating the precise message they require.

Sharing Successes

Clients in group counseling select precise activities to do between sessions. They learn quickly how to share with the group the success they experience in implementing change. Gradually they learn to differentiate between bragging to impress someone and sharing real successes, first with fellow clients and then, eventually, with those significant others who care deeply about helping the client implement desired changes. Increasingly, they learn to celebrate successes; they also learn to admit their failures and analyze them for the purpose of deciding how to revise unsuccessful tactics and try other approaches.

Termination

Termination of a series of group-counseling sessions can teach clients how to conclude a temporary relationship, appraise its worth, identify each one's unfinished business, and plan for follow-up. During the first or second session members should be encouraged to decide on starting and closing times; how and under what conditions members may arrange for individual sessions; approximately how many group sessions they will have; how they will decide on termination; and how the counselor will provide for those who are not ready to terminate counseling when their group disbands.

Sometimes clients resist termination because the group is providing them with some of the best relationships they have ever experienced, and they do not want to give them up. When the counselor senses such feelings, the feelings are reflected back to the group in order to help the members acknowledge and discuss them. They should explore what they must do to develop more-satisfying relationships with friends, relatives, and co-workers (and/or develop new and more meaningful friendships). They then should say their goodbyes to their fellow members. With the frequent moves most clients will be expected to make, they must learn to terminate some meaningful relationships, to sustain others despite separation, and build new relationships quickly.

The use of a closing ritual by group counselors has become markedly more popular recently. Several sessions prior to termination, those counselors who favor the idea encourage each client to review which goals have been achieved, which still need additional work; whose assistance will be required to make the desired changes remaining, or to reinforce the changes already achieved; and what problems are envisioned in implementing and maintaining new behaviors. Each client also is directed to give the group feedback on those instances in which help and hurt were most experienced.

After each client has reviewed gains and describes any unfinished tasks, they stand before each of the others to receive two final messages: (1) a statement concerning what each liked about the client, and in particular what was accomplished in the group; and (2) an "I urge you" message in which each member notes some specific area of growth on which he would like to encourage this particular client to pursue growing. In order to preserve these messages for each client, the counselor assigns each a partner who records the first of the two messages on the front side of a sheet of paper and the second message on the back of it.

Follow-up and Encouragement for Continuing Growth

Counselors who do not wish to conduct each group as a research project may still be able to complete an evaluation of the group which will be helpful both to the counselor and to the group members. Each client's goals from the initial intake can be grouped into a behavior inventory that each member can complete both for the individual client and for each member of the group immediately following the termination session. From this evaluation it is possible to identify how each individual sees the change that occurred for him individually, as well as for each of the other members. Some counselors offer to review these findings with each client individually, others use them for group feedback. They tend to encourage continuing growth.

When such an evaluation instrument is used, some counselors prefer to send clients a copy of it a few days prior to having a follow-up session to encourage them to review their own and others' goals, and to review for each person what unfinished business may remain. Some also request each client to complete an inventory for himself and one for each of the others early enough so that the counselor is able to summarize the results prior to the follow-up meeting.

Nevertheless, the purpose of a follow-up session is to review the degree to which each has maintained the goals he has made during counseling and the degree to which each has finished any business left undone at the end of the counseling group. Where it is difficult or impossible to reassemble the group for a follow-up session, the counselor can request a follow-up letter from each, with a copy of the letter to the other group members. Clients commonly comment on the fact that even though some at first failed to work on unfinished business, the prospect of the follow-up encouraged them to do so.

WHO PROFITS FROM GROUP COUNSELING?

Most who are willing to learn new behaviors can profit from counseling when they are troubled by problems or confronted with developmental tasks with which they feel they cannot cope by themselves or even with the assistance of friends, relatives, or co-workers. For example, people may have been hurt or let down by someone whom they love. They doubt the love from someone they love very much. They feel guilty about hurting someone. They are grieving for someone. They are conscious of a problem for which they lack the courage, self-confidence, or skill to attack. They are confronted with a problem for which they have the essential knowledge, abilities, and skills to solve, but they do not realize it; or they are confronted with a problem for which they have a good solution, but implementing it will disappoint or hurt someone whose acceptance they value very much.

Consequently, even similar personality types seek assistance for quite different reasons. Some require assistance in identifying and clarifying their problems. Others require information and feedback on themselves and their environment, training in decision making, skill building, and increased confidence in themselves. Those who require feedback from others, opportunities to give help and to accept help from others, and to practice interpersonal skills can be helped best in groups.

Those who seek assistance on their own are easier to help than those who are coerced into treatment by relatives and friends (Beck, 1958; Ewing & Gilbert, 1967; Johnson, 1963; Rickard, 1965). Lieberman, Yalom, and Miles' (1973) clients who profited most from treatment were open and trusting. They gave others frank but considerate feedback and requested feedback from others. On the other hand, they recognized the curvilinear nature of openness—with whom and under what conditions it is appropriate to be open. The authors' successful clients also took risks in implementing desired new behaviors outside their counseling groups. Stranahan, Schwartzman, and Atkin (1957) found that those who profited most from their group treatment had some capacity for insight, a degree of flexibility, a desire for growth, and some wholesome experiences early in life with an authority figure who possessed some measure of steadiness, helpfulness, direction, and maturity. Allport (1960) decided that ability to become ego-involved is an essential characteristic of any good group member. Such a member is able to invest in helping others and to reap satisfaction from seeing others solve their problems.

Ryan (1958) reported that clients' ability to become meaningfully involved in a treatment group seems to be related to a member's ability to empathize with others, to delay gratification of one's own needs, and to derive satisfaction from helping others gratify their needs. On the other hand, Sethna and Harrington (1971) established that those who failed to disclose and to become meaningfully involved early in the life of the group tended either to lapse from treatment or to become nonparticipating members.

Spielberger, Weitz, and Denny (1962) decided that those who profited most from group counseling had the personality characteristics that enabled them to participate fully (and possessed the commitment to attend counseling sessions regularly). Lindt (1958) found that those who were helped were able to make an emotional investment in helping at least one other client. Finally, the authors have found that those who are able to define precise behavioral goals are most apt to be helped (and those who cannot or will not do so are most apt to become resisting clients). Bach (1954) questioned the wisdom of including the decidedly resisting types of client: the culturally deviant, the chronic monopolist, and the impulsive.

Possibly most of those characteristics which McClelland (1971) discovered that differentiate achievers from others also describe good bets for counseling: (1) They are challenged by the opportunity for growth and willing to work hard to achieve some clear goals; (2) They prefer to work at a problem rather than to leave the outcome to chance or to others; (3) They require clear goals and criteria for growth in order to use their feedback to assess their own growth; (4) They habitually spend time thinking about doing things better.

Many clients who at first appear to be poor bets (and have not volunteered) can become good treatment risks when the treatment is described for them; their questions about it are answered; they are encouraged to explore alternative sources for help; they are permitted to decide for themselves whether to participate; and they accept the responsibility for convincing themselves and their counselor that they can discuss their problems openly, define precise goals, and encourage fellow clients to learn desired new behaviors. Perhaps even reluctant clients, including the resisting type, can be helped when they are included in a group in which most clients are strong enough to prevent them from intefering with the development of (or from destroying) therapeutic group norms. If, however, they are to profit from counseling they must not be forced to participate.

THE PRESENTATION

The presentation is a description of the treatment process for prospective group-counseling clients. It also includes a discussion of what is expected of clients; what they can expect from their counselor and from fellow clients; examples of the kinds of concerns that similar clients commonly discuss; and previous clients' goals and how they were helped. For example, a counselor began her presentation to a college freshman psychology class as follows:

> Students like you join a counseling group to discuss with peers the problems that really worry and upset them. They soon discover that a counseling group is a safe place in which to talk about anybody or any topic that worries them. They learn to share with fellow clients how they really feel, to decide precisely what new behaviors they want to implement, to listen to others, and to help them learn the new behaviors they require to cope with life more effectively. They also learn that when the problem involves conflict with someone the purpose of the discussion is not to determine who is at fault, but to discover what the problem is, what new behaviors must be learned to solve it, whose cooperation is required to solve it, how that cooperation can be elicited, and if it cannot be obtained how the problem can be solved without it.

Included among the expectations is a description of the intake interview. Its purpose and how it is scheduled is discussed at the end of the presentation, after prospective clients' questions have been answered.

Though the presentation is designed to provide prospective clients with the information they require to decide whether to volunteer for a counseling group, it also achieves several additional purposes: (1) It encourages clients to accept responsibility for getting themselves ready to talk openly about their problems and for learning precise new behaviors; (2) It helps ensure truth in packaging for the services; (3) To the degree that the presenting counselor is able to answer prospective clients' questions nondefensively, to give examples of meaningful problems that similar clients have discussed in groups, and to include some examples of problems of prestigious clients, it increases the attractiveness of group counseling. Some counselors have achieved these goals with the assistance of successful former clients. They make a videotape of the first session of a role-played counseling session, which the counselor plays for prospective clients. This approach enables former clients to produce on the basis of their own experiences as clients a highly realistic first session without running the risk of breaking confidences. It also provides prospective clients with a chance to quiz this particular counselor's previous clients and to obtain from them the answers to their questions.

Prospective clients' questions tend to deal with the degree of privacy in discussion topics, membership, expectations, and confidentiality. For example, "Will we feel really free to discuss anything that bothers us?" "How do we learn to do that?" "How will we behave differently in a counseling group than we do in a bull session with a group of friends . . . than participants do in an encounter or sensitivity group?" "How will you decide with whom you place me?" "How can we help others when we are upset ourselves?" "What can a counseling group do for persons like us?" "What can't or won't group counseling do for us?" "To what extent am I running a risk of being hurt in group counseling?" "Will I be permitted or encouraged to have individual counseling sessions with you between group sessions?" "How have others like us been helped?" "Where will the group meet?" "How often will it meet?" "Is attendance required?" "For how many sessions do such groups usually meet?"

When prospective clients seem to have their questions answered the counselor distributes slips of paper to everyone. Each prospective client indicates whether he or she wants to participate in group counseling by selecting one of these three answers: (1) yes, definitely; (2) no, not interested; or (3) maybe. In addition to name, where the student can be reached most easily, and the extent of interest in participation, each also records: (1) the best meeting times, (2) with whom he would like to be placed for group counseling; and (3) with whom he would prefer not to be placed.

Those who write "yes" are contacted first and scheduled for intake interviews. In the meantime, some who wrote "maybe" will seek out the counselor to indicate that they are definitely interested, and consequently are scheduled for intake interviews. Of course, others will report that they are no longer interested, or at least are not interested for the present.

Presentations are made whenever counselors meet their clients. Some of a counselor's individual clients are introduced to the idea during individual counseling. Others are introduced to the idea when they are referred for counseling. Group presentations have been made in classes, churches (especially for marriage counseling and parent education groups), special group-outreach meetings scheduled by community mental-health staff members, special after-work meetings scheduled in industrial plants, and special meetings called for the particular purpose of persons in mental hospitals and prisons. When such presentations are first proposed for inmates of mental hospitals and prisons, some staff members tend to be threatened by the idea until they can observe how it is done and discuss why it works.

THE INTAKE INTERVIEW

The following is an example of an intake interview. In this example, the individual intake interview occurred a few days after the counselor had made a presentation to a group of eleventh-graders. The counselor covered the highlights of the presentation and structured for the intake interview as follows:

When I visited your class I described what goes on in a counseling group, gave you a number of examples of what students your age talk about in counseling groups, reviewed how they were helped, and answered your questions. I also indicated that I scheduled these intake interviews to give you a chance to practice talking about what concerns or upsets you, to help you decide precisely how you would like to change [goals for counseling], and to help you decide precisely how you will be able to recognize when you have achieved your goals for counseling [criteria for evaluating personal growth]. Although I try very hard to help everyone who requests counseling, I accept for group counseling those who are committed to discuss from the beginning what really worries and upsets them, to learn desired new behaviors, and to help fellow clients learn and implement desired new behaviors. The more carefully we select clients the better are the chances that each will be helped. [Here I often give examples of who needs whom for what—both as models and as characters to role play significant others.] Tell me about you, what is worrying you right now? I will listen, try to understand how you feel in order to help you talk, and try to determine what you seem to be ready to deal with now.

For most this is sufficient. For those who require more help in getting started we often use one of these two approaches: (1) "Perhaps it would help if you could tell me what you wish you could share with me and what is keeping you from doing it."; (2) "Think of someone whom you admire who is doing what you would like to be doing, and tell me about that person."

Besides clarifying clients' expectations the counselor uses the intake interview to help each prospective client assess his commitment to talk openly about problems and concerns and to implement desired new behaviors; define specific goals (and criteria to appraise growth with reference to each); identify those significant others whose assistance and reinforcement would enhance chances for success; and decide how their assistance may be elicited. A few must be re-interviewed to help them define more-precise behavioral goals or help them develop the courage to make a commitment to speak first at the first meeting of the group and to begin their discussion with their most difficult problems. Obviously, such interviews take considerable time (30–60 minutes), but they are worth it. Consequently, even before clients join these counseling groups they are motivated to talk openly at a productive level and to accept considerable responsibility for helping to develop therapeutic norms and to enhance and maintain their own personal growth.

For those prospective clients who are not ready for group counseling, the counselor may help them decide whether it would be a good future source for assistance, and if so, what they may do to get themselves ready for a future group. When they decide that group counseling does not show promise as a source of help for them, the counselor helps them look at other sources for assistance. Thus, genuine caring for them is exhibited and this helps them learn to accept responsibility for their growth.

STRUCTURING

The purpose of structuring is to provide a framework within which clients can learn their desired new behaviors; develop therapeutic group norms; make input into their group; revise the structure when desirable; and use it to enhance their own growth. With the preparation used in this treatment model, most clients realize before the first counseling session how therapeutic talk differs from social conversations and classroom discussions, and how expectations in group counseling differ from those of other groups. Each learns to accept responsibility for developing trust and for preventing those situations in the group in which members may be tempted to break confidence. From the very beginning of the first session, good client and helping behaviors are recognized and reinforced. Thus, clients learn quickly to discuss genuine feelings openly and to accept them. Gradually they also learn to manage and enjoy them.

Some school counselors have failed to differentiate clearly between the teacher's function and the counselor's function in a group. In these schools, counselors must communicate these differences, and, more importantly, exhibit these differences in their daily relationships with clients. The real structuring is done by the way the counselor lives her professional role and responds to clients' behavior—knowingly encouraging certain behaviors and discouraging others. The way in which a counselor participates and encourages clients to participate, especially during early sessions, affects the amount and the nature of clients' participation throughout the life of the group (Psathas, 1960).

The more deep and meaningful group relationships that clients have had, and the safer they feel with their counselor, the easier the structuring will be. Similar previous experiences provide a base from which the counselor can generalize and differentiate to convey the unique nature of clients' expectations and responsibilities in group counseling. Even within the best working climate the counselor must be sensitive to detect and clarify inaccurate communications to ensure that the counselor's intentions are imparted in understandable language, taking cognizance of clients' maturity and cultural, ethnic, and racial backgrounds. Nevertheless, clients may understand their stated responsibilities and limits, but have difficulty accepting them genuinely. For these clients the counselor must be able to detect such feelings, reflect them accurately, and help clients explore whether they are committed to implement the essential norms for their own growth.

The primary structuring for this group-counseling approach is done during the presentation. Expectations are further clarified during the intake interview. From time to time the need for further structuring occurs whenever clients are either not certain what is expected or sense the need for new operating guidelines. Though it is appropriate for counselors to describe the conditions under which they are best able to help clients within a group setting, they also should encourage clients to define those guidelines that they feel they need. Effective structuring contributes to the therapeutic climate; overstructuring and rigid rules interfere with it.

SELECTING CLIENTS FOR A GROUP

Counselors should select only those clients who they feel reasonably certain can be helped by their method within the counseling setting. Rather than sit back and wait for clients to seek assistance or be referred, Wattenburg (1953) encourages school counselors to describe for teachers and administrators (and we do it for other clients too) who can be most readily helped by counseling. In other words, Wattenburg believes that counselors should know whom they can help and should solicit the assistance of relevant persons in attracting such clients. When, on the other hand, poor bets are referred, he believes that the counselor should accept them on a trial basis after communicating to the referrer why this particular client is a poor bet. When the referrer and the counselor decide cooperatively that the client cannot be helped by counseling, the counselor should help the referrer to explore other sources of assistance. Wattenburg notes that when counselors fail to follow this recommendation two harmful side effects result: (1) The counselor is discouraged with poor results; (2) Referrers tend to judge counselors' worth on the basis of their poorest treatment risks.

The methods described in the two previous sections tend to attract good bets for successful treatment. The literature reviewed in the section "Who Profits Most from Group Counseling" suggests that the counselor asks the following questions in selecting prospective clients for a group and in deciding to what group each should be assigned (and preferably these decisions should be made with the assistance of a trusted colleague): Are the clients able to talk openly about what worries and upsets them? Are they willing to do so in a group? Have they defined some specific new behaviors they are committed to learn and implement in daily living outside of the counseling group, and are they committed to help fellow clients to do the same? Are they committed to attend counseling sessions regularly and to work on problems? Do they understand and accept responsibilities for helping to develop and to maintain therapeutic group norms? Have they developed criteria for each goal that are precise enough to enable them to appraise their own progress during treatment? Do they seem to be the type of persons who have the courage to take the risks required to implement desired new behaviors? Are they capable of becoming ego-involved in helping fellow clients? Can they delay gratification of immediate personal needs in order to help others? Can they reap satisfaction from observing others achieve their goals? Are they challenged by their problems and are they willing to work hard to solve them? Do they prefer to work out their own solutions rather than let others solve them? Who needs whom for what?

Of all those criterion questions listed above perhaps the most-important criteria pertain to clients' commitment to discuss their problems openly beginning with the first session, to define specific behavioral goals, and to implement desired new behaviors. They also must be able to become involved in helping fellow clients and possess the courage to expect fellow clients to implement their own desired new behaviors.

From their review of the literature Peck and Stewart (1964) concluded that most therapists who provide group play therapy preferred homogeneity with reference to sex and age; 76 percent considered intellectual level important, but less than 50 percent considered religion or socioeconomic status important. Except for extremely withdrawn children, who they concluded should be treated by themselves, most therapists preferred heterogeneity with reference to personality or diagnostic types. Bach (1954) argued for heterogeneous personality types on the grounds that patients are provided with the opportunity to learn to relate to and to aid persons different from themselves.

Freedman and Sweet (1954) found that when they chose patients who were homogeneous in diagnosis they tended to reinforce each other's defense. For example, in the school setting a counselor can counteract this problem by placing gifted underachievers in groups with peers whom they admire, who are searching for ways to improve their academic performance, and who are highly motivated to adjust to their situation rather than to rebel against it; or by placing young drug users with attractive peers who can experience peak moments without drugs; or depressed persons with their spouses for group counseling. In the latter instance, the spouse discovers how she contributes to the depression, and what she can do to help her spouse cope with depression and reinforce the desired new behaviors.

On the other hand, clients can be assigned to groups with persons who have common problems. Clients can sense genuine affiliation feelings when they have assigned a problem the same name but still have very different underlying causes for it, or its diagnosis. Observing fellow clients openly discuss similar problems—seeing their efforts to empathize, their encouragement of those who implement new behaviors—motivates even one who is holding back, trying to decide whether to disclose and to learn new behaviors. Recognizing and reflecting affiliation feelings is highly therapeutic counselor behavior (Powdermaker & Frank, 1953). Discovering other clients with problems to which they have assigned the same name tends to make all clients feel that they belong and that they are understood, but it is especially potent for adolescents.

Most counselors prefer to counsel in a group of clients of approximately the same age, but the crucial factor is social maturity rather than chronological age. Even for his adult therapy groups, Bach (1954) selected patients with similar problems as well as similar social maturity:

> For example, with respect to age and maturity, we find it necessary to exclude the very young with little sexual and social experience from more-experienced adult groups. While we definitely like to mix married and unmarried members in the same group, we see to it that we have at least two of each category in the

same group. In general, we limit excessive heterogeneity by trying to place a patient in a group when he can find at least one other patient in circumstances which are similar with respect to some other central phase of his own life (p. 26).

Ginott (1961) reported that the prevailing practice in clinics is to separate boys and girls for treatment during the latency period. Ohlsen and Gazda (1965) noted that girls in their fifth grade groups were more mature, showed more interest in boys than boys did girls, tended to handle topics related to sex better than boys, were more verbal, and tended to dominate the discussion. Consequently, Gazda (1973) tended to prefer to separate boys and girls at this age while Ohlsen (1973) preferred to treat them together. Although there are difficulties in treating them together, perhaps the counseling group is one of the better places in which to help them face and deal with their differing rates of sociosexual development.

Most counselors agree that for adolescents both sexes should be treated within the same group. Moreover, adolescents tend to be very sensitive to opposite-sex peers' evaluations of them and have a very strong need to prove themselves (Ackerman, 1955): they want very much to learn to relate to the opposite sex. They also learn quickly to discuss their sociosexual development problems frankly and to practice skills required to help each other in role-played scenes, with less need to use language that they think may be offensive to the counselor and/or to some fellow clients, than when they are assigned to groups composed of only boys or girls.

Bach (1954) found that the less-educated and less-intelligent adults tend to feel out of place and reluctant to participate with persons much brighter and better educated. Perhaps those who work with children having a wide range of verbal fluency should take cognizance of Bach's recommendation of some homogeneity concerning verbal fluency. When most clients have better verbal fluency than a given client, they tend to talk over the head of that person. When, on the other hand, a client talks down to the rest of the group, he often rejects and, in turn, is rejected by fellow clients. A client's ability to profit from counseling is determined in part by communication skills. Nevertheless, persons with a narrow range of verbal fluency can learn to communicate, and the group can be the source of motivation for improving communication skills. Furthermore, bright adolescents who want to become leaders must learn to communicate with a wide range of persons, and a counseling group can be a place in which they begin this process.

For those who use the methods endorsed here, prospective clients are the primary source of data. Though the elaborate type of diagnostic testing used by Bach is rarely required by those who counsel normal clients, there are occasions when a counselor may wish to supplement the intake interview with other sources of data (and, of course, only with a prospective client's permission): the cumulative folder and case conference reports (Ohlsen, 1974); and interviews with teachers, relatives, friends, or employers. From such data a counselor can learn what primary roles prospective clients play in various settings, the ways they attempt to solve problems, the way they relate to significant others, and significant others' perception of their problems.

Once a counselor has the essential data from the pool of clients, the best possible combination for each group is selected. Best results tend to be obtained when several counselors assist each other in selecting clients and supervise each other during counseling (especially for their first several groups).

GROUP SIZE

Loeser (1957) concluded that four to eight clients are ideal for group counseling and group therapy, and that such a size is the largest that can function without a leader and some strong rules. As groups increase in size above this, transference tends to become weaker and weaker until members have little meaningful, involved relationships with each other; the group tends to function as a collection of subgroups; members tend to develop meaningful relationships only with leader, speaker, or performer; and members tend to function like a class with increasing dependence on the leader. The extent to which the leader is able to establish meaningful relationships with members determines the degree to which she can arouse emotion for action or quiet unrest.

Psathas' (1960) review of the literature also indicated that with increased group size, members experience less-direct involvement and participation. Instead of interacting with each other, they tend as the group gets larger to direct their communications to the highest-ranking initiator, who in turn responds to them as a group rather than as individuals. Most communications in larger groups flow through a selected or appointed leader.

When making a decision on group size, a counselor must consider clients' maturity, attention span, and ability to invest in others. Clients must feel that they are allocated adequate time during each session; that they do not have to wait too long to get the floor; and that the group is small enough for them to get to know the other clients and vice versa. Those who counsel children in groups tend to schedule shorter sessions for smaller groups and to meet with them more frequently than those who counsel adolescents and adults. Usually adolescents are counseled in groups of six to eight. In order for clients to function effectively, a client must be able to capture others' attention, to feel safe, to interact meaningfully with others, and to give, solicit, and accept feedback.

GROUP SETTING

Effective group counseling can be provided with minimal space and equipment: adequate space for a circle of nine chairs in a room in which clients can speak freely without being overheard. An attractive, spacious, well-equipped group room indicates institutional support for the service (and a successful practice for the private practitioner). Furthermore, a carpeted floor encourages clients to move back their chairs and to sit on the floor when they feel that it is appropriate. A more-spacious room is essential for those who use play techniques, informal exercises (such as trust walk), dance, music, and role playing as a basic part of their treatment process (Ohlsen, 1973). Regular audio recordings are essential in order to enable clients to review what happened in any given session, to criticize a proposal or role-played action, and to help an individual (including the counselor) to appraise his impact on others. Video recordings are even better for these purposes; often they are essential in order to help a member recognize unproductive behavior and unverbalized needs. Increasingly, counselors are learning to use video recordings to solicit feedback from their clients. Even young children can review a videotape and react to the following directions: (1) Watch for specific instances in which you were helped or hurt; (2) For each, indicate whether you were helped or hurt; (3) Watch for and tell us what helped or hurt you.

BEGINNING THE FIRST SESSION

Clients come to the first counseling session expecting to talk openly about what worries and upsets them and to explain to fellow clients precisely how they plan to change their behavior. Those who may otherwise be inclined to speak last are prepared by the intake interview to speak first and to begin with those problems that they think may be most difficult to discuss. For this courageous behavior they are reinforced by the counselor and fellow clients. As a consequence they tend to be pleased with their behavior; to feel that they have passed their most difficult test within their group; to conclude that they can cope with their problems; and to sense fellow clients' genuine acceptance of them. They recognize that their openness and courage helps others, too.

Early in the first session, the counselor comments very briefly on the importance of everyone being given a chance to talk about problems and goals. Usually the counselor also asks clients to help manage the use of time in order to give everyone a chance to talk, and finally to agree on operation guidelines. After each has discussed their major concerns and described their desired new behaviors, clients are encouraged to ask any questions they may have concerning expectations and to agree on any essential operation guidelines. Most groups develop some agreements on confidentiality, meeting time, attendance, approximate number of meetings, scheduling of individual sessions, and termination. Whenever the counselor notices (especially during the first several sessions) a client functioning especially well as a client or helper, she reinforces it by calling attention to the productive behavior. Some counselors even make video recordings of early sessions and critique them, looking for specific instances in which individuals were good clients or good helpers.

When the need for a new operating guideline surfaces, the counselor reflects the need for it and helps the clients define it. When they have a guideline but seem to be waiting for her to enforce it, the counselor tries to help them identify and accept their responsibility for maintaining their own guidelines. For example, "You seem to be annoyed with Jack's walking around the room when you'd like him to listen. I guess you wish I'd make him sit down and help Jane decide what she would like to tell her teacher." Thus, the counselor conveys to clients that they must accept responsibility for maintaining a working atmosphere that enhances their chances for being helped.

SUMMARY

Group counseling is a special relationship in which clients feel safe to discuss what really worries and upsets them, to define desired new behaviors, to practice essential interpersonal skills, and to implement new behaviors. Precisely how it differs from other group relationships and why each must demonstrate commitment to change and to help others change are discussed in this chapter.

Besides reviewing characteristics of those who tend to profit from group counseling, the chapter stresses why good prognosis for treatment is not sufficient. Clients must convince themselves as well as the counselor that they are ready for group counseling and committed to help develop and maintain the necessary and sufficient conditions for client growth.

Prior to being asked to decide whether they wish to participate in group counseling, a presentation is made to convey what clients can expect, what will be expected from them, and how they may be helped. The presentation also encourages clients to accept responsibility for getting themselves ready for group counseling and for defining behavioral goals and criteria that they can use to appraise their own growth. In addition, it tends to make the group experience more attractive. It is followed by an intake interview in which each prospective client is helped to define behavioral goals and criteria for appraising growth, to assess readiness for counseling, and to clarify expectations.

The primary structuring for group counseling is done in the presentation and the intake interview prior to the first counseling session. Further structuring occurs whenever clients are either uncertain what is expected or sense the need for new operational guidelines. Nevertheless, verbal structuring alone does not convey what is really expected: The counselor's expectations, at least, are communicated by the counselor's behavior in the counseling group—knowingly encouraging certain behaviors and discouraging others.

REFERENCES

Ackerman, N. W. (1955). Group psychotherapy with a mixed group of adolescents. *International Journal of Group Psychotherapy, 5,* 249–260.

Adler, K. (1972). Techniques that shorten psychotherapy illustrated with five cases. *Journal of Individual Psychology, 28,* 155–168.

Allport. G. W. (1960). *Personality and social encounter.* Boston: Beacon Press.

Ansbacher, H. (1972). Alderian psychology: The tradition of brief psychotherapy. *Journal of Individual Psychology, 28,* 137–151.

Alexander, F., & French, T. M. (1946). *Psychoanalytic therapy.* New York: Ronald.

Bach, G. R. (1954). *Intensive group psychotherapy.* New York: Ronald.

Bandura, A. (1977). *Social learning theory.* Englewood Cliffs, NJ: Prentice-Hall.

Barten, H. H. (1971). *Brief therapies.* New York: Behavioral Publications.

Beck, A. T. (1976). *Cognitive therapy and the emotional disorders.* New York: International Universities Press.

Beck, D. F. (1958). The dynamics of group psychotherapy as seen by a sociologist. *Sociometry, 21,* 98–128, 180, 197.

Bellak, L., & Small, L. (1965). *Emergency psychotherapy and brief psychotherapy.* New York: Grune & Stratton.

Buda, B. (1972). Utilization of resistance and paradox communication in short-term psychotherapy. *Psychotherapy and Psychosomatics, 20,* 210–211.

Cahill, T; Jessell, J.; & Horne, A. (1979). Peer and professional counselors: Prisoners' preference and evaluations. *Criminal Justice and Behavior, 6,* 400–415.

Carney, F. J. (1971). Evaluation of psychotherapy in maximum security prison. *Seminars in Psychiatry, 3,* 363–375.

Corrigan, J.; Dell, D.; Lewis, K.; & Schmidt, L. (1980). Counseling as a social influence process: A review. *Journal of Counseling Psychology, 27,* 395–441.

De Esch, J. B. (1974) The use of the Ohlsen model of group counseling with secondary school students identified as being disruptive to the education process. Unpublished doctoral dissertation, Indiana State University.

Dougherty, A. M. (1974). A study of the effects of two types of interpretation on subjects of different personality types from two education levels. Unpublished doctoral dissertation, Indiana State University.

Egan, G. (1985). *The skilled helper.* Monterey, CA: Brooks/Cole.

Ellis, A. (1984). Rational emotive therapy. In R. J. Corsini, (Ed.), *Current psychotherapies* (3rd ed.) Itasca, IL.: Peacock Publishing Company.

Ewing, T. N., & Gilbert, W. M. (1967). Controlled study of the effects of counseling on scholastic achievements of students of superior ability. *Journal of Counseling Psychology, 14,* 235–239.

Freedman, M. D., & Sweet, B. S. (1954). Some specific features of group psychotherapy and their implications for selection of patients. *International Journal of Group Psychotherapy, 4,* 355–368.

Gazda, G. M. (1973). Group procedures with children: A developmental approach. In M. M. Ohlsen (Ed.), *Counseling children in groups: A forum.* New York: Holt, Rinehart and Winston.

Ginott, H. G. (1961). *Group psychotherapy with children.* New York: McGraw-Hill.

Goldstein, A. (1971). *Psychotherapeutic attraction.* Elmsford, NY: Pergamon Press.

Goldstein, A., & Myers, C. (1986). Relationship enhancement methods. In Kanfer, F., & Goldstein, A. (Eds.), *Helping people change.* New York: Pergamon Press.

Helner, P. A. (1972). The effects of the use of interpretation as a counseling technique. Unpublished doctoral dissertation, Indiana State University.

Hilkey, J. H. (1975). The effects of video-tape pretraining and guided performance on the process and outcomes of group counseling. Unpublished doctoral dissertation, Indiana State University.

Hilkey, J. H.; Wilhelm, C.; & Horne, A. (1982). Comparative effectiveness of videotape pretraining versus no pretraining on selected process and outcome variables in group therapy. *Psychological Reports, 50,* 1151–1159.

Holmes, D. J. (1964). *The adolescent in psychotherapy.* Boston: Little Brown.

Horne, A., & Matson, J. (1977). A comparison of modeling, desensitization, flooding, study skills and control groups for reducing test anxiety. *Behavior Therapy, 8,* 1–8.

Hughes, J. (1983). The comparison of general and specific video pretraining on selected process and outcome variables in counseling. Unpublished doctoral dissertation, Indiana State University.

Ivey, A. E. (1983). *Intentional interviewing and counseling.* Monterey, CA: Brooks/Cole.

Johnson, J. A. (1963). *Group therapy: A practical approach.* New York: McGraw-Hill.

Jourard, S. (1964). *The transparent self.* New York: Van Nostrand.

Katz, E. W.; Ohlsen, M. M.; & Proff, F. C. (1959). An analysis through use of kinescopes of the interpersonal behavior of adolescents in group counseling. *Journal of College Student Personnel, 6,* 1, 2–10.

Lawe, C.; Horne, A.; & Taylor, S. (1983). Effects of pretraining procedures for clients in counseling. *Psychological Reports, 53,* 327–334.

Lieberman, M. A.; Yalom, I. D.; & Miles, M. D. (1973). *Encounter groups: First facts.* New York: Basic Books.

Lindt, H. (1958). The nature of therapeutic interaction of patients in groups. *International Journal of Group Psychotherapy, 8,* 55–69.

Loeser, L. H. (1957). Some aspects of group dynamics. *International Journal of Group Psychotherapy, 7,* 5–19.

McClelland, D. C. (1971). That urge to achieve. In D. A. Kalb; I. M. Rubin; & J. M. McIntyre (Eds.), *Organizational psychology: A book of readings.* Englewood Cliffs, NJ: Prentice-Hall.

Meichenbaum, D. (1977). *Cognitive behavior modification: An integrative approach.* New York: Plenum.

Mowrer, O. H. (1973). Group counseling in the elementary school: The professional vs. the peer model. In M. M. Ohlsen (Ed.), *Counseling children in groups: A forum.* New York: Holt, Rinehart and Winston.

Murphy, P.; Jessell, J.; & Horne, A. (1988). Model reinforcement and rational behavior therapy treatments for treating counselor anxiety. Unpublished manuscript, Indiana State University.

Ohlsen, M. M. (Ed.) (1973). *Counseling children in groups: A forum.* New York: Holt, Rinehart and Winston.

Ohlsen, M. M. (1974). *Guidance services in the modern school.* New York: Harcourt.

Ohlsen, M. M., & Gazda, G. M. (1965). Counseling underachieving bright pupils. *Education, 86,* 78–81.

Oxley, G. (1973). Short-term therapy with student couples. *Social Casework, 54,* 216–233.

Peck, M. L., & Stewart, R. H. (1964). Current practices in selection criteria for group-play therapy. *Journal of Clinical Psychology, 20,* 146.

Powdermaker, F. B., & Frank, J. D. (1953). *Group psychotherapy.* Cambridge, MA: Harvard University Press.

Psathas, G. (1960). Phase, movement and equilibrium tendencies in interaction process in psychotherapy groups. *Sociometry, 23,* 177–194.

Rhodes, S. L. (1973). Short-term groups of latency age children in a school setting. *International Journal of Group Psychotherapy, 23,* 204–216.

Rickard, H. C. (1965). Tailored criteria of change in psychotherapy. *Journal of General Psychology, 72,* 63–68.

Ryan, W. (1958). Capacity for mutual dependencies and involvement in group psychotherapy. *Dissertation Abstracts, 19,* 1119.

Schafer, R. (1973). The termination of brief psychoanalytic psychotherapy. *International Journal of Psychoanalytic Psychotherapy, 2,* 135–148.

Schmidt, L. D., & Strong, S. R. (1970). Expert and inexpert counselors. *Journal of Counseling Psychology, 17,* 115–118.

Sermat, V., & Smith, M. (1973). Content analysis of verbal communication. *Journal of Personality and Social Psychology, 26,* 332–346.

Sethna, E. R., & Harrington, J. A. (1971). A study of patients who lapsed from group psychotherapy. *British Journal of Psychiatry, 119,* 59–69.

Sifneos, P. E. (1972). *Short-term psychotherapy and emotional crises.* Cambridge, MA Harvard University Press.

Simonson, J., & Apter, S. (1969). Therapist disclosure in psychotherapy. Paper presented at the Eastern Psychological Association Conference, Philadelphia, PA.

Simonson, N., & Bahr, S. (1974). Self-disclosure by the professional and paraprofessional therapist. *Journal of Consulting and Clinical Psychology, 42,* 359–363.

Smith, M. L.; Glass, G. V.; & Miller, T. V. (1980). *The benefits of psychotherapy.* Baltimore, MD: Johns Hopkins Press.

Spielberger, C. O.; Weitz, H.; & Denny, J. P. (1962). Group counseling and academic performance of anxious freshmen. *Journal of Counseling Psychology, 9,* 195–204.

Stranahan, M.; Schwartzman, C.; & Atkin, E. (1957). Group treatment for emotionally disturbed and potentially delinquent boys and girls. *American Journal of Orthopsychiatry, 27,* 518–527.

Stroff, H. H., & Binder, J. L. (1984). *Psychotherapy in a new key.* New York: Basic Books.

Taylor, H. E. (1974). A study of comparison of reactions to four types of counselor response on the dimension of the locus of responsibility. Unpublished doctoral dissertation, Indiana State University.

Wattenburg, W. W. (1953). Who needs counseling? *Personnel Guidance Journal, 32,* 202–205.

Wolberg, L. R. (1965). *Short-term psychotherapy.* New York: Grune & Stratton.

2

THEORIES OF GROUP TREATMENT

Learning the intricacies of group process and developing skills for effective group leadership rests on a solid base of theoretical understanding. The purpose of this chapter is to stimulate the reader's interest in understanding how theory can be used by comparing and contrasting theoretical orientations and their relationship to group process and intervention. Therefore, the following questions will be used to explore this relationship: How do roles of leaders and group members change according to different theories? What stages do groups go through in the process of becoming a group? What is the nature of structural and technical intervention typical of various theories? What are the goals for process and outcome of various theoretical orientations? How can different theoretical orientations be used in an integrated and creative fashion? Theoretical models presented in this chapter are illustrations of how individual theories of psychotherapy can be used as a format for group counseling. The theories covered in this chapter are viewed as secondary to the goal for teaching theoretical integration and the development of multi-strategy interventions.

RATIONALE FOR THE USE OF THEORY: A CASE FOR ECLECTICISM

Theories of psychotherapy have common elements. They all have a philosophical basis that suggests an appropriate lifestyle capable of promoting health; or a belief system that, if subscribed to, will optimize adjustment, as well as foster change and growth. Theories of psychotherapy attempt to account for how people come to function poorly, as well as specify various methods for rendering assistance. Most theories provide some format for developing and assessing criteria which indicates the "nature" of changes that have taken place.

A general criticism regarding particular theories is they are either too specific or too general to account for all the elements involved in the complexities of human behavior. A problem frequently facing counselors is the conflict over choosing which theories to accept, or how to put together theoretical concepts to form a consistent system from which to work. This situation increases in difficulty when the counselor is faced with research findings that suggest that no significant differences exist between theoretical orientations and therapeutic effectiveness (Korchin, 1976).

The belief that one must be consistent with a theory, or have one theory that is known best, may be an attempt on the part of the counselor to gain a sense of security through mastering a portion of the field of psychology, which is vast, uncertain, and constantly changing. To align oneself with a particular theory often generates a political attitude in which the party member becomes a loyal advocate. Theoretical perspectives often polarize and practice can become rigid when the counselor develops a theoretical bias. Searching, experimenting, reflecting, and formulating strategies for providing help is a continuous process. Using a theory to build strategy for offering help must take into consideration the context of the client and the problems or issues being addressed. For example, theories that regard all human problems as caused by intrapsychic conflict and recommend insight and catharsis as important curative factors can be seen as being in conflict with theoretical procedures for learning to reduce anxiety by desensitization. Both provide explanations and procedures for rendering help; however, staunch believers in each theoretical perspective argue the truth and correctness of their position, while denigrating the value of the other, leaving the practitioner in a state of ambiguity and confusion. The choice of one perspective over another can limit the counselor's options to broaden the scope of the counseling process and reduces the potential benefit to the client that both perspectives might offer.

Combining insight with desensitization stretches the boundaries that limit both theories, and challenges the counselor to create a helping process that provides multi-methods for different aspects of the client's problem.

The Multi-Modal Approach

Albert Einstein referred to theory as a conceptual system created to order our thinking and to meet an intense desire for assured knowledge (Einstein, 1982). A system of theoretical conceptualization helps the counselor order the complexities and nuances characteristic of the human condition, as well as providing a method for testing the certainty of the knowledge generated by such a system. Maintenance of a critical attitude on the counselor's part is essential when integrating different theoretical perspectives. Accordingly, such attitudes recognize actual or possible theoretical contradictions. The resolution and interaction of theoretical differences broadens the base of theoretical understanding the counselor has, thus enriching the potential benefits for clients participating in group counseling (Slavson, 1979). Clients, according to Slavson (1979), profit more from a variety of integrated approaches, which seems to be especially true for group counseling due to its dynamic qualities of interaction which run parallel with many theoretical perspectives. Lazarus (1976) holds a similar view, suggesting that clients' problems stem from a combination of factors operating simultaneously, and that focusing the counseling process on only one element of a problem reduces the efficacy of counseling. We take the position that a multi-modal approach provides a good framework for supporting further theoretical integration and development. A multi-modal process need not be limited to the multiple variables suggested by Lazarus. There may be an infinite number of potential variable combinations, especially since no two human beings are alike or experience problems in the exact same way.

Theory Abuse and Limitation

In general, theories serve several purposes, ranging from providing assurance for the counselor, in the form of knowledge about group process, to a superstructure for conducting the scientific process of observing, formulating, predicting, implementing, and evaluating processes and outcomes of group counseling. Theory meets the need for stimulating the counselor's growth and development as a professional (Shertzer & Stone, 1974). On the other hand, theory can also be abused by counselors when they accept theoretical ideas that appeal to their needs for power and control instead of what may be best for the client. Theoretical abuse also occurs when counselors use it to justify and rationalize a lack of success or negative outcomes of group counseling in order to save face. Perhaps an even worse abuse of theory occurs when it becomes a self-fulfilling prophecy, in which the client's reactions to the therapeutic bias are used as criteria for proving the validity of the therapist's theory

All theories have limitations, are partially useful, and reflect the historical, cultural, and value perspectives of the time in which the theory was constructed. As Slavson (1979) suggests: "Contradictions are inherent in all human effort, especially in the intellectual domain. A tentative theory, and also a practice, approaches truth more closely than does doctrinaire positivism" (p. 282). The following theoretical frameworks may serve the beginning counselor as basic elements for theoretical integration. We will begin first with the basic elements of group dynamics.

GROUP DYNAMICS: COMMON CHARACTERISTICS OF GROUPS

Group dynamics is a branch of social psychology that deals with the processes of group structure and function. The following are considered characteristics of groups in general: all groups have some basic purpose for existing *(goals)*, a system in which members play various parts *(roles)*, and some form of evaluating and establishing expectations for members' behavior *(norms)*.

Some of the common goals frequently associated with counseling groups are gaining awareness and perspective of one's problems by comparing feelings and perceptions with others; enhancing one's self-image by receiving support and acceptance from others; developing an understanding and sensitivity for others; and learning new communication and coping skills (Goldenburg, 1983).

The various behaviors individuals display in group are often based on the roles they perceive appropriate for themselves and the expectations they believe others have for them. When these two factors are in harmony, the individual feels accepted, comfortable, and is able to function in the group with less anxiety or apprehension. However, when the individual experiences a conflict between the roles he or she wishes to play and those the group members think he or she should play, the individual may experience dissatisfaction, lowered group morale, and lowered self-esteem.

Common roles group members play are maintenance, task, and self. Members playing a maintenance role are concerned with promoting group morale and member satisfaction. Typically, members who support others, convey empathy, or wish to settle disputes are concerned with maintenance of group cohesion. Task role behavior generally involves promoting the group's goals by encouraging members to cooperate in accomplishing the task at hand. Self role behavior is based on satisfying personal needs which may be inconsistent with or irrelevant to the goals of the group. Monopolist and recognition seekers illustrate self role behavior (Bass, 1965).

The power of roles seems obvious when looking at the outcome of research, such as that of Philip Zimbardo's mock prison study, in which he randomly assigned students at Stanford University into either roles of guard or prisoner. Role instructions were minimal. Guards were told to keep order. The study was scheduled to last for two weeks, but had to be stopped due to the violent behavior of the guards. Hostility, expressed both physically and verbally, became indistinguishable from role play or reality. Perhaps such research points out the power of shaping and affecting behavior by psychodrama and role play.

Another characteristic common to all groups are norms, which are standards that govern and maintain behavior. Norms set up limits or boundaries for what is acceptable. A counseling group establishes norms for openness, congruent communication, and emotional expression on both a formal and informal level. Such norms are established formally by providing ground rules, and informally by the behaviors of group interaction and idiosyncracies. The power of norms greatly affects one's sense of acceptance by others. Fitting into and affiliating are determined by norms governing appropriate interpersonal relationship behavior. At times these norms can be coercive and damaging to an individual.

A great deal of group behavior is generated by the principles of social influence. Conformity is a type of social influence that shapes the norms of a group. Several factors affect conformity. The fear of being different, rejected, or labeled as a deviate increases the tendency toward conformity among group members. The more unanimous the group is in agreement, the more likely its members will conform. The greater the sense of group cohesion the more likely members will conform. The more members view the group as an effective means of testing reality, the more conformity will take place among them. The lower the individuals' level of self-esteem, the more likely they will seek acceptance in the form of conformity. The greater the need for affiliation the individual experiences, the more likely they are to conform (Stang, 1972).

According to social psychologists (French & Raven, 1959), social power and influence can be broken down into six categories. First, *coercive* power is said to exist when the influence is controlled by potential for punishment. Second, when the control of behavior is influenced by potential for *reward,* power is exerted by providing pleasure, gratification, and/or positive reinforcement. Third, influence and power may stem from the belief in the leader and/or group members as having some form of *expertise.* Fourth, *referent* power is said to exist when the group and/or leader serve as a point of reference for self-evaluation. Fifth, the leader, by virtue of his or her training and position in the group has a form of power known as *legitimate* power. And sixth, power and influence may also come in the form of providing *information,* which can lead to perceptual and behavioral change.

Group members may respond to social influence and power in a variety of ways. Kelman (1961) suggests that they respond in three basic ways. They either *comply* in order to gain a reward or avoid punishment, seek *identification* with the individual or group in order to be liked or affiliated, or they simply comply because they believe in the correctness and appropriateness of the behavior; in this last regard, the influence is said to have been *internalized.*

One of the major sources of influence characteristic of group counseling is based on the need for affiliation—the desire to be with and related to others. Several factors influence affiliative behavior. Schacter (1959) suggests that anxiety is a major reason people seek to affiliate, whereas Festinger (1954) believes the need is based on other social needs. For example, the need for feedback and/or some method of self-evaluation by comparison with others (known as the Social Comparison Theory of affiliation). Learning theories, in general, hold that individuals simply affiliate with each other out of the potential benefits, which is referred to as the Social Exchange theory.

A group leader needs to be familiar with the basic elements of group dynamics. The power and social influence of the group can be both devastating and therapeutic. When the group develops norms that are coercive or vigilante-like, members can easily become victims of conformity and uniformity of thought. The group has failed to foster the development of therapeutic norms. It is the leader's responsibility to assure that healthy group norms develop by their ability to model appropriate behaviors and to teach the same to group members. Let us now turn our attention to behavioral processes and group work.

BEHAVIORAL PROCESSES

Behavioral approaches to group counseling, as presented in this section, will include elements of cognitive, social learning, rational emotive therapy, and multi-modal behavior therapies. As a model for therapeutic intervention, behavioral therapy consists of the application of a set of principles based in learning theory (Lazarus, 1971). Most of these principles and procedures follow the scientific method. Clearly defining and specifying goals and objectives is the first step in this process. Clients are encouraged to state specific goals for behavioral change that can be measured objectively. The therapist's role in both individual and group work is to assist the client in clarifying and specifying desired changes in behavior. The initial phases of the change process are seen as requiring clarity and specificity.

The second step, which is based on the development of specific goals for behavior change, is the development of appropriately designed strategies for intervention relative to the client's purpose for change. Such intervention strategies are typically action oriented, and often involve the use of role playing to practice desired new behaviors in the counseling group. Measurement and assessment of the frequency of occurrence and rate of change in desired behavior is standard procedure, resulting in positive reinforcement for change. This process typically characterizes the last step in a behavioral program (Mahoney, 1977).

Clearly Defined Goals

An illustration of a clearly defined goal would be "to learn how to express one's feelings and thoughts assertively in the presence of others." This goal might be appropriate, as part of a treatment program, for a socially withdrawn or shy client. Such a client may be invited to role play initiating conversations in a group. For example, the group leader invites Bill, a shy withdrawn client, whose goal in the group is to learn to express himself openly and assertively without feeling anxious and overwhelmed, to role play initiating conversations in a semi-familiar setting. Initiating and being involved in a group on a spontaneous level is Bill's stated goal for this particular group session.

Role Playing: Action and Practice

The leader asks the group members to help Bill set the role-play scene. The group decides with Bill's input, to role play a situation frequently encountered by Bill, which involves withdrawing and avoiding others. The role play consists of Bill approaching and initiating conversation with a group of students who congregate outside a classroom in a lounge area. The role play starts with Bill initiating conversation: "Uh, hey, uh, (silence), uh, anybody read today's assignment?'' A group member replies: ''Yeah, boring stuff, huh? I had a hard time staying awake. I couldn't care less about rat studies on the schedules of reinforcement!'' Bill responds: ''Well, actually, uh, I, uh, (silence), thought it was sort of, well, kind of interesting, but maybe it was boring.''

Another group member interjects: ''I didn't think it was boring either, Bill; but I would rather have been watching the Celtics play the '76ers.'' Bill replies: ''Yeah, I wish I had more time to relax and watch a little tube once in a while. This semester seems like it's never going to end.'' Judy, another group member, joins in with: ''I know what you mean, I can't believe all the work I've got to do and there's only a few weeks left.'' Bill initiates again by extending and changing the conversation: ''I guess the only good point in all this is that we'll be getting a break soon . . . what do you guys have planned for the break?''

Feedback

After Bill has had an opportunity to practice new behaviors, the leader asks the group members and Bill to comment on what they experienced during the role play. Group members are invited to give feedback, and to reflect on their behaviors in the role play. Invariably, members will identify with issues similar to Bill's. In this regard Bill's problems are seen as problems people have in common. Bill may feel support and reassurance that he is not alone, and that others more interpersonally skilled have difficulties as well.

Reinforcement

After feedback is given, Bill is invited to try again to practice what he has learned. When the role play is concluded the leader asks Bill if he can think of situations he might encounter during the week in which he would be willing to practice his assertive behavior. At this point, the leader invites Bill to contract with the group to initiate conversations on three different occasions during the week with a selected group of people he would like to get to know better. Subsequent group work with such a client may include reports from the homework contract and further role plays or amended homework contracts designed to deal with specific aspects of this client's desired change. Group members, in accordance with behavioral approaches, assist by reinforcing desired behaviors during the process and feedback portion of the role play, model appropriate behavior during the role play, as well as reinforce members for behaviors that approximate their goals.

A summary of characteristics of behavioral approaches to group counseling, but not exclusive to behavioral counseling in groups are: specific, concrete goals for behavioral change implemented through action, practice, feedback, and reinforcement for desired change in behavior; an understanding that the client will continue to work at changing on their own between sessions; that clients will have prepared specific goals for each session; and a goal-attainment and progress scale designed to measure the outcome of behavior change (McCarthy, 1978).

Behavioral procedures are aimed at providing the client with a set of problem-solving skills appropriate and flexible enough for dealing with the client's current issues and concerns, as well as reducing the likelihood of future problems. Individuals in need of assistance are viewed by behavioral therapists as having deficits, deficiencies or excesses in their repertoire of coping and social skills. Personal concerns are perceived to result from learned habits and patterns of adjustment versus historical antecedents or intrapsychic conflict. Optimistically, clients are seen as being capable of learning new and more appropriate ways of behaving; likewise, growth and development are a result of learning.

ROLE OF THE COUNSELOR

The role of the counselor may be defined as a facilitator catalyst and teacher with more emphasis on the role of teacher than in other theoretical frameworks, such as client-centered. Initially, this role may involve assisting a client during the intake phase of group work to clearly and specifically define the elements of their concern. Careful documentation of the duration, intensity, and frequency of a client's problem is considered essential. Any attempt on the part of clients to experiment with changing their behavior is also recorded along with the success or failure of such attempts. Co-investigation and co-experimentation are shared responsibilities between clients and therapists. The behavioral therapist encourages the client to view the development of her concerns as problematic behaviors instead of hidden or unconscious elements of past relationships with parental figures, which are responsible for the client's current state or condition.

A major role of facilitation played by a group therapist, in general, involves implementing the process. For the behavior therapist, facilitation may take the form of assisting the client and group in the clarification, specification, and outlining of the parameters of a particular counseling session. The process goals of how the group session will be performed is detailed clearly to group members. (This may be done by giving clients handouts prior to the session, covering specific topics, such as giving feedback, self-disclosure, role playing, setting goals for specific behavior change, and the like.) The role of experimenter/investigator is a shared responsibility in which members are taught a process of change through experimentation and investigation. The combined roles of facilitator/teacher may involve teaching the clients to recognize the impact of their self talk (what they tell themselves) and its effects on their subsequent behaviors; or the therapist may teach group members how to determine which behaviors should be reinforced and how they should reinforced.

The behavioral counselor's approach to group counseling emphasizes the importance of the social environment in shaping and maintaining behavior. From this perspective, the leader is interested in developing a group environment in which members can assert their rights, opinions, thoughts, and feelings congruently. These congruent behaviors are taught, not just by the leader, but through reinforcement given by members when and how they attend to each other. The leader instructs members in life-enhancing prosocial skills, such as identifying inappropriate cognitions and, self-defeating statements that minimize adjustment and lower self-esteem. Members are taught how to stop and replace negative thinking with appropriate self-supporting statements which increase the clients' ability to cope, and enhance self-esteem.

The Counselor in Action

The following is an example of a typical group session using behavioral approaches. The group has been given a handout in the previous session regarding the nature of thought stopping and self-defeating statements. The focus is on a problem one of the members has been dealing with regarding her negative self talk. The member, Molly, has just finished telling the group that she has never had a good relationship with a man, and that she does not think she will ever trust or accept that someone could really love or care about her. The leader asks the group to respond to what they hear in Molly's self talk: "What did you hear about how Molly is describing her relationships with men?"

A male group member responding: "Molly, you seem to be making statements about yourself that are conclusive. According to you, you're no good and no one would want to have anything to do with you. You are making sweeping generalizations about yourself and your potential for relationships." A female member interjects: "I know what it's like to think like that. I feel lousy when I treat myself like I can't do anything right. But lately I've been catching myself making defeating statements. You know, I'm beginning to realize that I really don't have to be perfect to get respect or approval, and besides I think I spend too much time worrying about what others will think of me if I do this or that wrong. I mean who really cares if I don't get all As anyway! I'm a worthwhile person regardless of my grade point average." Other members join in the discussion, some making comments relevant to their own behaviors, and some giving Molly feedback.

The leader interrupts: "Molly, I wonder how you could use what others have been saying to help yourself?" Molly responds: "Well, I think I have a better understanding of how my negative thoughts affect me. I think I dwell too much on how others don't accept me. I also think I set myself up for rejection by assuming the worse will always happen." A discussion follows, led by the leader, which focuses on the concept of indirect self acceptance and the self-fulfilling prophecy. The session concludes with Molly agreeing to keep a record of the frequency and nature of her self-defeating talk as well as comments on her progress with stopping negative thinking and replacing it with positive, self-supportive statements. Molly is invited to bring this information back at the next session for further work.

ROLE OF GROUP MEMBERS

While carefully recording their efforts, group members are expected to actively participate in defining, developing, and experimenting with changes in their own and others' behavior. In this regard, members share in the responsibility for improving the quality of their lives by being actively involved in their own therapy, while giving assistance, through clear and specific feedback, to others—helping them to clarify and assess the various dimensions of their behavior change.

The roles of group members may vary with the particular format and focus of the treatment. The multi-modal approach of Arnold Lazarus (1976) illustrates such a framework. The multi-modal approach teaches clients to view problems along a continuum of different psychological indices. Group members and leaders learn to adapt their interventions according to the multiple dimensions of the client's problem through problem definition and treatment strategy, as well as through assessment and reinforcement of client change. The following is the multi-modal orientation.

DIAGNOSTIC CATEGORIES	PROBLEM DEFINITION
Behavior	Withdraws and withholds self from others.
Affect	Feels fearful, lonely, and isolated.
Sensation	Tense, constricted, and frozen in the presence of social conditions.
Imagery	Images of self being put down, ridiculed, and rejected in social group.
Cognition	Self talk. "Others always reject me—don't find me of worth—people are cruel—it's awful to be rejected."
Interpersonal	Nonassertion and denial of personal rights and responsibilities with others.

TREATMENT FORMAT	ASSESSMENT/OUTCOME DATA
Role play specific situations of interpersonal problems in group in which client practices self assertion and spontaneous contact with others.	Client learns to express feelings, opinions, and thoughts congruently and forthrightly.

TREATMENT FORMAT (cont'd)

Group interaction to learn how to give feedback and reinforcement for appropriate self-disclosure along with understanding and learning framework for disclosure and feedback.

Experimentation with body awareness with feedback and practice for changing nonverbal behaviors in group (contact/withdrawal exercise).

Leader and group members encourage client to develop mental images/scenarios of interpersonal effectiveness which are used for role play and behavior rehearsal.

Client is requested to keep records of self statements for purpose of recognizing errors in logic, judgment, and rationality as well as to explore self statements which are healthy and capable of engendering growth and change. Client's progress is reported in group.

In-group role plays are extended into contracts for out-of-group behavior in key situations pertinent to client's objectives for change.

ASSESSMENT/OUTCOME DATA (cont'd)

Client develops ability to give and receive feedback thus extending psychological freedom and enhancing self-esteem.

Client learns how to adjust body sensations in the context of interpersonal tensions.

Client learns to define self in multiple ways through positive mental imaging.

Client decreases deficits in coping skills and increases ability to cope more effectively through thought stopping and replacement.

Client transfers in-group learning to outside experiences, tries out new learning and celebrates progress as well as work on improving efficiency for behavioral change.

RATIONAL/COGNITIVE BEHAVIORAL PROCESSES

Closely associated and connected to behavioral models for group work are the *rational/cognitive* therapeutic approaches. Rational-emotive (RET) and Neuro-Linguistic programming (NLP) seem to have similar goals and processes aimed at helping the client adapt by way of altering or changing perceptions or mental programs. In general, such approaches do not stress the interpersonal dynamics of relationships as important therapeutic phenomena that enhance change; nor is emotional catharsis viewed as a key to therapeutic facilitation. RET views the group's objective as structuring experiences in which members learn more about the nature of their self-defeating beliefs. NLP stresses the importance of building mental program formats that increase effectiveness in coping.

RET

The RET group leader functions to structure the focus of participants on how to solve problems and live more rationally. Teaching people how to accept reality and to put their efforts into changing (instead of complaining and obsessing, in the presence of several others, about the woes of their existence) is seen as more powerful in effecting change than a single therapist/client relationship. Often clients are able to recognize irrationality in other members' behaviors more so than in their own, and can bring it to the attention of the participants, thereby enriching the potential for self-awareness among the group members as a whole. Group members in RET often take on the responsibility of helping others by offering suggestions, comments, and assistance in the form of reality-checking for rational thinking which enhances therapeutic effectiveness.

Similar to other group-based formats, RET employs role playing, behavioral rehearsal, and homework contracts to stimulate members to employ in-group learning to life situations outside the group. The group is also seen as a microcosm in which irrational member behavior is viewed as a demonstration of the typical kind of thinking and behaving that creates problems for the client in their outside lives. Homework reports given by members in group follow the ABCs of the principle for rational living. Members are taught to use a format consisting of a daily commitment to homework as a practice in which they fill out a homework sheet detailing *activating* events (a); rational and irrational *beliefs* (b); *consequences* of their irrational beliefs (c); *disputation* and challenge for their irrational beliefs (d); and their alternative thoughts and *emotions* (e) (Ellis, 1977).

RET, being a highly cognitive process, makes use of psycho-educational processes that help individuals tune into the irrational thought processes involved in their fear and catastrophic expectations over risking openly in a group; and to understand that such thoughts inhibit their psychological freedom and limit their contact with others.

NLP

Other cognitive approaches may be used to assist clients. A typical goal of NLP therapy is to increase the client's awareness of and insight into their dysfunctional and maladaptive self talk and to understand the relationship between such mental activity and self-defeating behavior, as well as the effects of lowered self-esteem and general stress and anxiety. Clients can be taught to stop negative mental programming (self talk) and to explore their thinking with contextually appropriate cues and self support, both verbally and with images relative to enhancing general performance. These objectives are generally accomplished in group by the leader acting as a teacher and the members as seminar participants.

Cognitive-behavioral approaches tend to focus more on the intellectual, perceptual aspects of human experience, in contrast to the client-centered approaches, which tend to emphasize the role of feeling and emotional expression. The leader assumes a more directive-prescriptive role in a cognitive-behavioral approach, while the leader in a client-centered approach is more nondirective, and sometimes participates in the group like a member. Contrasting behavioral approaches with those of Gestalt provides the group leader with the options of teaching group members, for example, assertive behavior by combining the Gestalt principles of awareness and body language with the behavioral tenets for assertiveness. In this way, the group members learn how to use behavioral skills and their awareness of the here-and-now to creatively satisfy their needs. Keeping in mind the purpose of integrating theory, the following is a brief introduction to Gestalt processes.

GESTALT PROCESSES

Gestalt processes of psychotherapy have roots in existentialism, focusing more on the "what is" of an experience than on the "what should be." There is strong valuing for awareness in general; and, in fact, Perls (1969) believed that awareness, in and of itself, could be therapeutic. Similar to existential philosophy, the emphasis in Gestalt therapy is on the client's freedom of choice and responsibility for choosing. Gestalt is a nondirective, experiential process that opposes interpretive or cognitive didactic processes, which are viewed as fostering dependency through telling or informing clients about themselves. Gestalt therapy is based in field theory where perceptions, focus of attention, energy, and action are components of a holistic orientation. Field theory is interested in understanding how the individual is organizing experience in the present; what is being differentiated, selected for attention, focused on; and, how such aspects influence the investment of energies necessary for the completion and satisfaction of a need (Wallen, 1970).

The Components of Gestalt

Gestalt is a German word meaning "whole," or the sum of the parts that make up the whole (Simkin, 1975). This sum of the parts, or in Gestalt terminology, *configuration,* consists of patterns made of foreground and background. Foreground is that which emerges or stands out from background. A need that is being focused on (for example, thirst) is considered foreground. Background consists of anything undifferentiated, that is, needs that are not the present focus of attention. The process of Gestalt formation is present-centered, dynamic, and constantly changing. The Gestalt process is considered to be natural, self-regulating, and sensorimotor based. The individual is considered to be healthy when she is in harmony with her sensorimotor experiences (when they are congruent). Needs generate behaviors, and the process of organizing one's needs with appropriate behaviors that satisfy needs, is the process of a Gestalt formation. A good gestalten is well organized when needs are clearly identified and behaviors are appropriate for satisfaction and completion of the gestalt.

According to Simkin (1975), the goal of therapy is to help the client regain the capacity for experience intellectually, emotionally, and sensorially: to use their own equipment. Much, if not all major work in Gestalt therapy, is done through sensory contact with the environment in the here-and-now. Teaching about or supplying insight, as other theories advocate, is considered a therapeutic mistake (Perls, 1969). Change begins when individuals accept themselves as they are rather than as who they think they should be. The primary vehicle of Gestalt therapy is awareness. Awareness is a state of consciousness that develops through the focusing of one's attention. Human beings develop problems when awareness is blocked (Perls, 1969).

Levels of Resistance

Blocks to experiencing awareness may be equated with resistance. In dealing with resistance, Gestalt therapists (Zinker, 1978) believe that it is important to accept the client's resistance as a natural part of the change process. Often resistance can be dealt with by increasing the client's awareness of sensations in their bodies indicative of holding back or repressing energy. The client's awareness may be heightened by asking them to reenact or repeat statements, gestures, and behaviors until the energy level is sufficient to sponsor movement toward completion. Perls (1969) provided a schema for resistance that characterized various levels of resistance in terms of contact with self and others. The cliché level of surface interactions and social amenities are distant and void of meaningful contact. The next level of resistance, the phony level, was characterized by structuring time to avoid contact, and to play games designed to maintain distance and avoid intimacy. In the next level, the phobic level, the individual not only avoids meaningful contact, but becomes phobic, trying to escape facing themselves or others.

The last level of resistance was characterized as the explosive level in which energy for expressiveness and completion of needs is trapped or bottled up. The explosion occurs as a result of the energy released during the expression of the emotion or behavior being repressed. The important point is that the energy for expression is released in a healthy fashion allowing completion and resolution to take place. The explosion dramatically need not be expressed in order to have release. It is the ability to use one's awareness of the release that provides for continuation of the natural processes involved in contact and withdrawal. Perls (1969, 1973) believed that much of the focus of therapy pertained to working through the various levels of sensitivity to provide release.

The Gestalt Therapist

Gestalt (Kepner, 1980) characterizes the role of the leader as a facilitator of interpersonal and intrapersonal interactions in the here-and-now of the group. The therapist's role is to be a phenomenological observer, who reports observations without biasing the client with interpretations. The therapist's interventions are made where the blocks are in the client's awareness/excitement/contact cycle (Zinker, 1977). This natural process of experience is directed toward the completion and satisfaction of needs. The first part of this cycle is the organization of experience into an awareness. Energy from unmet needs serves to organize the individual's perceptions. Once the needs or wants of an individual become figural, foreground (or the focus of her attention), the second part of the cycle occurs in which energy is released in the form of motion or movement toward environmental contact which leads to fulfillment or completion of a need. Completion or resolution in healthy individuals results in withdrawal from contact, and the cycle begins over again. The Gestalt therapist uses the experience cycle as a framework to diagnose client dysfunction, develop intervention strategies, and assess the outcome of therapy.

Awareness Blocks

An individual may develop difficulties in functioning by blocking the mobilization of energy at any or all phases of the awareness/excitement/contact cycle (Zinker, 1978). Blocks at the sensation-awareness phase of this cycle may be characterized as being out of touch with one's body, not feeling, hearing, or seeing what is presently available to sensation, or blunted/dulled, and only partially aware of a present experience. Individuals who suffer from chronic hypertension are often unaware of their skyrocketing heart rates and blood pressures and report no sensation of stress or tension. An intervention at this stage may be directed at the client's body sensations by having the client translate awareness into body sensations. In this regard, the client would be instructed to report awareness in terms of sensation, for example, "When I think about all the responsibilities I have, I feel tightness in my throat, and knots in my stomach, and my jaw seems tense."

Energy Blocks

At another level of the cycle, the individual may have blocks between awareness and energy mobilization. She knows what she wants but fails to take actions which would lead to satisfaction. The procrastinator may illustrate such blockage in that she recycles "should" messages and then withdraws and avoids actions that would lead to accomplishing her objectives. Such a person may say to herself, "I should get to work on that report," but engage in endless social conversation with fellow employees, or merely sit dazed in a blur of her own anxiety. She generally ends up feeling guilty, depressed, and complains of fatigue, or not having enough energy to get anything done.

Instead, the energies to accomplish become anxiety and tension, and the block is the avoidance behavior. Getting the individual involved with her energies may be facilitated by having her experiment with changing "should" messages to "I want" and notice the changes in energy in her body as she changes her thinking.

Contact Blocks

At another level of this cycle, a sense of powerlessness is experienced when the individual has blocks between the energy and action phase. At this phase of the cycle, the individual may have an overload of energy, be highly excited to the point of being overwhelmed, shocked to the point of immobility. Interventions at this stage may consist of having the client attend to urges or impulses and having her express these impulses in a psychodramatic fashion. Blocks between action and the contact phase result in a lack of a sense of completion. The individual may report vague feelings, confusion, or act impulsively. Energy may be discharged with great gusto, but the outcome of the actions are disconnected from the needs that would fulfill or satisfy the individual. An intervention here may consist of having the client experiment with making contact with immediate reality and then withdrawing and reporting awareness in body sensation. The contact and withdrawal cycle has a natural rhythm, similar to the rhythms in nature, like day and night. When this natural process is disregarded the individual has lost touch with the most basic elements of human experience: the satisfaction found in living fully (Zinker, 1978).

Applying Gestalt Theory to Group Counseling

The leader in Gestalt therapy groups acts to facilitate by stimulating and mobilizing energy necessary for contact and involvement between self and others. Helping members to focus their awareness and attention on what they are doing in the here-and-now is a major leadership role for the Gestalt therapist. This includes getting members to take responsibility for what they are currently experiencing (Enright, 1975). The therapist may intervene at different levels, at the individual-member level, at the level of interpersonal contact, and the group level. At the individual-member level the therapist may ask a member to identify and express what she is currently experiencing. On an interpersonal level, the therapist encourages members to use their current experiences and sensations to engage each other directly. On the group level, the therapist intervenes to mobilize the group's energies and awarenesses of issues that result from the group's combined interactions over time, the group's process, or how the group as a whole has decided to act. This process is often unconscious to members.

The leader may intervene sequentially at all levels on a specific issue. For example: "Jerry, you seem tense. Can you get in touch with what's going on inside you right now?" (Individual level). The client responds by reporting sensations of tightness in his chest. The leader asks the client to focus his awareness on what is happening in the group at that moment that might be connected with Jerry's sensation of tension (interpersonal level). The client is then asked to take this awareness and put it into direct expression to someone in the group. The client says: "I'm feeling angry with you, Jim! I didn't like what you said to Mary; it seemed righteous and pompous!" In this instance the group becomes silent, members withdraw, and there is tension in the group over how to deal with this new situation, one in which the first, direct confrontation has taken place by one member to another.

The leader intervenes at the group level by asking the group to get in touch with what they are experiencing. What they heard or saw as well as how they are responding. The leader may ask members to share their sensations on a body level, individual to individual level, or on a fantasy level regarding what the group seems like at the moment. Often metaphoric feedback from members at the group level is rich in energy potential for developing ways of interacting that strengthen the group. For example, one member shares a fantasy in the form of a metaphor about the group, "I feel like we've been walking on ice and the ice just cracked; and we all heard it and we've stopped in our tracks." This metaphor can then be processed by the group with individual members sharing their feelings, thoughts, and fantasies about walking on ice with each other, as well as how they would like to interact, and what changes would have to take place.

In the previous example with Jerry, the need may be to check in with each other to see how others are experiencing the confrontation and to process how confrontation is o.k. or not o.k. and to share their personal issues about being confronted.

Therapist Intervention

Intervention by the therapist is a continuous process in which the therapist facilitates the natural flow of energy, awareness, and contact on an individual, interaction, and group level. Members have needs at all of these different levels. As members get in touch with their unique experience in the group, various needs emerge. Contacting others—showing specific responses they are having with another member; checking out their perceptions and having them affirmed by others; feeling they belong and are accepted by the group; and that the group is open to their input for change—illustrates the needs involved in the development of a sense of group community.

Timing of intervention on the part of a group leader is crucial. Attending to the signs indicative of the group's energy level, which may be illustrated by body postures, eye contact, and the expressiveness of members, can serve as important criteria for deciding when and how to intervene. Energy varies from member to member and from the issues being addressed. A different group energy, availability, and attentiveness exist for a member going through a divorce than exist for a member talking about problems in working with computers. The amount of time left in a session, and how much energy may have been expended during the session, may also influence the group's energy investment. The essence of creative use of group time and energy depends on the leader's ability to assess the situational dynamics within the group that influence energy production and energy loss. Gestalt therapy is above all else a process therapy. The experience of being in the group is the major therapeutic vehicle for growth and change. The leader's awareness of group process is the essential criterion for intervention.

Role of Group Members in Gestalt Therapy

Traditional Gestalt approaches to group counseling limit interaction among members. The primary benefit of limiting interactions between members is based on the notion that vicariously working through issues takes place when members relate to the work going on between the therapist and the individual client (Perls, 1969). The center of attention is between the therapist and the client. However, much of what Fritz Perls did in terms of group work consisted of time-limited workshops and seminars which limited the use of interaction or process-related group work. Not all Gestalt therapists are the same in their view of the use of group and Gestalt therapy (Enright, 1975; Zinker, 1977).

Interactional Model

The Gestalt Institute of Cleveland's model, for example, uses a group-interaction process. Interactional or group process models view changes that are curative as coming from the interactions among members and the subsequent development of therapeutic forces in groups. The role of the therapist shifts from working with individuals in a group to the working with the group as a system (Kepner, 1980), similar to other models of group work that are interactional and process oriented (Yalom, 1975; Corey, 1981; Ohlsen, 1977; Gazda, 1975).

Dual-Focus Models

Some Gestalt therapists believe that it is possible to combine the individual and group focus (Harmon, 1984). This dual focus seems to imply that focus on both the individual and the group is possible and appropriate to Gestalt group therapy. This notion points out the conflict between traditional Gestalt approaches to group counseling, which amount to treating individuals in a group, as opposed to group dynamic or process models, which view the group as having inherent therapeutic benefit. When the focus is solely between the leader and a member, the group members become sidelined; the leader takes on the power of knowing how to help, and members become dependent on the leader for direction. These circumstances seem to be mutually exclusive to the curative forces outlined by the interactional models. A delicate balance exists between the individual and the group regarding the effects of the disposition of energy, time, and focus. The more the group norms (via behavioral frequency and group sanction) involve individual members taking turns with the leader (the hot seat model), the more the group power shifts to the leader. Consequently, the more the group power shifts to the leader, the more the interaction processes necessary for the development of a group are restricted.

Intimacy Model

A group is an intimate system (Zinker, 1978). Like any system of human encounter, there are barriers to intimacy. Lying, being phony, withholding, playing the social games of fitting in, disguising feelings, denying or suppressing one's feelings and thoughts are roadblocks to intimacy. The role of a Gestalt group therapist is to assist members in removing their barriers to being intimate. According to Zinker (1977), groups are systems of people that come together to form an atmosphere that fosters creativity. The group becomes a process capable of fostering creativity when it encourages and supports experimentation with ways in which members can develop a sense of community; when it is aware of its process of development and can change to meet the needs of its members and the community; and when it fosters intimate contact among its members.

Intimate contact among members is essential to the development of a group. Intimacy may be brought about by heightening the awareness of group members' contact with each other in the here-and-now, particularly on the how and what of encounters between and among members. Growth occurs as members contrast their experiences in terms of the similarities and dissimilarities they share with others. In this way, the group becomes a wealthy community sponsoring a variety of possibilities for impact. The group becomes a cohesive unit when it can accommodate and assimilate the various elements and styles of members' contact with each other (Zinker, 1977; Kepner, 1980).

For example, when Bob shares with the members of the group that he can understand how withdrawing (not expressing his thoughts and feelings in response to the expression and behavior of other members in the group) could be interpreted as not caring, and that he has difficulty trusting others to be caring toward him, he is both assimilating and accommodating to the processes of group work. His therapy becomes the therapy of the group as both profit from the interchange. On the group process level, the group becomes a safer place when members come to understand and accept their differences and similarities, and a deeper level of intimate contact is more likely now that barriers have been removed.

Basic principles of Gestalt therapy serve to orient the members to the process of group counseling (Zinker, 1977). Members are encouraged to focus their attention on present, here-and-now encounters. Members are invited to share awarenesses of their differences and similarities of experience with each other and the group. The emphasis is on contrasting how members experience themselves and the group. Active, present, centered, and authentic encounters between members and the group are considered an important operational procedure. The leader is an active authority who may be an energy source for stimulating the group to experiment with the dynamic qualities of the group's social Gestalt; or the leader may elect to be a participant-observer, sharing thoughts and feelings regarding the processes of group interaction.

Creative Experimentation

Typical of Gestalt process, experimentation is encouraged by members. The source of energy for experimentation comes from the needs of the members and the group. The leader need not have sole responsibility for inventing and engineering the experimentation, but instead, may help the group decide on how it wishes to use its energy in a creative experiment. A leader may act as a stimulator and support-provider for sponsorship of group creativity. Creative experimentation by the group can take many forms. The group can be transformed into any number of social and/or metaphoric symbols capable of sponsoring exploration, discovery, and growth for its members.

For example, the group can be a courtroom dealing with the conflict over the behavior of a member that has broken a group norm. In this way, the group has a chance to explore its expectations for member behavior as well as to experiment with roles played in the group by various members. Being a judge, member of a jury, witness, prosecutor, or defending attorney gives members a rich source of experience and energy to play out in a lively fashion. As members experiment with the different configurations of the social microcosm, individual problems, themes, and archetypes are often uncovered in the gestalt of the group. The issues brought up by individuals as they experience them in the group and elsewhere in their lives, stimulates the exploration of creative alternatives for change and growth.

The blend of Gestalt therapy with group process and interaction models combines the flexibility, creativity, and the development of group dynamics (found in the experiential process) with the structural aspects of directed therapy (Zinker, 1977). Leader interventions are aimed at directing attention to what is being experienced by the group in the here-and-now and the emergent needs members have in the milieu of the group's ongoing process. The process of the group is seen as an unfolding social drama, and blocks which inhibit the ongoing process become the focus of awareness directed by the leader. Unlike the nondirective group leadership style, where the leader maintains a more passive role, the Gestalt leadership style is directive and active. The leader does not impose direction on the group but, instead, actively intervenes in the process of the group's experience to further energize the actions of the group to facilitate the satisfaction and completion of the needs of group members.

Thus far we have explored behavioral and Gestalt approaches to group counseling. Each having their unique benefits and limitations for assisting clients. Keeping in mind that no one theory has been demonstrated to be superior over others as a method for delivery of counseling services (Korchin, 1976), we will now explore what the client-centered model has to offer.

CLIENT-CENTERED GROUP COUNSELING

Client-centered counseling has become synonymous with the work of Carl Rogers. Typical of Rogerian group process, the group is viewed as having the inherent resources capable of developing and determining its own direction. This distinction places both behavioral and Gestalt processes in contrast with nondirective or client-centered processes. While there are many similarities, there are also differences regarding the function of the leader and the group members. In both the behavioral and Gestalt approaches, the leader is a stimulator and energizer and much more action oriented than the typical leader of a client-centered group. The leadership style of client-centered groups is generally more passive and nondirective. The leader is a model for interpersonal effectiveness, modeling the therapeutic norms of openness, congruence, warmth, genuineness, and acceptance. However, this is not meant to imply that other models for therapy do not advocate the same. The relationship dimension of client-centered counseling is considered critical to positive therapeutic outcome.

Developing a Group Climate

The identifying facilitative characteristics and objectives of client-centered groups may be formulated as follows. The development of a psychological climate in which members feel free to express themselves, without fear of ridicule or rejection, is a crucial quality of the client-centered approach. Group members gradually develop a sense of trust and identify with the group as a result of learning to express their feelings spontaneously and directly with each other. Members in client-centered groups are encouraged to take responsibility for their feelings and express them directly. Trust and open expression of feeling develops when members risk self-disclosure and discover that the expected catastrophic rejection or emotional collapse does not occur. Change becomes possible when the individual's psychological state is flexible and nondefensive. A group atmosphere of warmth, openness, and acceptance allows members to drop their defensive behaviors, and face themselves and others openly and honestly. The freedom to explore, adapt, and modify behaviors is considered to be an outcome of developing a therapeutic group climate (Rogers, 1970).

Experiences which may be growth providing often involve a sense of being in contact with others on a deeper and more meaningful level. Such experiences may be viewed as therapeutic in that changes in emotional states, or transitions in thoughts and viewpoints, frequently influence change in the way a person communicates. Individuals seem more willing to accept themselves and their experiences which are communicated in the form of "I" statements instead of "you," "one," or "we," which are typically disowning and distancing. New and old ways of behaving stand in contrast to each other, which often provides a new awareness of self and others. Often this experience is based in a recapitulation of old behaviors but under the above conditions the old pattern gives way to a new experience of "I'm o.k.! I can accept myself for who I truly am, even if others don't!"

Stages of Group Interaction

A client-centered approach to group counseling is based on the assumption that with the facilitative conditions of warmth, empathy, genuineness, and accept-ance, stages of group interaction sequentially emerge. Curative forces develop through the resolution of the issues involved in these various stages of group interaction (Yalom, 1975; Corey, 1981). For example, due to the nondirective nature of client-centered group work and the subsequent lack of structure, members may, at times, feel frustration, confusion, tension, and sometimes boredom. This condition is considered a stage of group process and is seen as part of the struggle of the group to get the leader to do something to take care of them. At this stage members may direct anger or resentment toward the leader. One of the goals at this stage of group interaction is to assist the group in resolving the issue of dependency on the leader to direct and conduct the group. As members learn to take responsibility for the direction of the group, the group becomes a product of their choice and making, thus the process is said to be group centered.

Initial Stage

In the early stages of a client-centered approach, contact between members is characteristically superficial, and generally void of energy and feeling. The topics of conversation are often social, like a cocktail party. Very little, if any, genuine contact occurs at this stage. The group seems to be in search of a leader, someone to guide, direct, and relieve them of the frustration and chaos they experience; someone who will reassure them and make something meaningful happen to relieve the stagnation and tension often experienced by members at this stage of the group's development. Leaders who have experienced this phenomenon know the pressure from the group can be intense. Resisting the pull to provide structure can prove very challenging. It is easy for a leader to give in to the bid to take responsibility. However, the group-centered process considers this to be a mistake. Giving in to the demands of the group to be taken care of blocks the development of the inherent facilitative characteristics and qualities of the group-centered process. When the leader takes responsibility for the structure of the group, he also supplies the energy, thereby hindering the group's ability to generate its own response.

Middle Stages

The process of moving from the cliché level of superficial interchanges is not always smooth and linear. Members may risk venturing beyond their façades and find others not ready or unwilling to grant them the asylum of acceptance. At this point the risking member may feel misunderstood, disappointed, and hurt. Others in the group may feel threatened and uncertain about how they should respond to such overt disclosures. The leader's role is to aid the group by helping members clarify and express their feelings about the experience, both to each other and about the group. The leader may be of further assistance by inviting members to disclose their own struggle to being open and to understand the process of the group at this stage. In other words, understanding group process means understanding the combined similarities and differences in the experiences shared by group members. Each member comes to a greater understanding of his or her own interpretations, meanings, and behaviors in the context of the same in others.

The energy and psychological movement inherent in this process of group interaction is continuous and dynamic. Without such awareness, expression, and understanding, the group stagnates and becomes blocked, and may regress to the superficial talk of previous stages in an attempt to produce a sense of safety. Essentially, the group statement is: "We aren't sure it's safe to venture further self-disclosure." The issues most often involved at this stage are trust and safety, generally based in fear of rejection and ridicule after being open and vulnerable. However, once members begin to risk openness it becomes increasingly difficult for them to return to the previous state of surface talk. The difficulty in returning to superficial-level interchanges is in part due to the lack of energy and stimulation that such encounters provide. The social "hunger" for genuine contact encourages open expression of feelings. As the group develops a sense of trust and safety, patterns of interaction and communication among members change. Expression of feelings becomes more spontaneous, genuine, and open between members, and interchanges tend to be more present centered, less a reporting from the past (a point in common with Gestalt therapy).

Advanced Stages

As members become less guarded with each other the expression of feelings toward each other may become negative or critical. A shock wave may go through the group at this point, as the vow of mutual support has been broken. The price of free, open, and genuine self-expression is often paid for in pain and struggle by group members. Trust among members may be temporarily damaged, but generally as members work through their hurt feelings trust is reestablished on a deeper level. The leader's role at this point is crucial. The leader can help group members deal with their hurt feelings, and help the group decide how feedback can be given without harm or undue pain to its members.

The level of safety and comfort that results from the ease and openness of expression by members not only varies with the developmental stages of group transition, but also from member to member. The ability of members to engage each other intimately can be an index of a particular individual's capabilities or limitations, the group's norms (prescription for appropriate behavior), and the developmental stage of the group. It behooves a leader to understand the variety of factors operating simultaneously in any given interchange in order to tailor their interventions effectively. It is important to keep in mind that in nondirective group work one of the roles the leader plays is expert process observer; this role is similar to the role of phenomenological observer played by the Gestalt therapist. The difference, other than semantics, is the Gestalt therapist is often more directive and active.

Client-centered group work is rooted in phenomenological existential philosophy, which characterizes the modern human conditions as cut off from the kinds of human contact once found in the extended families of previous decades. The desire to escape from loneliness, despair, and alienation supplies the motivation for seeking group counseling as a method of finding more meaningful relationships with others. The curative factors of group work correlate with these existential needs. The continuous interplay between members and the collective exchange of the group becomes the forum for developing, defining, and operationalizing the curative factors and healing potential of a group.

The Client-Centered Therapist

The work of a client-centered therapist is harmoniously linked to the human experience itself. If the benefits of client-centered group therapy are found in experiencing the inherent forces considered curative and natural to groups of human beings, then the technique and facilitation is found in the personhood of the therapist. In this regard, the therapist is not a role, but fully human and vitally present in all phases and aspects of the group's development. Accepting the responsibility as leader means willingly risking to be genuinely present and authentically involved with group members. Being open to self reflection, aware of personal shortcomings, and actively involved in one's own growth and development is seen as a responsibility involved in the process of self-actualization.

The emphasis on authentic and genuine encounter, coupled with the nondirective orientation of client-centered group work, makes this philosophy a difficult one for many therapists to adopt. A therapist who desires action, and who believes that more of the responsibility for the change of their client lies with them than with the client, may not be well suited for client-centered counseling.

When the conditions of the client-centered group have been fully developed, the potential outcome may be characterized as follows: the individual becomes more vitally and fully involved in all phases of their life. The individual's communication with self and others is more freely, congruently, and spontaneously expressed. The vitality the individual experiences is in part due to the increase in risking behavior to become actively involved with self and others. A general valuing for, and trust in, one's experience is enhanced and a profound belief in the potential for change, development, and growth in oneself and others is held in high regard (Bugental, 1963; Rogers, 1961).

Role of Clients in Client-Centered Group Counseling

Existentially, client-centered group work emphasizes each member's responsibility to be the author of his or her own feelings and experiences in the group. The level of self-disclosure, the impact of self-disclosures, and the subsequent feedback, learning, and change that may occur are seen as individual responsibilities. The nature of one's freedom to experience oneself in the eyes of others and to transcend the limitations of one's own personal concerns for the purpose of new freedoms, growth, and change is indeed a matter of individual responsibility. The potential for self-actualization is based in one's ability to be a responsible agent for one's own change. As members become aware of the freedom they have to behave as they choose, they recognize their responsibilities to shape the group to meet their needs. The extent to which members can behave in accordance with their self responsibilities may also serve as a diagnostic framework for their resistance to experience the group as therapeutic. Yalom (1975) suggests that group leaders aid group members by helping them become aware of their personal responsibilities for seeing themselves through the eyes of others; the impact and subsequent perceptions other members have for them; and how members can use the group to evaluate and change behaviors they believe are inappropriate.

The Will to Change

According to Yalom (1980), the "mainspring of action" in the process of change is *will*, and therapy requires movement and action. Much of one's will for change comes from the faith and hope one has in the processes involved in change (Frank, 1973; Rank, 1945; May, 1953). The existential elements of one's faith and hope supplies energy for the development of curative forces in group work. The faith and hope that a member has in his ability to change, and the faith and hope that the group can help him change, greatly influences the cohesiveness and attractiveness of a group. The courage to risk, to trust, to give and receive support, to be compassionate and understanding, and to commit to change hinges on faith and hope. The success or failure of a group depends, to a great extent, on the development and maintenance of therapeutic forces. Client-centered group work advocates that responsibility and expectations for developing and maintaining such a climate are shared by both the leader and group members. As each member of the group learns how to develop and maintain a therapeutic climate in the group, they can also learn to apply this process in their lives outside of the group.

Freedom

Interwoven with hope and faith as crucial phenomena of group work is the existential issue of freedom. The freedom we experience with others occurs as a result of our ability to express ourselves openly without fear of ridicule and rejection. The process of client-centered therapy rests upon the assumption that the individual can and will become congruent, self-regulating, and indeed self-actualized as a consequence of feeling free to experience and express herself openly and authentically. Interpersonal relationships are dependent and built upon the notion of expression of feelings. We come to know, understand, accept, and love ourselves and others primarily as a result of expressing ourselves freely. Nowhere else does the role of sharing feelings spontaneously play a more important part than in client-centered group therapy.

The freedom one experiences may be likened to the room one feels to express the variety of feelings one can experience in general. Such freedom may typically characterize the relationships a person has with others. Additionally, the nature and amount of what one selects to disclose is also an illustration of one's freedom to regulate one's distance and contact with others. The interpersonal freedom one experiences in sharing contact with others is an important aspect involved in the interpersonal learning process of group work (Yalom, 1980). At the same time, the climate of safety and trust in the group is also an illustration of the freedom members feel to be self-disclosing. The ability of a member to be aware and in touch with their feelings, to accept and understand them, as well as to express them, are prerequisites to functioning freely in the group. The aforementioned are the freedom issues of the individual. Freedom on the group climate level involves the feelings of safety and trust among members. A group member's freedom to express, then, varies with how free that member is in expressing herself, and how safe and trusting the group climate.

The meaningfulness of a therapeutic experience in group is a combination of the member's ability and availability to invest in and commit to expressing as freely as possible all the feelings typical of the human experience. To be a group member means to be open to participating in the development of a group climate of warmth, safety, acceptance, trust, and understanding, as well as to share the feelings of loneliness, isolation, frustration, and rejection. In a client-centered group, therapy is the process of allowing the curative forces which are inherent and natural to take their course.

SUMMARY AND CASE ILLUSTRATIONS

Case examples will be used to illustrate and characterize the major theories covered in this chapter.

Behaviorism

- Scientific method applied to human concerns.
- Carefully defined precise goals for behavioral change.
- Intervention program designed to teach specific skills necessary to reduce problematic behavior and/or increase adaptive behaviors.
- Concrete, observable, and measured outcomes for assessment of change.
- Human problems are seen as resulting from faulty learning.
- Role of therapist is scientific investigator, teacher, model, and facilitator.
- Role of group member is student, participant, co-investigator, and an advocate and support for change.
- Technical, eclectic format of intervention and specific treatment for various elements of individual concerns.

Case Example

Bob, a 19-year-old college freshman seeking help at a university counseling center, joins a group to learn social skills for dating and relating to his peers. During the group intake the counselor asks Bob to describe the nature of his difficulty in meeting others and developing good relationships. Bob reports having a long standing problem of several years in developing and maintaining friends. His interpersonal-relationship profile consists of no close friends. At the end of the intake, Bob is instructed about the group in terms of what will be expected from him as a member and how he can help himself in the group. The counselor and Bob have agreed that Bob will express his concerns within the first half hour of the first group meeting and will ask for feedback from the group members regarding how clear his objectives are for being in the group.

At the second session, Bob is asked by the therapist if he would be willing to share with other members what he is thinking and feeling about what is going on in the group; what has been stated that he finds himself in agreement with, and if he has experienced anything similar to what other members have been talking about. Successive approximations of behaviors seen as interpersonally appro-priate are being shaped by gradually encouraging and reinforcing Bob's in-group behavior. In future sessions, Bob's work can be more detailed and specific, but initially Bob needs to be desensitized to his interpersonal anxiety by gradual encounters with group members with reinforcement for his participation.

At the third session, Bob may be invited to role play initiating conversations in a mock social gathering in which group members play assigned parts based on the particular skill being rehearsed, that is, talking with members of the opposite sex regarding such social skills as breaking silence during conversation, changing the topic of conversation, extending and continuing conversation, and ending conversation. At the conclusion of the role play, Bob is invited to process his thoughts and feelings regarding his self talk during the role play. The group is then invited to give him feedback regarding what they observed that was positive and how he might improve his skills in subsequent social encounters. The group may then be invited to brainstorm for an idea for restructuring thoughts that hinder Bob's ability to initiate contact with others. At the conclusion of this work with Bob, a homework assignment may be recommended in which Bob is requested to make a list of positive self statements and practice them prior to and during the initiation of conversations with others. Further, Bob is invited to continue his social-skills training by initiating conversation with at least two people outside the group whom he would like to get to know better. He is asked to report back to the group at the next session on the outcome of his homework.

Fourth session, out of Bob's homework request, additional role plays, in-volving giving and receiving compliments, take place—as well as group discus-sion on expectations for friendships, opening up to others, and developing trust —in which group members share their ideas, struggles, issues, and strategies for success. In this way both Bob and the group can profit from each other, reinforce change, as well as generate new ideas for continued growth and social skills development. Future sessions may follow a similar format in a group with a behavioral emphasis.

Gestalt

- Emphasis is on contact among group members in the here-and-now.
- Focus of therapeutic interventions are on blocks in client's awareness.
- Leadership style is action oriented and experiential, such as psychodrama.
- Goal of therapy is resolution and completion of unfinished business, satis-faction of needs, and the assumption of responsibility for self actions.
- Therapy is seen as a process of experimentation directed at getting group members to integrate and assimilate their experiences instead of frag-menting, separating, and suppressing themselves from the natural process of being. Owning experiences means surrendering to being as you are instead of what you think you should be.

- The group is viewed as a microcosm, a social gestalt where members play out the various elements of their unfinished business.

Case Example

Susan, a 31-year-old computer programmer, was seeking help from the group regarding a recent divorce. Susan seemed withdrawn and out of touch with her feelings, and was somewhat isolated from other members. The leader noticed that Susan began to cry as one of the other members was expressing frustration regarding difficulties with her boyfriend's family. The leader asked Susan what she was experiencing as she listened. Susan reported that she felt sad, but was not sure exactly why. The leader then asked if she would be willing to experiment with her sadness to see if she could increase her awareness regarding the incompleteness between her feelings and her lack of understanding. Susan agreed to the experiment.

The leader asked Susan if she would be willing to use her imagination and create a fantasy regarding her sadness, and to report what she visualized as if it were happening in the present. Susan reported that she was standing in the living room of her ex-husband's parents, but that nobody was home. At this point, Susan began to cry and said, "I can't say goodbye if nobody is home." The leader asked the group if they had any ideas regarding how to help Susan say goodbye to her in-laws. Members suggested that they might play her ex-husband's family and give her a chance to say goodbye. The leader asked Susan to select and cast members of the group as her in-laws. She was then instructed to express whatever she felt or wanted to say to the various family members in order to complete her unfinished business.

This work episode ended with Susan processing her experience with the group in terms of awareness, feelings, and sense of completion. Group members were invited to share their experiences in the roles and with Susan, as well as any awareness and insight they discovered while role playing. In this way, both Susan and the group members benefit from the experience through contrasting the differences and similarities of their experiences, as well as feeling good about their contributions to the process of helping.

Client-Centered

- Group has the inherent resources for determining its own direction.
- Leader is the facilitator of group process. The primary focus is on member-to-member interactions and group development.
- The psychological climate is viewed as crucial in terms of beneficial therapeutic outcome.
- Self-actualization responses among group members are facilitated when the psychological climate for core conditions of warmth, empathy, and genuineness are developed and maintained by group members.

- Group process is stage related and a therapeutic climate develops as a result of group resolution of the issues involved in the various stages.
- Group success is seen as an increase in self-actualizing lifestyles; communication between self and others is more freely, congruently, and spontaneously expressed; and value of, respect, and belief in potential for change are vitally involved in all phases of their lives.

Case Example

The first session opens by members discussing why they are in the group. The interaction between them has a strong flavor of underlying tension masked by polite interchanges. Bill talks with Jim about an aunt he has who lives in a town near Jim's hometown, and other members join in with loose associations aimed at attempting to share commonality. The group continues to interact at this level until a silence begins to lull over the group, as if the energy of surface level interchange has been drained out of the group. A member turns to the leader and says, "Is this what we're supposed to be doing?" The leader responds, "Sounds to me like you aren't sure about what's o.k. or not o.k. to talk about in here." Another member states, "Yeah, I could talk about stuff like this with my friends. I thought that being in a group would be different."

At this point, the leader's interventions may be aimed at helping the group process their perceptions, expectations, and feelings about what is going on and what changes they would like to see in the group. It is important to bear in mind that several attempts on the part of members to find contact that is satisfying may occur before success is experienced. The leader's role is to assist members in owning and understanding their feelings and to express them as openly and honestly as possible. The leader needs to help the group focus on the issues involved in opening up to each other that are stage related. Encounters among members will follow patterns set by implicit norms that will need to be addressed and brought into the open for work and resolution. The issues in this example are initial stage issues involving identification, commonality, and how the group time can be used. (Note: These example issues do not always occur together as the group may jump into issues that would normally occur at a more advanced stage, and then recede to elementary, surface-level identification. The key issue for the leader at this stage is to aid the group by helping it tune into its process, model, and facilitate interaction that assists members in making contact with one another.)

Fifth session: Bill begins the group by sharing his thoughts and feelings regarding difficulties in dealing with his father, and expresses that he feels frustrated and angry toward his father. Susan, a group member, says she has had a similar experience with her father and has felt the same way. Mary brings the focus more directly to the present, stating that she sees a pattern between Bill's interaction with his father and how he relates to the leader. Bill snaps at Mary, "You always seem to act like you know it all." Jim and Peter join in simultaneously sharing that they think Bill is getting defensive and that maybe Mary has a point. The group then begins to work more with Bill helping him sort out his feelings with his father and how he seems to relate to the leader in a similar way. Bill asks the leader for feedback regarding the ways he comes across which seem angry and hostile.

The group at this stage is much more open, spontaneous, and present centered. The energy is coming from the group, and the members are learning to deal with each other as people and not as objects. The focus by members is on important life issues and their relationships with others. As in any group interaction, there is much the leader can do, several places in which to intervene. In this episode, the leader steps out, remaining on the sideline, allowing the group to work. In this way the leader is trusting members. The message is: "You are capable of directing the group by yourselves; I'll be here when you need me."

Subsequent sessions may involve greater levels of openness without defensiveness; intimate contact surrounding important life issues becomes a group norm; and the group takes on more importance and meaning in the lives of its members.

The case illustrations have been designed to provide a flavor of the kinds of interactions that are typical of the various theoretical frameworks covered in this chapter. In reality, most group leaders form a style of leadership that combines and cuts across theories. The next chapter on procedures of group counseling will address the issues involved in the formation of leadership style.

REFERENCES

Achacter, S. (1959). *The psychology of affiliation*. Stanford, CA: Stanford University Press.

Bass, B. (1965). *Organizational psychology*. Boston: Allyn and Bacon.

Bugental, J. T. (1963, August). The person who is the psychotherapist. Paper presented at the APA annual meeting, Philadelphia, PA.

Corey, G. (1981). *Theory and practice of group counseling*. Monterey, CA: Brooks/Cole.

Einstein, A. (1982). *Ideas and opinions*. New York: Crown.

Ellis, A., & Grieger, R. (1977). *Handbook of rational emotive therapy*. New York: Springer.

Enright, J. B. (1975). An introduction to gestalt therapy. In F. D. Stephenson (Ed.), *Gestalt therapy primer*. Springfield, IL: Charles C Thomas.

Festinger, L. (1954). A theory of social comparison processes. *Human Relations, 7,* 117–140.

Frank, J. (1973). *Persuasion and healing: A comparative study of psychotherapy*. Baltimore: Johns Hopkins.

French, J., and Raven, E. (1959). The bases of social power. In D. D. Cartright (eds.), *Studies of Social Power*. Ann Arbor: University of Michigan, Institute for Social Research.

Gazda, G. M. (Ed.) (1975). *Basic approaches to group psychotherapy and group counseling* (2nd ed.). Springfield, IL: Charles C Thomas.

Goldenberg, H. (1983). *Contemporary clinical psychology.* Monterey, CA: Brooks/Cole.

Harmon, R. L. (1984). Recent developments in gestalt group therapy. *Journal of Group Psychotherapy, 34,* 473–478.

Kelman, H. C. (1961). Process of opinion change. *Public Opinion Quarterly, 25,* 57–58.

Kepner, F. (1980). Gestalt group process. In R. Feder & R. Ronald (Eds.), *Beyond the hot seat: Gestalt approaches to group* (pp. 42–78). New York: Brunner/Mazel.

Korchin, S. J. (1976). *Clinical psychology.* New York: Basic Books.

Lazarus, A. (1971). *Behavior theory and beyond.* New York: McGraw-Hill.

Lazarus, A. (1976). *Multi-modal behavioral therapy.* New York: Springer.

Mahoney, M. (1977). Personal science: A cognitive learning therapy. In A. Ellis & R. Grieger (Eds.), *Handbook of rational emotive therapy* (pp. 352–366). New York: Springer.

May, R. (1953). *Man's search for himself.* New York: Norton.

McCarthy, B. (1977). Acquisition of coping skills. In G. Harris (Ed.), *The group treatment of human problems: A social learning approach.* New York: Grune & Stratton.

Moreno, J. L. (1946). *Psychodrama* (Vol. 1). Beacon, NY: Beacon House.

Ohlsen, M. M. (1977). *Group Counseling* (2nd ed.). New York: Holt, Rinehart and Winston.

Perls, F. (1969). *Gestalt therapy verbatim.* Lafayette, CA: Real People's Press.

Perls, F. (1973). *The gestalt approach and eyewitness to therapy.* New York: Bantam Books.

Rank, O. (1945). *Will therapy and truth and reality.* New York: Alfred A. Knopf.

Rogers, C. (1961). *On becoming a person.* Boston: Houghton Mifflin.

Rogers, C. (1970). *Carl Rogers on encounter groups.* New York: Harper & Row.

Schachter, S. (1959). *The psychology of affiliation.* Palo Alto, CA: Stanford University Press.

Shertzer, B., & Stone, S. (1974). *Fundamentals of counseling.* Boston: Houghton Mifflin.

Simkin, J. (1975). *Gestalt therapy: Issues and approaches in the psychological therapies* (pp. 147–161). London: John Wiley.

Simkin, J. (1975). An introduction to gestalt therapy. In F. D. Stephenson (Ed.), *Gestalt therapy primer* (pp. 3–12). Springfield, IL: Charles C Thomas.

Slavson, S. R. (1979). *Dynamics of group psychotherapy.* New York: Jason Aronson.

Stang, D. J. (1972). Conformity, ability, and self-esteem. *Representative Research in Social Psychology, 3,* 97–103.

Wallen, R. (1970). Gestalt therapy and Gestalt psychology. In J. Fagan & I. L. Shepherd (Eds.), *Science and Behavior.* Palo Alto, CA: Stanford University Press.

Yalom, I. D. (1975). *The theory and practice of group psychotherapy* (2nd ed.). New York: Basic Books.

Yalom, I.D. (1980). *Existential Psychotherapy.* New York: Basic Books.

Zimbardo, P.; Haney, C.; Banks, W.; & Jaffe, D. A Pirandellian prison: The mind is a formidable jailer. *New York Times Magazine,* April 8, 1973, 38–60.

Zinker, J. (1978). *Creative process in gestalt therapy.* New York: Vintage Press.

3

PROCEDURES FOR GROUP COUNSELING

This chapter is aimed at illustrating the use of technical processes for group leadership. Case examples of group facilitation on the individual, interpersonal, and group levels will be presented. The technical procedures outlined in this chapter are based on the following assumptions: group counseling is primarily based in group process. The process of the group is the therapy. The dynamic qualities of group process touch on a variety of theoretical orientations that may be integrated to form a comprehensive technical process. Finally, the needs and issues of group members serve to guide the development and implementation of the group process. Based on these assumptions, this chapter will attempt to demonstrate the role of leader facilitation of the group process.

THE GROUP LEADER

The repertoire of skills and techniques possessed by a leader reflects the leader's assumptions about the process of helping, and about the individuals seeking help. Perceiving the group and its members as capable, reliable, and responsible for governing the direction and development of the group is indicative of the leader's trust in the group process. Effective leadership in the group depends on the ability of the leader to make an appropriate response to the needs and conditions of the group, which are in a continuous state of change. The definition of leader effectiveness is based on a combination of knowledge, awareness, skill, and technique (Dyer & Vriend, 1980). Skilled interventions are a product of the leader's continual efforts at expanding knowledge and experience with technical process. In this regard the leader is both a scientist and a practitioner.

FACILITATING GROUP CLIMATE AND RELATIONSHIPS

The group climate and relationships are important factors in the process of change. Group relationships are the foundation for the interpersonal process. Such relationships facilitate learning to be more open to others, more vulnerable, more known, more understood and accepted, as well as to create a place to deal with the conflicts, barriers, and problems that limit intimate contact (Yalom, 1975). The outcome of the action (process) of these relationship conditions allows the inherent curative forces in the group to emerge and develop.

The following are examples of therapeutic forces typical of the group process mentioned by Yalom (1975). Group members learn to be sensitive and helpful to others which in turn produces a sense of group cohesion. The feeling of belonging also aids in developing an awareness of similarities and differences, providing a sense of universality. As members learn to calculate risking openly with others, they learn how others perceive them, which stimulates the interpersonal learning process. At times, members may wish to check out their thoughts, feelings, and perceptions, and discuss their plans and decisions with the group for the purpose of seeking guidance from others. Members often benefit from group by having a safe place to express their feelings—a place to release emotional tension and to learn how to express themselves assertively. As members interact with each other, especially under role-playing conditions, they act as models for behavior change. At times, the group process may seem like a family. Members, under these conditions, can come to understand the roles they play with parents and siblings that block their growth and limit relationships with others. As a result of seeing others change, members can gain a sense of hope and faith that they can also change. The basic life-issues of freedom of choice and responsibility for the consequences of one's choice are often associated with the general outcome of membership in a group.

How to facilitate and work with these therapeutic forces is the subject matter of this chapter. In the preceding chapter on theories, the point was made that therapeutic conditions are an inherent part of the group process, and also build on and interact with each other, so that facilitation of one therapeutic force enhances and influences the development of others.

The pattern of relationship development that occurs as a result of group interaction is essential to group process. The ideas, feelings, and behaviors of members are a dynamic source of influence shaping the group. Any aspect of group activity involves some form of process. Probably the major aspect of group process from the standpoint of building a counseling group climate is the sense of cohesion that members feel with each other in the group. Essentially group cohesion is the amount of liking and acceptance members feel toward and from each other and the group (Bach, 1951). Developing group cohesion depends on several factors. In order to feel connected with others, members need to experience some degree of commonality or affiliation. That "you and I are alike" means we have a way to relate and the basis for a relationship. Cohesion is a dynamic process and, from this standpoint, can change from moment to moment and from member to member. The more members have in common, at least initially, the faster a sense of group cohesion is likely to develop. Furthermore, the group's ability to direct itself, resolve its issues, and understand its process of development is also characteristic of a highly cohesive group.

Facilitating cohesion can be done by working directly with the need that members have to affiliate with or to belong (Hansen et al., 1976). In this regard, the role of the counselor is to introduce members to the similarities they have in common. These similarities are readily found in the feelings, perceptions, and behaviors members share for any experience. It should be mentioned that a prerequisite to the development of a cohesive group is the careful selection and screening of members prior to the beginning of the group. Screening and selecting members allows the leader to select only those members that are suitable to the objectives and make-up of the group.

Facilitating Cohesion

Case Examples

The following cases illustrate the use of affiliating responses aimed at linking clients together. The first group session begins with the leader asking members to share their reasons for being in the group. Members take turns disclosing the issues that they are seeking help for from the group.

Case 1.   Jim, a 19-year-old college sophomore, tells the group he wants to learn how to build closer relationships with others. In describing his concern, he talks about how he feels like he is on the outside looking in, and how it seems that others know how to communicate. The leader observes another member nodding his head and says, "Fred, you seem to understand what Jim is saying. Have you had similar experiences?" The leader invites Fred to share what he has experienced that is in common with Jim, thereby linking them together. The leader facilitates identification among group members by clarifying and reflecting the feelings Jim and Fred share in their common experience, and invites others to contrast their experiences with those of Fred and Jim. At the same time the leader attempts to remove barriers that may limit or block clear communication among the members. An example of a barrier to open expression of feelings may be illustrated by members' not owning their feelings or thoughts, by using words that distance, such as "one feels" or "you make me mad," or talking about feelings toward others—"it's frustrating when people don't seem to listen to you." The effects of such communication often leave members feeling confused or uninterested. Interventions, such as those previously described make the group a safer place to share. By helping members experience contact with each other in an affirming fashion, the group is developing a sense of cohesion and, by sharing common experiences, a sense of universality. As "I find experiences in common with others, I feel less alone, and at the same time I feel more hopeful because someone else also has felt and experienced as I have and is striving to change."

A key element linked with sharing common experiences is the interplay between self-awareness, acceptance, and the ability to be aware of and accept others. The quality of relating is like the I–thou relationship that Martin Buber (1958) describes. As members learn to express themselves openly and feel acceptance from others, they become more accepting of themselves and less defensive with others. The members' ability to be sensitive, understanding, and accepting becomes the basis of group support. As in any support system, how members give and receive support is a major part of the group's therapeutic potential.

FACILITATING THE INTERPERSONAL PROCESS

The leader's role in facilitating this process is to educate members in the interpersonal processes involved in communication (sharing with others and listening to others) as well as to teach members how to assist each other in accurate self-expression. This largely amounts to teaching and modeling empathy. The following case example illustrates how this process can be facilitated.

Case 2. Roger (in a resentful and bitter fashion) is addressing the group with a testimonial regarding how others really cannot understand him, and how unimportant it would be even if they did. The leader intervenes with, "Well, Roger, it doesn't sound like you've got much to lose either way. I wonder if you'd be willing to let people here respond to what you've been saying." The leader then invites group members to convey what they think they understand from Roger's disclosure. The leader also encourages members to share the impact of Roger's message on them. Kim, a female member, responds first: "You seem so bent on keeping us away; I think you want to be closer, but maybe you don't know how or are afraid of being hurt or rejected." Another member adds, "Yeah, I get that same feeling . . . like you want us to risk trying to understand you but you're afraid that if we do, you won't know what to do. You might feel awkward and embarrassed." Another member suggests, "I don't think you trust us yet. You seem tense and anxious about what's happening right now."

Ralph, another member, responds, "Roger, my reaction is confusion and frustration. You say you want to learn how to trust others, that your parents were never close to you and that they expected you to be like they were. I mean you seem to understand why you want to open up, to trust or you wouldn't have joined this group or said you wanted us to help you change." Group members nod in agreement. The leader notices Bill, a quiet and somewhat withdrawn client, nodding his head. The leader says, "Bill, I notice you seem to be in agreement with the others. What's your reaction to Roger?" Bill replies, "Well, I agree that Roger said he wants to change, and he does know why he wants to change; but that's just it—I don't think we can expect Roger to open up, trust us without having trouble. It's like he wants to learn how to swim, but he's afraid to get in the water." The leader says, "I think you've said some important things, Bill, and so have the rest of you. Roger, I wonder what you heard from what others have been saying?" Roger goes on to say how he feels some comfort in the acceptance shown by Bill and other members of the group; and that he felt challenged by Ralph, yet feels some trust and respect toward Ralph as well.

In ending this encounter between Roger and the group, the leader asks Roger to clarify and take responsibility for his goals and behaviors that are congruent with his reasons for being in the group, as well as for those that are inconsistent and self-defeating. The leader shifts the focus back to the group by asking the group to get in touch with the issues, on both an individual and group level, that have been brought up by the focus on Roger. Individuals are encouraged by the leader to share with the group how they connect with Roger's issues; how they have similar or different issues and experiences.

Case Analysis.   The counselor encourages members to share whatever they would like, including any feeling, thoughts, impressions, images, or metaphors that might characterize their response. In this way, the leader is continually sifting through member-to-member experiences, linking members to each other, removing blocks in communication and barriers to intimacy. The basic tools are simple: it is the *when, where, what,* and *how* to use the tools that equals skill.

In the case above, the tools were clarification, reflection, confrontation, support, summarization, and termination. Notice that these tools were not just used by the leader. In fact, most were used by group members. The leader's role was based in the theoretical knowledge of the process (cohesion, universality, interpersonal learning) of group building, plus her awareness of how to structure members' communications (their tools) to facilitate group building. This last point may be further illustrated by how a session such as this one might end.

Terminating the Session.   In closing on issues raised by the focus of attention with Roger, the leader needs to be mindful of tying up loose ends, finishing up communications, reinforcing work done, acknowledging progress made by both the individual members and the group, bringing the group's attention to issues not resolved, and setting the agenda for future group work. As mentioned earlier, members in this instance are given opportunities to deal with their feelings and concerns related to the focus on Roger. In this example, trusting, letting defenses down, risking, changing, feeling angry, feeling frustrated and hopeless, allowing others to help, and feeling hopeful for trying were dealt with on a member-to-member level. The leader, aware of the breadth of material and the time and energy left to continue, elects to begin processing the experience. The focus is one of reflecting on what took place during the group experience.

PROCESSING GROUP MEMBERS' EXPERIENCE

Processing members' experience in the group is a primary method of creating a group climate in which members can help each other change. The here-and-now awareness of group members is a constant resource for interpersonal learning. Processing the awareness of members' here-and-now experience aids group members in understanding how others view them and/or feel toward them; and, in turn, form relationships with them. The patterns of relationships they develop in the group also serve to heighten their awareness and understanding of other relationships outside the group, such as family relationships. The goal is to stimulate learning about their process of relating and forming meaningful relationships with others.

Processing, as a general skill for group leaders, may be broken down into six steps or phases. First is the experience or awareness phase, what is being experienced in the present. Second is the sharing phase: Who would be willing to share their experience? What were you aware of and when? The interpreting phase follows, and facilitative questions are directed at understanding the meaning of an experience. What does this experience mean for you? How was it significant? How does this help you understand yourself and your relationship with others? Next is the generalizing phase, in which members are encouraged to organize their experience into more abstract principles for the purpose of application. Examples of structural questions include: What can you draw from _____? How does this relate to other experiences or what do you associate with this experience? The application phase is next, with such questions as, How can you use this information? What would you prefer to do with this information? Finally, there is the wrapping up or closing phase. How was this experience for you? How might it have been more meaningful? What changes would you make? What would you continue?

The leader may begin processing by responding to the group in general. For example, after a pause in which members have naturally ended by reflecting on their personal issues generated during the session, the leader may intervene by saying, "We covered a lot of ground today. What has this session been like for you?" The leader continues by encouraging members to identify feelings, thoughts, images, and the like related to the session by asking them specific questions, for example: "What feelings do you associate with _____?" "How open were you today?" "Were you able to express what you wanted?" "If you held back, what do you imagine would have happened if you had not held back?" "What could we do (more of/less of) that would encourage openness and trust?" "What can we take from this session that we need to continue to do as a group?" These examples of processing questions for closing a session cannot be used by rote or without consideration of the context of members' reactions; nor can they be completely and neatly answered. They are designed to help the group find its own way of developing.

In Case 2, it may be important to note that Roger is not seen as psychopathic or ill. He is a college sophomore; a high school student; the man next door who just got divorced; or any of us at some point in our lives for that matter. He feels discouraged, hopeless, angry, and resentful, and has a pattern of relationship dynamics and perceptions that block his ability to meet his needs for closeness and relationships with others.

STAGES OF GROUP DEVELOPMENT

The stages of development a group goes through are similar to the stages of development in any meaningful relationship (Dyer & Vriend, 1980; Gazda, 1971). In general, these stages are the beginning or initial stage, the work or productive stage, and the termination stage.

Stages of development may vary from member to member and from group to group. In some groups the stages are clear and progress moves in a smooth, linear fashion. In other groups the progress is erratic; the group may move forward in one session and have to begin all over in the next. The leader's role generally varies as do the goals, objectives, and needs of group members.

The ability of a group to develop and progress through the various stages is greatly dependent upon the issues and characteristics of members and their willingness to be open in identifying and dealing with emotions. If the group norms reflect members' withdrawn and silent behaviors, the progress and quality of the group will be affected at all stages. In this regard, screening and selecting members for heterogeniety of problems and concerns is crucial for process-oriented group counseling.

Initial Stage

The first stage involves the group's need for safety, trust, and cohesiveness. At this early stage, group members want the leader to direct and protect them. They are characteristically guarded, uncertain about how much or what to reveal about themselves. Self-disclosure is usually superficial, polite, and generally aimed at keeping things safe. At times group members can be defensive.

In this initial stage, the leader is generally involved in helping members open up, learn to trust one another, calculate risk, give straightforward and honest feedback, and build an accepting, caring environment. Members learn to take responsibility for their behaviors and to be actively involved in governing the direction the group takes.

Case Example.   The following case illustrates leader intervention typical of initial stages. The issues are trust, acceptance, and cohesion. In this instance, the third session, members are avoiding contact, and the group begins with talk that is external and superficial. As group members file into the room and take their seats, they begin chatting about their weekend. When everyone has arrived, the group continues to circulate the weekend review. Members seem content to continue to talk at this level. The leader remains silent. Members begin to lose interest in the conversation and a tension develops in the group. One member makes a joke and others laugh, but quickly return to fidgeting and looking around. Typically this behavior is a search for a leader. "Who is willing to take responsibility for this lack of direction?" Finally, one member asks the leader if this is what they are supposed to be doing, and how this silence is getting the group nowhere. The leader responds, "You sound frustrated, Ted. What's your awareness of what's going on in the group right now?" Ted begins with, "I don't think anything is going on, that's the problem. You just sit there and do nothing." The leader says, "I think you're angry with me for not making something happen, for not taking control." Ted replies, "Yes, that's right, you're the leader, aren't you?"

Addressing the group, the leader asks, "How do the rest of you feel right now about what's happening between Ted and me?" One member states that she feels anxious about Ted's confrontation. Another member shares his agreement with Ted about wanting the leader to take control. Another member makes the point that it is their group and they have the right and responsibility to talk about what's important to them if they so choose, and they do not want the leader to call on them as if they were students in a classroom. This interchange continues, with the leader intervening to assist members in clarifying how they want to use group time and who will be responsible for what. The discussion ends with agreement by the group that it is their group, that they are there for the purpose of improving their ability to relate to others, and that they want the leader's help with opening up in front of each other.

The leader then intervenes by asking members to think about what would happen to them if they were to risk being more open. Mary, the woman who reported feeling anxious about conflict, states that she thinks someone would attack her, put her down, or not care what she had to say. The leader intervenes to ask if anyone else feels the way Mary feels. Others join in, sharing their expectations about what might happen if they risk being open. The leader reminds the group about the ground rules for listening, conveying acceptance of the person, and the like to assure the group that they have agreed to a guideline structure for the safety and well-being of the members.

The leader then invites the group members to focus on those in the group they feel would give them support and understanding, and those they think might be confrontational and harsh with them. This intervention allows members to specify their fears based on past experiences they may have stored, or to share their impressions of others in the group toward whom they may have distorted perceptions and feelings, some of which may be based on interactions learned in their families. The group, with the leader's help, is structuring itself by building rules and setting up boundaries and limits appropriate to its needs.

Case Analysis.   In this example, the overriding needs are for meaningful relationships and safety. This case example also illustrates the tension members feel when there is no specific goal on which to focus. Process-oriented groups frequently encounter such tension in the initial stages. At this point the leader's role is to help the group use its own process and resources to shape and build cohesion. This example further illustrates the leader's handling of the confrontation of members. It is important that the leader deal with such confrontation in a nondefensive manner and understand the tension members feel in the initial, unstructured stages of a beginning group that leads to the search for a leader who will supply direction and reduce tension. It is also important for the leader not to give into the pressure of structuring the session for the group. As illustrated in the case example, the leader keeps the focus on the members' issues related to risking open self-disclosure, safety, trust, and how they experience these issues in the group.

Typical of issues involved with the initial stage (safety, trust, openness) illustrated by the case example are fears based on past experiences and/or future possibilities. Members may have either stored a previous experience from an interchange in the group in which they felt anxious or threatened, or they have fantasies about what they fear might happen. In other words, they either have unfinished business with each other (or someone outside the group), or they are projecting and forecasting their fears about what might happen in the group. In either case, the results are the same: limited self-disclosure, withholding behavior, and a reduction in the benefits of the group process. The danger of not resolving issues such as those illustrated is that limitations in intimate contact create loose bonds among members. Group cohesion is above all else a process of bonding together. When the barriers to this process are not adequately resolved, the group may begin to deteriorate.

Working Stage

In the middle or working stages of group development, the group has generally been successful in resolving the issues of trust, openness, and cohesion. If these issues are not resolved by the majority of group members, the group will falter and will have difficulty being productive. An attendance problem is one of the major symptoms of groups that have not successfully dealt with the issues involved in the initial stages. Members will come late, miss sessions, or drop out completely. In such instances, the therapeutic forces have not been sufficiently developed to provide for meaningful experiences in the group.

In a working group, the curative forces are well-established. Members feel safe about risking openly because they have experienced acceptance of who they are, even when they do not like the things they have disclosed to others about themselves. In fact, the working group characteristically provides a place where members can risk disclosures they have never risked with anyone before. The therapeutic aspects of modeling, interpersonal learning, hope, and caring culminate in a sense of family, a way in which members frequently describe the group. Some whose experiences with their families have been troubled report that the group offers more than their families in terms of consistency, openness, warmth, and caring.

The leader's role at the working stage may vary. In general, like the group members, the leader may feel more freedom to experiment with different strategies than in the initial stages because the group is established and the sense of fragility is gone (Hansen et al., 1976). A firm sense of trust has been developed. The focus of interpersonal contact in the group is more consistently in the here-and-now, and members have come to value and respect the rights and responsibilities of others to make their own decisions (Dyer & Vriend, 1980).

Time Value.   Typical of a group in the working stage, a session begins with members checking in with the group. Yalom (1975) refers to this strategy as "making the rounds." Members are given time to discuss what they have been working on during the week, progress they have made, and issues they are currently dealing with that they would like to spend some time with during the session. Making the rounds allows both the leader and the group to set priorities for that particular session, to determine who needs time, or who would like time to focus on specific issues. A distinction between a working group and a beginning group is the value seen for use of group time. In a beginning group, members are unsure and anxious about how the time will be spent, and often members want to avoid having the group's time and attention focused on them; after members have witnessed the benefits of group, time becomes valuable. It is important to note that the value of having time in group, at the working stage, creates a different set of problems for the leader and members. Working-stage time problems tend to center around not having enough time to cover all the issues and concerns that members would like to bring up. However, in a working group, members are much more able to assert their requests for time, take turns, and benefit from the time others spend with issues; they are also more able to provide support, feedback, and help the group create and invent ways to help others. Making the rounds with members assures all members of receiving some of the group's time, as well as giving them the responsibility for determining what they wish to deal with during that session.

Case Example.   Mary begins the group by sharing her recent success in assertively dealing with her roommate. She characterizes how she behaved differently and shares with the group the positive outcomes of her assertive behavior in terms of her feelings of increased self-esteem. The group reinforces and praises her efforts, and Mary sets another goal for continuing her assertive behavior. The leader intervenes to clarify and assist group members in helping Mary set reasonable goals. The leader then assists the group in making the rounds by shifting the focus to another member.

Bill shares his efforts at working on being more sensitive and open with others. He invites the group to give him feedback on how they see him now as compared to the way he came across earlier in the group. He also asks for changes in their feelings toward him and how that affects their relationship with him now. Members are invited to give feedback and the leader helps Bill clarify and understand what the group's feedback means to him. After Bill concludes with the group, the leader may shift the focus to another member. The leader noticed that Craig responded emotionally to what others had been saying to Bill. Craig reports to the group that he's feeling anxious about going home over spring break, and that he dreads spending time with his parents. He asks for group time to role play how he wants to handle his interactions while at home. The leader and the group agree to allot time for Craig in this session. The leader intervenes to continue the process of making the rounds: "It sounds like Craig has some important issues he'd like to spend time with this session. I think we also need to hear from others who might be needing time as well, before we start with Craig."

The group moves on with other members sharing their issues and reporting on progress they have made and their accompanying good feelings. Janet, interjecting feelings and issues similar to Craig's, states that she would also like some time from the group to deal with her feelings toward her father. After everyone has had the opportunity to check in with the group, the leader invites the members to look at some of the common themes mentioned during the checking-in phase of the session. For example, the leader intervenes to facilitate reflection on common issues and feelings by saying, "After listening to Janet and Craig's concerns, I wonder what kind of feelings or thoughts you might have had about relationships with your families, and how these relationships reflect your behavior in this group." The leader briefly processes (with the group) their feelings and thoughts, conflicts and resolutions regarding their family experiences. In this way, the leader is preparing the group for the work with Craig and Janet, as well as planting the seeds for personal exploration and discovery by group members in general.

The focus is then shifted to Craig, the leader asking him to think about what he would like to accomplish in the role play, and how the group might be involved. During the phase of setting the stage for the role play, members and Craig are encouraged to brainstorm ideas for the actual role play. The leader works with Craig and the group to set up the roles, depict the scenes, and clarify the objectives and goals of the role play. For example, Craig has assigned the roles to various group members. The leader and Craig have given members their basic scripts (how they are to talk and act during the role play). The scene takes place a few days after Craig's arrival home. Craig and his mother are having a conversation in the kitchen regarding Craig's relationship with his girlfriend. The purpose of the role play is to help Craig express his emotions, assert his rights, and avoid potential "guilt hooks," as well as resolve some of his feelings toward his parents.

The Role-Playing Scene.   The role play begins:

CRAIG:	Mother, I don't know if I can talk about Sara with you without getting into a fight. I really want to enjoy spring break with you, and I don't want to end up fighting and arguing. I don't feel like anything good comes from it.
ROLE-PLAYED MOTHER:	Well! I just want you to know how much your father and I are worried about how you're living your life. We don't approve of her, and we don't think she's good for you! I talked with your father the other day, and he's thinking about sending you to another college we think would be better for you. Besides, why should we pay for your college education if all you are interested in is finding a girlfriend?
CRAIG:	(visibly angry): I resent the implied threat. I will not let you intimidate me into giving up my relationship with Sara. Besides, I don't think you are concerned about my welfare or my feelings in this relationship. No, Mom, I think you don't like Sara because of her religion. You and Dad are hypocrites. I thought you taught us to be accepting, tolerant, and respectful of other people, including their religious views.

The role play continues with an argument between Craig and his mother. The leader decides to interrupt the role play after Craig has had sufficient time to express his feelings and practice assertive responding. The group is invited to give feedback connecting that which they have seen in the role play with what relates to the role play's objectives. The group gives Craig the feedback that his expression of feelings needs to be clearer and more congruent; that more "I" statements and feeling words need to be present in his communication; and that his assertive responding could be improved by deleting the retaliatory remarks and countermanipulations (for example, "You and Dad are hypocrites"). Craig is then invited to practice role playing once more to incorporate the feedback and extend the learning experience. The role play with Craig concludes with the leader debriefing and processing with Craig and group members regarding work done vicariously by members during role play on issues relevant to their family experience.

Case Analysis.   A role play with similar issues may also take place in this session, say, with Janet and her issues with her parents. The leader at this point needs to be sensitive to the group's availability to work with another client (Janet) as well as to that client's level of interest and energy to use the role-play format. The intensity, length of involvement, and the vicarious learning (modeling) that was gained from the role-play exercise with Craig may have been sufficiently thorough to provide members with awareness, insight, and learning how to enhance interpersonal behavior (role-play modeling). The leader may process with members what their experiences were during the role play, helping them contrast their similarities and differences shared in the group session. This process includes their understanding and learning of more effective interpersonal behaviors.

The role-play strategy is one way of working with particular issues with common themes among group members. The more members have issues in common with the role-play issues, the more they are likely to benefit vicariously; this is an important consideration in the choice of role-play strategy. A group psychodrama or sociodrama could have been used that would have involved more members. Psychodrama as a technical strategy will be discussed later in this chapter. In using a role-play format, in which the leader is initially in a more directive role, the leader may wish to involve the group more, by brainstorming several alternatives for working with common issues among members, and let the group decide what procedures they would like to use. In this way, the leader is blending the expertise of a consultant with the group's responsibility for deciding its own course of action.

Termination Stage

According to Hansen et al. (1976, p. 414), "Termination is one of the most significant aspects of the group process. If handled inappropriately, it may not only conclude this experience without effective change for the member or members, but also so adversely affect individuals that they may not seek further help when necessary. If handled adequately, the process of termination in itself can be an important force in helping individuals develop new behaviors."

The termination stage of group work is influenced by several factors: the length of time the group has been meeting, the meaningfulness and intensity of the group experience and the relative success of the group in meeting the goals, expectations, and needs of its members all influence the quality of the termination stage. When the group is an open-ended one—meaning that members come and go as they accomplish their goals and objectives—the issues involved in termination are more individual in nature.

During a group's closing stages, the leader summarizes with members the progress, or lack of progress, made toward the various individual goals and objectives that each member set (Hansen et al., 1976). In closing, consideration is given to the amount of investment in terms of energy and commitment made on the part of members, and the subsequent meaning that underlies such investment and commitment. Some members may feel abandoned, reluctant, and/or angry about ending the group. Often, therapeutic issues emerge in termination that need working through. Sensitivity on the part of the leader to these conditions is a necessity. Part of the reluctance to terminate may be avoided by supplying members with advance notice and opportunity to deal with the termination. In general, members will need time to understand and process their thoughts and feelings regarding the meaning of their group experience; such conditions vary from member to member. For some, a referral to another counselor to continue with individual counseling or with another group may be an appropriate solution.

General guidelines for closing and terminating a group or, for that matter, a particular group session include wrapping up, reviewing issues covered, examining feelings generated, establishing what has been left unfinished and what progress has been made, and projecting future directions, goals, and objectives. In order to keep the focus on termination, the leader will need to remind members that no new business or rehash of old issues on which work would be necessary is permissible or possible. In the case of ending a session, the emphasis will be on linking issues covered in that particular session to future work and sessions.

Structuring and facilitating the closing of the group varies with the issues and feelings members bring to closing and ending. Some members may feel abandonment, some may withdraw to avoid dealing with the painful issues of ending, some may get angry, and others may feel a sense of loss and sadness. Embedded in the process of termination are issues of the individual's separateness, autonomy, and independence from the group. It is hoped that individuals have learned from their group experience a set of skills and abilities that allow them to cope with such existential issues so that, on the one hand, they can appreciate the importance of separateness as vital to their self-development, and, on the other, can eagerly engage in developing relationships with others that respect the boundaries of others in a caring, loving, and nonpossessive way.

Case Example.   The leader in this case has prepared the group for termination by reminding them that the group's termination has been approaching, giving members ample time to work on the issues they brought to the group, and helping them explore their feelings about ending. The purpose of this session is to review the group experience; assess the progress made by members; encourage members to continue to work on issues that still need attention to use what they learned in group to maintain their progress; and, finally, to say goodbye.

The group opens with the leader inviting members to share with each other what the experience in group has been like for them. One of the members begins by telling the others how much he will miss not seeing them. The leader asks the member if he can share exactly what he is going to miss. "I'm going to miss the honesty and openness that all of you have shared. I've never experienced anything like this before; it's going to be hard for me to give this up." Another member, extending on what has been shared, states that she feels the same way: "We've come a long way in the time that we've been together and I feel sad that it has to end. I feel very special in this group, and you've all given me the kind of care and understanding that I wish I would have had in my family." Members continue to share their feelings about the meaningfulness of their group experience. The leader shares her feelings as well, and when members have had sufficient time to express themselves, the leader asks them to share with each other the progress they have made and seen each other make.

Structuring Termination.   Several intervention strategies and structural formats may be used at this point. Have members express appreciations and regrets for helping efforts made and missed by themselves, members, and the leader; or, use sentence completions:

- "I think you benefited most from or by _____ , and I urge you to continue working on _____ ."
- "The one thing I learned most about myself in this group is _____ ."
- "I became more aware of _____ in terms of my relationship with others."
- "If I were starting a group today, I would work more on _____ ."
- "The thing I regret most about this experience is _____ ."
- "The thing I liked most about the group was _____ ."
- "The thing I did not like about the group was _____ ."

Structuring Feedback.   Let us now return to the case example in which the leader is attempting to assist the group in closing and terminating. Interventions are focused on getting members to reflect on efforts they made at changing goals for future efforts for continuation of progress, and to share this with each other. Members are also encouraged to give each other feedback on progress they have seen others make in the group.

One member starts by stating that she feels less anxious and tense around others, that she doesn't hide her feelings or thoughts as much as she did when she first entered the group, and that she has less fear of rejection or disapproval. Members respond by giving feedback and testimony to what they have seen regarding her changes. By structuring the feedback, the leader encourages members to be specific, supportive, and honest. For example, the leader asks, "Jim, you said that you thought Mary had made a lot of progress in the last three sessions. Can you think of an example of a specific instance in which she was behaving as she's described?" Another member urges Mary to continue work on changing her critical self-evaluation by building a more supportive, nurturing, and self-accepting attitude.

Fantasy.   Parallels, metaphors, and guided fantasies may also be used to facilitate termination. In such strategies, the leader assists members by equating termination with other life events, such as leaving home, moving away, going on a trip, or ending a relationship. Members are asked to reflect on these previous life experiences and to share how they handled such experiences and to express how the group ending is similar. Guided fantasies and metaphors may be used to depict the development, roles played by members, and outcomes of the group experience. A fantasy camping trip may be used, for example, in which members fantasize about what happened on the trip, the roles they played, relationships that were developed, what they expected, what they received, and how they felt about the trip in general. These fantasies can then be translated to the group experience. Such fantasies help facilitate expression of feelings and reduce the tension that surrounds termination. However, it is important for the leader not to supply structure here to avoid the important and natural aspects involved in termination (sadness and a sense of loss).

The Goodbye.   When members have finished sharing progress made, as well as discussing how to continue working without the group, the leader intervenes to bring the group to the final phase of closing—saying goodbye. The leader may set the tone for the closing moments by sharing feelings of satisfaction with the work the group has done, and by inviting members to express themselves in a farewell. Sometimes, for some members, there is a need for touching, shaking hands, or hugging. Some members want to make contact with others after group is over. Generally, these issues are discussed openly and members come to their own decisions and preferences. The needs that members have to try to continue the group experience after or during the phase of termination are discussed openly (the issues of being dependent and fear of separation). The focus, facilitated by the leader, is on life after the group, how what has been learned and developed in group can be applied elsewhere. In some instances, a follow-up session can be planned, the purpose of which is generally to assess progress and encourage maintenance of behavior change. The follow-up session should not be a postponement of termination. The ending of a group has as much potential for learning, growth, and development as do all other stages.

WORKING WITH INDIVIDUALS IN A GROUP

There are times when working with individuals in a group is necessary for maximizing the potential for change. In this case the leader is the central help provider, the expert. Techniques aimed at working with individuals in a group involve accessing the clients' resources for change. Guided fantasies, covert rehearsal, and imagery techniques are examples of processes aimed at helping clients get in touch with personal resources: positive self-esteem, hope, faith, will, self-confidence, and self-nurturance. The following techniques are aimed at illustrating the use of imagery in groups.

Creative Imagery

According to Robert Assagioli (1982), the ability to imagine creative images is one of the most important functions of the psyche, both unconsciously and consciously. Imagery increases one's ability to concentrate, which enhances problem-solving skills. Images influence the body (for example, imagining self as relaxed), which in turn can influence the autonomic nervous system. Imagery is also an important prerequisite for action. The ability to use imagery and visualization processes can be expedited by having members go through some relaxation exercises prior to a fantasy exercise. It may also be helpful to practice visualizing some simple geometric shapes or innocuous images, such as an apple, as a warm up to working with imagery.

Exercises Using Imagery

The leader in the first exercise guides group members by asking them to imagine a classroom with a gray or dull black blackboard (Assagioli, 1982):

Imagine that in the middle of the blackboard appears a figure, number five, in white chalk. Hold this image, keep it vivid and steady in your inner mind's eye. Now, to the right of the five place a number two: fifty-two. Hold these figures in your mind's eye. [Pause] Now try adding another number, number four, which makes five hundred and twenty-four. The leader may wish to check with group members in terms of the vividness, clarity, durability, and frequency of figures. This warm-up period may be extended to include the use of color and geometric shapes (for example, having the members image the figures as blue triangle, green square, yellow circle).

Fantasy Work and Emotions

Group members may find it easy to envision a meadow. The symbolic value of *meadow* is rich for creative fantasies. A meadow is a neutral starting point, a symbol of nature which can evoke peaceful, calming emotions or playful, energetic emotions. Visual stimulation may be guided by requesting that members explore the meadow and the feelings evoked. The meadow symbol can be used to facilitate the development and expression of emotions. Another symbol that can be used is *climbing a mountain* to explore feelings of motivation or aspiration, as well as blocks or limitations perceived to goal attainment. A guided fantasy of *following a stream* may be used to explore conflicts the individual perceives in setting goals, experiencing blocks or frustration, and in self-expression (Assagioli, 1982). Fantasy work is largely a creative process that is open to the imagination and inventiveness of the leader. With the use of fantasy, a creative group leader has a powerful technique to aid group members in identifying, understanding, and expressing feelings, as well as dealing with unconscious material and discovering personal resources for stimulating creative problem solving for further growth and development.

Fantasy Work and Interpersonal Issues

Disapproval

In working with issues of interpersonal conflict, rejection, autonomy, and independence, the leader may intervene by having members imagine receiving disapproval from someone in the group and picture that person's face, voice, posture, gestures, and statements. A follow-up intervention on the part of the leader might consist of asking the members to focus their attention on their own responses and what they imagine themselves doing (for example, defending or counterattacking). The leader can bring the experiences generated by the fantasy back to the group so that members can process with each other what they are experiencing that results in conflict (Lazarus, 1977).

This exercise may be used to facilitate members' attention on how they deal with disapproval, from whom they want affirmation, fears they have of rejection from each other, and to increase the climate of trust and safety in the group, as well as to encourage members' self-disclosure regarding important interpersonal issues. Additionally, members may become desensitized to fears and anxieties over disapproval, paving the way to a greater sense of independence and self-reliance. The quality of openness and genuine interpersonal feedback may increase, and assertive responding from member to member may also be facilitated by such group fantasy work.

Resistance

A similar fantasy can be used to deal with resistance expressing oneself honestly by asking members to imagine sharing openly and honestly with group members. In similar fashion to the previous example, the leader then processes with the group the feelings members experienced during the fantasy, difficulties they anticipated from group members, and the impact they think the openness would have on group members.

Additionally, fantasies such as taking psychological risks in the group, appearing foolish to others, saying no, disagreeing, expressing anger, among others, may also be used to aid group members in opening up to each other and dealing with tough interpersonal issues. Working with imagery and fantasy in this way allows the leader to deepen the level of interpersonal contact among members, remove barriers to intimacy, and help members cope with interpersonal tensions and anxieties. Imagery gives members an opportunity to rehearse and play out their fears, hopes, wishes, and needs in a safe way (in the privacy of their own fantasies) and to process their fears and calculate their risk in view of what others fantasized before they engage in a potentially threatening interpersonal encounter.

The following guided fantasies can be used to help members gain a sense of physical sensations of release of tension or fear, as well as to access feelings of well-being such as strength and acceptance. Such fantasy work may also be a warm-up for additional work with psychodrama.

Letting Go

Relax, deepen, and protect yourself. Travel easily to a safe mind space. Here in this space you can recreate your day, a day that has been difficult for you. Conjure up each thought, each act, each word that you regret. See them all very clearly. *Pause about three to five minutes.*

Now take the images one at a time and watch as they grow smaller, smaller, and smaller. Help the images grow smaller. They are dissolving, growing smaller and fainter until they no longer exist. This image no longer has the power to hurt or disturb you in any way. It is dissolved, washed away, completely erased.

Now conjure up each word, each act, each thought that you enjoyed, that you consider important, anything that you feel positive about. Conjure up each happy thought, fleeting smile, pleasant experience. Let these images grow. Let them become larger and larger. Let them spill over into your consciousness. You are bathed in the joy of the remembered experience. *Pause about three to five minutes.*

These positive experiences will continue to grow and develop. They will remain a part of you always. Swim in these images now, remembering, recreating, and rejoicing in them. They will remain a part of you now and always.

And now when you are ready, you may return to your usual awareness, released of all pain and fear and filled with a joyful and loving energy. Take your time. Then open your eyes and stretch your body (Mariechild, 1981).

Develping resources for solving problems fosters a sense of personal growth and inner wisdom. Resolving conflicts between the mind, body, and emotions allows us to change, grow, and actualize our potential. Accordingly, the following guided fantasy is offered:

Body, Mind, and Emotions

Relax, deepen, and protect yourself. And now as you continue to relax, to float on down, you realize that you are going to a meeting, a very important meeting where you will converse with three aspects of yourself. This meeting will be held at the top of a mountain. To carry you to this meeting is a bird, a beautiful creature, lovelier than any you have seen. And she is here now, calling you by name and you fly with her to the top of the mountain. *Pause about one minute.*

And now the bird alights on the mountain top and leaves you there in the quiet and stillness of that cool and airy space. And here you see your emotions, manifesting themselves before you. Notice the form they take and talk with your emotions, realizing that thoughts and emotions flow through you, they are not you. *Pause about three minutes.*

And now, as suddenly as they appeared, your emotions leave. And again your mind manifests itself before you. Notice the shape it takes. Talk with your mind, knowing that you have a mind but you are more than your mind. *Pause about three minutes.*

And now, as suddenly as it appeared, your mind leaves. And once again another manifestation of you appears, your physical body. Notice the form it takes and talk with your body, knowing that you have a body but you are more than your body. *Pause about three minutes.*

And now, as suddenly as it appeared, your body leaves. And to your right you see the bird, ready to carry you off the mountain top. And you fly with the bird up and back to your usual waking reality. Return relaxed, refreshed, and filled with energy. Open your eyes and stretch your body (Mariechild, 1981).

Processing the Guided Fantasy

In processing the previous guided fantasy, the leader may begin by simply inviting members to share their experiences of the fantasy. "Who would volunteer to share their fantasy?" The leader may then ask members to reflect on and interpret their experiences by asking open-ended questions such as "What does that mean to you?" In assisting members in generalizing from the fantasy, the leader might ask members questions like, "What do you associate with _____?" To begin to apply the information generated by the fantasy, the leader may ask group members to think about what they discovered in the fantasy that they can apply in their daily lives, how they might go about doing so, and what benefits or liabilities they could anticipate as a result? In concluding the guided fantasy, the leader may invite members to contrast the use of fantasy as a method of working together in the group with other experiences, and to evaluate the pros and cons of spending the group's time in such a fashion.

The emotions generated by the fantasy experience may dictate the nature of what will take priority in terms of the issues and amount of time members need for identifying, experiencing, and expressing their feelings and awarenesses. In general, the more intense the emotional experience, the longer it takes to work through and process the fantasy experience. Various needs may also emerge which serve to focus the group's time and energy on providing satisfaction. Members, for example, may have a need to share personal reactions to each others' fantasies.

WORKING WITH THE GROUP AS A COMMUNITY FOR CREATIVE PROBLEM SOLVING: PSYCHODRAMA

One of the most creative processes available for group work is psychodrama, developed by J. L. Moreno in the 1930s. According to Moreno (1946), psychodrama includes both individual and group therapy. As a technique, psychodrama provides an activity in the form of drama that teaches through experience rather than by thought. The goal of psychodrama is to work out emotions (catharsis) through action, and to use understanding and insight developed by the process of acting out to solve problems and resolve conflicts (Greenburg, 1974). According to Moreno (1946), a psychodrama has no past or future; it is completely a spontaneous and here-and-now endeavor. The outcome of psychodrama is the reorganization of the individual's perceptions, which leads to increased problem-solving abilities and reduction in tension, as well as increases in self-awareness, control, integration, and acceptance.

Components of the Psychodrama

Director/Producer (Leader and/or Group)

The director of the psychodrama sets the stage, warms up the actors and the audience, opens the communication channels among the group, stimulates participants to be involved emotionally, and helps determine the goals and objectives for the psychodrama (Moreno, 1946).

Protagonist (Client)

The goal of the protagonist is to freely express thoughts, feelings, concerns, and issues relevant to the objective of the psychodrama. The key element of spontaneous expression is crucial to the role of protagonist.

Auxiliary Ego

Auxiliary ego is a role taken by members of the group to assist the protagonist with playing out issues and attitudes toward significant others. Auxiliary egos are generally selected by the protagonist to represent key figures appropriate to the psychodrama. The auxiliary ego needs to be sensitive to the cues received from both the director and the protagonist in order to play out the psychodrama.

Audience

The audience is composed of remaining group members who are not directly involved in the psychodrama. The purpose of the audience is to give feedback regarding what they saw, heard, and felt during the psychodrama. Moreno (1946) encourages members of the audience to identify and personalize issues triggered by the psychodrama, and share their insights and understandings relevant to the protagonist and auxiliary egos.

Psychodrama Techniques

The Warm-Up

The warm-up, a method for dealing with reluctance to get involved in the psychodrama, is especially important in assisting group members with overcoming their apprehensions, fears, and anxieties regarding performing, expressing, and being the center of attention. A warm-up is a relatively neutral activity which allows members the choice of how much and what to share on a personal level. The warm-up is also a demonstration of what is expected in terms of using technical procedures that are dramatic and experiential in nature (Leveton, 1977).

According to Greenburg (1974), the warm-up is a phase of the psychodrama in which the director (group leader) stimulates group members to open up channels of communication; arouses the group emotionally, exciting their interest and curiosity; and fosters the group's sense of creativity and playfulness. With such objectives in mind, the leader may facilitate the warm-up phase by leading general discussions on topics relative to the purpose and goals of the psychodrama. For example, the group may be assisted in warming up to emotional expression or catharsis in the psychodrama by dealing with their resistance to open, emotional expression, as well as by reminding members of the ground rules which state that each member has the right to choose how far he or she wishes to go with emotional expression.

Warm-Ups for Creative Imagery.   Warm-ups may be specific to psychological processes such as guided imagery or fantasy work. In warm-up for imagery work, the leader may ask group members to envision innocuous scenes such as geometric shapes or a piece of fruit to assist members in concentrating and focusing with the mind's eye. Creative imagery is an important resource for spontaneous improvisation. Group members may also be assisted in warming up by the use of structured exercises such as sentence completions (I have to, I want to . . ., I should . . ., I need . . .).

Sculpting.   Sculpting is a warm-up exercise that involves having members characterize their relationships in their group, family, or any set of relationship possibilities (how they appear to the individual doing the sculpting in terms of distance, influence, and impact) by positioning the various members into a tableau, or, in general, any setting that can be characterized by body posture and physical configuration. The goal is to depict the perceptions and responses of group members regarding their interpersonal dynamics. After members have had an opportunity to experiment with the sculpting, the leader processes the experience with the group and may then use information generated by the sculpting to set up psychodramas. A primary goal of warming up is to give members permission to behave spontaneously (Leveton, 1977).

The Double (Auxiliary Ego)

Essentially, doubling is empathy in action. A group member stands in for the protagonist (doubles for the protagonist) and expresses another point of view or an underlying feeling that has not been expressed but is implied in the context of the protagonist's dramatization of the issue being addressed.

Case Example.   Mary, the protagonist, is dramatizing her relationship with her parents in which she portrays herself as controlled, guilty, and fearful of expressing herself openly and honestly. The goal of the psychodrama is to help Mary learn to express herself, stand up for her rights, and explore how she relates to her parents in ways that reduce her self-confidence and self-esteem. The leader asks a group member to play Mary standing up to her parents' demands. The theme of the psychodrama is based on the premise that Mary's low self-esteem and lack of self-confidence are a result of allowing others to take responsibility and control from her. The first scene involves Mary turning her checking account over to her parents because, according to her father, she is incapable of managing her life. The double can be used to model the expression of feelings and behaviors that Mary in turn incorporates in the psychodrama.

Applications of Doubling.   The double is a technique based on a true and meaningful understanding of the inner issues relevant to the protagonist. It therefore requires that the double be sensitive, aware, and in touch with the protagonist's feelings and perceptions. From this standpoint, the double needs to be flexible to the cues given by the protagonist so that doubling is done correctly. Several experiments with doubling may be necessary until the double accurately reflects the protagonist's inner expressions and desired responses (Leveton, 1977).

Several group members may serve as doubles in a given psychodrama. Group members learn to double by being instructed by the leader about the role, as a result of feedback from both the director and the protagonist during the experiencing of doubling, and by watching other members double. The double may experiment with a variety of portrayals (for example, exaggeration of voice tone or nonverbal gestures depicting qualities of interaction that serve to block or hinder the protagonist from adequately expressing needs or wishes clearly). The double may also characterize emotional tones of the protagonist's behavior, such as understated or only partially expressed feelings of love, anger, rage, and the like. The entire group can also be called upon to give their improvisational expression of what they feel and how they would like to respond if they were the protagonist. In general, the doubling process gives the leader a technique to structure member behaviors that help the client resolve concerns.

The Soliloquy

By use of the soliloquy technique, the leader instructs the client to talk out thoughts and feelings as they come to the client spontaneously around the issue being addressed.

Case Example.   Bob, a group member going through a divorce, is instructed by the group leader to do a soliloquy of his thoughts and feelings regarding the ending of his relationship. The scene of the psychodrama has Bob just finishing a phone conversation with his wife which involved everything that went wrong in the relationship. This topic was chosen by Bob and was based on an actual experience during the week prior to the group meeting. The soliloquy allows Bob to survey, clarify, and get in touch with emotions, thoughts, and perceptions relative to working through his feelings and coming to closure and resolution with the ending of his relationship (Greenburg, 1974).

Role Reversal

Role reversal is a psychodrama technique that involves members' taking each other's place and understanding, feeling, and thinking as that other. The other may be a teacher, friend, lover, boss—anyone with whom interpersonal conflict exists. The goal is to open up channels of communication by helping members become more aware of the projections (assignment of responsibilities to the other), blame, and perceptual biases that limit resolution and sustain conflict. Leader interventions in role reversal generally occur where members seem blocked or unaware of the pattern of communication that sustains the conflict. The goal is to clear up distortions and to foster direct and clear communication.

Case Example.   Bill, a group member involved in a scene characterizing his father as critical, uncaring, and distant, is asked to play his father. Bill (as his father) begins by countering with, "I'm very much concerned about you. I wish I were better at showing you how I feel, but I end up feeling angry and frustrated and my words seem to come out wrong. I say things I really don't mean." The effects of the role reversal provide Bill with a sense and perception of his father as caring, but struggling. Under this perceptual condition, Bill is more willing to try to resolve, more able to understand the nature of the conflict between him and his father, and more open to possibilities for resolution.

The Magic Shop

An example of improvisation, the "magic shop" technique may be used as a guided fantasy, or members may actually be assigned the roles of shopkeeper and shopper. The idea is that qualities, personal resources, and values may be obtained through fantasy and imagery. The magic shop's goods may be traded or purchased only by bartering. The individual must be willing to give up or sacrifice something of importance to obtain something of importance (for example, a sense of well-being, self-confidence, courage, freedom). The leader's role is to stimulate the bargaining process.

Case Example.   Jim, a member of the group who is frequently withdrawn and distant, takes the role of shopkeeper. Karen, a member who frequently struggles with low self-esteem, plays the part of the customer. Jim's fantasy as shopkeeper involves setting up the magic shop on a quiet street in a small town (metaphoric of his withdrawn behavior). Karen plays a fantasy character who is uncertain, lacks confidence, and defers to others. Karen approaches the shopkeeper, who informs her that he has the kind of self-worth she needs, but wants to know what she is willing to give in return. Karen says, "I don't know if I have anything worth giving." The leader intervenes, asking the group to assist by making suggestions about what they think Karen might give in return for a sense of self-worth. Having listened to the group's suggestions, Karen decides to give Jim some of her ability to express feelings openly. The two continue to negotiate and bargain on the merits and importance of the exchange.

Application of the Magic Shop.   Processing the feelings, thoughts, and aware-nesses of the bargaining encounter allows members to explore their relationships with themselves as well as with others (how I see me and how you see me). What we want and how we go about giving and receiving become the focal points of exploration. Other aspects of psychodrama may be introduced, such as doubling, to help members further explore the various roles they play in bargaining to get what they need and want, or, conversely, how they avoid or block themselves from getting what they need and want. The leader can structure the role-play double to focus on the needs members struggle to satisfy, as well as on the methods, energies, and behaviors they engage in to satisfy those needs.

Imagination and fantasy are important abilities for group members to engage in to benefit from the magic shop. A sense of playfulness and an atmosphere of openness and willingness to experiment with creative fantasy are important prerequisites for the positive outcome of the magic-shop strategy. A spirit of imaginative playfulness is an essential prerequisite for a leader employing strategies like the magic shop. Getting people in touch with imagined resources and abilities can be a powerful method for fostering change. Uncovering resources, dealing with emotions, enhancing self-understanding and acceptance, and promoting internal rehearsal, as well as testing reality, may be creatively facilitated by the use of fantasy (Starker, 1982, pp. 139–140).

Summary of Psychodrama

Psychodrama consists of stages similar to group work in general. The beginning stage is the warm-up. Members are encouraged to use this stage as an open period to explore, identify, and develop their awareness, perceptions, and target behaviors for the future work of the psychodrama. Psychodrama is open; members need to be free to explore and act out in a spontaneous fashion. Therefore, the leader must encourage and model the norms of permission, choice, and responsibility on the part of group members to decide how, when, and what they wish to bring up in the warm-up.

The acting-out stage involves assisting the protagonist in the spontaneous expression of scenes representing the protagonist's conflict, and is similar to the work stage in this regard.

As the psychodrama concludes, the leader shifts the focus to the audience and discusses the impact of their experiences, parts of the psychodrama with which they identified, issues they got in touch with, and what they learned from the psychodrama in general. Before the psychodrama is concluded, the protagonist is given an opportunity to hear from the group. The leader at this point may help by facilitating from the group identification, understanding, and empathy for the protagonist. Having center stage in front of the group and exposing the vulnerabilities is a sensitive matter that calls for sensitivity from both the leader and the group.

Working with the group as a creative problem-solving process involves a number of important leader behaviors and resources. These include the ability to visualize how the group can experiment with its creative energies, the willingness to risk, a sense of timing, sensitivity to the emotional energy of the group, and a trust in the group as having the capacity for providing its own creative experiences.

The procedures illustrated and covered in this chapter are considered basic tools for group work. How they are used depends on the leader's personal style, group members' concerns, and the group's willingness to act in the capacity as a creative system for change.

SUMMARY

As presented in this chapter, how, when, and why the leader intervenes is related to several factors. The leader's philosophy or personal orientation toward helping; the context or stage of the group; and the individual member's issues, goals, and needs all influence the nature and choice of the leader's intervention. The orientations and technical strategies covered in this chapter focus on the crucial ingredients of the interpersonal process. The goals of process-related group counseling are to develop a system, climate, and/or subculture which characteristically embodies a set of norms that make the group process therapeutic. Being in a healthy environment can be therapeutic in and of itself; however, being a participant in building and maintaining a therapeutic climate provides even greater benefits. From this point of view the leader's role and primary task is to help the group develop and maintain therapeutic norms.

The choice of a particular method or technique on the part of a leader is viewed as experimental. What may have been an effective and helpful intervention in one instance may be met with failure in another. As a scientist/practitioner, the leader is open to experimenting, discovering, and learning about the fascinating process of human interaction. The goal is to develop technical processes that are open to change, addition, and integration. The techniques and processes covered in this chapter are offered as examples to demonstrate the use of technique, and are not by any means seen as conclusive. They were selected on the basis of their potential for illustrating the art of practicing creative and innovative methods of group counseling.

REFERENCES

Assagioli, M. D. (1982). *Psychosynthesis*. New York: Penguin.

Bach, K. (1951). Influence through social communication. *Journal of Abnormal and Social Psychology, 46*, 9–23.

Buber, M. (1958). *I and thou*. New York: Scribner.

Dyer, W. W., and Vriend, J. (1980). *Group counseling for personal mastery*. New York: Sovereign Books.

Gazda, G. (1971). *Group counseling: A developmental approach*. Boston: Allyn and Bacon.

Greenburg, J. A. (1974). *Psychodrama: Theory and therapy*. New York: Behavioral Publications.

Hansen, J. C.; Warner, R. W.; and Smith, E. M. (1976). *Group counseling: Theory and process*. Chicago: Rand McNally.

Lazarus, A. (1977). *In the mind's eye: The power of imagery for personal enrichment*. New York: Rawson.

Leveton, E. (1977). *Psychodrama for the timid clinician*. New York: Springer.

Mariechild, D. (1981). *Mother wit: A feminist guide to psychic development*. New York: Crossing Press.

Moreno, J. L. (1946). *Psychodrama* (Vol. 1). New York: Beacon House.

Starker, S. (1982). *Fantastic thought*. Englewood Cliffs, NJ: Prentice-Hall.

Yalom, I. D. (1975). *The theory and practice of group psychotherapy*. New York: Basic Books.

4

THERAPEUTIC FORCES IN A COUNSELING GROUP

Effective leaders try to understand and manage the forces within the group that either contribute to, or interfere with, the group's achieving its goals. The extent to which the leader trusts members and shares leadership functions with them determines the extent to which he will be able to enlist their assistance in diagnosing the group's problems; in developing therapeutic norms; in recognizing and using therapeutic forces; and in keeping the antitherapeutic forces from interfering with members' achieving their goals. Therefore, the counselor must learn to use his special status to facilitate client growth rather than to gain recognition for himself.

Democratic leadership supports Lewin's (1944) early findings for counseling groups: (1) a discussion can clarify issues better than a lecture, but it does not necessarily produce either a decision or an action; (2) improved production (and/or changed behavior) follows meaningful participation in defining specific production goals; (3) a "we" feeling (belonging) is experienced in a democratically led group; and (4) friendliness and cooperative behaviors in democratic groups tend to replace hostility and competition experienced in autocratically led groups. Klauss and Bass (1982) concluded from their review of various laboratory studies that high morale and satisfaction were usually associated with unrestricted open communication, and that performance, too, was enhanced in more-complex task environments.

Gordon's (1955) leadership model also lends itself well to counseling groups. He urged the leader to listen empathically; test his understandings with carefully stated reflections; try to discover relevance of each member's contributions; try to detect and convey linkage to others' contributions; and reinforce members' efforts in becoming increasingly independent. He contended that the leader should trust members, exhibit confidence in their ability to help manage the group, and recognize each member's unique contributions. By his example, Gordon encouraged leaders to develop members' leadership skills as they help members achieve their goals.

Whenever an individual joins any group, participates in formulation of its norms and in definition of its goals, makes a commitment to help its members achieve its goals, and invests genuinely of herself, she can expect—even in a short-term, task-oriented group—to have some impact on the other members, and they upon her. This notion holds even more strongly for the type of counseling group in which, even before members contract for counseling, they have been given the opportunity to explore precisely what will be expected of them and what they must do to achieve their idiosyncratic goals while helping others to achieve their own unique goals. Moreover, having practiced discussing their worries and concerns, they have been provided the opportunity to appraise how adequately the counselor is able to help them before they become members of the counseling group. Consequently, change is not as threatening as it could be in other group settings. Nevertheless, some clients will wonder during the course of treatment whether they may be hurt—or, at least, not helped sufficiently to be worth the pain they experience. At such times the counselor's competency shows both in detecting such a client's fears and in teaching fellow clients to help the threatened one cope with her doubts.

This chapter discusses the therapeutic forces that are available to the counselor in a counseling group and suggests ways of managing them to facilitate clients' maximum growth. It also helps the counselor recognize antitherapeutic forces so he may teach his clients how to help prevent these forces from interfering with clients' achieving their own unique goals. We then discuss the impact of leadership on clients' growth.

LEADERSHIP

The counselor is a powerful therapeutic force in a counseling group, and one which must be seen by clients as a source of support. Yalom (1985) believes that the instillation and maintenance of clients' hope is crucial in all psychotherapies:

> Research substantiates that it is vitally important that therapists believe in themselves and the efficacy of their group. I sincerely believe that I am able to help every motivated patient who is willing to work in the group at least six months. In my initial meeting with patients, I share this conviction with them and attempt to imbue them with my optimism (p. 7).

The counselor (therapist) is the observer-participant in the group. He is the historian. He notes and connects events that occur over the life of the group. He remembers the individual's goals and helps each discover the connection between those goals and the material with which she is currently struggling. He moves the focus from outside the group to inside, from abstract to specific, and from generic to personal (Yalom, 1985).

This therapeutic relationship emphasizes positive feelings and interpersonal attitudes, reciprocally held by counselor and clients; feelings of liking, trust, and respect. Once achieved it can serve as a powerful force in facilitating clients' openness, communication, and willingness to change (Kanfer & Goldstein, 1986):

> . . . In general, it may be concluded that helper expertness and status serve to increase client respect, which in turn leads to the client being more open to the helper's attempts to influence him or her and subsequently, more likelihood of client change (p. 33).

> . . . the clearer it is to the client that it is his or her interests, not the helper's own, toward which the helper is working, the greater the helper's credibility (p. 34).

> . . . research has consistently shown that a helper's empathy with the client's feelings strongly influences the quality of the helper-client relationship that develops, and subsequently, the degree of client change . . . (p. 34).

> The unilateral aspect of the helping relationship reflects the fact the participants agree that one person is defined as the helper and the other as the client. It is also agreed, explicitly or implicitly, that the focus of the relationship and all of its activities is on solving the problems of the client. In this respect, the change process is unlike most other interpersonal interactions. The personal problems, the private affairs, the worries and the wishes of one person, the helper, are not focused upon. Treatment, therapy, or whatever the helping relationship is called, is one-sided and concentrates exclusively on the client (p. 2).

However, in group counseling the counselor does teach clients to be effective helpers as well as successful clients. In the intake interview, he teaches clients to discuss their worries and concerns, define precise goals, develop criteria for detecting their own growth, appraise their commitment to learn new behaviors, and decide whether or not to contract for counseling. Early in their group sessions, clients are taught to recognize and use therapeutic forces, to recognize and manage antitherapeutic forces (including their own resistance), to develop productive group norms, and to be good helpers as well as good clients. Thus, they discover gradually that they have decisional control over their treatment; that they are real partners in the process. Furthermore, group counseling is made more attractive by the care with which clients are selected. Consequently, clients' respect for the counselor, confidence in the treatment process, and hopes for successful results are enhanced. Though Roberts (1985) develops her case for such participant involvement out of an experience in managing a school crisis, her generalizations seem to apply to counseling groups as well: it creates hope and a belief that the world is knowable, understandable, and manageable.

Some counselors are bothered by the notion of the counselor managing the therapeutic forces within the group. Of course, a counselor must be concerned lest he misuse this power. In particular, he must make a conscious effort to ensure that a given client is learning to implement *her own new behaviors* rather than the ones he, or his other clients, desire for her. He also must be sensitive to the collective attempts to force that client to discuss her pain lest they merely tear away her defenses, forcing her to face and deal with the pain with which she is not yet ready to cope. When, however, clients are taught to discuss the pain with which they *are* ready to cope—and be good helpers as well as clients, to provide considerate feedback, and to celebrate their successes—these mistakes rarely occur.

EXPECTATIONS

Before members of any group will take the risks required for therapeutic participation, they must reach some agreements on the following topics (Thelen & Stock, 1955): (1) What operational roles will be required to achieve their goals? (2) How will these assignments be made and by whom? (3) To what degree are persons encouraged to discuss their personal feelings and needs? (4) What can members expect of each other? (5) How will disputes be settled and by whom? (6) How will group norms be developed and changed? Those who are considering group counseling also want answers to questions such as: With what problems will other clients be seeking assistance? How will group counseling differ from encounter and therapy groups? What is the likelihood that participants can expect to profit from this type of assistance? What is done in these groups to maintain confidences? How are clients selected for these groups?

Clients profit most from group counseling when they understand *what will be expected from them and what they can expect from others* prior to contracting for group counseling. Besides getting the answers to their questions, clients are very sensitive to how the counselor answers their questions, and to what questions he seems to give defensive answers. Though they want to participate in developing therapeutic group norms, and to be taught how to change the norms, they also want to know the conditions under which their counselor functions best—what norms will enable them to make the best use of his therapeutic skills. Even young clients recognize the *need for carefully developed structure;* and clients do need to be taught to be good helpers as well as good clients. Nevertheless, the counselor must be careful to establish himself in his unique role as counselor rather than as a teacher. Inasmuch as there are many occasions early in the life of a counseling group when it is appropriate for the counselor to give information and teach clients new skills, he must realize that these behaviors can establish him too much in the role of a teacher and not sufficiently as a counselor.

Until clients know what to expect, and feel secure in asking questions concerning expectations, spontaneity is limited; they feel uncomfortable and self-conscious and are reluctant to take risks required to function effectively in their counseling group. From their research on therapy groups designed for World-War-II veteran outpatients, Powdermaker and Frank (1953) concluded that when there was too little structure, intense competition developed among patients; and when there was too much structure, patients became too inhibited and spent too much energy trying to please the therapist. Kanfer and Goldstein (1986) reported that structuring increased clients' liking of their helpers and the openness with which they discussed their problems.

Dies (1985) concluded that genuineness, empathy, and warmth are not sufficient. The therapist must provide clients with assistance in deriving the therapeutic benefits of the group. This may be achieved in a variety of ways. Dies discovered that facilitative techniques are preferred over manipulative ones. Facilitative leaders use techniques such as structuring, modeling, reinforcement of clients' successful behaviors, and offering of process commentary. They are generally supportive and encouraging and favor positive over negative methods for delivering feedback and confrontation.

A counselor who has the opportunity to get to know clients outside of counseling in schools, colleges, and other institutional settings has the benefit of former clients conveying expectations. He also can arrange to meet with prospective clients to describe group counseling and answer their questions prior to meeting them in the intake interview. When such presentations can be made, clients come to counseling better prepared to help the counselor establish therapeutic group norms, to participate more effectively, and to use the therapeutic resources within their group.

CLIENT COMMITMENT

Those who profit most from group counseling recognize their need for counseling and are committed to discuss their pain openly; to define precise new behaviors to be learned; to implement these new behaviors; and to help fellow clients learn new behaviors. They are aware of at least some of their problems and are willing to surrender their defenses in order to profit from counseling (Beck, 1958). They usually insist that fellow clients do the same. In short, if a client is to be helped, she must know what will be expected of her and how she may expect to be helped, accept the conditions, and develop the commitment to do what is expected (Kelman, 1963). The way the counselor develops a therapeutic relationship facilitates a client's discussion of her pain, answers her questions concerning expectations, and encourages the development of this commitment. It is further reinforced by the techniques used by the counselor, especially in early group sessions, to involve clients in developing and maintaining group norms and in reinforcing their successful client and helper behaviors.

On the other hand, when clients fail to disclose and become meaningfully involved in the therapeutic process early in the life of the group, they tend to drop out of the group or become nonpatient members (Sethna & Harrington, 1971). In early sessions especially, the counselor must watch for signs that suggest that a client cannot accept group norms, or accept responsibility for maintaining and/or redefining them, or meets with resistance for which she does not know how to cope, or is hurt by someone in the group. Moreover, the counselor must recognize and reinforce a client's willingness to take risks and discuss painful material and implement her desired new behaviors.

Where prospective clients have many opportunities to learn from friends and relatives what to expect from group counseling and the counselor is endorsed by them, clients find it much easier to make a commitment. On the other hand, when prospective clients' relatives and friends were hurt—or, at least, did not feel that they were helped—by some group procedure (which appears to be something like group counseling), their commitment is much harder to achieve because of these failures.

ATTRACTIVENESS OF THE GROUP

The more attractive a group is to its members, the greater the odds are that it will have an impact on them. A group's attractiveness tends to be determined by the extent to which it seems to meet prospective members' needs; its goals are appealing to prospective members; and it includes prestigious members (Cartwright, 1951). Making admission to a group difficult makes even a dull group more attractive (Festinger & Aronson, 1960). When, therefore, the counselor selects his clients with great care, and explains why he does so, he increases the attractiveness of the counseling group. Furthermore, the client should play an important role in assessing whether she accepts the admission criteria and the responsibility for helping to develop therapeutic group norms; this participation also increases the attractiveness of the group. It is preferable that a client recognize when she is not ready for group counseling before entering a group than to undergo the discomfort of dropping out. A client can make a judicious decision, however, only when provided with sufficient information concerning the nature of the group experience; expectations of clients, including criteria for assessing readiness to meet these expectations; treatment duration; and costs (Yalom, 1985).

The greater the prestige of a group member, the greater will be her impact on the group (Cartwright, 1951). When, therefore, a counselor selects a prestigious person for membership in a group, he must be certain that the person is admired by his clients rather than only by the staff of his institution. He also must take special care in selecting and preparing that person to ensure that she is committed to being a good client and helper—otherwise she may prove to be a poor model during treatment.

Kelman (1963) demonstrated that changes produced by counseling and therapy may result from three processes: compliance, identification, and internalization. New behavior learned through compliance tends to manifest itself under conditions of surveillance by the influencing agent and tends to be continued only when it is observable by that agent. Identification-based change depends on the salience of the learner's relationship to the influencing person. Perhaps, therefore, the counselor should facilitate a client using a prestigious figure as a model, and apply identification-based learning rather than mere compliance. Nevertheless, the practice of the new behavior relies on others' expectations and approval, and consequently the maintenance of the new behavior is tied to an external source.

Finally, when motivation to learn new behaviors results from internalization, it depends on neither surveillance nor on salience; the new behavior is implemented whenever the learner believes it is appropriate. Such new behavior is internalized into the learner's own values and needs—into her own unique self. Though it is appropriate to include prestigious members to serve as models, just as the counselor helps clients identify their heroes and copy from them selectively, the counselor still must help individuals develop their internal motivation. Lasting change results from internalization.

BELONGING

Both those who are to be changed and those who influence change in a group must sense a strong feeling of belonging (Cartwright, 1951). In order for a client to feel that she truly belongs, she must feel accepted, needed, and valued and feel that her fellow clients give of themselves without ulterior motives.

Many clients enter treatment with the disquieting thought that they are unique in their wretchedness, that they alone have such frightening or unacceptable problems, thoughts, impulses, and fantasies (Yalom, 1985). The problems in family life, and loss of extended family influences resulting from frequent moves, have left many Americans with devastating loneliness and feelings of rootlessness. Discovering others in their group with similar problems enhances the feelings of belonging and affiliation.

Powdermaker and Frank (1953) encourage counselors to make a special effort to note affiliation feelings among members. The counselor can use a reflection to point out similarity of one client's worries and concerns with another's and generalize from one's successes to encourage another to implement her own desired new behaviors. As the feeling of belonging increases, a client becomes more ego-involved in anothers' problems, participates more meaningfully, and increases her own and fellow clients' commitment to learn new behaviors. Belonging to such a group also helps the individual to recognize and accept her need for intimacy, desensitizes her to the fear of intimacy, and offers her an opportunity to learn relationship skills. Developing satisfying relationships which she can recognize and enjoy is especially critical for the neurotic. This need for belonging is essential for normal clients, too, and for adolescents in particular. The preparation and selection of clients for groups helps them discover affiliation feelings and accept responsibility for developing a feeling of belonging in their group.

Though acceptance by fellow clients is not as predictable nor as unconditional as the counselor's, it is powerful because clients recognize that it is more representative of society at large (Kelman, 1963). Moreover, unlike other groups, an individual can discuss deficiencies openly without losing status in a counseling group (Dreikurs, 1957). Nevertheless, clients should be reinforced when they discuss their pain openly, take the risks required to implement desired new behaviors, ask volunteers to help them practice new behaviors, and participate in solving the problems which arise in developing and maintaining group norms. Thus, they discover that they can contribute, and that their contributions are valued by fellow clients as well as the counselor. Poey (1984) urges the counselor to reinforce these signs of cohesiveness *whenever they are exhibited.*

CLIENT READINESS

During the presentation clients are told what they can do to increase their readiness for group counseling. They are encouraged to think about what really worries and upsets them, think how they would like to change, and come to the intake interview prepared to convince themselves and their counselor that they are committed to learn new behaviors. As this commitment grows in the intake interview, in subsequent group sessions, and in implementing their new learnings, their self-esteem increases. Moreover, this new self-image is reinforced by fellow clients.

The better clients understand what is expected of them, adopt these expectations, and accept responsibility, the more ready they feel for group counseling. Obviously, a counselor can facilitate this process, but he must convey to clients that they must accept responsibility for achieving readiness. When clients experience this readiness they increase their self-esteem and their willingness to take the risk required to implement new behaviors. Thus, they also increase their hope for successful results and their own personal potency. They gradually discover that they do not have to be victims—that they can do some things to achieve a better life for themselves.

CLIENTS' ACCEPTANCE OF RESPONSIBILITY

The way group counseling is presented to clients, how their questions are answered concerning expectations and their readiness for counseling, and the nature of their participation in development of group norms influences clients' acceptance of responsibility. Teaching prospective clients to ready themselves facilitates their acceptance of responsibility too. Kanfer and Gaelick (1986) believe that such decisional control also increases clients' intrinsic motivation and their chances for successful results.

Hobbs (1962) argued that the locus of control must be placed with clients rather than with the counselor; clients must be taught to accept responsibility for developing and modifying their cognitive structure in order to make personal sense out of the world. That insight, as it is usually perceived, probably follows rather than precedes changed behavior. He believes that emphasis must be placed upon clients' immediate experiences and their learning new behaviors. Clients must practice making decisions, learn to accept responsibility for themselves, learn new ways of relating to others, and discover that they are capable of managing their own lives.

Clients' acceptance of responsibility for formulating and maintaining their group norms does not mean that norms so developed will never be ignored or challenged. From time to time, individuals will have difficulty disciplining themselves, listening to others, sharing time, suppressing their own immediate needs in order to help fellow clients, and recognizing and managing their own and others' resistance. When norms are not maintained, and clients do not recognize and cope with the problem, the counselor teaches clients to recognize and to cope with that problem rather than managing it for them. For example, a reflection of a distracting client's underlying feeling is usually sufficient: "Perhaps Joe is uncomfortable with the way we are trying to encourage Sue to complete her unfinished business with her boyfriend." Sometimes the counselor must ask the group to review what is expected of clients when a client questions whether she wants to keep the previously agreed-upon norms. For example, it may be difficult for a client to accept sharing time when she is hurting and wanting to talk; she eventually learns to do so because she is helped to recall the rationale for that guideline, and she realizes that reasonably soon she will be given another chance to talk.

Dealing with Irresponsible Behavior

Whenever a person is faced with debilitating emotions (for example, intense anger, despair, distrust, fear, grief, jealousy, or feelings of inadequacy), she may be tempted to behave irresponsibly and excuse herself. For such clients, the counselor tries to detect and reflect the debilitating emotion and encourages her to discuss these feelings and to learn how to manage them. With encouragement, and specific instruction on how to help a fellow client, she can be very helpful. Furthermore, her assistance tends to be more readily accepted than the counselor's. When, in particular, such a client states that she feels helpless and excuses her own irresponsible behavior, fellow clients can be taught to explore with her the logical consequences of such a conclusion. They also can be very powerful in encouraging her to identify and discuss the underlying feelings that allowed her to behave irresponsibly and to identify the new behaviors that she must master in order to cope with similar problems in the future. Such a client also should be encouraged to note and report back to her group instances in which she was tempted to behave in her old irresponsible way, what she did to prevent it, and what new behaviors she must learn to manage it more effectively next time.

Following the process of helping a client with irresponsible behavior clients often discuss (and can be encouraged by the counselor to discuss) instances in which they used irresponsible behavior to achieve something that they did not believe could be achieved with responsible behavior. The individual learns to act insane or takes drugs, including alcohol, to free herself of the controlling inhibitions of her conscience or the threat of arrest and/or punishment. For example, she gets drunk (or pretends to be drunk) in order to tell off someone who has hurt her; she excuses her behavior on the grounds that she did not know what she was doing. From their participation in such discussions, clients discover many instances in which they behaved irresponsibly; why they did so; what were the logical consequences of the behaviors; and what new behavior each must learn to handle similar situations better next time.

Case Example

Following an instance in which he helped a fellow client discuss ways she believed her roommate behaved irresponsibly to her, Mel became very upset. He realized that his behavior with his girlfriend often paralleled his fellow client's roommate's behavior. Though he admitted his shame to the rest of the group, he was reluctant to stop behaving so because it seemed to work well for him. The other clients were disturbed by this reaction, but they did not argue with him. Instead, they encouraged him to role play a scene in which he used bullying to get his way with his girlfriend—beginning first by instructing a female client to play his role so he could demonstrate how his girlfriend seemed to accept his bullying.

After listening to and discussing members' feedback, he played his own role and the same woman played his girlfriend's role. The group then processed the role playing again. The role playing and fellow clients' feedback enabled him to grasp the impact of his behavior on his girlfriend and helped Mel to define new, more-productive behaviors to be learned to replace the old, thoughtlessly hurtful ways of controlling her. At the conclusion of several sessions devoted to this problem, the counselor generalized for them as follows: "Even when your crazy irresponsible behavior gets you what you want, it erodes your own feelings of self-respect."

COUNSELOR'S ACCEPTANCE OF RESPONSIBILITY

Important as it is for the counselor to encourage client participation in establishing group norms, and in maintaining them during counseling, the counselor *must accept and use wisely* his special status in the group. He is a qualified professional with a reputation for helping his clients. He makes the presentations to prospective clients, selects the clients (preferably with client participation), helps them define their therapeutic goals, arranges for a place for them to meet, schedules sessions, monitors their progress (and again, preferably with their participation), and helps them to decide when to terminate.

SECURITY

From the very first contact with his clients, the counselor begins developing a special therapeutic relationship. His way of initiating the helping process, his sensitivity to the clients' fears and reservations, and the way he is able to help them discuss these feelings facilitate the development of a feeling of security. As clients feel increasingly secure within their counseling group, they learn to give up their façades, discuss their pain openly, listen to others' discussion of their problems, accept feedback, and provide others with considerate feedback. They learn to discuss those reservations that threaten their security and help others take responsibility for making their counseling group a safe place. These discussions also desensitize them to the many common sources of threat in a group.

The way the counselor deals with behaviors and feelings that threaten client security, and the confidence he exhibits in dealing with them, particularly in the early life of the group, contribute significantly to the development of security. The genuineness with which the counselor responds is important, too.

Case Example

When, for example, at the beginning of the second session, a junior-high-school client questioned whether certain confidences had been broken, the counselor said, "Wow, that threatens me, too. First, we must be certain that we know precisely what our rule is; secondly, what can we do when we think that we have been let down; and finally, how can we help those who have been deceived." On the one hand, he admitted the threat. On the other, he demonstrated that though it would be hurtful to be deceived, together they could figure out some way of coping with it.

When the source of threat is a particular person, role playing can be used to prepare a client to deal with that person both within and outside their counseling group. Although such role-played scenes can surface pain and frustration, it also can give clients a chance to clarify what they need to do, and with whom; to identify and practice new behaviors; and to enhance their chances of successful results. It enables them to practice new behaviors and to obtain considerate feedback from fellow clients.

The counseling group is a good place in which to learn to discuss threatening material (Beck, 1958): it is more easily learned with peers; peers provide uncensored, realistic responses; peer feedback is accepted less defensively; peers listen, accept another's problems, and offer helpful feedback.

SELF-DISCLOSURE

Readiness to openly discuss worries and concerns early in group counseling can be enhanced by a presentation in which prospective clients are given an opportunity to clarify expectations. The intake interview also gives clients a chance to practice discussing pain. The counselor helps each client discover the relationship between each pain and the new behavior to be learned (goal). During early sessions he helps clients discuss their genuine pain and reinforces their behavior when they do it. Stone and Gotlib's (1975) principal finding was that both instructional and modeling procedures increased self-disclosure. Lieberman, Yalom, and Miles' (1973) successful clients self-disclosed.

Perhaps nothing is as powerful in encouraging self-disclosure, especially for adolescents, as for clients to discover that they are members of a group in which clients believe that self-disclosure is essential in order for them to define relevant goals, to learn desired new behaviors, and to implement them. When they discuss their pain openly, they experience increased acceptance. Furthermore, they are encouraged to take the risk required to implement new behaviors; and when they fail, they believe that they can return to the group for assistance in deciding either what they must do to succeed or what new alternatives to try next. In other words, they are encouraged to believe that they can learn from their failures, too. During the course of trying to help others, they also discover that other clients whom they admire have problems as difficult or more difficult than their own—and those clients believe that they can solve theirs!

CLIENT PARTICIPATION

A human being wants to become meaningfully involved in solving her own problems and in making the decisions that affect her at home, at work, and at every level of government. She likes to believe that she can help improve the social order in which she lives. When she is allowed to help shape the events that influence her life, she finds life more meaningful and consequently accepts more responsibility for improving the conditions within which she lives. Kanfer and

Gaelick (1986) believe that such decisional control is important in developing intrinsic motivation in psychotherapy, too.

When clients are given the opportunity to participate in appraising their own readiness for group counseling, defining their own goals, developing criteria that they can use to assess their own progress, developing their own group norms, and determining when they terminate their own group counseling, they like it. Furthermore, participation enhances effective operation of the counseling group and results. Bach (1954) claims that client participation produces group cohesiveness. Lindt (1958) concludes that those clients who most readily accept responsibility for helping others as well as themselves tend to profit most from his therapy groups.

On the other hand, those who do not feel that they are allowed to participate adequately in their groups become reactive. They attack, complain, and look for scapegoats. The ego is clamorous, jealous, possessive, and cantankerous; this results from constant threats. A reactive ego tends to perceive neighbors and associates as threats rather than as collaborators (Allport, 1945): "In other words, a person ceases to be reactive and contrary in respect to a desirable course of conduct only when he himself has had a hand in declaring that course of conduct to be desirable" (p. 122). Reluctant clients' first response to an invitation to participate in group counseling tends to be reactive. They must be convinced that they can be helped and that the natural consequences of doing nothing will be more painful than accepting conditions under which they can be helped in a counseling group. Finally, they must be taught how to be collaborators. They must be taught how to be clients as well as helpers and to allow others to help them.

COMMUNICATION

Effective communication among members is essential in a counseling group. However, this can be difficult to achieve. First the message sender (source) is struggling with distracting thoughts as she formulates her message; consequently, her message may be unclear or even distorted. Normally, the channel is not a problem, because sender and receiver are sitting reasonably close to each other and talking directly to each other. Nevertheless, the receiver may not be listening very carefully because he may be distracted by his own pain. Moreover, the message sender's nonverbal behavior may not be congruent, or the message receiver's perception of it may not be congruent with the sender's verbal message.

Congruence is essential for effective communication among members. When the message sender is congruent, the feelings expressed in her message match those feelings that she is experiencing (Rogers, 1961). To illustrate lack of congruence, Rogers used the case of a man whose flushed face, angry tone of voice, and pointing finger clearly suggested anger; but, in a calm voice, he denied anger. Rogers noted that at a physiological level, he was experiencing anger that was not matched by his awareness. Therefore, there was real incongruence between experience and awareness; consequently, a communication problem resulted.

Rogers also noted that the individual (neither sender nor receiver) is not a sound judge of her own degree of incongruence. Therefore, the counselor must teach clients to recognize this phenomenon and assist both relevant parties to cope with it. Usually the incongruent member responds better to a reflection rather than to an interpretation or confrontation: "You want to discuss this issue calmly," rather than, "You are angry. Admit it. It is obvious to all of us." Moreover, when communication problems first occur in the group session, the counselor would do well to describe briefly the basic elements in good communication, suggest clues that indicate communication problems, and teach clients ways of responding to them (Klauss & Bass, 1982; Morran, Robinson, & Stockton, 1985; Rogers & Rogers, 1976).

> Merely being told what can be done to improve one's communication skills obviously is unlikely to produce much improvement. The desire to improve must be there. We think that the desire is heightened by diagnostic feedback. But again more must be done. Skills require practice. Practice requires taking chances that mistakes made will be tolerable. Skill learning requires subsequent feedback (1982, p. 185).

In order for good communication to be achieved:

1. The message sender (source) must be reasonably congruent.
2. She must formulate a clear message.
3. The receiver of the message must be reasonably congruent and listen carefully to the message.
4. When in doubt the message receiver must be taught to clarify rather than challenge and/or make inferences from the sender's nonverbal behavior.
5. The observers' (counselor and fellow clients) role is to help clarify the message, detect incongruence, and help either and/or both parties manage incongruence.

Feedback for Counselor

Of course, there will be times when the counselor's messages are not clear and/or he is not congruent. He must convey to clients at the first opportunity in the life of the group that he requires their assistance, too. Thus, he encourages them to use feedback in order to improve his communication skills. Finally, those who counsel children must develop competency in use of play media.

Even when clients are prepared to recognize and manage communication problems, they may experience some reluctance to make such suggested reflections. They have learned from past experience in other types of groups to confront and/or to keep quiet and share their impressions privately in sub-groups. Most do not want to be hurt or to hurt others. Therefore, the counselor must convince them that their assistance is required, that they can learn to help the message sender and receiver to detect and manage incongruence through use of helpful techniques. Thus, the counselor enlists clients' assistance in diagnosing the group's problems and teaches them strategies for solving them. Such tactics enhance client participation as well as congruence; recognize that cohesiveness can be maintained even while managing conflict among clients; and reinforce confidences in members' ability to accept responsibility in the therapeutic process.

FEEDBACK

Feedback is designed to help the source send a clearer message. Teaching clients to use feedback is essential in order to improve communication among the members of the group. Rogers and Rogers (1976) suggest:

> Feedback may be thought of as messages to the source conveying knowledge of the effectiveness of a previous communication. Positive feedback informs the source that the intended effect of the message was achieved; negative feedback informs the source that the intended effect of a message was not achieved. As such negative feedback is disruptive of the source-receiver relationship, and it can generate hostility between source and receiver (p. 13).

> In general, the more feedback-oriented a communication process is the more effective it is. . . . If a source has false assumptions about his receivers, his efforts to communicate are likely to be less effective (p. 14).

Teaching clients to accept and use feedback facilitates their own personal growth as well as their helping skills. It also can be used to teach them to copy selectively from models and heroes, and to solicit feedback with reference to proposed actions.

Everyone has blind spots. By soliciting, accepting, and using feedback, individuals can learn how they are perceived by others, and discover their blind spots. Bradford, Gibb, and Benne (1964) noted how feedback may be used to stimulate changes in behavior, feeling, attitude, and perception. Feedback enables individuals to check out their perceptions of themselves against others' perceptions of them—even to explore the natural consequences of proposed actions before they act.

During counseling, clients frequently solicit information about themselves and their problem situation. Counselors who use tests to help clients answer their questions about themselves must, in interpreting test results, take account of the clients' readiness to accept and use what they learn. Client participation in the selection and interpretation of test results facilitates acceptance of results, but the counselor still must be very sensitive to a client's feelings about herself and what she learns about herself, to reflect these feelings back to the client in order to help her accept and use what she learns. Even when a competent counselor really understands a client's reluctance to accept new information that is not congruent with her perception of herself and responds supportively to the client's feelings, the client may still distort those data that are difficult for her to accept (Ohlsen, 1983).

Increasingly, those who assist youth in formulating educational and career goals are beginning this process by first soliciting clients' perceptions of their interests, aptitudes, abilities, and values before they help clients formulate the questions for which they require more information. Where tests seem to be a good source of desired information, counselors are increasingly recognizing that research findings encourage them to involve their clients in the selection and interpretation of the tests. Recent findings suggest that test results are much more difficult for clients to accept than was previously believed. Not only must the client be congruent to accept and use the results, the counselor also must be congruent to communicate the test results and to respond to the client's underlying feelings concerning the new test data.

Generalizations from Research

Just a few generalizations from research are cited here. Successful clients learned to give frank, but considerate feedback to fellow clients (Lieberman et al., 1973). Feedback to an individual is more effective than feedback to a group (Smith, 1972). The creditability of positive feedback is enhanced when presented in a positive emotional climate. Negative feedback that is stated in behavioral terms is more creditable than negative emotional feedback. In general, positive feedback is rated as most creditable, more desirable, and impactful (Jacobs et al., 1973).

Reinforcement of successes is more productive than criticism of failures. Most clients, but especially adolescents, can accept precise behavioral feedback with reference to a specific instance better than general feedback. They can accept criticism better when the critic states precisely what he wishes the actor would have done instead of what she did.

Clients can be taught to request, give, and accept feedback in the type of therapeutic atmosphere described in Chapter 1. For example, Ralph and his girlfriend (Jill) were members of an undergraduate college, student-counseling group. During his efforts to improve their relationship the counselor helped Ralph organize a role-played scene in which Sandra played Jill's role. After five or six minutes, Ralph stopped the role play with this request for assistance: "Sandra is upsetting me as I try to use her to help me work out my problems with Jill. I can't tell whether I am reacting to Sandra as Sandra or Sandra as Jill. I can't tell whether she is putting me down or I am setting her up to put me down just the way Jill does." First they helped him discuss how he really felt toward Sandra and what he would like to tell her as Sandra, then they helped him state what he would like to say to Jill. Finally, they encouraged both Sandra and Jill to give him suggestions on how he could talk to Jill more productively in order to improve their relationship—or terminate it if it cannot be developed into a good one.

Clients profit most from feedback from others whom they trust and believe are motivated to help them. They profit most from feedback from those who previously have exhibited genuine caring for them. When they learn to accept and apply the feedback they receive from fellow clients, clients also can be taught to solicit and accept feedback from significant others outside their counseling group. They also can learn to apply these learnings to complete unfinished business with significant others.

THERAPEUTIC TENSION

Most great public performers experience tension just before they walk on the stage or athletic field. They also realize that it can be productive. It can get them up to perform at their best. It also can debilitate them to such an extent that they perform badly. When such tension is first exhibited in the counseling group, the counselor describes the phenomenon and explains how fellow clients can help the suffering client recognize it and use it therapeutically.

Even when the client comes to the intake interview committed to discuss her pain openly and to learn new behaviors, she may merely experience catharsis, reduce emotional tension, and lose some of the motivation required for her to continue counseling and profit from it. This is why the counselor does not try to relieve her of all of her pain. Instead, he teaches her to discuss only the pain for which she is ready to define precise behavioral goals and for which she is ready to implement new behaviors. He also makes certain that she understands what will be expected of her and what she can expect from others—including learning to manage the tension she experiences as she learns to participate in a counseling group.

Most clients who seek treatment in a counseling group do experience tension as they struggle to discuss their worries and concerns; try to decide what they can do to improve the quality of their lives; and develop the courage and self-confidence to initiate desired new behaviors. Though they are threatened by what they uncover and by the notion of learning to change, they also develop early in the life of the group a sense of genuine support; they are taught to develop sources of support outside their counseling group. They sense considerable tension at times, but like the talented performer, they learn to manage it so that it does not become debilitating. Moreover, when they fear that it may become debilitating, they are pleased to discover that their fellow clients and counselor have detected the depth of their pain and are prepared to help them cope with it.

They also are taught the real difference between a quality support system and a rescue service.

SUMMARY

The counselor helps clients recognize and manage the forces that contribute to and interfere with their achieving their counseling goals. He teaches clients to use the group's resources to facilitate their growth, accept responsibility for detecting problems that arise during counseling and participate in diagnosing and solving those problems.

He accepts the notion that he is a special person in the counseling group who has responsibility for selecting clients; scheduling a time and place to meet; helping clients develop precise behavioral goals and criteria that they can use to appraise their own growth; teaching them to be good clients and good helpers; teaching them to define and maintain therapeutic norms; and encouraging them to participate fully in their own and fellow clients' growth. He realizes that mere talking is not sufficient—that clients must learn to function better.

A group's therapeutic potential is most fully realized when clients:

1. believe that the *counselor is competent* to help them and has confidence in their ability to profit from counseling
2. enter counseling *committed* to discuss their problems openly, to learn new behaviors, and to help fellow clients learn new behaviors
3. find the group *attractive* on the basis of members' mutual needs, goals, and commitment
4. feel that they truly *belong*—that fellow clients give of themselves without ulterior motives
5. are *ready* to discuss their problems and learn new behaviors—that they have been prepared to profit from counseling
6. *accept responsibility* for learning new behaviors, for helping others learn, and for developing and maintaining a therapeutic climate in their group
7. feel *secure* in their counseling group
8. enter counseling committed to discuss their problems openly and discover fellow clients modeling *self-disclosure*
9. enter counseling prepared to *participate* in making the decisions that could influence the outcomes for themselves and fellow clients
10. learn to *communicate congruently* with one another in the counseling group and to implement these communications skills outside their counseling group
11. learn to give *feedback* and apply it in improving their problem-solving skills
12. are taught to recognize and use *tension* productively

REFERENCES

Allport, G. W. (1945). The psychology of participation. *Psychological Review, 52,* 117–132.

Bach, G. R. (1954). *Intensive group psychotherapy.* New York: Ronald.

Beck, D. F. (1958). The dynamics of group psychotherapy as seen by a sociologist: Part I. The basic process and the dynamics of group psychotherapy as seen by a sociologist: Part II. Some puzzling questions on leadership, contextual relations, and outcomes. *Sociometry, 21,* 98–128, 180–197.

Bradford, L. P.; Gibb, J. R.; & Benne, K. D. (1964). *T-group theory and laboratory method.* New York: Wiley.

Cartwright, D. (1951). Achieving change in people: Some applications of group dynamics theory. *Human Relations, 4,* 381–392.

Dies, R. R. (1985). Leadership in short-term group therapy. *International Journal of Group Psychotherapy, 35,* 435–455.

Dreikurs, R. (1957). Group psychotherapy from the point of view of Adlerian psychology. *International Journal of Group Psychotherapy, 7,* 363–375.

Festinger, L., & Aronson, E. (1960). The arousal and reduction of dissonance in social contexts. In D. Cartwright & A. Zander, *Group dynamics: Theory and practice* (pp. 125–136). New York: Harper & Row.

Gordon, T. (1955). *Group-centered leadership.* Boston: Houghton Mifflin.

Hobbs, N. (1962). Sources of gain psychotherapy. *American Psychologist, 17,* 741–747.

Jacobs, A.; Jacobs, M.; Feldman, G.; & Cavior, N. (1973). Feedback II: The credibility gap: Delivery of positive and negative emotional and behavioral feedback in groups. *Journal of Consulting and Clinical Psychology, 41,* 215–223.

Kanfer, F. H., & Gaelick, L. (1986). Self-management methods. In F. H. Kanfer & A. P. Goldstein, *Helping people change* (pp. 309–355). New York: Pergamon.

Kanfer, F. H., & Goldstein, A. P. (1986). *Helping people change.* New York: Pergamon.

Kelman, H. C. (1963). The role of the group in the induction of therapeutic change. *International Journal of Group Psychotherapy, 13,* 399–432.

Klauss, R., & Bass, B. M. (1982). *Interpersonal communication in organizations.* New York: Academic Press.

Lewin, K. (1944). The dynamics of group action. *Educational Leadership, 1,* 195–200.

Lieberman, M. A.; Yalom, I. D.; & Miles, M. D. (1973). *Encounter groups: First facts.* New York: Basic Books.

Lindt, H. (1958). The nature of therapeutic interaction of patients in groups. *International Journal of Group Psychotherapy, 8,* 55–59.

Morran, D. K.; Robinson, F. F.; & Stockton, R. (1985). Feedback exchange in counseling groups: An analysis of message content and receiver acceptance as a function of leader versus member delivery, session, and valence. *Journal of Counseling Psychology, 32,* 57–67.

Ohlsen, M. M. (1983). *Introduction to counseling.* Itasca, IL: Peacock (pp. 90–116).

Poey, K. (1984). Guidelines for the practice of brief, dynamic group therapy. *International Journal of Group Psychotherapy, 34,* 331–354.

Powdermaker, F. R., & Frank, J. D. (1953). *Group psychotherapy.* Cambridge, MA: Harvard University Press.

Roberts, N. C. (1985). Transforming leadership: A process of collective action. *Human Relations, 38,* 1023–1046.

Rogers, C. R. (1961). *On becoming a person.* Boston: Houghton Mifflin.

Rogers, E. M., & Rogers, R. A. (1976). *Communication in organizations.* London: Free Press, Collier Macmillan.

Sethna, E. R., & Harrington, J. A. (1971). A study of patients who lapsed from group therapy. *British Journal of Psychiatry, 119,* 59–69.

Smith, K. H. (1972). Changes in group structure through individual and group feedback. *Journal of Personality and Social Psychology, 24,* 425–428.

Stone, G. L., & Gotlib, I. (1975). Effects of instructions and modeling on self-disclosure. *Journal of Counseling Psychology, 22,* 288–293.

Thelen, H. A., & Stock, D. (1955). Basic problems in developing a mature and effective group. *National Education Association Journal, 44,* 105–106.

Yalom, I. D. (1985). *The theory and practice of group psychotherapy* (3rd ed.). New York: Basic Books.

5

LABELING CLIENTS' PROBLEMS

On the basis of our own experiences counseling our clients and supervising our practicum students and interns, we concluded that most clients' problems can be assigned to one of the following labels: (1) unfinished business with significant others (relatives, friends, classmates, and co-workers); (2) self-defeating beliefs and behaviors; (3) managing crises; (4) inaccurate or inadequate information about one's self or problem situation; (5) learning developmental tasks; and (6) learning to manage passages. Naturally, others' professional experiences and research influenced the identification and definition of these categories—especially Williamson and Hahn (1940), Bordin (1946), and Pepinsky (1948).

We believe that such labels help clients discover that they have learned to be what they are; that they can learn the new behaviors that will enable them to function better; that they do not have to be victims; and that they can learn to manage their own lives. These labels also can be used by counselors to help clients define precise behavioral goals; develop criteria that they can use to detect their own growth; accept counseling for themselves and communicate to significant others why it is appropriate for them (rather than to apologize for needing it); enlist their significant others' assistance in reinforcing their desired new behaviors when they occur; and decide for themselves whether or not to contract for counseling. These nonthreatening labels also increase their hopes for successful outcomes. Furthermore, a counselor can use the labels to select the techniques that she and fellow clients may use to help each other within the group.

Moreover, the way a counselor uses these labels is important. From Chapter 1, the reader will recall that the counselor is encouraged to develop a therapeutic relationship with each client, to make certain that each understands what will be expected of him as a client; what others may expect from him, and how he can expect to be helped (truth in packaging); and to ensure that a client's goals are his own goals (and not his significant others' or his counselor's goals for him). From the very first contact, a client is taught to accept maximum responsibility for his own growth. He is helped to realize that he is a partner in the growth process—including labeling his problems and selecting new behaviors to be learned. Kanfer and Gaelick (1986) state:

> In general, motivation is increased if the client has decisional control over the treatment, has confidence in his or her ability to execute the plan, and believes that treatment will lead to desirable outcomes. Decisional control is also important in establishing intrinsic motivation. . . . When employed with care, external rewards can be very useful in the initial stages of the change program, when the client requires additional incentives to initiate new behaviors. The negative effects of external rewards can be minimized if the client retains decisional control over the change program and if the reward conveys information about the client's competence at the new tasks. Rewards also can be more effective if the content is related to the tasks, such as rewarding weight loss with a new dress instead of money or other general reinforcers (p. 301).

Consequently, the client realizes that the labels for *his* problems and *his* therapeutic goals can be redefined whenever he feels that redefinition is required. And, of course, these discoveries in and of themselves reinforce the basic notion that he can change, that he can learn to manage his own life, that he no longer has to view himself as a helpless victim.

UNFINISHED BUSINESS

When someone hurts another, or is hurt by someone, and fails to resolve his problems with the relevant person, unfinished business results. In order to complete the unfinished business he must identify the hurtful event and develop the courage, self-confidence, and interpersonal skills to confront the person and resolve their differences. Many find this difficult; and, consequently, they cumulate more unfinished business.

Perhaps even more frequently, unfinished business arises out of a person's failure to note and communicate clearly his positive feelings to the relevant individual, and consequently misses an opportunity to enrich an established relationship or to nurture a new, potentially satisfying relationship. Even in a well-established relationship, the one expressing the positive feelings cannot assume that the other realizes how he feels. He must communicate clearly; and when he does, both lives are enriched. In order for accurate communication of either positive or negative feelings to occur, the message sender must be reasonably congruent (accurately matching those feelings that he is experiencing with those with which he is aware); he must state his message clearly, and the message must be heard and understood by a reasonably congruent, message receiver.

Case Examples of Unfinished Business

Case 1

Cheryl complained about Tom's inability and/or discomfort in expressing his positive feelings to her. Consequently, his counseling group encouraged him to use role playing to practice this skill. Following the role playing, they provided him with helpful feedback. A few days later, Cheryl and Tom went on a walk. Tom thought to himself, "Cheryl is especially pretty tonight, and that was a good dinner; but, of course, she knows that"; but instead of saying nothing as he would have done in the past, he stopped, hugged her, and said, "I feel uncomfortable and silly, but I promised to practice saying these positive feelings. You look especially attractive, and the dinner was delicious." After reporting his success at the next counseling session, Tom concluded as follows to his fellow clients, "Perhaps Dr. John's statement is correct that positive feelings must be stated to be communicated and fully enjoyed by both parties."

Case 2

Another client, Jeff, a good-looking engineer, reported similar results as a consequence of using role playing in a singles' group to develop interpersonal skills required to communicate positive feelings to a female colleague. During the first counseling session, Jeff discussed his loneliness and shyness. Though he thought he had been fairly successful as a conqueror in one-night stands, he had never developed lasting relationships with any female. Moreover, Jeff rarely developed any close friendships. Recently, he had had two dinner dates with a female colleague, and felt that he could learn to like her a lot, but never even told her he enjoyed their dates. When pressed by fellow clients, Jeff admitted reluctantly that he felt uncomfortable stating positive feelings to a female with whom he would like to develop a relationship, and perhaps was afraid of being rejected.

When the counselor suggested that role playing could help him, Jeff asked for a volunteer to play the female role, and was shocked to discover that all four females volunteered. Inasmuch as the volunteers did not know the girlfriend, they asked him to play her role as he thought she would act when he tried to convey his positive feelings (role reversal is discussed in Chapter 3). He also was asked to tell the female playing his role the positive feelings he wanted to communicate. Then another client suggested that the girl playing Jeff's role conclude the talk by asking for another date. After this practice, the group gave Jeff feedback; then Jeff played his own role and the volunteer played Jeff's friend's role. Again, the group gave helpful feedback.

The following week, Jeff reported on his talk with his female colleague. It did not go as well as it did in the role-played scene; but he perceived it to be a great success, and he did get another date. A female fellow client's concluding remark was reinforcing, too: "You could learn to be a great date. Your friend should be patient with you. You are worth the effort." Besides completing his unfinished business with his colleague, he improved his intimacy-building skills and found persons with whom to practice them—both with his friend and fellow clients.

Case 3

Another example illustrates how negative unfinished business can continue to hurt one for years after being hurt by significant others. Sally, aged 32, was a member of a doctoral students' group designed to help formulate and clarify their professional goals as they sought their first post-PhD positions. Earlier in this particular session, one of the fellows complained about pressure from his father to take a certain position close to home. Sally reacted very negatively to this father, and another client remarked that it was unlike her—perhaps the other client's problem uncovered pain for her. At first, she denied it and explained why her father would not do that; then she described an incident when she, at age ten, told her father that she wanted to be a doctor, and he laughed and said: "We can talk about your plans when you get older."

She also shared her dream with her fifth-grade teacher; he listened and helped her locate a career pamphlet on medicine. Unfortunately, her high-school counselor also discouraged her from becoming a doctor and told her to consider nursing instead. After a number of years of successful, elementary-school teaching and counseling, she enrolled in a PhD program in counseling psychology, where she did very well. Her fellow clients encouraged her to complete her unfinished business with her father and high-school counselor.

First they helped her write to each of them telling them how their behavior had hurt her and why she wanted to complete her unfinished business now. For her letter to her father, they urged her to write a brief introduction followed by her positive feelings toward him expressed in her most-convincing language, her negative feelings expressed considerately, and a request for time to sit down to talk and complete this unfinished business. Her letter upset her father, but both felt they profited from their discussion. Though her session with her high-school counselor did not go as well because she felt Sally was too critical of her, the session completed Sally's unfinished business with her, too.

Later fellow clients helped her explore whether or not she still wanted to enter medicine rather than to seek a counseling psychology position. She decided to seek a counseling psychology position. In the group's follow-up session 90 days after termination of counseling, she reported that the help in completing this particular unfinished business proved to be the highlight of the treatment for her.

Reviewing Unfinished Business

Clients with unfinished business must be taught to discuss the specific unfinished business they have with particular persons; to explore alternative ways of approaching relevant persons to discuss and complete their unfinished business; to select an approach; and to develop the interpersonal skills and self-confidence required to complete the unfinished business. Role playing often can be used to achieve this last objective. When, in their eyes, they have failed in trying to complete their unfinished business, clients are encouraged to review their efforts with the help of fellow clients to determine whether or not they wish to take what they have learned and try again, or give up on the relationship for now. Frequently, it helps to precede the confrontation with a letter in which they convey the positive feelings they failed to convey; or tell how they were hurt or how sorry they are because they hurt the other; *or explain why it is important for them to complete their unfinished business, what they need from the other now,* and where they would like to meet *to begin the mending process.*

Even when a significant other rejects their efforts to complete their unfinished business, clients experience some relief when they conclude that they have genuinely tried to complete it. Consequently, a counselor uses a number of different approaches to facilitate clients' completion of their unfinished business: client-centered approaches to uncover their pain and develop the courage to learn desired new behaviors (Rogers, 1979); behavioral approaches to help clients define goals and learn the new behaviors (Horne, 1982); and skill training to develop the self-confidence and the interpersonal skills required to implement their new behaviors in daily life outside their counseling group (Cantor & Wilkinson, 1982; Goldstein et al., 1982; Lange & Jakubowski, 1978).

SELF-DEFEATING BELIEFS AND BEHAVIORS

Whenever an individual hurts himself or someone he claims to love, or does something that interferes with achieving his goals, including refusing to master the knowledge or learn the new behaviors required, that behavior is self-defeating. For example, a bright girl met with difficulty in a high-school chemistry course and decided to give up her goal of becoming a nurse. She also refused tutoring and the counselor's assistance in appraising her chances for success in nursing. Other common examples are: poor eating habits; smoking; procrastinating on completing assignments; criticizing and/or nagging someone whom one is trying to help replace an undesirable habit, instead of reinforcing successes; and angry outbursts against persons for whom the individual cares or with whom he must learn to work. Most who seek counseling can readily identify some self-defeating behaviors. Other self-defeating behaviors are identified by fellow clients as they struggle to help an individual learn and implement his own desired new behaviors. Fellow clients also help such an individual realize that his self-defeating behaviors should and can be replaced with productive ones, thereby providing him with a critical factor for successful results: hope (Yalom, 1985).

Case Examples of Self-defeating Behavior

Case 1

Our first example is a common one in which a *self-righteous spouse genuinely believed* that criticism and nagging facilitated a spouse replacing self-defeating behavior with productive behaviors. Her husband, Max, is a likable fellow, and a reasonably successful professional, who embarrassed her by exaggerating. Her usual reaction was to embarrass him by correcting his statements, especially in the presence of colleagues and certain of her relatives whom Max admired. When Max first told her in the group how she hurt him, fellow clients helped her grasp that criticism and nagging kill love, and that she was unknowingly embarrassing him to satisfy her own need for revenge. As she wept and discussed how she was hurt by the feedback, fellow clients helped her communicate to Max that what he had accomplished was good enough so that he did not have to exaggerate. Fellow clients also helped them to reinforce desired behaviors and use considerate touching to deter temptations to fall back into the use of their old self-defeating ones.

Case 2

A different type of case illustrates how confrontation with the natural consequences of doing nothing enables a self-defeating client to accept counseling and profit from it. In this case, an abused wife (Marsha) sought counseling. When her husband (Jack) refused to join a counseling group with other abusers, she left him and filed for divorce. At this point, Jack scheduled a session with the counselor in which the counselor helped him learn to accept and discuss his own pain, to define some personal goals, and to schedule a session for him and Marsha together. During the intake interview with them, the counselor talked to them together, then separately, and finally together again. Though the counselor was able to help Jack state his goals more precisely and contract for counseling in the abuser's group, Jack could not accept Marsha's suggestion that he work on his drinking problem. Consequently, they agreed to schedule still another intake interview in which Marsha agreed to discuss why she was afraid of him, especially when he drank, and to discuss further her own reasons for desiring counseling—whether they continued their marriage or not.

During the next intake interview, they both defined precise behavioral goals; agreed to help each other learn to function better, whether or not they elected to continue their marriage; to continue their separation under carefully specified conditions; and to contract for counseling. In the group, they were surprised how readily fellow clients saw through the dumb games they played; how they detected their pain and helped them discuss it; how they learned to tolerate the pressure fellow clients put on them to own their unrecognized pain and learn the new behaviors required to manage it; and how fellow clients provided quality support while they struggled in implementing their new behaviors.

Case 3

This case also illustrates how a client (Darlene) accepted counseling when she was confronted with the natural consequences of doing nothing during an intake interview with her husband, and two additional intake interviews with her husband and two adolescent children. Her husband and children explained to her why they were no longer willing to make the sacrifices required to maintain her in an expensive, private mental hospital. (They did not have the money required, and she had made little effort to profit from treatment.) The counselor also helped her convey what she wanted from them: genuine love, respect, and acceptance of her—something she began to realize that she had to earn, and she could not earn it sitting in a mental hospital. Darlene's family and counselor also helped her replace the psychotic labels with specific self-defeating labels for which they helped her define specific new behaviors to be learned in the counseling group with the help of her fellow clients and family.

Though most of Darlene's and her husband's treatment was provided in a couple's group, periodically the counselor scheduled a family session that was observed by the other couples. Most of the observers' comments focused upon things family members could do to encourage and reinforce each parent's growth, but the children also were encouraged to request help for themselves. Moreover, other clients solicited the children's assistance in helping Darlene accept her adult parenting and homemaking responsibilities (previously she had ignored these). When Darlene decided she was ready to accept a part-time accounting position, observers were very effective in teaching her children to reinforce her success, to be supportive.

Reviewing Self-defeating Behavior

Most clients' self-defeating behaviors can be corrected primarily with behavior-modification techniques. First, however, some must be helped to discover that they can profit from counseling. Many depressed clients have profited from reading and discussing in their groups the ideas gleaned from Burns' (1980) *Feeling Good.* Ellis' (1973; Ellis & Greiger, 1977) rational-emotional approach also has been used successfully with depressed, grieving, anxious, and other-controlled clients. Moreover, it is especially important *for these clients* to define precise criteria that they can use to detect growth *with reference to each goal.* Fellow clients' assistance is also often required to teach these clients to note and record observations that confirm their growth. Discovering their own growth increases self-esteem and the determination to continue treatment when the going gets tough.

On the other hand, there are some very different clients whose problems are self-defeating behaviors, such as drug addicts and delinquents who require assistance in detecting and accepting the natural consequences of their behavior. Until they recognize precisely how their self-defeating behaviors hurt themselves as well *as those whom they claim to love, and accept blame for hurting others*, they will not be sufficiently motivated to learn and implement desired new behaviors. They *require tough love*, encouragement, reinforcement, and recognition for learning their new behaviors. Perhaps most of all, they need help in discovering that there is hope for them; that they can learn the required new behaviors; and that fellow clients are strong enough to confront them and provide tough love.

MANAGING CRISES

A crisis is a disruption. Everyone is confronted with crises such as life-threatening accidents and illnesses, death of a significant other, divorce, arrests, and loss of a job. Some merely survive a crisis, do not deal adequately with it, and consequently it becomes unfinished business.

Case Examples of Managing Crises

Case 1

Connie is such a case. Her father died unexpectedly and she fell apart. Previously she had been an honor student for two years in a very exacting college major. The semester in which her father died, she sat around and grieved, and ended up on probation. The next semester she dropped out of school. Almost a year after her father's death, she joined a counseling group that included two other young singles with grieving problems. Besides assigning her a book to read on grieving, the counselor helped her in an intake interview to discuss her pain, define specific goals, and begin exploring what she wanted to achieve during the rest of her life. Fellow clients encouraged her to give up her victim status; review her sources for support, and cultivate new and better sources; and decide what she must do now to achieve her dreams. Gradually, they helped her recognize that though she would always miss her father, she was more fortunate than most: she had the good fortune to have had a great relationship with him, and she was not left with unfinished business. However, she did have to say goodbye to him and get on with her life; and they convinced her that she could do that.

Case 2

Terry represents a very different type of case. When he graduated from high school, he had little notion of what he wanted to do except to attend the state university. On the spur of the moment, he decided to steal a neighbor's pick-up and rob a bank to obtain money for college. He was caught and sent to prison. A few months later, he was given the option of enlisting in the army, where he made a fabulous record during World War II. Upon discharge, he was pardoned and used his G.I. Bill and fellowships to earn his bachelor's degree, and then later his PhD at his state university. When he learned about a counseling group for those completing their doctorates he joined it.

Since he had never resolved the crisis of his arrest, it surfaced in his counseling group; he was afraid to discuss the problem with his fellow clients lest they would reject him and probably break confidences. Consequently, he requested a private session with the counselor. Before scheduling such a session, the counselor indicated to him in the group that such sessions were scheduled to help a client get ready to discuss problems he did not feel he could discuss at that time in the group. He discussed the crisis in detail in the private session and explored how he could assess whether or not fellow clients could be trusted to keep confidences. Later in the group, fellow clients convinced him that they could forgive him for anything he had done, and that they could keep confidences. As he grieved about the arrest and hurting his parents, they encouraged him to explore with whom he had left unfinished business.

Eventually, he decided to tell his parents and siblings how neglected he felt when he committed the crime, how sorry that he still feels for embarrassing them, and how much he would like a close, loving relationship with them. Both parents were deeply touched by the letter he wrote to initiate the development of the relationship he desired; and his siblings were willing to talk to him, but did not feel that it was crucial anymore. Though they were all threatened by the idea of having a family session prior to the group's regular meeting (with other clients observing and providing feedback), they all came and participated. Terry genuinely profited from both, and so did his parents and siblings; that was a first step in a markedly improved family relationship.

Reviewing Managing Crises

In both instances, the counselor was surprised to learn how little her clients knew about managing crises; why all people need significant others upon whom they can call for help during a crisis; how to use their assistance without becoming dependent upon them; how to differentiate between a support group's assistance and a rescue service; how to develop a support group; how to provide help to others during a crisis; and when to seek professional services. The counselor also helped them to recognize that those who are able to accept professional services and profit from them are generally healthier than those who need them but cannot accept them.

INACCURATE OR INADEQUATE INFORMATION ABOUT ONE'S SELF OR PROBLEM SITUATION[1]

For one who possesses inaccurate or inadequate information *about himself or his problem situation,* fellow clients can be very effective in helping him identify and clarify the questions for which he must seek answers; discover where the required information may be found; assume maximum responsibility for obtaining the information; and accept what he learns when it differs from his perception of himself or his problem situation. Usually clients are able to accept new information about their problem situation easier than they can accept new information about themselves. For example, it is usually easier for a client to accept new information concerning what the foreman expects on the job than it is for him to accept new information that suggests he is much brighter than he thought he was; and, consequently, he should accept a challenging opportunity for special on-the-job training. Under such circumstances, a private session with the counselor may be required to interpret test scores (and thus respect the confidential data), help him recognize and examine his feelings toward these new data, and accept the new data and challenges thaty are associated with accepting the information. He also must be prepared to decide what must be shared with fellow clients and how he wants to enlist their assistance in accepting and using the new information.

Case Examples of Inaccurate or Inadequate Information

Case 1

Elaine joined a counseling group for assistance in career planning and development. She was employed in a situation where she liked her co-workers, but her position did not make full use of her ability and professional preparation. During the course of counseling she sought information from her college placement service. They told her about an interesting position in another part of the country. She applied and was invited to come for an interview, but after some study of the situation she was about to reject the invitation because she felt that she was a country bumpkin moving into a group of sophisticated, ivy-league workers.

The group helped her decide what she would like to know about the company and those with whom she would work most closely. They asked her for what questions did she need answers. They also asked her how she could use the answers to decide whether to take the position if offered. They used reflections to

[1]This label was suggested by Dr. Allen Ferreira, Clinical Team Leader, Midtown Mental-Health Center, Indianapolis.

try to help her discover what really worried her, and how she could manage those fears. They also helped her prepare for the job interview and plan the trip. In other words, they helped her plan, encouraged her, and increased her self-confidence. She was offered the position and she accepted it. When she returned, they helped her learn to cope with the problems associated with moving to a new community, especially in developing new friendships and a support group.

Case 2

Another client joined a counseling group made up of employed young adults. Eric, aged 33, was an unusually successful restaurant owner who was now wondering if he should have decided at the last minute not to attend medical school. Though he had good grades and was admitted to medical school, he questioned his ability to succeed. Fellow clients helped him explore the satisfactions he could expect from medicine that he could not get from business management; whether he could satisfy his needs better in some other business; whether he could support himself during medical education; and for what questions did he still require information to make a decision. Using this last group of questions the counselor, in an individual session, helped Eric select some tests that helped him determine his chances for success in medicine. Then Eric asked for a period to review his science courses with a tutor's help, completed the testing, and found that the state university medical school would still admit him. Nevertheless, he still had trouble accepting the high test scores.

Here was where his fellow clients and counselor were most helpful. First, they helped him examine his reluctance to accept his high test scores and its implications for his success in medicine. Then they used the fiddler game[2] to help him decide whether to go to medical school or to manage his business. To begin the process, they asked him whether he was leaning toward going to medical school or continuing to manage his business. He said he was leaning toward going to medical school. Then he was asked to present, on the basis of his data, the best case he could for going to medical school. When he seemed to run out of material, several people in the group added new points. Then the counselor asked him to take another chair labeled "business manager" (the first had been labeled "doctor") and make his best case for continuing to manage his business. When he seemed to run out of material again, others added points. Finally, the counselor said, "Decide." Eric was quiet for a while, and then said he was going to medical school. He went and completed the program successfully.

---

[2]Perhaps most readers will remember "Tevye" in *Fiddler on the Roof* playing his violin—discussing first the pros and the cons of an issue. It is applied here to help Eric make a decision.

Case 3

Phil was a junior-high-school student held back twice for poor academic performance. After several individual sessions, a new school counselor decided that Phil was really bright but probably had some learning disability. Fortunately, one of the counselor's professors was an expert on dyslexia and recognized Phil's problem. After considerable diagnostic testing and conferences with Phil's parents, Phil was placed in a learning-disability program. He also was included in a counseling group with two other learning-problem students and four regular students. Like Eric, Phil found that his fellow clients were able to help him accept his newly discovered potential and apply it. Their encouragement and caring also increased his hope for successful results.

Reviewing Inaccurate or Inadequate Information

During the process of growing up, humans seek answers to varied questions about themselves and their problem situations. They wonder what makes them feel and behave as they do, and why success comes so easily sometimes and why it is so difficult at other times. They often question whether or not they have the aptitudes, abilities, interests, values, drive, commitment, and funds to achieve their goals. Fortunate are those who grow up in homes in which they are listened to and encouraged to ask their questions and to accept what they learn. They also tend to be more willing to take the risks required to explore new interests, develop newly discovered talents, and implement their goals. Those who have been less fortunate often require professional services in order to learn about themselves and accept what they learn in order to achieve their goals (Ohlsen, 1983, Chapter 5). Many persons find that they are impressed when fellow clients see through the self-defeating games that they play in order to avoid accepting the information about themselves and/or their problem situation and apply it to achieve their goals. In these three instances, fellow clients were able to help them accept the information that a professional helped them to obtain.

LEARNING DEVELOPMENTAL TASKS

During the process of growing up, everyone is expected to *learn mental as well as physical tasks* that facilitate still further learning. For example, the child learns to stand by an object, to balance his weight, and finally to walk before he can learn to run. Intellectually, home training and pre-school experiences provide reading readiness for the introduction of formal reading instruction. "With regard to mental growth, in particular, it is likely that many of the children who in the past were considered 'dull' or even retarded were, in effect, made so in early life by restricted environments, to the extent that they were never able to succeed at tasks expected of normal individuals" (Havighurst & Neugarten, 1968, p. 130).

The developmental tasks that must be learned and the difficulty with which each is learned are a function of the individual's inherited characteristics, the situation in which he is reared, and the society in which he is reared. Mastery of these tasks contributes to the development of an individual's self-esteem and success in later life. When, therefore, an individual discovers that he has failed to learn a task that is normally learned earlier in life, he has to learn it when the deficiency is discovered. For example, the 27-year-old married man who did not learn during latency to cope with an assertive female's request for affection must learn to respond to it appropriately in order to achieve quality intimacy.

Fortunately, more and more elementary schools are employing counselors to consult with parents and teachers; assist teachers in conducting classroom discussions that deal with their pupils' developmental tasks; and provide counseling for children. In order to introduce these services, counselors go into classrooms to tell students about these services and answer their questions concerning the services (see Chapter 12). Usually while making these classroom presentations, the counselor describes common developmental tasks with which children of that particular school grade are learning to cope. Classroom discussions are developed and counseling groups are formed to meet the students' needs revealed at these presentations.

Similar presentations have been used to reach secondary school and college students. Increasingly, personal-growth type of groups as well as counseling groups also are being developed to help adults learn developmental tasks. For example, parenting the first child, assertiveness training, learning to live alone again, weight management, preparing for retirement, and so on. Frequently, the counselor encourages participants to read relevant self-help books and discuss implementation of their new learnings in their group. This approach encourages clients to take maximum responsibility for their own growth and to use peers' assistance in implementing what they have learned. Adolescents, in particular, can become very fascinated with books on adolescent psychology that describe in meaningful language their developmental problems and use good case materials to illustrate various ways for coping with their problems.

Case Examples of Learning Developmental Tasks

Case 1

Tony grew up in a small town in the Midwest where he was an excellent student and school leader. His high-school counselor encouraged and, perhaps, even pressured him to apply for a scholarship to Harvard. At first, he was very pleased when he was admitted and won the scholarship at Harvard; but as time came for him to leave for college, he began to have doubts about being separated from his family and living in a big city. He did not believe he knew how to cope with these developmental tasks.

Like other developmental tasks in his life, Tony required assistance from fellow clients in defining the tasks to be learned and from whom he would require assistance in learning the tasks. His counseling group also provided him with a variety of opportunities to practice, through use of role playing, desired new interpersonal skills.

Case 2

Billy's case also illustrates how such a client can be helped. Shortly before school started when Billy was ready to enter seventh grade, Billy's family moved from a big city to a small farming community. Fortunately one day, his social studies teacher in the new school noticed a boy picking on him, and used this material for a class discussion. This helped Billy convey how tough it is to move into a new town and, in particular, how lonely he felt. Because she was such a good discussion leader, and knew how to use role playing effectively, she was able to help his classmates discover precisely what happened on the way into school; to solicit their assistance for coping with, as it turned out, the one bully who picked on him; and to use Billy's classmates' suggestions for developing some new friendships in the school. The discussion also encouraged a few students to reach out and help Billy get acquainted. Thus, what at first appeared to be an unmanageable situation became manageable. It also helped the hurtful boy get in touch with the natural consequences of his hazing behavior.

LEARNING TO MANAGE PASSAGES

With each passage the individual sheds a protective structure, feels exposed and vulnerable, discovers new potential, and enters another stable period in which he regains equilibrium (Sheehy, 1976). A person moves from a sheltered home into a less-protected school environment, into more and more challenging educational experiences in which he is expected to assume ever-increasing responsibility for his learning, from schools into the labor force, from single life into married life, from living alone with a spouse into rearing children, from work into retirement, and so on. And, of course, there are many more passages in between. What is right for one stage in one's life may become boring or lack challenge, or even be overwhelming, at another stage.

Many require professional assistance in learning to adapt to change, and the counseling group is a good place to learn it—especially when the counselor helps participants generalize what can be learned from a challenging passage. This cannot be assumed; it must be taught. Furthermore, it usually can be most readily taught after several clients have dealt successfully with passages. Usually they require assistance in answering for themselves these questions: (1) With what passage do I require assistance? (2) What is unique about this change? (3) What makes it so threatening for me at this time? (4) With what new personalities must I learn to work closely? (5) With whom am I least prepared to work? (6) What new skills and knowledge must I master to meet this challenge? (7) With whom can I practice these new skills?

Whereas learning developmental tasks requires that the individual master the knowledge and skills with which he is confronted as he matures, managing passages requires that he learn to cope with change and generalize from each successful passage in order to manage better subsequent passages. For example, Tony's problem was one of learning the developmental tasks required to take responsibility for himself in a big city with strangers and separated from his family and friends. On the other hand, since he was the youngest child, his parents' problem, and especially his mother's, was learning to manage a passage: the empty-nest syndrome.

Married couples must learn to adapt to change as well as learn new developmental tasks; deciding with whom they will develop and/or maintain close friendships; communicating expectations and negotiating those for which they do not agree; doing cooperative career planning; learning to manage conflict and the power struggle; achieving intimacy and satisfying sex; deciding whether or not to have children and how many; learning to share responsibility for maintaining a home and rearing children; and managing finances. Thus, they must learn to cope with some problems that are primarily adjustment to change whereas others are primarily new tasks and responsibilities to be learned. Counselors and leaders of discussion groups have found that books such as Sheehy's (1976) *Passages* and Cole's (1970) biography of Erik Erikson can be useful in teaching participants to manage passages. Clients also profit from selecting biographies and autobiographies of their heroes, and as they read them, try to identify their heroes' critical passages, note how they handled them, and discuss the implications for themselves and their fellow members.

In any case, there are common elements in helping clients learn to manage passages as well as to learn developmental tasks: (1) identifying the particular passage or developmental task with which each requires assistance; (2) deciding what is unique about it that makes it threatening; (3) identifying the knowledge and/or skills to be learned; and (4) practicing the required skills. During the process of learning to manage passages it is important for clients to discover that everyone must learn to adjust to change; though change is threatening to most, it also stimulates growth; the way each adjusts to change enables him to develop into his own unique self; and that it is important to generalize new learning in adjusting to change. Frequently, during the process of helping clients learn to adjust to change, group members also can be taught to identify their sources for support, to develop other needed sources of support, and to differentiate between a source of support and a rescue service.

SUMMARY

Most clients' problems can be assigned one of these six labels: (1) unfinished business with significant others; (2) self-defeating beliefs and behaviors; (3) managing crises; (4) inaccurate or inadequate information about one's self or one's problem situation; (5) learning developmental tasks; and (6) learning to manage passages.

The way in which counselors involve clients in assigning labels and using the labels to help them define desired new behaviors and define criteria to appraise their own growth helps clients discover that they do not have to be victims; that they can learn to manage their own lives; and, consequently, that they can expect to profit from treatment. Furthermore, the counselor can use the labels to select the techniques she will use to help clients achieve their goals.

REFERENCES

Bordin, E. S. (1946). Diagnosis in counseling and psychotherapy. *Educational and Psychological Measurement, 6,* 169–184.

Burns, D. D. (1980). *Feeling good: The new mood therapy.* New York: Signet.

Cantor, S., & Wilkinson, J. (1982). *Social skills manual.* Somerset, NJ: John Wiley & Sons.

Cole, R. (1970). *Erik H. Erikson: The growth of his work.* Boston: Little Brown.

Ellis, A. (1973). *Humanistic psychotherapy: A rational emotive approach.* New York: McGraw-Hill.

Ellis, A., & Grieger, R. (1977). *Handbook of rational emotive therapy.* New York: Springer.

Goldstein, A. P.; Sprafkin, R. P.; Gershaw, N. J.; & Klein, P. (1982). *Streamlining the adolescent.* Champaign, IL: Research Press.

Havighurst, R. J., & Neugarten, B. L. (1968). *Society and education* (3rd ed.). Boston: Allyn and Bacon.

Horne, A. M. (1982). Counseling families—Social learning family therapy. In A. M. Horne & M. M. Ohlsen, *Family counseling and therapy .* Itasca, IL: Peacock.

Kanfer, F. H., & Gaelick, L. (1986). Self-management methods. In F. H. Kanfer & A. P. Goldstein, *Helping people change .* New York, Pergamon.

Kanfer, F. H., & Goldstein, A. P. (1986). *Helping people change.* New York: Pergamon.

Lange, A. J., & Jakubowski, P. (1978). *Responsible assertive behavior: Cognitive behavioral procedures of trainees.* Champaign, IL: Research Press.

Ohlsen, M. M. (1983). *Introduction to counseling.* Itasca, IL: Peacock.

Pepinsky, H. B. (1948). *The selection and use of diagnostic categories in clinical counseling.* Stanford, CA: Stanford University Press.

Rogers, C. R. (1979). Groups in two cultures. *Personnel and Guidance Journal, 58,* 11–15.

Sheehy, G. (1977). *Passages: Predictable crises of adult life.* New York: E. P. Dutton.

Williamson, E. G., & Hahn, M. E. (1940). *Introduction to high school counseling.* New York: McGraw-Hill.

Yalom, I. D. (1985). *The theory and practice of group psychotherapy* (3rd ed). New York: Basic Books.

6

CLIENTS' COUNSELING GOALS

When clients seek assistance they are usually troubled about something with which they hope to learn to cope. More often than not, they require help in learning to relate to some significant others (relatives, friends, classmates, co-workers, or authority figures). A function of counseling, then, is to help people learn more-effective ways of managing their lives. Skills of living have been identified as personal competence—the ability to do life planning, to be self-reliant, and to seek the resources of others in coping (Brown & Lent, 1984); and as social-life skills (Larson, 1984). Most human problems are seen as social problems. Thus, group counseling generally is a more-effective medium for helping people learn social skills.

SETTING GOALS FOR A HEALTHY LIFESTYLE

Beginning with the intake interview, each client is helped to define specific, individualized goals that are clarified and restated in more precise, behavioral terms during counseling. In an effective counseling group, members discover that they can each face and cope with crises as they meet them. They learn to accept themselves and others; to give and to accept love; to build meaningful relationships with significant others; to work and play with others; to find meaningful work; to recognize reality; and to change what can be changed, or learn to live with those disturbing situations that cannot be changed (or are not worth the effort to change). Clients gradually discover who they are; what they can do; what gives them greatest satisfaction; what they would like to do; how to recognize sources of conflict early; and how to cope with conflict (rather than ignore or deny it). Clients do not wish to have problems in living. They have ideas, beliefs, and expectations about how life could be different and more fulfilling. In group counseling, clients clearly identify how they would like for their lives to be different and, as the group progresses, see how they are

144

gradually moving toward accomplishing the changes they anticipated: the real and ideal selves come closer together. In other words, therapists' and counselors' general counseling tends to reflect their theoretical orientation and their perception of the good life.

The Adlerian Model

There are many similarities among various models of helping for describing what healthy lifestyles are like for people. For example, Adlerians (Sonstegard & Dreikurs, 1973) help their clients give up the faulty premises and faulty logic that have produced their guilt feelings, their feelings of inferiority and isolation, and their desire for prestige. By helping their clients experience genuine feelings of belonging and a meaningful exchange of ideas, they help their clients discover goals for more-effective lifestyles. They help clients understand the consequences of their behavior and goals; teach them to cooperate with others, to relate more wholesomely, to seek healthier sources of satisfaction, to experience increased self-esteem (or remove feelings of inferiority), and to take life in stride.

Like Adlerians, Glasser (1965) stresses the importance of his clients' learning to accept responsibility for their behavior:

> Therapy is a special kind of teaching or training which attempts to accomplish in a relatively short, intense period what should have been established during growing up. The more irresponsible the person is, the more he has to learn about acceptable, realistic behavior in order to fulfill his needs. However, the drug addict, the chronic alcoholic, and the severely psychotic are examples of deep irresponsible people with whom it is difficult to gain sufficient involvement so that they can learn to relearn better ways to fulfill their needs (Glasser, 1965, pp. 20–21).

Glasser is concerned about helping each client satisfy two basic needs: the need to love and be loved; and, the need to feel worthwhile, by oneself as well as by significant others. Glasser tries to help each take cognizance of others' needs in fulfilling one's own needs. Like Adlerians, he uses encouragement to reinforce desired behaviors, and natural consequences to extinguish undesirable behaviors. To that extent, and, perhaps (as they perceive it), with more human compassion for their clients, Glasser and the Adlerians are able to help their clients change their behavior by learning more-effective living skills.

The Dynamic Model

Not all orientations toward helping place the same emphasis on behavioral change of living skills. Bross (1959), for example, states quite different goals for her analytically oriented groups: to develop ego resources; to improve functioning as a group member; to resolve transference and resistance; to gain pleasure from purposeful activities; to develop self-confidence, greater assertiveness, and greater self-realization with contemporaries; and to formulate and implement one's plans.

Both Frank (1957) and Kelman (1963) also take cognizance of clients' needs for improved interpersonal skills. Frank's general treatment goals are: (1) to facilitate constructive release of feelings; (2) to strengthen patients' self-esteem; (3) to encourage patients to face and resolve their problems; (4) to improve their skills for recognizing and resolving both interpersonal and intrapersonal conflicts; and (5) to fortify them to consolidate and to maintain their therapeutic gains. Kelman's goals are: (1) to overcome feelings of isolation; (2) to enhance self-esteem and increased acceptance of self; (3) to develop hope for improved adjustment; (4) to help clients learn to be themselves and to express their feelings; (5) to accept responsibility for themselves and for solving their problems; (6) to develop, practice, and maintain new relationship skills; and (7) to enhance their commitment to changing their attitudes and behaviors, and to generalize insight and skills by implementing them in daily life.

Such goals are desirable and, in fact, can include specific guidelines for behaviorial change; but, as presented, it is often difficult to judge how a client is doing with regard to vague treatment goals because of the general way in which they are stated. Behavior therapists pioneered the area of goal setting. Recently some of their critics have adapted behavioral techniques for their use. More-precise behavioral goals are required to encourage client change, to appraise counseling outcomes, and to help counselors determine whether to continue a given client's treatment and/or refer the client for more-appropriate treatment. In particular, early in the therapeutic relationship more counselors are helping their clients define specific objective goals. Some critics of counseling practices recognized this need some time ago.

Critics of the Dynamic Model

Krumboltz (1966) states:

> Brayfield (1962) argued that counseling psychologists had placed undue emphasis on egocentric, self-regarding internal states and should, instead, use a performance criterion that would stress dependability, accountability, obligation, and responsibility. Similarly, Samler (1962) cited three instances in which problems of prejudice, self-pity, and poor workmanship were brought to the counselor. In each case, Samler argued the important objective was that the client change his behavior in relevant ways whether or not his subjective feelings changed. Such logic finds a foundation in the concept of efficiency as advocated by Wishner (1955) and the concept of competence that was brilliantly developed by White (1959). Ultimately counselors of all persuasions look to client behavior changes as justification for their procedures.

. . . The use of behavioral goals would result in (a) a clearer anticipation of what counseling could accomplish, (b) a better integration of counseling psychology with the mainstream of psychological theory and research, (c) a facilitation of the search for new and more effective techniques for helping clients and (d) the use of different criteria for assessing the outcome of counseling with different clients (Krumboltz, 1966, p. 153).

GOAL SETTING IN THE WORKPLACE

There has been a long history of studying the use of goal setting in industrial settings. Many of the findings from industry apply equally well to group counseling. For example, Locke (1968) found that goals that are more difficult to achieve result in a higher level of performance than do easy, simple goals; and that more-specific and objective goals result in better performance than vague, general goals ("Do your best."). Further, Locke reported that a person's commitment to a goal plays an important role in determining how easily that person will give up when encountering difficulty—the more commitment to the goal, the less likely the person is to abandon the goal, regardless of the difficulty. Locke's work is supported by McClelland (1971) who also found that motivated workers like to be challenged. They set moderately difficult, but potentially achievable goals for themselves, and they worked hard to achieve their goals.

Locke, Cartledge, and Knerr (1970) also studied the effect of goals on performance. They found that an individual's performance was determined by that person's goals, and that goals were determined by the person's satisfaction and value judgments. Interestingly, the level of performance that was satisfying in the past was not necessarily that which produced satisfaction in the future. Rather, an individual's anticipated, not past, satisfaction best predicted subsequent goal setting.

Steers and Porter (1974) further found that when employees set specific objective goals, they had improved attention and effort, and they had improved task performance. Also, they learned that, when properly reinforced, more-difficult goals led to increased performance. Notz (1975) relates the findings to deCharms' (1968) hypothesis that man's primary motivation is to be effective in producing changes in his environment:

Because of the desire to be the "origin" of his behavior, man is constantly struggling against the constraint of external forces—against being moved about like a pawn. Thus, deCharms hypothesized that when a man perceives his behavior as stemming from his own choice (i.e., sees himself as an origin), he will cherish that behavior and its results; when he perceives his behavior as stemming from external forces (i.e., sees himself as a pawn), that behavior and its results, though identical in other respects to behavior of his own choosing, will be devalued (Notz, 1975, p. 884).

Notz's review lends credence to the emphasis presented in Chapter 1 for describing counseling: letting clients decide if they want to participate; helping them accept and truly be responsible for getting themselves ready for treatment; encouraging their full participation in defining behavioral goals; and making them responsible for implementing their desired new behaviors. These conditions also tend to contribute to a client's intrinsic motivation.

Perhaps the following generalizations from all of the findings presented above on employees' behavior apply to clients' behavior in group counseling: (1) specific goals serve to focus a client's behavior on learning specific new behaviors; (2) commitment to goals enables clients to sustain their efforts at times when otherwise they may be tempted to stop; (3) the expectation of succeeding (anticipation) may enhance clients' chances for achieving their goals; (4) clients want to be challenged, but can be discouraged by unrealistic goals; (5) the definition of goals must enhance clients' intrinsic motivation; and (6) encouragement and reinforcement are required to maintain a client's motivation to achieve goals.

CLIENTS' INVOLVEMENT

Though a number of studies had attempted to assess the impact of counselors' goals and clients' awareness of goals on counseling outcomes for clients, no research was identified that focused on either the impact of clients' participation in formulating their counseling goals or on each defining his or her own individualized goals. Four studies using the model described in Chapter 1 determined that the clients did make significant growth with reference to clients' defined goals (Bartell, 1972; Bush, 1971; De Esch, 1974; Hilkey, 1975). Each of these studies examined involving clients in the process of goal setting. Each found that if clients are involved, through intake interviews, in setting their individual goals, defining goals for the group, and in helping each other to achieve the goals established, that the outcome is positive.

On the other hand, when clients are not actively involved in an intake interview specifically for helping determine goals for change, the outcome is less successful. An exception to this was the study by Hilkey (1975). He found that, as in the other studies, when groups had goal-setting intake interviews, the members of those groups moved more quickly to accomplishing change. For the groups in which there was no intake, if the group leader was experienced and effective, goal setting occurred as part of the group process; and the members still made positive changes. Groups with no intake and with less-experienced or effective counselors were not able to make positive changes.

The Threat of Change

The threat of change and what may be done to reduce this threat for clients was discussed in Chapter 4. Several of the elements that reduce the threat of change associated with counseling pertain to a client's participation in deciding whether to volunteer for group counseling; to accept responsibility for learning to trust the counselor and the other clients; to cooperate in formulating specific, behavioral goals; and to cooperate in defining criteria that enable the client to appraise progress during counseling. With the definition of behavioral goals, clients discover that group counseling is designed *to help each learn desired new behaviors.* This is much less threatening than the inferred need for basic personality change—something that threatens most clients, especially adolescents who tend to wonder whether treatment will disrupt their search for identity.

The importance of goals in effective group counseling is well summarized by Yalom (1985):

> I cannot overemphasize the importance of setting clear and appropriate goals: It may be the most important step you make in your therapy. Nothing will so inevitably ensure failure as the presence of inappropriate goals.
>
> It is imperative to shape a set of goals that is appropriate to the clinical situation and achievable in the available time frame. The goal must be clear not only to the therapist but to patients as well . . . I emphasized the importance of enlisting the patient as a full collaborator in treatment. You facilitate collaboration by making the goals and the group procedures explicit and by linking the two: that is, by clarifying how the procedure of the therapy group will help the patient attain those goals.
>
> In time-limited, specialized groups, the goals must be limited, achievable, and tailored to the capacity and potential of the group members. It is important that the group be a success experience: Patients enter therapy feeling defeated and demoralized; the last thing they need is another failure (pp. 458–459).

In establishing lifestyle change, Kolb, Winter, and Berlew (1968) found that many persons are able to set and achieve self-selected goals. They found that lifestyle change was more likely to occur and endure if the process of change was seen by the individual to be under her own control. Perri and Richards (1977) examined those who were successful lifestyle changers versus those who were not. They found that successful changers used more techniques for change, over longer periods of time, with self-reward techniques and with strategies individualized for the problem. Doerfler and Richards (1981) found that clients who were successful in managing depression had made dramatic changes in their social environments, whereas those less effective in changing depression had not made changes in their social environment. This was perhaps a result of the lack of social support, support that a group-counseling environment could provide.

COUNSELORS' NEED FOR PRECISE BEHAVIORAL GOALS

Every profession is obligated to appraise the worth of its services. One of the guidelines for group leaders established by the Association for Specialists in

Group Work is that group leaders must assist clients in developing personal goals; and that it is unprofessional to conduct a group without clearly stated goals. Specific goals stated in precise, measurable, or observable terms are necessary in order to appraise treatment outcomes, whether the purpose is to assess a client's progress or a service systematically.

Even the practitioner who does not think that there is the time or inclination to do research must accept the ethical responsibility to seek the necessary data to answer questions such as: Which members of this group are profiting most and least (and/or are being hurt most) by this treatment? Which goals has each achieved? For which of the goals discussed has each openly related painful material? For which of those problems discussed does each require mini-goals, training in interpersonal skills before being able to implement the desired new behaviors, or assistance in determining how to request (or practice in requesting) reinforcement of desired new behaviors from significant others? For those who do not or cannot profit from treatment (or are hurt by it), what changes may enable them to profit from it? What other sources of help are available?

Besides keeping case notes in which counselors record descriptions of specific behavior, they can ask clients and clients' significant others to note specific behavior changes and/or evidence concerning implemented desired new behaviors. Counselors are expected to be accountable for their actions. The delineation of goals is an important way to do this.

Case Example

A practicum student's request for help from her supervisor with a countertransference problem can be used to illustrate how a counselor helps the client develop behavioral goals for the purposes discussed above. When her supervisor reflected the student's reluctance to respond therapeutically to a particular client's painful feelings (as the supervisor had done several times previously), the student discussed her reluctance to expose this client's painful material. Without going into all the details of the conference it will suffice to review the primary topics that they discussed: How does she feel toward this client? What feelings does she experience when this client approaches therapeutic material? Why has she (the practicum counselor) avoided earlier treatment opportunities? What is the impact of her fear of being a client on her counseling behavior? What unfinished business does she have with the person of whom this special client reminds her?

Following the conference, the student sought membership in a counseling group at the counseling center. With the assistance of her counselor, she defined the following goals for group counseling (her criteria for appraising growth is added to each parenthetically): (1) to volunteer to play recorded counseling sessions during class supervision, to solicit feedback from peers, and to use their feedback for improving her counseling skills (come to every practicum class session with a tape marked at the spots where she would like help; and following the criticism of the tape, to solicit feedback from her peers on the extent to which she listens to their feedback and uses it to improve her counseling); (2) to determine of whom this particular client reminds her, what her unfinished business is with this person, and how to finish it (identify the person on or before the close of the third counseling session, decide what must be done, and begin work on the problem with the target person immediately); and (3) to examine whether she really wants to be a counselor; and if she cannot be satisfied with her level of success in practicum, to define a new career goal (sources of data for adequacy of counseling performance will be peers', practicum professor's, and another professor's [selected cooperatively by the student and professor] rating on their standard, practicum rating sheet).

Of course, another criterion is whether she makes the decision to stay in counseling or to leave it and define a new career goal. With these goals and criteria for appraising her growth, this client and her counselor were able to determine to what extent she was helped by group counseling. She also was able to use her criteria to appraise her own growth during treatment. Her success encouraged her to work harder on goals not yet achieved. With such criteria, a counselor can discover growth in clients and solicit better feedback from clients and their significant others.

FORMULATING CLIENTS' GOALS

In counseling literature, the major emphasis has been upon helping clients establish goals to alleviate a particular problem, or more recently, to help clients identify ways of behaving opposite from current behavior (aggressive to assertive, depressed to encouraged). In order to accomplish this, the counselor and the client must have a collaborative relationship: helping clients to identify their goals for change and develop plans for achieving those goals is an act of empowerment; the counselor is helping the client develop the skills for positive change.

For the model described in this book, clients define their initial goals with the assistance of their counselor in the intake interview. Additional goals are often developed during counseling with the help of fellow clients and counselor.

When clients learn from the presentation what is expected from them in group counseling they come to the intake interview prepared to discuss what worries and upsets them and to define desired new behaviors (goals for counseling). Even when clients have learned about group counseling from a friend or relative, or are referred by someone, and have not heard a presentation, they learn to discuss what bothers them. The counselor helps develop specific behavioral goals out of their therapeutic materials. The counselor listens empathically and tries to decide when the client has discussed a problem in sufficient detail and experienced sufficient relief to understand precisely what to do with whom to improve adjustment: what desired new behaviors must be learned. On the other hand, the counselor must not permit a client either to wallow needlessly in painful material or to cathart to such an extent that catharsis alleviates both the pain and the motivation to change. Instead, clients are helped to define and implement behavioral goals at the earliest possible moment to achieve some goals while they are still discussing and formulating relevant goals for other painful material.

The goals that are set must include identification of the specific, positive change desired. It is more appropriate to express what *is* wanted rather than what *is not* wanted. Clients should move toward, rather than away, from a goal. The client needs to recognize and agree to the importance of the goal; and in doing so, establishes steps for measuring movement—for without achievement of small steps, discouragement may occur.

Barriers to Achieving a Goal

There are a number of roadblocks that can occur as a barrier to successfully achieving a goal. Brown and Lent (1984) have identified four possible road-blocks: (1) a lack of knowledge; (2) a lack of skills; (3) an inability to assess risks involved in changing behavior; and (4) a lack of social support. The counselor can help identify which of the four roadblocks would likely hinder a client from making change; and the group setting can provide the vehicle to overcome each of the four roadblocks. For a withdrawn person who wishes to become more outspoken and assertive, the group may:

- Help the person understand the importance of being confident and assertive, and circumstances when such behavior would be appropriate (knowledge).
- Teach the skills through demonstrations, role plays, and behavioral rehearsals: modeling (skill acquisition).
- Help the client learn to evaluate the risks involved in being assertive by sharing examples and experiences (risk assessment).
- Provide a social support system for helping the client decide to try the new behaviors and experiment with behavior change (social support).

Defining New Goals

During the course of treatment, when clients uncover additional therapeutic material, fellow clients help them define new goals. Frequently, such new-goal material surfaces as another client struggles with a similar problem. In any case, clients want fellow clients *to listen* carefully and allow them to share what worries them. When clients think the group pushes toward precise goals too quickly, they tend to wonder whether the members care or whether they have obtained enough data to be helpful. Like the counselor, they must listen; win the client's trust; help develop individualized goals; and see that the client perceives the goals as stemming from her own needs and desire to change. Melby (1972) found that:

- Appraisal instruments should be designed to measure change in terms of individuals' goals.
- Mean change scores on common goals were significantly higher than mean change scores on individual goals.
- Significantly more change was reported on items that were selected by individuals as goals than on items not selected by individuals.

Example 1

CLIENT: I'm not certain why I'm here. I guess one reason is the problems I have with co-workers. I'm sick and tired of the constant battle.

COUNSELOR: What is the constant battle?

CLIENT: They are always shoving off all the work on me that they can so they can do other things. Fun things, their own things on company time.

COUNSELOR: Sounds like you'd like to do something about this.

CLIENT: Yeah, but I don't know what. If I complain, it will only make matters worse.

COUNSELOR: What if there was another way?

CLIENT: That would be great, but I don't know of any.

COUNSELOR: O.K., let's consider making one of your goals finding alternative solutions to the problem. That's what group counseling is particularly good at doing: expanding one's options.

Example 2

CLIENT: I hear this group stuff is o.k., but I feel awkward in social situations. See, I have trouble making conversation. I end up getting red in the face and saying things I don't always mean. I mean sometimes I feel really stupid afterwards.

COUNSELOR: I think that is a good reason for joining the group. At first, you can just get to know everyone. Once you feel more comfortable, during the first session, you will be able to share with others why you are there. Gradually you'll be able to express yourself better. What do you think your goal could be?

CLIENT: To relax and talk more freely?

COUNSELOR: Sounds good. Let's be even more specific. With whom, when, where, how often, et cetera. Let's explore this further now.

Setting Unrealistic Goals

Usually counselors ask: "What about clients who develop unrealistic goals?" Schwartz (1974) found that subjects with higher depression scores were less accurate in setting goals than subjects with lower depression scores. His more-depressed subjects tended to set unrealistically high goals. He indicated that Adlerians (Dreikurs, 1962) believe clients set unobtainable goals in order to fail, thus reinforcing the client's feelings of inferiority. Bieliauskas (1966), on the other hand, saw unrealistic goal setting as a compensatory reaction, exaggerating the value of the individual by overaspiring. In either case, the goal-setting strategies of people experiencing depression or inferiority are unrealistic and result in overestimation of goals.

Setting unrealistic goals tends to be a part of some clients' lifestyles. Krumboltz and Thoresen (1969) describe them as follows:

> The problem of unrealistic high aspirations is a difficult one. High aspirations are undoubtedly instilled at an early age by perfectionistic mothers, fathers, and teachers as well as mass media. . . . The difficulty is that they compare their own successes with those of the most successful people in each field of endeavor (p. 13).

For such clients, best results tend to be achieved when they are placed in a group with at least one or two clients whom they admire and who have had the same difficulties to a lesser degree. Such peers model more-realistic goal setting and are able to react frankly and considerately, but bluntly if necessary, to their unrealistic goals and generally self-defeating behavior. Clients with unrealistic goals also witness these models openly discussing painful material and getting real help.

Dealing with Unrealistic Goals

When a counselor discovers such a client, even at the first contact in the intake interview, an attempt is made to convey caring and willingness to help that person become the best possible—with reference to the client's most-cherished goals—without setting up for failure. As the counselor listens to such a client discuss unrealistic goals, an appropriate response may be: "Jim, it is really important for you to please _____. I guess you feel that you just about have to be perfect to please him."

Within the counseling group, the counselor also often detects and reflects other clients' feelings toward such a client as follows: "Jim seems to feel like a failure at times when you think he should feel o.k. Perhaps you feel that he is already doing as well as he should expect himself to do. His goals for himself could not be achieved even by a superman." Such a reflection enables other clients to respond in a caring, empathic manner; to express admiration for motivation to do well; and to encourage the client to explore whether the unrealistic goals are essential. They encourage the client to explore what else may be done to build the kind of relationship that would be desired with the target person.

Correcting Unrealistic Goals

Sometimes a client who seems to have unrealistic goals learns that some goals could even be achieved if deficiencies, such as learning disabilities that block progress toward goals, could be corrected. Eventually the client with unrealistic goals learns, with peers' assistance, either to define more-realistic goals or to correct deficiencies that make some of the goals unachievable. Such discussions also often surface into awareness of other valued goals that have been neglected. This encourages clients to examine how they want to spend their time and energy; whether they are willing to continue to ignore valued goals now that they are no longer possessed by certain goals.

Even for such a client some realistic, behavioral goals can be defined in the intake interview. The counselor helps develop goals in terms of specific attitudes, behaviors, and skills and helps define precise criteria to determine whether, and to what extent, the client is being helped. The counselor and client also discuss what data they must collect from whom to help them appraise the client's change during and after counseling. In other words, the counselor merely helps each client define her own goals. Moreover, when for any reason the counselor questions whether goals are the client's or the counselor's, an examination of that particular recorded session is conducted with great care. Thus, the counselor ensures that clients define their own desired new behaviors.

Counselors' Evaluations of Clients' Unethical Goals

Krumboltz (1965) answers two related questions for counselors: Whose criteria shall be used to evaluate counseling? What may a counselor do when the counselor thinks that a client's goals seem to call for unethical or immoral behavior?

> Some people may be offended by the notion that we should permit the wishes of our clients to determine the criteria of our success and would prefer to establish universal criteria applicable to all clients. It should be remembered that all professional groups and all professional persons are ultimately evaluated by the extent to which they bring about the conditions desired by their clientele. When a client requests his lawyer to write out a last will and testament, the client expects the lawyer to write the document in such manner that the client's requests will eventually be executed in precisely the manner that he wishes. In a like manner a physician is successful if, let us say, a patient with a broken leg can walk normally again as he desires. In the case of both the lawyer and the physician, there come times when the professional man cannot carry out the wishes of his client either because the request is not within the scope of his interests, or because it is beyond his power, or because it violates his ethical standards. In such cases the professional man explains the reasons why he cannot carry out the specific requests of the client, perhaps indicating alternate courses of action, including referrals when appropriate. When a professional

man does accept a client, however, he is implicitly agreeing to exert whatever efforts he can to accomplish what his client requests. The use of clients' request as a basis for generating the criteria of success is as appropriate for counselors as it is for lawyers and physicians. In the case of counselors, it means that the same criterion measures cannot be applied to evaluating all counseling contacts (Krumboltz, 1965, pp. 383–384).

To what extent is a counselor free to respond to new therapeutic material during counseling, and thereby infer the need for new goals? Counselors and fellow clients will detect new therapeutic material from clients in the group and respond to it, when appropriate. As long as clients realize that they decide whether to add new goals and how to rank their goals (either for the order in which they work on them or on the level of relative importance to them), the counselor has protected the clients' rights.

EVALUATION OF CLIENTS' GOALS

Once clients have defined their goals and developed criteria to appraise their own growth, the counselor examines their goals to ensure that the clients' best interests can be served. A few criteria that may be used for that purpose are discussed here.

1. *Is this the client's goal?* To what extent does the goal reflect the counselor's values and ambitions for the client? Walker and Peiffer (1957) believe that counseling goals are influenced too much by the counselor's middle-class values. Krumboltz (1966), on the other hand, contends that a client's goal must be at least compatible with, though not necessarily identical to, the counselor's values. Most counselors agree that it would be unethical to accept a client whose goal involves breaking a specific law, but many have great difficulty deciding whether they should be expected to accept a client for counseling whose goal involves actions that they perceive to be immoral; for instance, a request for assistance in planning a robbery versus a request for help in deciding whether to seek an abortion. If the counselor feels that he cannot help a client achieve her goals, the counselor must refuse treatment, give reasons for refusal, and help the client find other resources for help. Perhaps the danger comes when the counselor thinks the client's goals have been accepted, but unconsciously reinforces behaviors that divert the client away from the goal. Wolberg (1954) believed that even when a therapist is objective and tries to help a patient plan action consistent with the patient's values, the patient tends to be influenced by the therapist's values: to use the therapist as a model.

Because counselors exhibit tolerance for values different from their own, and not usually accepted in the community, does not mean as some critics have suggested, that either they or their clients condone unlawful or irresponsible behavior. It does mean that members of a counseling group can accept others' goals that are not appropriate for themselves. When there is imminent danger that someone may be hurt by a client's anticipated plans, usually fellow clients encourage the client to examine the consequences of such behavior. When they do not, the counselor may do so; the counselor may also need to explain to the group the necessity to take action to protect the person who may be hurt. Very, very rarely are those who only do individual counseling required to break confidence for such reasons. It is even less likely that group counselors would be required to do so.

A major point of group counseling is to provide the individual with consensual validation of goals. In the end, however, it is not the counselor's evaluation nor the group's evaluation of the individual's goals that is important. What is important is how the person utilizes the feedback and support. In the end, only the client can evaluate how successful the efforts have been to accomplish goals. Only the individual can evaluate the extent to which effective change has occurred.

2. *Does the goal statement convey that client's unique, individualized need?* Krumboltz (1966) contends that the unique feature of counseling is the individualization that it provides. Consequently, counselors must be willing to help each client state and work for solving her own unique objectives. For treatment purposes alone Krumboltz is correct. When, however, a counselor sets out to appraise the worth of a technique, it is usually necessary to paraphrase and combine very similar goals into common, behavioral statements just to reduce the number of goal statements on the Q-sort or behavior inventory (Bartell, 1972; Bush, 1971; De Esch, 1974; Hilkey, 1975). Furthermore, such common, behavioral goal statements so developed tend to be perceived as clearly their own. Most clients also adopt and work on others' goals.

3. *Are the goals stated in clear, precise, behavioral terms for which a client and the counselor can readily obtain essential measures and/or observations to appraise outcomes?* Do the goals focus attention on specific desired new behaviors? Though Walker and Peiffer (1957) endorse the need for specific goals they still warn counselors about the dangers of symptom removal and substitution. Few counselors are bothered about the latter point today. They do not believe that symptom substitution occurs when symptoms are removed by effective counseling. Ample support for this point of view is provided by behavior therapists; for example, Ullman and Krasner (1965).

4. *Do the goals reflect the client's language and are the goals expressed in the client's own words?* When clients truly believe that the goals arise out of their own needs and unresolved problems, they invest more fully of themselves to achieve them. They realize that they participated fully in their development. They make a greater commitment to achieve the goals.

5. *What observations of the client's behavior suggest that the client believes that the goals can be achieved; that there is an anticipation of success?* Expectation of succeeding enhances the chance for success.

6. *Are the goals challenging to the client and still perceived as achievable?* The case was made earlier for both this criterion and the previous one.

7. *And finally, what happens when a majority of the group elect to terminate? Does it make any difference whether those voting for termination have achieved their goals? What about those who have not achieved their goals?* Unless the group is not functioning therapeutically, most who support termination will have achieved their goals. When, on the other hand, the counselor senses that someone who is suggesting termination has given up or is confronted with goals that are very difficult to handle, a reflection of these feelings helps the client discuss them. Sometimes this discussion produces either new goals or mini-goals for the old goals. If, nevertheless, the client still elects to terminate, this is permitted.

Often the other clients encourage the client to explore the natural consequences of running away from unresolved problems. In any case, clients decide when they terminate. When they decide to terminate, each is usually helped to explore: What has been accomplished? What is still to be done? Whose help will be required to do it? How can the assistance of significant others in reinforcing gains and in helping complete unfinished business be enlisted? Among those who achieve their goals first, there is usually considerable commitment to help the others achieve their goals. Nevertheless, groups often terminate before everyone achieves set goals. These clients are either counseled individually or referred to other groups.

Perhaps some readers will be concerned because none of the criteria dealt with what is good for society. Well-adjusted persons are concerned about what is good for society as well as for themselves; they work very hard to correct social injustices. They accept the need for a balance between what is required of them for self-actualization and what must be done to improve society. Some learn to express genuine concern for others as they learn to help fellow clients achieve their goals.

Summary

Group counseling is designed to help reasonably healthy clients recognize their problems, seek help with them, define precise new behaviors that they would like to learn, and implement their new learnings in daily living. When a counselor accepts a client's reasons for seeking counseling and can involve each client in stating clearly and simply the changes in behavior and attitude that she desires, the counselor facilitates the clients' readiness for counseling and commitment to change.

More often than not, clients want assistance in improving their relationships with relatives, friends, or co-workers. Consequently, they require help in deciding what they want to learn to do with whom. During counseling they often have to break their goals into mini-goals: "Tomorrow I will talk to my husband about _____ . After we decide what we are going to do about _____ , I can talk to my mother about _____ ." Frequently a single problem has several facets. A client requires help in deciding where to begin with whom for each facet.

Most counselors have general goals for their treatment, but they are not sufficient. Precise, behavioral goals are needed to focus a client's attention and energy on learning desired new behaviors. Genuine participation in the development of the goals is necessary for a client to develop acceptance of the goals and the commitment required to sustain her efforts when she might be tempted to stop. Helping the client establish criteria for each goal facilitates problem-solving skills. One of the purposes of group counseling is to facilitate the generalization of effective living skills from the group learning experience to the general environment in which the individual lives.

REFERENCES

Bartell, W. (1972). *The effect of the intake interview on client-perceived outcomes of group counseling.* Unpublished doctoral dissertation, Indiana State University.

Bieliauskas, U. J. (1966). Shifting of the guilt feelings in the process of psychotherapy. In J. L. Moreno (Ed.), *The international handbook of group psychotherapy* (pp. 265–269). New York: Philosophical Library.

Brayfield, A. H. (1962). Performance is the thing. *Journal of Counseling Psychology, 99,* 3.

Bross, R. B. (1959). Termination of analytically oriented psychotherapy in groups. *International Journal of Group Psychotherapy, 9,* 326–337.

Brown, S. D., & Lent, R. W. (1984). *Handbook of counseling psychology.* New York: John Wiley.

Bush, J. (1971). *The effects of fixed and random actor interaction on individual goal attainment in group counseling.* Unpublished doctoral dissertation, Indiana State University.

deCharms, R. (1968). *Personal causation: The internal affective determinants of behavior.* New York: Academic Press.

De Esch, J. B. (1974). *The use of the Ohlsen model of group counseling with secondary students identified as being disruptive to the educational process.* Unpublished doctoral dissertation, Indiana State University.

Doerfler, L. A., & Richards, C. S. (1981). Self-initiated attempts to cope with depression. *Cognitive Therapy & Research, 5,* 367–371.

Dreikurs, R. (1962). *Fundamentals of Adlerian psychology.* Jamaica, W. I.: Spaeleng, K. E. S.

Frank, J. D. (1957). Some determinants, manifestations, and efforts of cohesiveness in therapy groups. *International Journal of Group Psychotherapy, 77,* 53–63.

Glasser, W. (1965). *Reality therapy.* New York: Harper & Row.

Hilkey, J. H. (1975). *The effects of videotape pretraining and guided performance on the process and outcomes of group counseling.* Unpublished doctoral dissertation, Indiana State University.

Kelman, H. C. (1963). The role of the group in the induction of therapeutic change. *International Journal of Group Psychotherapy, 13,* 399–432.

Kolb, D. D.; Winter, S. K.; & Berlew, D. E. (1968). Self-directed change: Two studies. *Journal of Applied Behavioral Science, 4,* 453–471.

Krumboltz, J. D. (1965). Behavioral counseling: Rationale and research. *Personnel and Guidance Journal, 44,* 376–382.

Krumboltz, J. D. (1966). Behavioral goals for group counseling. *Journal of Counseling Psychology, 13,* 153–159.

Krumboltz, J. D., & Thoreson, C. E. (Eds.) (1969). *Behavioral counseling: Cases and techniques.* New York: Holt, Rinehart and Winston.

Larson, D. (Ed.). (1984). *Teaching psychological skills.* Monterey, CA: Brooks/Cole.

Locke, E. A. (1968). Toward a theory of task motivation and incentives. *Organizational Behavior and Human Performance, 3,* 157–189.

Locke, E. A.; Cartledge, N.; & Knerr, C. S. (1970). Studies of the relationship between satisfaction, goal setting, and performance. *Organizational Behavior and Human Performance, 5,* 135–158.

McClelland, D. C. (1971). That urge to achieve. In D. A. Kalb; I. M. Rubin; & J. M. McIntyre (Eds.), *Organizational psychology* (pp. 123–129). Englewood Cliffs, NJ: Prentice-Hall.

Melby, D. J. (1972). *Individual and common goals: An analysis of the criterion problem in group counseling.* Unpublished doctoral dissertation, Southern Illinois University.

Notz, W. W. (1975). Work motivation and the negative effects of extrinsic rewards. *American Psychologist, 30,* 884–891.

Perri, M. G., & Richards, C. S. (1977). An investigation of naturally occurring episodes of self-controlled behavior. *Journal of Counseling Psychology, 24,* 178–183.

Samler, J. (1962). An examination of client strength and counselor responsibility. *Journal of Counseling Psychology, 9,* 5–11.

Schwartz, J. L. (1974). Relationship between goal discrepancy and depression. *Journal of Consulting and Clinical Psychology, 42,* 309.

Sonstegard, M. A., & Dreikurs, R. (1973). The Adlerian approach to group counseling of children. In M. M. Ohlsen (Ed.), *Counseling children in groups: A forum* (pp. 47–77). New York: Holt, Rinehart and Winston.

Steers, R. M., & Porter, L. W. (1974). The role of task-goal attributes in employee performance. *Psychological Bulletin, 81,* 434–452.

Ullman, L. P., & Krasner, L. (Eds.) (1965). *Case studies in behavior modification.* New York: Holt, Rinehart and Winston.

Walker, D. E., & Peiffer, H. C. (1957). The goals of counseling. *Journal of Counseling Psychology, 3,* 204–209.

White, R. W. (1959). Motivation reconsidered: The concept of competence. *Psychological Review, 66,* 69–80.

Wishner, J. A. (1955). Concept of efficiency in psychological health and in psychopathology. *Psychological Review, 62,* 69–80.

Wolberg, L. R. (1954). *The technique of psychotherapy.* New York: Grune & Stratton.

Yalom, I. (1985). *The theory and practice of group psychotherapy* (3rd ed.). New York: Basic Books.

7

RESISTANCE

Failure to cooperate in the therapeutic process is *resistance*. In individual counseling, clients may exhibit resistance by arriving late for an appointment; skipping or postponing sessions; appearing unable to talk about problems; refraining from the definition of precise behavioral goals; questioning whether or not they can be helped; dwelling on earlier events in their lives; becoming preoccupied with side issues or small talk; acting distracted or confused; acting out impulses; demanding or pleading for advice; being spontaneously cured (flight to health); and dropping out of treatment without getting the help they need. These resistance tactics are exhibited in groups as well.

In addition, clients protect themselves and fellow clients by advice giving, protective talking, and monopolizing; selective silences (which may go unnoticed in a group setting); talking about persons outside of the group; wondering whether or not the group is really a safe place to discuss personal problems; questioning whether or not confidences will be (or have been) kept; requesting further clarification on what is really expected of clients in a group; and acting overwhelmed about their responsibility for helping to develop and maintain therapeutic group norms.

Resistance, though, should not be seen as bad. As Corey, Corey, Callanan, and Russell (1982) explain:

> All resistance is not negative. After all, to some extent, it is perfectly normal to be cynical or to want to check out a situation before acting or to hold back making oneself known until it seems safe to do so (p. 65).

Yalom (1985) supports this, saying:

> I have yet to encounter the improblematic patient, the patient whose course of therapy resembles a newly christened ship gliding smoothly down the slip into the water. Each patient must be a problem: the success of therapy depends

161

upon each individual's encountering and mastering basic life problems in the here-and-now of the group. Each problem is complex and unique . . . (p. 373).

RESISTANCE WITHIN THE GROUP SETTING

Within a group setting, resistance is either individual or group behavior that slows the group progress toward group goals. Almost any behavior can be a form of resistance. The two keys are behavioral excess (whether too little or too much) and the needs underlying such behavior. For example, silence and overtalking may represent resistant behavior, depending upon the circumstances. Both extremes of talking can prevent the client and the group from experiencing threat, anxiety, and involvement. It is helpful to remember that at the root of most resistant behavior is fear: the fear of being exposed, the fear of being disliked, and the fear of losing control. The choice of approach to addressing resistance depends upon the counselor, the client, the form of resistance, and the group environment. Spinks and Birchler (1982) have said:

> The choice of intervention strategy will depend on the form the resistance takes and on what the therapist already suspects concerning the nature of the underlying issues (p. 174).

The overall thrust, though, is to start with the most-obvious and straightforward methods and, if not successful, proceed to more complex procedures.

Resistance Due to Ethnic Differences

It is important to be aware that, in group work, clients of ethnic origins different from that of the counselor may resist group pressure to conform. Recognition of the context of the resistance is essential. In a multicultural society such as ours, resistance can occur because clients do not understand the process of counseling as "middle-class America" has come to practice it. For some cultures, there is great shame associated with having to participate in a process such as counseling. Other cultures may value seeking guidance from others, but expect direct information giving: being told what to do. Still other cultural groups may respond well to the specific model of change presented in this book, but reject affective involvement. Counselors must become and remain aware of the cultural norms of the target population and then work within the restraints placed upon the process by cultural differences.

The Nature of Resistance: Slowness to Change

Resistance is a natural part of the group-counseling process and has been recognized as a function of personal change throughout the history of psychology. It is natural for people to resist change, to be hesitant to exchange the known—painful as it may be—for the unknown. Freudians refer to the slow change people allow as *repetition compulsion*, while behaviorists have described the same inertia as *reinforcement history*. Regardless of the terms selected to describe the process, counselors must be sensitive to the difficulty clients experience as they trade their familiar behavior for the unfamiliar.

Slowness of change can be frustrating, but is to be expected. Systems theory explains that an individual's behavior is not only influenced by the behavior of others, but also influences others; that is, a person's interactions with significant others influences how the others think and behave, and vice versa. Reciprocity of behavior develops, much like a dance, with each person in a system simultaneously influencing and being influenced by others.

The Systems Perspective

The family, friend, and work relationships clients have outside the group are systems that have included the client. When we attempt to help a client make changes, even when changes are desired by the client and the client's family, we are changing the system in which that person lives. The system, while not necessarily conducive to good mental health, provides stability for all involved: each person's role is known, predictable, and congruent for that system. When the counselor introduces methods of change, the client's system is going to work against the change process. When the client changes, the homeostasis of the system is broken, which poses a threat to all involved in that system.

Given the systems perspective, an aspect of counseling in groups that is important is to address how change may impact the other systems in which the clients live and work. Helping clients be aware that resistance is not just a response from within the person but also reflects the feelings of persons unknown to the group is important. By helping clients identify how their changes will influence other people in their lives, clients can then be prepared to recognize the system resistance and how to work with it to help themselves and others in their lives make the changes smoothly.

The counselor must be aware, not just from a therapeutic perspective, but also from an ethical/professional stance, of the impact that change can have on clients and their significant others. So often, counselors enter into contracts with clients for change programs without reviewing both the positive and the negative outcomes that are possible. While in the long run, change may be positive and consistent with the value system most counselors hold, it can be very painful for those experiencing it, or for significant others of the client who may not even understand what is happening.

Case Example

John was a freshman in college who joined a group to explore career options as he looked ahead at his college program. John was from a rural, low socio-economic family. As the group progressed, John seemed to be having great difficulty moving toward his goal of exploring career options. He seemed to have many different reasons for not looking up information, interviewing relevant persons, and reading materials provided. When the lack of progress was pointed out to John in the group, group members helped him explore what the block seemed to be toward the topic. It turned out that John had a cousin, older, who had also gone to college—one of the few in his family to have done so. After finishing college, John's cousin moved to a distant city and now had very infrequent contacts with his family. It turned out that John also had a fear of losing contact with his family, and he saw making career selections as moving toward the loss of family. Members of his family had indicated John would have to choose between family and career, as his cousin had, and that he would not be able to have both. The group at that point helped John develop a second set of goals to work toward: how to be a success and to make career choices while maintaining close family ties and making certain that drifting away would not occur.

CLIENTS' AMBIVALENCE

Sometime or other, most clients experience ambivalence when they try to change: wanting and not wanting the services for which they have contracted (Osborn, 1949). Although clients who have heard the type of presentations and participated in the intake interviews described in Chapter 1 tend to exhibit less resistance and take more responsibility for coping with it than most clients, they still experience the type of ambivalence described by Osborn. Occasionally, even highly motivated, confident clients will have difficulty admitting even to themselves what really worries and upsets them; wonder whether or not other clients will continue to accept them when the others discover what the clients are really like and/or what they have done; question whether or not they are willing to suffer as much as may be required in order to solve their problems; abhor the thought that opening themselves up to some problems also may uncover still others of which they are unaware; and doubt whether or not they can really achieve the goals that they and their counselor have cooperatively identified. Thus, resistance arises out of a broad spectrum of fears, not a desire to do battle with the counselor or therapist. Schlesinger (1982) has pointed out that resistance is not a word that describes behavior; it is a term that explains it. Strupp and Binder (1984) support this by saying:

> While resistances may take many forms, all dynamic therapists agree that
> they serve to protect the patient from experiencing painful affects which are
> related to conflicts (p. 181).

Perhaps the most-powerful source of help for assisting clients to deal with
resistance is the genuine self-respect they experience as they struggle to discuss
painful material, find that they can do it, and discover the extent to which they
are admired by fellow clients for doing it. Moreover, discovering that their fellow
clients can provide quality support (and where it is not forthcoming, the
counselor is able to detect their need for it and teach fellow clients to provide it)
reinforces further risk taking.

Resistance is not something that is good or bad; rather resistance is simply part
of the process of change. And in the process of identifying resistance, the
counselor can gain important clues to the client's lifestyle by attending to the
client's personal, emotional reactions to the ongoing process. When counselors
address issues that are of importance to clients they often respond with habitual
patterns (anger, silence). When the counselor, in a supportive manner, points
out the behavioral pattern, the client can learn how they respond to problems in
the group setting and probably outside the group as well.

IMPACT OF RESISTANCE ON THE COUNSELOR

At one time or another, most counselors and therapists have had difficulty
accepting the resisting client, detecting precisely what the person is feeling, and
responding to those feelings. When counselors are most effective, they can listen
to the resisting client, detect the resisting client's underlying fear, reflect it, and
enlist the other clients' assistance in these activities, too. Counselors are also able
to enlist group members' assistance in trying to answer questions such as: Why is
this client having this impact on me right now? What unfinished business, and
with whom, does it suggest that I try to discuss? How can I use these data to
respond to the client now?

When a counselor is less effective, it is easy to react personally to the resisting
client's behavior: to feel rejected, unappreciated, frustrated, and angry. On such
occasions, the counselor must try to determine the extent to which techniques,
counseling methods, and/or the counselor's own unresolved problems might
account for the client's resistance. Goodman, Marks, and Rockberger (1964)
describe how they met together weekly for mutual supervision for two and a half
years, and what they learned from these experiences:

> The focus shifted slowly, almost imperceptibly at first, from patient dynamics
> to exposing and exploring the irrational and distorted in our own perceptions of
> the therapeutic situation.

It became apparent that not only were our distortions interfering with our role as group therapists but that each one of us had specific islands of sensitivity (repetitive familiar situations) which had not been brought to light or resolved in his personal and control analysis. We found that the setting of peer group supervision permitted shades and nuances of emotional working through which contrasted with the authority-bound setting of the traditional supervisory experience.

The procedure in these sessions was for one of the therapists to choose for presentation and discussion the group which was not meeting his expectation for movement and in which he was encountering stiff resistance. The presenter would often present a tape recording of a session of his problem group, and his colleagues would question his interventions as well as the meaning of the interaction of group members. They would speak of the feeling they got as they listened to the session, and the presenting therapist would speak of what he saw as the resistance. The focus would then shift to some excess or lack of effective response in the presenter, a particular defensive attitude or position, and the feelings and reactions of his colleagues ... As we studied our countertransference to our groups, our patients, and each other, we became increasingly aware that these in turn induced reactions in our patients and led, at times, to seemingly impenetrable resistance phenomena within our therapy groups (pp. 335–336).

We have found the peer supervisory group an excellent setting in which to bring into consciousness many of the binding images that may interfere with our work. These professionals helped each other recognize how lack of congruence influenced the therapist's ability to detect and respond helpfully to therapeutic material. Their experience endorses peer supervision. Even better results can be achieved when peers use video rather than audio recordings as their source of data and help each other define precise, behavioral goals *for their professional growth.*

Peer groups that assist the counselor in examining resistance, transference/countertransference, and other counseling issues are highly recommended. It has been our experience that counselors in agencies or schools can develop a support supervision group with full encouragement from supervisors.

It is important that counselors not blame clients for resisting; rather, as Bergman (1985) suggests in his *Fishing for Barracuda*, a book on brief therapy with resistant families, we should assume that the counselor has failed to provide the proper conditions for helping people change. The counselor can gain important clues about the client's life through the interviewing process. Knowing what conditions the client needs in order to make healthy changes is one aspect of the interviewing process.

PREVENTION

Of course the best method for coping with resistance is to do everything possible to prevent it; and when it occurs, to recognize it early and deal with it (and to teach clients to recognize it and deal with it sensitively). A presentation on group counseling or an explanation about what happens in groups prior to ever beginning will help with resistance: clients will have a clear understanding of what to expect and from whom. Providing clients with the data they require to decide whether to participate; helping them accept responsibility for convincing themselves and their counselor that they are committed to discussing their problems openly, to formulating clear behavioral goals, and to learning new behaviors; and helping them establish and maintain therapeutic group norms help prevent resistance or, at least, how to cope with it when it occurs.

Careful explanation of what occurs in the group, what the process will entail, and the benefits of the group experience develops a positive attitude toward the process. Ruppel and Kaul (1982) report that joining techniques, the process whereby clients and therapists join to work together on problems, rests on the principle of reducing anxiety to a level such that growth and change can occur. After anxiety is lowered to a safe level and anxiety tolerance is enhanced, then other methods of group therapy can be used. Developing a relationship that is trusting, congruent, and facilitative leads to reductions in resistance. Larrabee (1982) found that counselors perceived as:

> . . . illegitimate, because of their role or behavior and influence attempts based on power incongruent with the predominant established power base tend to be more resistant to their influence than do legitimate counselors and congruent attempts (p. 238).

In working with reluctant clients, clients who are other-, rather than self-, referred, relationships can be built where anger, anxiety, and frustration are not experienced, or are not experienced very strongly. This occurs when counselors are able to accept the resistant position of a reluctant client and guide exploration of the positive and negative aspects of being in a group (Larrabee, 1982).

> If direct positive communication is established, an environment is created in which self-exploration can occur and the reluctant [client] is free to consider . . . negative as well as positive aspects of a particular behavior that is viewed by others as undesirable (p. 109).

This includes the use of paraphrasing, reflection of feeling, use of open-ended questions, use of leads while avoiding judgments, or negative implications.

The Ways and Means of Prevention

Careful selection and assignment of clients to groups can help prevent group resistance. With the type of structuring described in Chapter 1, most clients begin their first session by talking openly about what really worries them. The counselor takes note of her therapeutic client behavior, reinforces it, and helps clients reinforce each other. For example, "Dan, you are really impressed with the way Marjorie is able to discuss what really bothers her." Her norms encourage open discussion of problems, enhance self-respect, and reinforce those who do it first—to such an extent that clients soon tend to perceive failure to admit resistance, or not coping with their own resistance, as deviant behavior.

We assume that client ambivalence, skepticism, and caution are reasonable given the risk involved in making change. Change is scary. (Readers should review how they felt if ever they were asked to make changes as significant in their lives as routinely as we ask of our clients.) Clients lives are predictable; the effects of changing are unknown.

When clients seek help, they are admitting they cannot solve their own problems. Pride can cause clients to resist change; so it is important for counselors to reframe the process in such a way that clients understand how seeking help can show a wise and reasonable approach:

> I'm glad you all agreed to be in this group. You've all had an intake interview with me, and we've clearly identified goals for each of you. We all know the whole is greater than the sum of its parts, and that's why we've decided to work on your goals in a group setting: We can move faster, more effectively drawing upon the resources of all who are here. I appreciate your commitment to an effective learning experience.

Counselors should be cautious about attributing clients' nonperformance of tasks or activities to resistance. Rather, failure to complete tasks or to follow through on assignments may be the result of a communication or comprehension problem. If clients do not fully understand what they are to do, or how to do it, they are likely to appear resistant. Fleischman, Horne, and Arthur (1983, p. 45) suggest:

- Use simpler language to explain concepts.
- Slow down the pace.
- Use more examples to illustrate points.
- Incorporate more modeling and rehearsal.
- Engage in more-extensive problem solving before sending them home to use the techniques.

They also recommend:

- reassuring ("We really covered a lot last week. Did you have any difficulty remembering parts of what we discussed?")

- sharing the responsibility ("I may have explained it in a way that was confusing")

COUNSELOR MODELING

When clients are threatened, they exhibit resistance. From the first time a client exhibits resistance, the counselor should model facilitating behavior and help clients learn to do it, too. The counselor empathizes with the resisting client; tries to capture precisely what is being experienced; helps share fears; helps the client develop the determination to face the problem and discuss it; and reinforces the client's courage to deal with it. The extent to which the counselor can detect and reflect accurately in meaningful, concrete terms helps the resisting client perceive feeling that there is support that can be relied upon. Thus, the counselor models acceptance of the client's struggle with resistance and encourages the client to face the problem rather than excusing and retreating from it.

The supportive, empathic model is not subscribed to by all. Some believe that resistant behaviors must be relentlessly attacked as a way of moving on to the important issues at hand (Davanloo, 1980). However, this approach can lead clients to affectively withdraw, causing them to develop more-subtle ways of resisting.

Clients who are resistant by not adhering to group rules can be particularly troublesome. The group leader who fails to enforce group rules or to address infringement of rules can experience a significant impasse with clients (Weiner, 1983). A legalistic attempt to develop compliance with group rules often produces or increases the impasse; whereas a neutral explanation of the issue, involving all group members, avoids this problem.

Responding to Resistance

Counselors can learn to selectively respond to the statements group members make, choosing to respond verbally and nonverbally to those statements that the counselor believes will facilitate change and growth.

Case Example

In a group, Bill had not shared much yet. While Betty talked about difficulty at work the counselor noticed Bill paying particular attention to her:

COUNSELOR: Bill, you seem to be listening closely to what Betty is saying. It seems her concerns strike a chord in you. Is this an issue you can join us on?

BILL: Well, I know what she's talking about, but I don't have anything as serious as she does.

COUNSELOR: I'm sure you do know what Betty's talking about. Will you share with
her, and the rest of us, how this affects you, how you've had a similar
experience?

BILL: I don't know.

COUNSELOR: Betty, I noticed it was difficult for you to talk about your work problems.
Bill, you saw that Betty shared and all of us learned and were able to be
helpful to Betty even though it was tough for her, and she had trouble
presenting it. We'd be pleased to hear from you, too, even if you don't
think it is as important.

Modeling Techniques

In dealing with the client's resistant behavior, the key is not to ignore it or be
intimidated by it. Egan (1982) states that "the counselor should let clients know
how you experience it and then explore it with them" (p. 299). The counselor
needs to model openness through immediacy. Hopefully, by clarifying their own
response to a client's resistance, the counselor can achieve two goals. First,
clients can begin to understand their impact on others; second, members of the
group can learn a method to deal with their own and others' resistant behaviors.

Confrontation

A more-powerful technique can be used also, such as confrontation. The focus
would be on challenging discrepancies when the counselor chooses to confront.
Egan (1982) suggests that counselors should try to point out discrepancies
between what a client says and does, feels and says, thinks and says. However,
for confrontations to be effective, there must exist a strong relationship between
leader and group members.

There are several situations in which this method may be appropriate. For
example, confrontation may be highly useful in handling the following situations:
the client who fails to make any progress toward goals due to an apparent lack of
effort—as opposed to a lack of skills; the client who maintains a realizable wish
to be open to feelings, but continues to intellectualize; or the client who states a
realistic desire to be more direct with negative feelings, but continues to use
sarcasm. One of the main objectives of confronting resistance is to move the
client toward the identification and discussion of underlying, unspoken issues or
feelings that are inhibiting growth.

Paradox

If all else fails, an indirect technique, such as paradox, may be the technique of
choice. The successful use of paradox depends on a thorough understanding of
the client and a strong and well-developed therapeutic relationship. The technique of paradox would typically involve instructing the client to engage in the

resistant behavior. The goal would be for the client to become more aware of the problematic behavior.

Corey et al. (1982) presents an example of the use of paradox with a client who avoided self-disclosure through repeated questioning of other members. They suggested having the client "go around the entire group and ask every question that he possibly wanted to ask everyone in the group" (p. 70). Afterward the client can explain what he was feeling and also explore the reactions of clients in the group. The hope is that paradox will make a strong impact on resistant behavior.

Midway Assessment

After resisting clients have experienced some success in their struggle with resistance for the first time, the counselor may elect to review why they did what they did for the entire group; discuss the phenomenon of resistance, and why it is important to help clients face whatever painful material there is involved (but not force them to do so); and help them to decide what they must do, and with whom, to learn their desired new behaviors. Earlier in the treatment process, the counselor predicted resistance and taught clients to recognize resistance and to help each other cope with it. This way of dealing directly with resistance led to it having less power.

There is more to be gained by addressing directly the ways in which people guard against changing through counseling (their quietness, suspiciousness, or anger) than is to be gained by using techniques designed to elicit self-disclosures that are inappropriately shared. Yalom (1985) says:

> Acceleration that results in material being untimely wrenched from individuals may be counterproductive if the proper context of the materials has not been constructed (p. 451).

Requests for Private Sessions

Sometimes when clients recognize resistance in themselves, they may request a private session with the counselor. To enable such clients to reap the full benefits from group counseling, the counselor should encourage them to discuss their reasons for such a request with fellow clients prior to the private session. Several benefits follow: (1) Other clients are more likely to accept the client's need for time alone with the counselor without the usual "sibling" rivalry. (2) In helping clients discuss why they are unable to discuss certain topics, they discover in others the support and encouragement they require to discuss the issue—and without a private conference. (3) Such discussion enables the counselor to structure the private conferences for other clients as well as for the specific person making a request. (Here we agree wholeheartedly with Bach [1954]:

that such private sessions should be group centered, getting the client ready to discuss and resolve problems in the group setting. As long as a client is a member of a treatment group, the group should be identified as the primary source of help. This approach also prevents the drainage problem discussed by Bach, in which clients save personal material for the private conferences, allowing group sessions to degenerate into superficial material.) (4) It strengthens group solidarity by preventing rivalry, one-upsmanship, secrecy, and triangulation.

GROUP RESISTANCE

Occasionally, clients will exhibit resistance simultaneously: group resistance. This is most apt to occur when clients with similar problems (underachieving adolescents, for example) or similar motivating forces (ways of disengaging from families) are placed in the same group (Freedman & Sweet, 1954). In a situation where all or most of the clients are threatened by the same relevant, but feared, discussion topics, they may support externalizing the problem. They may, for example, begin to blame a teacher or their parents for their problems. The group can then reinforce this position by citing similar examples about teachers or parents.

Obviously, the counselor should have detected the problem in intake interviews and assigned no more than two of a type to the same group. Even when clients have been selected and placed in groups with care, there will be times when clients exhibit group resistance. On such occasions, the counselor should merely note that several, and perhaps all, of them are faced with something that is difficult to discuss; suggest that each try to guess what each of the others wants to, but is reluctant to, discuss; convey a willingness to help each, and if that does not work, at least review why it is so difficult for each to talk about the problems with which they are struggling privately at the moment. Yalom (1985) advises:

> I never cease to be awed by the rich lode of subterranean data which exists in every group and in every meeting. Beneath each sentiment expressed there are layers of invisible, unvoiced ones. How to tap these riches? Sometimes when there is a long silence in a meeting I express this very thought: "There is so much information that could be available to us all today if only we could excavate it. I wonder if we could, each of us, tell the group about some thoughts that occurred to us in this silence which we thought of saying but didn't." The exercise is more effective, incidentally, if the therapist himself starts it or participates. For example, "I've been feeling antsy in the silence, wanting to break it, not wanting to waste time, but on the other hand feeling irritated that it always has to be me doing this work for the group," or "I've been feeling torn between wanting to get back to the struggle between you and me, Mike. I feel uncomfortable with this much tension and anger, but I don't know yet, how to help understand and resolve it." When I feel there has been a particularly great deal unsaid in a meeting, I have often used, with success, a technique such as

this: "It's now six o'clock and we still have a half an hour left, but I wonder if you each would imagine that it is already six thirty and that you're on your way home. What kind of disappointments would you have about the meeting today?" (pp. 137–138).

Handling Group-Resistant Episodes

If counselors video record sessions, they may, after a group-resistant incident, merely say, "Let's roll the tape back a few minutes, and, perhaps if we observe ourselves for a few minutes, we will be able to figure out what we need to say to whom to make it easier for each of us to talk about what's really bothering us." Counselors also may ask the group to review what they think is expected of them on occasions like this, what each has accomplished, and what each has left to do. Usually, such a request calls forth a commitment from individuals similar to that called for in the intake interview. It also may cause members to question whether certain members have the essential commitment required for membership. When this occurs the counselor may be tempted to schedule an intake for all or just those members about whom the other members have doubts. Inasmuch as this is a group decision, it is much better to help members get the problem out into the open, giving the questionable members a chance to demonstrate their commitment to discussing their problems and to learning their desired new behaviors.

Frequently such discussions clarify doubtful members' goals and convey to them others' commitment to helping them change. When, however, they choose to drop out or are asked to leave, the problem can be handled in such a manner that they leave with a clearer notion of what is required of them to change; the consequences of failure to change; increased confidence in their potential for learning new behaviors; and increased appreciation of why others cannot and should not allow them to block their growth. When the group permits the doubtful client to remain on probation, the counselor must help them state precisely what their new expected behaviors will be to remain and achieve full membership again. Usually, when even reluctant clients are treated so honestly and are given a chance to demonstrate their readiness for growth, they come through convincingly—or voluntarily withdraw from the group. Thus group cohesiveness is used to cope with group resistance. Within the basic treatment model described in Chapter 1, group cohesiveness need not be feared as Slavson (1957) suggested it is in psychoanalytic groups.

NEED FOR STRUCTURE

What in the early group sessions may appear to be group resistance may actually be clients' reactions to inadequate structuring. From their research with World War II veteran outpatients, Powdermaker and Frank (1953) concluded that intense competition results from *too little* structure, but that clients are inhibited by *too much* structure. For coping with resistance they recommended that:

1. The therapist give the group considerable responsibility for coping with resistance, especially when there is a patient with initiative with whom the resistant patient can identify. In such a case, she can devote her efforts to facilitating the process of identification. Often this is best done by maintaining an interested silence. Therapy also is often facilitated when the therapist does not attempt to meet a challenge from a resistant patient but leaves it to the group.
2. In a newly formed group, the therapist should not pressure a withdrawn patient to talk about himself until others have set an example. In a mature group, she may not need to be concerned about this, since others will have already done so.
3. In a newly formed group, the therapist should provide support to the resisting patient when the group fails to provide it. Essentially, support consists of taking the patient seriously and conveying the idea that members want to understand his problem and help him discuss it.
4. She should be alert for situations in which members of the group express feelings that seem to be similar to those of the resistant patient and call these similar feelings to the attention of the resisting client.
5. She should seize the opportunity to take advantage of a response by the resistant patient to any occurrence in the immediate situation related to his feelings.

Strupp and Binder (1984) have said:

> In long-term work, as a result of nonexistent time pressures, the therapist may be in greater danger of becoming a victim of passivity or lethargy. This may be true particularly with patients whose resistances are characterized, to varying degrees, by emotional aloofness. In turn, this may create a chronic, if subtle, state of boredom (masked as patience) in the therapist. We propose that each session be viewed as a minitherapy, with palpable progress as its aim. If no progress can be discerned, the therapist should scrutinize the process more intensely (p. 304).

CLIENT'S ROLE

Bry (1951) also encouraged the therapist to help the group deal with the resisting client. Early in the life of the group she encouraged the therapist to devote considerable effort to helping patients understand why the phenomenon occurs; how it may be detected in oneself and others; and how they may respond to resistance. With such preparation she says that patients learn to manage it and to use it to detect therapeutic material. When, for example, patients exhibit protectiveness, sooner or later the other patients detect what is happening and urge the resisting client to stop "beating around the bush."

On the other hand, Bry believes that there are situations in which the therapist must take over. She says that this is usually required in the early stages of the group; but it also may be necessary later when the resistance results from an unusually complex situation or when members of the group do not recognize it. When this occurs the counselor should use process statements to share with the group what has happened: "I noticed that when Sam was talking about his relationship with his wife, he got very angry. When that happened the group seemed to pull away, to back off. I stopped Sam from sharing his anger further at this point because I want us to review what this means for each of you, how it fits in with the concerns you've got." Among those types of behavior that patients do not tend to recognize are intellectualization and advice giving.

Bry claims that the objective is to recognize and overcome resistance in order to proceed with the task of understanding the nature of the basic conflict and/or unfinished business with the significant other. Her interpretations are directed at the basic anxieties as well as toward the characteristic defense mechanism used. With reference to acting out, she interprets it immediately and focuses attention on the emotions displayed. Though she relies heavily on the use of interpretation, she realizes the therapist must take cognizance of her treatment goals and the patient's readiness to accept and use that which is uncovered by the interpretation.

Client Empathy

Obviously, Bry is correct: clients can detect another client's resisting behavior and confront that client. Moreover, clients can use confrontation productively with each other. For us, better results tend to be achieved by teaching clients to empathize with the resisting client; to detect precisely what that person is feeling; and to reflect those feelings to help expose the resistance rather than to help them dig it out with a confrontation. Similar techniques are used to help clients recognize and to reflect resisting clients' underlying feelings associated with their tendency to act out (also resistance). They learn to accept readily why, whenever possible, they should try to detect and to reflect desires to act out and to help others discuss those feelings openly prior to acting out on them impulsively, thereby having to deal with the resulting guilt. They also recognize readily why acting out decreases a client's motivation to face and resolve the problems associated with acting out. However, this type of discussion can become very attractive to clients and can be used by them to divert their attention away from relevant therapeutic material.

In any event, clients will pressure the resisting client to talk when they want to help him or when they are not certain they can trust him until he has shared his problems with them. However, it is questionable whether the counselor should encourage other clients to put the resisting client "on the hot seat." A few have even gone so far as to designate a given chair for the resisting client when it is his turn to face up to the problems that he seems to be resisting to face. Rather than trying to force such a client to talk, the counselor should help the other clients encourage him to talk. In order to profit fully from the therapeutic interaction within his group, every client must play two roles simultaneously: helper and client—listening very carefully to what other clients say; helping the speaker express clearly what is being experienced; allowing the speaker's discussion to uncover therapeutic material within the person; and dealing with personal problems as they come into awareness.

In psychoanalysis, interpretation is the primary method used to cope with resistance. Perhaps better results can be obtained by use of reflection to help clients surface their feelings related to resistance, learn to manage them, and use them as energy for change. The four reasons that were presented in Chapter 1 for using reflection in preference to interpretation apply to management of resistance, too: (1) Clients are encouraged to assume more responsibility for their own growth; (2) they feel more like a partner in the process rather than someone who is treated by a superior; (3) reflection focuses upon underlying feelings and harnesses them for change rather than encouraging clients to intellectualize; and (4) clients often feel attacked when a counselor or therapist interprets their behavior.

Adolescents are especially sensitive and vulnerable to any adult's judgment of their worth (Ackerman, 1955). Except for the dependent client, adolescents resent the air of superiority conveyed by interpretation. On the other hand, genuine participation in the recognition and management of their own resistance to growth enhances clients' self-respect; makes them more sensitive to underlying feelings in other situations that produce conflict and misunderstandings; and generally improves their relationship skills outside of their counseling group. They become more sensitive to their own inner feelings and learn to manage them more effectively.

SUMMARY

Resistance is a natural phenomenon in the therapeutic process that occurs when clients are threatened by change. Its impact can be minimized by carefully preparing clients for the therapeutic experience, by helping them accept responsibility for talking openly, by helping them learn new behaviors and by teaching them to help others change. Perhaps nothing reinforces these commitments as much as the increased self-respect they feel when they discuss their problems openly; discover that they can learn specific new behaviors; realize the extent to which they are admired and accepted for facing painful material early; and sense the degree to which members can learn to provide a quality support system.

When resistance is first observed by the counselors she tries to detect precisely how the resisting client feels, to reflect those feelings, and to provide quality support while the client discusses those feelings. Immediately after her first successful experience in helping a client cope with his feelings of resistance, the counselor describes the phenomenon, describes how it is exhibited, explains why it occurs, and describes what clients can do to help each other deal with it. The need to resist is further reduced when clients observe peers modeling self-disclosure and behavior change.

Resisting clients usually are reacting to the fear of change, the fear that the change will be too painful, or the fear that the change will not be for the good. When, therefore, the counselor detects the resisting client's feelings behind the resistance, she is less inclined to feel rejected, unappreciated, frustrated, and angry. Consequently, she can more effectively use her energy to help the resisting client share his fears, sense the group's real support, and try to learn desired new behaviors. She also learns to use her responses to the resisting client to better understand the resisting client and to help him—and to teach others to help him. Clients do learn readily to recognize others' resistance and use it therapeutically—and to recognize and cope with their own resistance.

REFERENCES

Ackerman, N. W. (1955). Group pschotherapy with a mixed group of adolescents. *International Journal of Group Psychotherapy, 5,* 249–260.

Bach, G. R. (1954). *Intensive group psychotherapy.* New York: Ronald.

Bergman, J. (1985). *Fishing for barracuda.* New York: Norton.

Bry, T. (1951). Varieties of resistance in group psychotherapy. *International Journal of Group Psychotherapy, 1,* 106–114.

Corey, G.; Corey, M.; Callanan, P.; & Russell, J. (1982). *Group techniques.* Monterey, CA: Brooks/Cole.

Davanloo, H. (1980). *Short-term dynamic psychotherapy.* New York: Jason Aronson.

Egan, G. (1982). *The skilled helper: Models, skills, and methods for effective helping* (2nd ed.). Monterey, CA: Brooks/Cole.

Fleischman, M.; Horne, A.; & Arthur, J. (1983). *Troubled families: A treatment program.* Champaign, IL: Research Press.

Freedman, M. B., & Sweet, B. S. (1954). Some specific features of group psychotherapy and their implications for selection of patients. *International Journal of Group Psychotherapy, 4,* 355–368.

Goodman, M.; Marks, M.; & Rockberger, H. (1964). Resistance in group psychotherapy enhanced by countertransference reactions of a therapist: A peer group experience. *International Journal of Group Psychotherapy, 14,* 332–343.

Larrabee, M. J. (1982). Working with reluctant clients through affirmation techniques. *Personnel & Guidance Journal, 61,* 105–109.

Osborn, H. (1949). Some factors of resistance which affect group participation. *The Group, 2,* 2–4, 9–11.

Powdermaker, F. B., & Frank, J. D. (1953). *Group psychotherapy*. Cambridge, MA: Harvard University Press.

Ruppel, G., & Kaul, T. (1982). Investigation of social influence theory's conception of client resistance. *Journal of Counseling Psychology, 29*, 232–239.

Schlesinger, H. (1982). Resistance as a process. In P. Wachtel (Ed.), *Resistance in psychodynamic and behavioral therapies* (pp. 25–44). New York: Plenum.

Slavson, S. R. (1957). Are there group dynamics in therapy groups? *International Journal of Group Psychotherapy, 7*, 131–154.

Spinks, S., & Birchler, G. (1982). Behavioral-systems marital therapy: Dealing with resistance. *Family Process, 2*, 169–185.

Strupp, H., & Binder, J. (1984). *Psychotherapy in a new key*. New York: Basic Books.

Weiner, M. F. (1983). The assessment and resolution of impasse in group psychotherapy. *International Journal of Group Psychotherapy, 33*, 313–332.

Yalom, I. D. (1985). *The theory and practice of group psychotherapy* (3rd ed.). New York: Basic Books.

8

TRANSFERENCE AND COUNTERTRANSFERENCE

THE NATURE OF TRANSFERENCE

Transference is displacement of affect from one person to another. Whenever a client assigns another the role of a significant other with whom she has unfinished business and treats him as though he were that person she is experiencing transference. That significant other need not be someone from her early childhood. It may be a spouse, friend, lover, fellow worker, supervisor, or a teacher as well as a parent or sibling. It may be that she failed to say important goodbyes; that she let a relationship die which could have offered great potential; that she failed to convey how deeply she appreciated a relationship and/or something a valued friend did for her; that she had hurt someone or was hurt by someone (unfinished business).

Glatzer (1965) described transference as an unconscious attempt to imbue relationships with old attitudes that are inappropriate for those present. Nevertheless she recognized that transference is not confined to the therapist and the therapeutic session. It occurs among clients in the group and with others outside their therapeutic group. Glatzer claims that deeply neurotic patients are unable to love tenderly because their unconscious fantasies are so centered around the oedipal and pre-oedipal figures that they feel guilty about these fantasies. Though they need very much to belong, neurotic patients often have concluded that it is dangerous to trust others and seek intimacy. Therefore, their transference objects are both loved and feared. Neurotics require the assistance of fellow clients as well as their counselor to work through these feelings in order to give and accept love.

Transference occurs whenever a patient seeks to satisfy unfulfilled regressive needs with inappropriate persons (Bach, 1957). They do not necessarily limit themselves to reexperiencing early childhood experiences; fellow clients also entice each other into dealing with their here-and-now unfulfilled needs or unfinished business with significant others. The counselor who treats clients in groups not only must recognize transference and develop a client's readiness to complete her unfinished business with significant others, but he must teach her fellow clients to recognize it and help him to help her complete it.

The Group as Surrogate Family

Brown and Beletsis (1986) believe that there is a natural tendency for clients treated in groups to view their counseling group as the family of origin and to behave in their group as they did in their families. They believe that their clients (adult children of alcoholics) recognized intuitively that by joining such a group they awakened a bond to their families in the long-term interest of achieving a physical and emotional separation not accomplished at the appropriate time in their development. They appreciated being with fellow clients who were suffering with similar problems and fears. These clients recognized that they needed to go back, to say what really happened, to feel that intensive bonding, and to complete their unfinished business. Such clients also require the encouragement and support of fellow clients to develop self-confidence and interpersonal skills to complete their unfinished business.

Transference within the Group

Thus, the classic analytic definition of transference can account for only part of what occurs. Much of the interaction within a counseling group is a reaction to reality. The transference object may look like, and even behave much like, the client's significant other with whom she has unfinished business. When, therefore, either a male client or counselor responds to a shy, naive female with understanding and acceptance, and facilitates her discussion of her feelings for him, this may be her most-wholesome interaction with a male. Consequently, she responds to him; and it is difficult to tell whether she is responding to him personally or to him as a transference object. Bach (1957) noted that it is difficult even for an experienced therapist to distinguish between unreal projections and justified reactions, between healthy self-assertions and acting out of infantile wishes. On the other hand, clients also react negatively when they are bombarded with transference demands. In addition to helping clients recognize and manage such reactions, they also can be taught to report how it feels to be used as transference objects and to discuss why individuals want to be loved or rejected for what they are and for what they have done, rather than as transference objects.

Case Example

Under the right circumstances, perhaps everyone assigns another the role of a significant other with whom he has unfinished business, and responds to that person as though he or she were that significant other. After using role playing to prepare him to complete his unfinished buisness, Stephen (case example in Chapter 5) described this phenomenon to transference as follows:

> At first I thought to myself Connie [a fellow client] reminds me of Debbie [his former girlfriend]. Then without realizing what was happening I began reacting to Connie as Debbie; it was like I put a mask of Debbie's face on Connie and began reacting very warmly to her as Debbie.

Perhaps this explains why a person spontaneously likes some new acquaintances and dislikes others.

THE COUNSELOR'S NEEDS

A counselor's own needs, values, clinical experience, and professional preparation all influence the degree to which he knowingly or unknowingly elicits transference. Very likely, and perhaps unconsciously, he reinforces certain client behaviors and discourages other behaviors (later in the chapter, we explain why we strongly endorse peer supervision). The nature and extent of transference elicited from clients in his groups seem to depend on how he answers questions such as: Does he believe that he knows what most of his clients should do in order to function better? What does he do to involve clients in the definition of their therapeutic goals? How does he involve clients in the process of selecting clients and of managing the group? What criteria does he use to select clients for the group? Does he convey to clients what will be expected from them in the group and what they can expect from others, or does he do only the minimum of structuring—perhaps deliberately leaving expectations rather ambiguous? How do dependent clients make him feel? What does he do to reinforce clients' dependency? Is it important for him to impress clients with his insightful interpretations? How does he encourage clients to use his or their fellow clients as transference objects? Does he encourage clients to express their feelings to each other? To what extent does he encourage clients to discuss early childhood experiences rather than to discuss their current problems? What does he do that may suggest to clients that they must understand why they behaved as they have in the past before they can learn new behavior? What does he do to encourage clients to be good helpers? How does he teach clients to accept responsibility for developing and maintaining a therapeutic climate in the group, for learning their own desired new behaviors, and for appraising their own growth?

Ambiguity evokes transference. The more unstructured or ambiguous the situation is, and the more all-powerful the counselor is perceived to be, the more clients will project and experience transference (Patterson, 1959). Even when the counselor tries not to be ambiguous and involves clients in the selection of clients and in managing the therapeutic process, he is still a very special person in the group. Hannah (1984) states:

> ... The uniqueness of the group lies in its interpersonal nature with the opportunity for the experience and clarification of the patient's abject relationships and the conflicts and emotions related to them. In this regard the therapist takes on the challenge of providing an environment and a type of abject relationship that the patient most probably has not experienced in a sustained or reliable manner.
>
> The therapist accepts and attempts to understand the communications of each patient and of the entire group; ... and demonstrates to the group whenever possible the link between inner feelings and behavior (p. 375).

IMPACT OF THE GROUP

In a counseling group, clients do not perceive their counselor as ambiguous, or as a blank screen the way a patient does lying on a couch or in more traditional therapy. Clients observe how he reacts to clients as well as how he attempts to help them. They recognize that he is a real person with his own feelings, values, needs, and expectations. Where the counselor sits and what he does, as well as his words, determine what clients expect from him. If he sits in an open circle of chairs, occupies a chair like the clients, and encourages them to react frankly to him as they do to fellow clients, he will be accepted more as a member. On the other hand, even a group-centered counselor is someone special whose words are valued more than other members. Clients do, and should, expect him to describe the conditions under which he seems to be most effective and to teach them to be good clients, to be good helpers, and to help develop and maintain therapeutic norms in their group. The way he involves them in achieving these conditions determines the degree to which he makes them dependent on him and himself a primary transference object.

Where the counselor works in an institutional setting, such as a school or college, and prospective clients may meet him first in another role such as a teacher, he must convey early what will be unique about his relationship to them as a counselor in a group. Nevertheless, while they are clients in his group he should not have responsibility for evaluating or disciplining them. On the other hand, the institutional setting offers the advantage for him to describe his services in a presentation and answer prospective clients' questions even before they schedule an intake interview.

Finally, the counselor can never be completely objective in his relationships with every client. Participation in group counseling as a client (especially with other counselors) can increase his awareness of his own needs, values, expectations of himself and his clients, and his own unresolved problems. Besides facilitating his own personal growth, participation as a client in a counseling group also can help him discover how these factors influence his effectiveness as a counselor. Moreover, Goodman, Marks, and Rockberger (1964) make a strong case for peer supervision. In particular, they argue for peer supervision to help counselors detect and manage countertransference. Continuing professional growth on the job is still another argument for peer supervision.

MANAGING TRANSFERENCE

When clients are encouraged to accept responsibility for their own growth and for maintenance of a therapeutic climate as suggested in Chapter 1, clients can learn to recognize and manage transference. Beginning with the very first group sessions, clients are taught to communicate, considerately, positive as well as negative feelings to the members of their group, and to develop the interpersonal skills required to complete their unfinished business with significant others. Whenever any member suspects that another member is experiencing transference, the observer is encouraged to help that person express her feelings to her transference object and, where problems arise, to resolve their problems.

Case Example (revisited)

Recall the incidence of Stephen talking about transference with Connie. The counselor then could try to involve fellow clients in helping Stephen decide whether or not he was experiencing transference by a comment such as:

> Now that you have learned to express your real feelings to Connie, we are wondering whether or not you were experiencing Connie as Debbie and whether you have some unfinished business with Debbie that you'd like to complete. Perhaps you would be willing to tell us what that unfinished business with Debbie is and use role playing to prepare you to complete that unfinished business with Debbie.

First, then, Stephen is encouraged to deal directly with his transference object. If he decides that he has been experiencing transference, then he will be encouraged to use role playing to help him develop the courage, self-confidence, and interpersonal skills required to confront the relevant significant other and complete their finished business.

Application

Usually when clients have been taught to recognize transference, they can detect when someone else is experiencing transference. Once the first client has successfully dealt with transference, members of the group are encouraged to explore how it feels to be treated as a transference object. Even the more-traditional group therapists have noticed that clients treated in groups tend to focus on their present relationships rather than on early childhood problems. Inasmuch as adolescents usually are primarily concerned with present and future, it may explain why some therapists have concluded that adolescents rarely experience transference in group therapy. Our experience is that once they understand the phenomenon, they admit to experiencing it. However, their unfinished business tends to be with persons with whom they are currently having problems.

Interpretation of Transference

On the other hand, classic analysis encourages transference with the therapist, and to a lesser degree with the other members of their group, and uses interpretation of it as a central element in the treatment.

Glatzer (1965) succinctly described this process as follows:

> As the patient repeats his infantile relationships in his relationship to the analyst, his buried feelings emerge and become accessible to interpretation. The repetition of the infantile conflicts under controlled analytic conditions enables the maturing ego to reevaluate and handle more objectively the early repressed conflicts (p. 167).

Fried (1965) noted that there is a rather pronounced tradition among group therapists to focus attention on the transference objects. She believes this focus is of limited value; that, instead, the therapist should help the patient understand the emotions being transferred—especially the related, entrenched defenses.

When a counselor or therapist uses interpretation, he enhances his status in the group, thereby making clients more dependent. Use of interpretation also tends to encourage clients to expect prescriptions: to be told what to do. Clients also often find that it is easier to discuss their past, to discover the crucial elements that shaped their behavior, and to discover why they continue their unproductive behavior, than it is to discuss their pain and to define the new behaviors to be learned. As a matter of fact, clients often know what they should do, but they lack the courage, self-confidence, and interpersonal skills required to implement their desired new behaviors. Fellow clients can provide essential support as a client struggles to implement desired new behaviors. When she fails in this endeavor, she is assisted in appraising why she failed and what she must learn to increase her chances for success, and in determining whether she should try again to implement the previously selected solution or select a new one to be implemented. In other words, they help her learn from her failures as well as to celebrate her successes.

The Transference Object

When transference is elicited, clients are more apt to act out impulses toward the transference object and the person with whom they have unfinished business. (For example, a client attacks her foreman who is a hurtful authority figure.) Such acting out does reveal therapeutic material that can be dealt with afterwards; nevertheless, it should be prevented whenever possible. Prevention protects the transference object (and sometimes the relevant person) from being hurt and the client from the subsequent guilt and natural consequences. When these complications are avoided, it is also easier to help the client discuss her feelings for the relevant person, discover new ways of relating to that significant other, and complete her unfinished business with him.

Within the Group

Naturally, counselors are concerned about the impact of transference on the transference object. Though a client may be hurt, frightened, or confused, she can certainly learn to cope with these problems in a counseling group. When the counselor discovers that the transference object is having difficulty accepting the roles he has been assigned by the client expressing transference, he may use a reflection to facilitate his management of the situation: "You can't understand why she responded to you as she did," or "Her responses don't seem to be appropriate for you." In other words, the counselor begins by helping the persons involved deal with their feelings for each other without even labeling them as transference. After these feelings have been dealt with, the counselor may use a reflection again to alert the transference object to what is happening and help her accept it: "It seems like she assigned you another's role and began treating you as though you were that person." To the client experiencing transference, the counselor may say: "Perhaps you could tell us who he reminded you of. And then, let us help you decide what unfinished business you have with him and what you must do to prepare yourself to complete that business with him."

Outside the Group

With clear expectations, minimal use of interpretation, and primary focus on the here-and-now, much of the dependency that clients often experience in treatment groups can be prevented. A client is less inclined to become dependent when the counselor selects her with great care; prepares her to accept responsibility for her own and fellow clients' growth; communicates confidence in her ability to profit from treatment; and teaches her fellow clients to reinforce independent behavior. Throughout the process, clients learn to cope with transference and related dependency and develop the skills to complete their unfinished business with their significant others rather than merely understanding why they experience transference. Moreover, what clients learn about this phenomenon must be generalized and applied outside their counseling groups. During counseling, clients are encouraged to note instances in which they experienced transference outside of counseling and learn to use their new knowledge to discover with whom they have what unfinished business and what they must do to complete it. Even when a good friendship results from positive transference, it tends to lack quality and depth. The transference object often feels at least slightly uncomfortable because the relationship was not fully earned. He is loved as a transference object rather than as a friend who earned the love.

COUNTERTRANSFERENCE

What is countertransference? When the counselor assigns a client in his group the role of a significant other *with whom he has unfinished business* and responds to her as though she were that significant other, he is experiencing countertransference. Inasmuch as he is not fully congruent, he can neither send a completely clear message nor hear accurately what the transference object says. Consequently, his communications with that particular client are apt to be distorted.

According to Crasilneck and Hall (1985), countertransference is the distortion of clients in the mind of the counselor. They contend that there is no more-evident example of this than the therapist experiencing a light trance while working with a patient.

Hannah (1984) believes countertransference includes all the emotional responses that the counselor or therapist has toward his clients. Furthermore, the recognition and management of these responses may determine how accurately he perceives clients and how effectively he facilitates their growth.

Detecting Countertransference

Based upon Korner's (1950) and Cohen's (1952) papers, we formulated the following questions that a counselor may use to detect his own countertransference and teach his clients to use to detect it:

1. Do I have an unreasonable dislike or excessive liking for a particular client?
2. Do I have an overemotional reaction to her pain?
3. Do I dread a treatment session that includes her?
4. Do I experience undue concern for her between sessions?
5. Do my thoughts wander and/or do I have difficulty focusing my attention on her communications?
6. Do I have difficulty comprehending what this client is trying to convey?
7. Do I become impatient with this client's progress?
8. Do I feel at a loss how to help her?
9. Do I feel insensitive or indifferent to her needs?

10. Am I bored with her?
11. Do I feel too protective of her?
12. Where did I distort her communications?

Whenever a counselor notes any of these feelings he should *listen to a recording* (preferably a video one) *of that session with a trusted colleague* to analyze the nature of his participation, to detect his emotional reactions, and identify distortions in his communications. Goodman et al. (1964) contend that countertransference distorts the counselor's communications and interferes with his ability to manage resistance. They encourage counselors to use peer supervision to cope with countertransference.

PEER SUPERVISION

Whether a counselor who has completed the group counseling course and the practicum in group counseling applies his new knowledge and skills on the job seems to be determined largely by whether or not his supervisor believes group counseling is effective, encourages him to use it, and provides quality supervision, and/or encourages peer supervision. Some counselors and therapists have elected to seek peer supervision from respected colleagues employed in neighboring schools and/or agencies rather than from their own agency. Where we have helped counselors organize peer supervision, we have encouraged the use of video recordings—otherwise, much valuable and subtle data are missed. In preparation for the supervision period, we urge the counselor seeking feedback to use a worksheet which consists of six columns:

1. *Therapeutic material revealed by a client.* (We urge the supervisee to transcribe the client's statements and significant nonverbal behaviors.)
2. *The counselor's response to the therapeutic material* (if any). He can expect that there will be times when the therapeutic material will not be detected. Hence, no response will have been made to it. Furthermore, when the counselor is experiencing countertransference he may not either hear accurately or respond therapeutically.
3. *Alternate responses.* Responses that he wishes he would have made.
4. *Client's goals.* Responses that were made or could have been made to help the client formulate a goal for a particular pain.
5. *Mini-goals.* Reflections that were made or could have been made to help the client identify first steps to be taken to achieve her larger goal.
6. *Genuine feelings.* Feelings he thinks he may have been experiencing at that moment during the session.

Usually, we encourage the counselor to view the entire tape and complete as much of these six columns as he can prior to analyzing the tape with the assistance of his supervisor (regardless of whether he is a peer or official supervisor). Thus, we encourage the counselor to initiate the diagnostic process; noting, especially, *instances in which he recognized that he required assistance.* Moreover, the use of this worksheet encourages his supervisor to *provide him with specific input* that enables him *to formulate better responses in the very next session.* Such a simple worksheet helps counselors recognize new therapeutic material; clarify clients' goals, formulate new goals, and develop mini-goals; obtain suggestions for coping with difficult instances; recognize countertransference and manage it; and formulate precise goals for both professional and personal growth.

The Ideal Model

Best results tend to be achieved when the supervisor perceives supervision as a leadership function rather than as a regulatory function. He stresses support, encouragement, and reinforcement of desired new behaviors rather than criticism, evaluation, and enforcement of the institution's policies. The counselor believes that his supervisor respects him, genuinely wants to help him, and is competent to help him. Besides exhibiting such caring, the supervisor helps him define specific behavioral goals for improving his helping skills, recognizes his strengths, and builds new competencies upon them. Under these conditions it is easier for the counselor to recall how he really felt in completing column 6 above, to admit his mistakes, and to request assistance with troublesome situations.

Participation in a counseling group as a client, both during the practicum in group counseling and the beginning of a group-counseling program on the job, helps a counselor recognize and cope with countertransference. Besides experiencing how it feels to be a client in a group, he learns how clients can be helped in a group; discovers how they expedite and block each other's growth; and observes how an experienced counselor facilitates the growth process.

Such experiences, in both peer supervision and as a client in a counseling group, help the counselor accept the notion that he does not have to perform perfectly. Though he is a human being with unfulfilled needs and unresolved problems that interfere with his effectiveness as a counselor, he, too, can learn to function better personally as well as professionally.

Acknowledging Countertransference

Whenever a counselor notes any of the symptoms that suggest countertransference during a session, he must learn to manage it for the rest of that session. He must determine what the distracting feelings are (see column 6, above), who triggered them, and how to disengage himself in order to respond productively to his clients. Bob's case, below, illustrates why sometimes the problem becomes progressively worse until the counselor acknowledges it.

Case Example

Bob was married; but he convinced the counselor to admit him to a single-parent's group whose members had sought counseling to cope better with their gifted, underachieving, ninth-grade sons. Whereas most of the women were college graduates, only one of the men (Chuck) had attended college. During the first eight sessions, all of the clients except Bob openly discussed their pain and worked hard to implement their desired new behaviors. Several times Bob had criticized fellow clients for stressing improved school achievement. He belittled the value of college education and frequently complained about his college professor's wife's ambitions for their son, an only child.

At the beginning of the ninth session, two of the women and one man shared some successes concerning their sons. Then Chuck said, "I can't seem to get my kid excited about improving his school grades. He doesn't seem to give a damn. He is doing the same thing I did in high school. I don't mind working two jobs to save enough money to send him to college, but it really gripes me that he won't do what is required to prepare himself for college." The counselor (Jane) responded to Chuck as follows: "You'd like for him to have it better than you have had it." That set Bob off and he attacked the counselor as follows: "So you think that college graduates are better than the rest of us—that you are better than I am. If you are so damn good why don't you tell Chuck what to do." Jane paused for several moments, then said to the group, "I need some time to collect my thoughts, to think about why Bob reminds me of my brother; to decide who I will respond to first—Chuck or Bob; and to decide how I can respond to Bob's anger in a way that will encourage him to discuss his real pain openly."

After several more minutes, Jane turned to Bob and said, "I guess you don't believe that I am really trying to understand how you feel; that I am also concerned about helping these very bright boys learn to achieve; that doing well in school is better than being a top-flight plumber." This evoked another attack on the counselor by Bob in which he said no one had been helped. At the end of it he threatened to quit the group. Though heretofore other clients let him bully them, this time they really told him off. After everyone *had* been given a chance to respond, Jane turned to Bob and said:

> I am pleased that the others now feel strong enough not to let you bully them anymore. Nevertheless, I'd like you to continue counseling in our group if you can develop the courage and self-confidence to discuss what really worries and upsets you and allow us to help you learn the new behaviors which you decide that you must learn to be a better father, husband, and friend. You have made it very difficult for us to like you, but I for one will give you another chance to develop a positive relationship with me.

The Outcome

After a brief discussion of their feelings for Bob, and his for them, one of the women asked Bob to discuss his real worries and concerns. They listened and responded therapeutically (to his obvious surprise). Had her clients dwelt on Jane's unfinished business with her brother, she would have explained that now that she is aware of it she will assume responsibility for completing it; and if she concludes that she needs professional help in doing it, she will seek counseling for herself: they have purchased her time as a helper rather than as a client. She had leveled with them to clear the air and thus disengaged herself from her own problems sufficiently to be a productive helper. She also provided support for the other clients and communicated to Bob what would be required of him to profit from further counseling. Perhaps she should have offered to schedule a special individual session to help him appraise his readiness to profit from counseling, to practice talking therapeutically, and to formulate clearer, more behaviorally oriented goals.

MANAGING COUNTERTRANSFERENCE

Frequently, when a counselor detects countertransference in a group, he can merely sit back for a few moments and listen to the interaction until he tunes back into it. Sometimes the counselor needs to ask clients to review what occurred in the group during the period in which he was distracted by countertransference. Occasionally, he may need to admit that he was distracted by his own unfinished business in order to disengage himself sufficiently to function well therapeutically.

The more effectively the counselor involves his clients in the therapeutic process; teaches them to be good helpers as well as good clients; teaches them to recognize transference and manage it; and encourages them to give him feedback in order to increase his effectiveness as a helper, the more readily they will respond to help him recognize and manage countertransference. They can accept him as a human being with unfinished business with significant others. Though some clients will want the counselor to discuss his own pain openly and let them help him complete his unfinished business, they can accept the notion that this is their time—that they have paid for his professional services. However, they usually are pleased to have their counselor report back that he did follow through to complete his own unfinished business and whether professional assistance was required in order for him to achieve it.

SUMMARY

An individual is experiencing transference when she assigns someone the role of a significant other with whom she has unfinished business and responds to that person as though he or she were that significant other.

Instead of eliciting transference and using interpretation to help clients work it through, we encourage counselors first to help clients learn to relate to their transference object, then to use role playing with them to prepare the person experiencing transference to complete her unfinished business with relevant significant others.

When the counselor experiences transference with a client, we label it countertransference. Inasmuch as he teaches clients to recognize and manage this phenomenon and be active participants in the therapeutic process, he encourages them to help him detect and manage countertransference, Whenever he, or a client, detects countertransference, he must determine what distracted him; who triggered these feelings; and how to disengage himself in order to function therapeutically for the rest of that counseling session. We strongly endorse the notion of counselors using peer supervision to help them recognize and manage countertransference. We described a technique that can be used, with video recordings, to achieve this end.

REFERENCES

Bach, G. R. (1957). Observations on transference and object relations in the light of group dynamics. *The International Journal of Group Psychotherapy, 7,* 64–76.

Brown, S., & Beletsis, S. (1986). The development of family transference in groups for the adult children of alcoholics. *International Journal of Group Psychotherapy, 36,* 97–114.

Cohen, M. B. (1952). Countertransference and anxiety. *Psychiatry, 15,* 231–243.

Crasilneck, H. B., & Hall, J. A. (1985). *Clinical hypnosis: Principles and applications.* New York: Grune & Stratton.

Fried, E. (1965). Some aspects of group dynamics and the analysis of transference and defenses. *The International Journal of Group Psychotherapy, 15,* 44–56.

Glatzer, H. T. (1965). Aspects of transference in group psychotherapy. *The International Journal of Group Psychotherapy, 15,* 167–176.

Goodman, M.; Marks, M.; & Rockberger, H. (1964). Resistance in group psychotherapy enhanced by the countertransference reaction of the therapist. *The International Journal of Group Psychotherapy, 14,* 332–343.

Hannah, S. (1984). Countertransference in inpatient group psychotherapy: Implications for technique. *The International Journal of Group Psychotherapy, 34,* 257–272.

Korner, I. J. (1950). Ego involvement and the process of disengagement. *Journal of Consulting Psychology, 14,* 206–209.

Patterson, C. H. (1959). *Counseling and psychotherapy: Theory and practice.* New York: Harper & Row.

9

CHALLENGING CLIENTS: THE EMOTIONALLY DEBILITATED

The emotional issues and difficulties that clients bring to the group are often, if not always, a source of challenge to all who attempt to offer help. The beginning counselor, taking a group practicum and leading a group for the first time, may be especially challenged by clients presenting intense emotional debility. The sources of challenge and/or difficulty seem to be based on a combination of suppositions and perceptions regarding emotional states, some of which have their roots in cultural norms and prescriptions stating how, what, with whom, and under what conditions various emotions may be expressed.

In this chapter, the counselor's attention is directed to emotionally debilitated clients: the grieved, dying, anxious, or crisis victim, the hostile, the depressed, and the learning disabled.

EMOTIONAL DEBILITATION

Several sources of challenge can be found in the background, or underlying reactions, to the individual in a state of debilitation. Human beings often fear the intensity of emotional expression. Some of this fear is based in the belief that once the dike of emotional suppression is released, they will lose themselves in their emotional release and be totally controlled by their emotions. Additionally, the debilitated may be suspicious that others see them as weak or crazy for releasing such emotional intensity, and ''being out of control''; a belief that is based in their own perceptions regarding emotional expression.

Chronic Suppression

Often, individuals with a history of chronic suppression and/or emotional denial will rationalize to the group that they do not believe the group could possibly understand, or even care to understand, the depth of their emotional pain.

Case Example

The case of Mr. D. illustrates these emotional dynamics. Mr. D. had, for years, a marked feeling of grief and depression over the loss of his wife. When Mr. D. reported his wife's death, it was from a distant cognitive position, and when members attempted to reach him on the level of emotional intensity that he had hidden behind his defenses, he would withdraw and rationalize that the group could not possibly understand, and what good would all that do anyway; while ignoring the fact that he was stuck in his life, neither able to move forward nor effectively deal with the trauma of his past. His life simply went on without joy, pleasure, or fulfillment. He was emotionally frozen.

Hopelessness

An underlying feeling often accompanying the emotional conditions described above is one of hopelessness. The emotionally debilitated client may feel that nothing can be done; that this is how life is—and how it will remain. He may, as well, fear vulnerability in front of others: being overexposed to ridicule or rejected. The norms of openness and value for the expression of feelings in a particular group, especially early in a group's development, may not be sufficiently clear to support a need for feeling safe enough to deal with the emotional intensity felt by a particular group member. Likewise, the goals for working through emotional states may not be concrete enough to demonstrate the benefits, or facilitate the process, of the emotional release. Working through and resolving emotional turmoils (loss of support, death of a loved one or pet, personal trauma, anxiety attacks or panics) may produce intense stress to the individual.

Dealing with Intense Emotions

The Counselor's Own

An inexperienced group leader, or one who has not dealt with her own emotional blocks or issues, often has difficulty when the group encounters individuals with intense emotional issues and debilitation. For example, a counselor may feel reluctant to involve the group due to a distrust of her own experience and lack of skill to facilitate what is seen as overwhelming emotional intensity—as in depth release of intense grief and depression. Such inexperienced leaders may wish to steer the group away from the issue or avoid it entirely by doing nothing.

Supervision is the key to assisting the group counselor in developing the skills necessary for working with the emotionally debilitated client. A particularly difficult emotional issue may often reveal important information for the growth and development of the group leader. Questions such as: (1) What are my uncomfortable feelings regarding this client's emotional condition? (2) What is his impact on me? (3) What clue or dynamics suggest countertransference? (4) How am I reacting as a transference object? (5) What is his impact on the other group members? (6) How can I use this information to help this person confront and work through this intense and debilitating emotional condition? (7) If he is having an antitherapeutic experience or impact, what may I do to cope successfully with it?

The Client's

As with other clients, a counselor must try to discover the answers to these questions about a difficult client: (1) What is unique about him? (2) Where does he hurt? (3) What unfulfilled needs does his behavior suggest? (4) How may I facilitate open discussion of these therapeutic materials? (5) How may I make a reflection that relates his pain and unsatisfied needs to desired new behaviors? (6) What may I do to sensitize the other clients to his therapeutic material and involve them in the therapeutic process? (7) And finally, if I am experiencing countertransference, what must I do to disengage myself and once again become therapeutically reengaged?

In order to involve the other clients in treating a difficult client, a counselor must search for the answers to questions such as: (1) What feelings does he have in common with other clients? (2) How may I respond to these common feelings and facilitate affiliative feelings among them? (3) How may I prepare him to request and use feedback from his fellow clients?

The Emotional Episode

There are times when everyone is at least temporarily disabled by debilitating emotions such as anger, anxiety, embarrassment, depression, disappointment, distress, failure, fear, grief, hate, loneliness, or self-doubt. On such occasions, one is tempted to blame others for one's emotional state, to withdraw or give up, or to act irresponsibly. Furthermore, it is tempting to feel sorry for and indulge in self-pity with these clients. That does not help them. Counselors who are most effective with such clients are able to detect the client's debilitating emotion; reflect it accurately; help that client discuss it; and decide what he must do to manage it more effectively. Usually, debilitating emotions involve significant others. Consequently, the client must decide precisely what he must do, and with whom, in order to cope with his debilitating emotion. Furthermore, he must come to believe that he can cope with these emotions and make the commitment to himself and to his group to behave responsibly.

Some clients also must express their hopeless feelings, explain what a rotten deal they got, or even explore whether or not they must express more revenge before they can take the risks required to honestly try to cope with the relevant process involved in learning the required new behaviors. In order to define the desired new behaviors and eventually act responsibly, clients must decide: (1) What are their alternative behaviors (to get off the dead center of their anxiety state)? (2) Which of the alternatives are most appropriate for them; fit their lifestyle? (3) What special satisfaction would each alternative action provide? (4) For which do they have the most confidence to act? (5) What new interpersonal skills must be learned to implement each alternative solution?

During the course of these episodes, some will appear too disorganized or discouraged to participate meaningfully and accept responsibility for their behavior. Even when clients are grieving, the counselor would do well to help them express their grief and begin exploring what they are willing to attempt now and when they will be willing to take more-responsible action in managing their own lives. Encouragement to act with the known support of the counseling group (and their help in developing a support system outside of their counseling group) is preferred to self-pity and no action. It is surprising what debilitated persons can do with such support. Nevertheless, some may still be unwilling to do anything for themselves until the group helps them explore the consequences of their failure to act (or to stop their irresponsible behavior).

THE GRIEVER

Freud suggests that grief is due to cathexis (bonding) by way of the libidinal energy invested in the love object as well as that which may resemble the love object or be associated with it. Recognizing the loss of such a love object causes the griever to obsess about the loved object, with the goal being to decathect from the libido in order to complete the work of mourning and free the ego. Abnormal grief reactions are seen as ambivalence toward the love object. The aggressive part of the ambivalence when turned inward produces depression (Freud, 1917).

Lindemann (1944) believes that grief reactions are composed of a five-component syndrome consisting of somatic complaints and problems; preoccupation with the image of the dead; guilt; hostility; and disorganized behavior. Grief syndrome may also be delayed, lasting for many years, or distorted such as becoming socially isolated, having hypochondriacal thoughts about the dead person's symptoms, and manic overactivity. The goal of grief work, according to Lindemann (1944), is the emancipation of the griever from the deceased, readjustment to the environment, and the formation of new relationships.

Bowlby (1969) believes that the grief states an individual experiences are similar to those seen in infant loss or separation, which are protest, despair, and detachment. The protest stage of a grieving person is characterized by searching, crying, anxiety, pining, total preoccupation with the loss, and hostility. As the grieving person begins to accept his loss, active searching and striving begins to give way to apathy and disorganized behavior. The final stage is complete when the person grieving begins to detach himself from the deceased and to adjust to his situations appropriately. Pathological reactions to grief are seen as a result of fixation in the first stage.

Behavioral approaches to grief work may be illustrated by the work of Gauthier and Marshall (1977). The antecedents or circumstances surrounding the loss are seen as crucial factors affecting the grief responses, such as the griever's predispositional condition entering grief, abruptness of loss, significance, availability of replacements, social reinforcement for grieving, and avoidance behaviors. They believe that grief work consists of shifting reinforcement for grieving to reinforcement for new activities and recovery.

The Nature of Grief

Clients seem to grieve for a number of reasons. Most experience loneliness and hopelessness for the future. Many feel helpless. Often, after a long illness of a loved one, the response to death may be relief, followed by feelings of guilt. Many also feel guilt and self-condemnation because they wish they had treated the deceased better or differently, or because they wonder whether everything possible had been done to save their lives. On the other hand, if they really rejected the deceased, grievers may at first feel relief and possibly even pleasure; but a guilt reaction may follow. Most counselors and therapists believe that the principal feeling is one of self-pity.

Children often experience feelings like those described above when a much-loved neighbor, friend, or relative moves away. They also experience *real* grief over the loss of a pet.

Case Example

When someone denies the loss or is not helped to grieve, related problems may be exhibited years later. This is what happened to Frances, a 50-year-old widow who sought counseling. In her intake interview, she said she wanted to learn to cope with her grieving sister. Her sister's husband had been dead a year, but her sister still refused to go out with their friends and relatives, often cried herself to sleep, would not return to work, and seemed to be completely helpless. In response to another client's reflection, Frances admitted reluctantly that she resented her sister very much.

Early in the next session, she cried and discussed the death of her own husband. Though she had lost her husband five years earlier, Frances felt that she had to be strong and to deny her deep feelings over the loss of her husband; but the group helped her discover that they could accept her grief, provide quality assistance in working it through, and help her to decide how she could learn to live without him. Once she had worked through her own grief, she was able to help her sister obtain the treatment she required and to accept the affection of an old friend and neighbor who had recently lost his wife.

Lindemann's Studies: The Manifestations of Grief

Lindemann (1944) studied psychoneurotic patients who lost a relative during treatment; the relatives of patients who died while hospitalized; disaster victims from the Coconut Grove fire and their relatives; and the relatives of servicemen. For acute grief he reported a common syndrome:

> . . . sensations of somatic distress occurring in waves last from twenty minutes to an hour at a time, a feeling of tightness in the throat, choking with shortness of breath, need for sighing, and an empty feeling in the abdomen, lack of muscular power, and an intense subjective distress described as tension or mental pain. The patient soon learns that these waves of discomfort can be precipitated by visits, by mentioning the deceased, and by receiving sympathy. There is a tendency to avoid the syndrome at any cost, to refuse visits lest they should precipitate the reaction, and to keep deliberately from thought all references to the deceased (Lindemann, 1944, p. 141).

He also found that reaction to grief could be delayed, and that morbid grief reactions represented distortion of normal grief. These distorted reactions included (1) overactivity; (2) acquisition of symptoms of the deceased; (3) a recognized medical disease; (4) alteration in relationships to friends and relatives (patients are irritable, do not want to be bothered, and gradually isolate themselves); (5) hostility toward specific persons; (6) efforts to hide hostility, giving appearance of schizophrenia; (7) a lasting loss of social interaction; (8) actions detrimental to their own social and economic existence (they behave in foolish ways that damage friendships, and they waste financial resources or permit themselves to be cheated out of them by unscrupulous persons); and (9) agitated depression (their grief is exhibited with insomnia, feelings of worthlessness, bitter self-accusation, and self-punishment; they may even become dangerously suicidal).

Nonhelpful Ways of Dealing with the Grieved

Unknowingly, friends and relatives often protect the griever from facing reality and dealing with grief. Rather than letting him discuss his real feelings and weep, they block his grieving with empty reassurances, suggesting that he will soon forget, that time heals all wounds. Even the suggestion that he will soon forget is perceived by him as an attack: it seems to challenge the sincerity of his love for the deceased, when in fact he feels the loss so keenly that his whole future looks bleak. Until they learn to react more therapeutically, even fellow clients tend to respond in these nonhelpful ways.

With reference to these nonhelpful practices in which persons try to help, Kübler-Ross (1969) wrote:

> Once the patient dies, I find it cruel and inappropriate to speak of love of God. When we lose someone, especially when we have had little time to prepare ourselves, we are enraged, angry, in despair; we should be allowed to express these feelings. The family members are often left alone as soon as they have given their consent for autopsy. Bitter, angry, or just numb, they walk through the corridors of the hospital, unable often to face the brutal reality. The first few days may be filled with busywork with arrangements and visiting relatives. The void and emptiness is felt after the funeral, after the departure of relatives. It is at this time that the family members feel most grateful to have someone to talk to, especially if it is someone who had recent contact with the deceased and who had anecdotes of some good moments toward the end of the deceased's life. This helps the relative over the shock and the initial grief and prepares him for a gradual acceptance (p. 117).

Helping the Grieved

What the griever needs to know is that friends and relatives care about him; that though they cannot understand fully how much his loss hurts, they want to help him express his grief and discover the strength to deal with it. Furthermore, they provide real support when they exhibit confidence in his ability to cope with it by helping him express it, rather than deny or conceal it. Even though he may prefer to withdraw, they patiently involve him appropriately in their relationships. They also help him to move back into other meaningful social relationships and to reestablish himself in his work. With such considerate responses, they may be given opportunities to protect him from those who would take advantage of him during his grieving period.

Lindemann describes this grief work as follows:

> The duration of a grief reaction seems to depend upon the success with which a person does the grief work, namely, emancipation from the bondage to the deceased, readjustment to the environment in which the deceased is missing, and the formation of new relationships. One of the big obstacles to this work seems to be the fact that many patients try to avoid the intense distress connected with the grief experience and to avoid the expression of emotion necessary for it. The men victims after the Coconut Grove fire appeared in the early psychiatric interviews to be in a state of tension with tightened facial muscula-

ture, unable to relax for fear they might "break down." It required considerable persuasion to yield to the grief process before they were willing to accept the discomfort of bereavement. . . . They became willing to accept the grief process and to embark on a program of dealing in memory with the deceased person. As soon as this became possible there seemed to be a rapid relief of tension and the subsequent interviews were rather animated conversations in which the deceased was idealized and in which misgivings about the future adjustment were worked through (1944, pp. 141–148).

To illustrate how a patient moved out into the mainstream of life and developed a future for herself, Lindemann went on to describe the case of a 40-year-old widow: "She then showed a marked drive for activity, making plans for supporting herself and her little girl, mapping out the preliminary steps for resuming her old profession as secretary, and making efforts to secure help from the occupational therapy department in reviewing her knowledge of French" (p. 143). For some persons (like this griever) counseling includes assistance in choosing a vocation.

Dealing with Grief in Group

Group counseling provides a climate in which clients experience more readily than in individual counseling the genuine encouragement to discuss the intense pain associated with the loss of the loved one; to cry; to learn to make requests of significant others; to accept others' love and companionship; and to decide what they must do to begin a more meaningful life. In addition to helping the primary grieving client, the counselor watches for clues that suggest that other clients also have unfinished grieving problems and helps them admit their problems and deal with them. When one client deals with a grief problem, this usually uncovers unfinished grieving problems for several clients who did not request help originally with grieving.

Group work with the bereaved client may take on a variety of different formats and forms. Separate groups may be needed for the victims of suicide focusing on issues of societal stigmas, denial of the cause of death, and delayed or unresolved grief (Wrobleski, 1985). A similar need may exist for parents' bereavement groups. Over 30,000 children die each year from catastrophic illness (Kirschenbaum & Zeanah, 1984). Additionally, groups can be helpful with such issues as the appropriate duration of bereavement, the importance of anniversaries, typical family problems, and the significance of social role in grief work (Roy & Sumpter, 1983). Outcome data for group work with the bereaved client suggests the cognitive-behavioral therapy format to be slightly more helpful with widowed females. Group treatment emphasizing cognitive restructuring reported a qualitative reduction in depression and significantly less social anxiety, which often leads to social isolation and withdrawal for the bereaved client (Walls & Meyers, 1985).

Children and Grief

Often adults do not realize that most children experience grief. They fail to notice how deeply a child feels about the loss of a pet or how much he misses that friend or relative who moved away. He also worries about what may happen to loved ones. Beginning elementary-school counselors are often surprised by the number of children who seek assistance with grieving problems—especially when they mention grieving in their presentation. They also tend to be impressed with the sensitive way in which children can help each other. Counselors also are encouraged to help teachers and parents of a grieving child. Seminars and discussion groups can be used effectively to help teachers and parents work through their own grieving problems and prepare themselves to help children cope with such problems. Counselors also are encouraged to conduct small discussion groups in the community (for example, in churches) to help adults cope better with the phenomenon of grieving and to refer those who require treatment for grieving.

DYING

When those closest to the terminally ill can be helped to accept death—facing death with the dying; helping the dying to accept it as well; helping them to complete their most important unfinished business—the griever is motivated to face death. He may then decide what he wants most from life for himself; look at his failures and lost opportunities in a new light; and complete his unfinished business with significant others, including the dying. Hopefully, the griever will be encouraged hereafter to express beautiful, positive feelings when those feelings are first experienced. In counseling groups, clients learn to express positive feelings when they are experienced; express angry feelings less hurtfully; recognize the problem's underlying conflict; and cope with that conflict. Thereby, they reduce the amount of unfinished business to be dealt with as one faces death. In order to help others learn to face death, the counselor must learn to face it herself.

Kübler-Ross: The Stages of Dying

Kübler-Ross (1969) found that most of the terminally ill patients whom she interviewed knew that they were terminally ill (even before they had been told) and appreciated her help in facing death. Her patients moved through five stages in learning to accept death: (1) denial and isolation; (2) anger; (3) bargaining; (4) depression; and (5) acceptance. She described this last stage as follows:

> If a patient has had enough time (i.e., not a sudden, unexpected death) and
> has been given some help in working through the previously described stages,

he will reach a stage during which he is neither depressed nor angry about his "fate." He will have been able to express his previous feelings, his envy for the living and healthy, his anger at those who do not have to face their end so soon. He will contemplate his coming end with a certain degree of quiet expectation. He will be tired and in most cases quite weak. He will also have a need to doze off to sleep often and in brief intervals, which is different from the need to sleep during times of depression. This is not the sleep of avoidance or a period of rest to get relief from pain, discomfort, or itching. It is a gradually increasing need to extend the hours of sleep very similar to that of the newborn child in reverse order . . .

Acceptance should not be mistaken for a happy stage. It is almost void of feelings. It is as if the pain had gone, the struggle is over, and there comes a time for "the final rest before the journey" as one patient phrased it. This is also the time during which the family needs usually more help, understanding, and support than the patient himself (pp. 112–113).

Children and Dying

Children as well as surviving adults must be considered in helping the dying person's significant others. Moreover, Kübler-Ross' findings suggest that those who attempt to help their grieving (and dying) child must know how children perceive death: (1) up to age three, they are concerned primarily with separation; (2) the next age group is concerned about fear of decay and mutilation (from seeing pets killed by cars or birds mutilated by other animals); (3) around age nine, children begin to understand the permanence of death; and (4) during adolescence the loss of a significant other, such as a beloved parent, appears to be too much to endure.

All should be listened to and encouraged to express whatever they feel; and after they have expressed their grief, discovered their sources for support, and developed the strength to endure it, they should be able to find a new life without the loved one. Working through the grief also should be used to help the griever, especially the young griever, to understand and accept death. With the assistance and cooperation of a child's teacher and parents, a counselor can use such a technique as classroom discussion to enlist classmates' assistance in helping the grieving child and his classmates deal with the death taboo. Berg (1973) advises:

> Becoming aware of the death taboo, confronting the facts and reality of its existence, and working through the distortions and emotions which surround it are the counselor's responsibility if communication is to remain open. Adults must especially allow children to inquire about death, share their memories and anxieties about it, and encourage them, when necessary, to accept the naturalness of their feelings without guilt or embarrassment. One hopes that as we all learn to acknowledge and accept our deepest feelings unashamedly, we are creating a philosophy of life that promotes equal regard and respect for the value

and rights of others' feelings. In helping children develop wise and beautiful ways of coping with death, we may hopefully provide them with a new and stronger dimension to life (p. 32).

Dealing with Dying in Group

Group counseling seems particularly well suited to the conditions and needs of those dealing with terminal illness. Anxiety, despair, loneliness, and alienation are feelings frequently surrounding terminal illness and loss due to death. Dealing with these feelings in a group setting can enable the individual to come to terms, finish the necessary business with relevant others, and complete the natural process of life. A number of research studies verify the benefits of group counseling with terminally ill clients. For example, in work with the families of terminal patients, a multifamily approach was successfully used to help families participate together to reduce anxiety regarding death, express pain, rage, injustice, impotence, and to accept and prepare for death (Greaves, 1983). Helping terminal clients and family members put death into perspective, and maximize the quality of the remaining life span, as well as to demystify death, and clarify personal meaning of an individual life, have been important outcomes of support groups for dying patients (Spiegel & Yalom, 1978).

A study by Kornfeld and Siegel (1979) successfully demonstrated the use of a group process enabling parents to express their fears and concerns surrounding the death of their children, and to problems created by progressive fatal diseases in their children. A hospital cancer unit found the use of weekly group sessions helpful in meeting needs for emotional support for family members of terminal patients (Kopel & Mock, 1978). Needs to express feelings and talk openly about fears—concern and doubts on a variety of topics regarding death which are difficult to deal with—seem to be best dealt with in groups of individuals with similar issues and concerns. Group work and grief work seem ideally correlated as a means of facilitating the working through of issues related to life's last conflict: death.

THE ANXIOUS CLIENT

Being anxious is not the same as being tense. An individual experiences tension when he anticipates some exciting or challenging event; for example, when he waits in the wings to go on stage to perform, when he waits for the whistle to begin an athletic contest, or even when he effectively studies for an examination. In this last instance, one would expect the tension to be discharged by the completion of the examination. Furthermore, when he is functioning well, such an experience creates a minimum of anxiety. On the other hand, when he doubts his ability to perform well on the examination to an extent that it interferes with his preparation or his performance during the examination, he is experiencing debilitating anxiety. Whereas tension tends to focus attention on action, anxiety tends to interfere with effective action.

The Anxious Client

Various theoretical orientations and interventions have been demonstrated as effective in dealing with anxious clients in groups. A study (Elizabeth, 1983) that compared psychoanalytic and client-centered group treatment methods on dependent measures of anxiety and self-actualization found the psychoanalytic group to have higher levels of anxiety among group members than did the client-centered group. In addition, the client-centered group evidenced more tendencies toward self-actualization than the psychoanalytic group. Findings such as these may suggest that clients with anxiety problems may profit more from group procedures other than psychoanalytically based groups.

Group instruction in rational-emotive therapy has also demonstrated efficacy in significantly reducing anxiety in individuals with achievement anxiety (Maxwell & Wilkerson, 1982). Group therapy per se was also found to be an effective treatment for reducing anxiety, fear, and hostility in rape victims (Cryer & Beutler, 1980). Group cognitive-behavioral therapy was found to be effective in reducing client symptoms of anxiety and depression (Shaffer et al., 1981).

The Anxious Client in Group

Sometimes the anxious client will frighten the other clients, and even the inexperienced counselor, with tears, apprehensions, and disorganized behavior. They are afraid that he will talk too freely and expose more material than he can manage. Under these circumstances, especially during the first few sessions, clients are tempted to reassure the anxious one. Though such efforts are meant to provide support, the underlying attitude conveys doubts concerning the client's ability to cope with their problems and, possibly, a lack of confidence in the treatment process. Thus, the precise feelings of the reassurer as well as the anxious one must be detected and reflected in order to get them out into the open where they can be managed.

In actuality, anxious crisis victims rarely uncover material that they cannot handle. Anxious clients can be hurt by penetrating interpretations, however, and by the feeling that they may be abandoned when they reveal very disturbing material. Usually they feel safer in the type of group described in Chapter 1 than they do in everyday interactions. Although clients face and relive hurtful events during counseling, and are pressured to change their behavior and attitudes, fellow clients learn to provide genuine support during painful moments. Even when another uncovers painful material with a penetrating reflection, the anxious one realizes that his helper is trying to help him in facing and learning to cope with relevant therapeutic material rather than confronting him with his maladaptive behavior; the helper is trying to empathize with the anxious one, convey confidence in his ability to solve his own problems, and provide support while the anxious one is learning desired new behaviors. Not only is the counselor able to convey that she cares and dares to suffer with the suffering client, and will not abandon him in distress or "chicken out" and try to minimize the extent of the hurt, she is able to teach the other clients to provide this quality support.

Preventing the Anxious Client from Disrupting the Group Process

Some readers may wonder, nonetheless, what they can do when they believe in an early session that a client is revealing too much too fast; they are afraid that later the client may regret what he revealed, or that he may continue to self-disclose too freely outside of the counseling group. When a counselor begins to feel uncomfortable with such a client, she should listen to the client and try to assess whether she is worried about the client or herself. If she suspects that the client may continue to reveal inappropriate private thoughts and feelings to others outside of counseling and be hurt by it, the counselor is obligated ethically to clarify expectations—differentiating between what is appropriate behavior in a counseling group and what is appropriate elsewhere. If she feels later that a client regrets what he shared, the counselor reflects these feelings, helps the anxious client discuss them, and helps fellow clients respond to the threat. When doubt about keeping confidences or continuing to be accepted by a certain fellow client arises, the counselor and the other clients, too, help the anxious one express his feelings and resolve his problems with that particular fellow client.

Slowing the Anxious Client Down

Sometimes a member cannot follow what the anxious one is saying. He may be talking too fast or incoherently. By making a reflection that clarifies, the counselor can convey that she is interested, slow the client down, and encourage him to clarify what he is trying to communicate: "Pardon my interruption, but I'm afraid I did not understand what you are trying to convey. I'm not sure whether you tried to speak to your Latin teacher and failed to get help, whether you are afraid to speak to her, or you don't think that it will do any good." When the counselor merely wants to slow the client down, she may say something like: "I'm having difficulty keeping up with you, trying to understand everything you are telling us. Apparently, a number of things are upsetting you. Perhaps we could understand you better if you could select one or two of the problems with which you would like help first and discuss them a little more slowly." In any case, the counselor must try to identify the anxious client's therapeutic material and respond to it helpfully; enlist the other clients' support and assistance; help them cope with any threatening material that the anxious one uncovers in them;

and help the anxious one implement his new discoveries and learnings with his significant others outside the counseling group.

Fellow Acceptance of the Anxious Client

With the structuring, careful selection of clients, and the definition of precise behavioral goals described in Chapter 6, clients come better prepared to help the anxious client than most readers may realize. The counselor also tends to have more confidence in the anxious client's ability to face threatening material and deal adequately with it. When clients realize that they have been selected with care to maximize their chances for getting help in the group, their counseling group becomes more attractive; and they are able to respond more spontaneously to each other. They are able to let the anxious one cry and express his feelings. The better they accept each other, the more they believe in each other—and accept the fact that it is worth the pain experienced to achieve the benefits of counseling—the more productive their group is. Talland and Clark (1954) found that their patients were helped most when they discussed their most-painful topics. Clients can accept essential pain to learn and implement their desired new behaviors.

THE HOSTILE CLIENT

When clients, especially adolescents, are pressured by others to accept counseling, they often appear hostile. Even when they seem to cooperate in the intake interview, they spend an undue amount of time complaining about their significant others who require treatment more than they do.

The Adolescent

Before hostile adolescents are encouraged to join a group, the counselor should try to convey that she understands how they feel and that, perhaps, the group is not appropriate for them unless they are willing to discuss how they have been hurt and learn specific new ways of relating to their resented significant others and whatever else they would like to work on.

The Badgered Client

Another client may appear to be hostile when he actually feels inadequate or lacks the human-relationship skills to cope with some specific persons or situations. Frequently, he is "badgered" by an employer, co-worker, spouse, parent, or teacher who is an intellectual bully, and he strikes back (or is afraid that he will explode and hurt his adversary) because he feels trapped, cornered, or overwhelmed. Like a trapped animal who is tormented, he would run away if he could, but he is caught and forced to deal with the threatening situation. He needs to learn to widen his repertoire of human relations and verbal skills in order to deal with his hurtful adversary.

The Overdisciplined Client

Still another type is the client who has had a very strict, moralistic upbringing. He may seek relief from obsessional thoughts concerning normal reactions to a target person for justified anger (or similar guilt-arousing sexual thoughts toward appropriate sex objects). Helping such a client define precise behavioral goals and obtaining feedback from peers that these are normal reactions helps such a person, but usually these are not sufficient. He must practice expression of anger to relevant target persons in role playing and listen to feedback from fellow clients. Some also require assertiveness training in order to cope with such feelings. Rowen (1975) believes that such clients must be taught systematically to accept these normal feelings. Assertiveness training in groups has been demonstrated to effectively reduce hostility (Fiedler, 1979).

The Abandoned Client

Finally, there is the genuinely hostile client who has been rejected, hurt, let down, or abandoned by someone whose love and acceptance he requires. Whereas aggressive clients may step on others as they move toward their goal with minimum regard for others' rights, they hurt others accidentally; the really hostile person, however, is often distracted from his goal in order to hurt others. He tends to be demanding, brutal, sullen, and defiant. Even when he turns to a counselor for help, it is difficult for the counselor and fellow clients to prove to him that they want to understand him, accept him, and help him. Consequently, the counselor who helps him must be strong and have the courage to help him make a genuine commitment to change; define precise goals; disclose hurts openly in the group; and, perhaps, even admit him to the group with probational status.

When such a client tends to gloss over the depth of his pain, it takes courage, on the part of the fellow clients as well as the counselor, to be assertive, empathic, and demanding—that is, to state the wish to help and not let the hostile client's anger and defensiveness keep them from hanging in there—patiently, caringly insisting that he own his pain; complete his unfinished business; decide what relationships cannot be salvaged; and discover what new behaviors he must learn to function more effectively with those with whom he replaces the unsatisfactory significant others. Expressing empathy through accurate reflections is important for every challenging client, but for this client it is especially important, and it requires a great deal of courage.

Dealing with Hostile Clients

Difficult as it is for hostile behaving clients to accept other members' efforts to empathize with them, this is what they require. Members need to learn to refuse to let a hostile client brush them off and respond helpfully with warmth respect that conveys understanding of how he really feels and help him express those feelings. Expressing their willingness to help him cope with those who hurt him, their confidence in his ability to learn desired new behaviors, and their expectation for him to change, motivates change. Most hostile clients have learned to expect and to deal with receiving hostility in return. When they do not get it, they look for it anyway. When a hostile client receives empathy and support from his fellow clients instead, he may be surprised: he does not feel like attacking them, his usual response. As he gradually discovers the extent to which the others can detect and reflect how he feels and are able to provide encouragement for him, he is motivated to help others rather than to push them away and attack them.

THE DEPRESSED

Understanding the nature of depression as an emotionally debilitating phenomena is important in developing a method for assisting the individual in a state of depression (Whitaker & Deikman, 1980). A depressed state may result when anger, hostility, and aggression become self-directed, or turned inward. The depressed person's cognitive perspective may typically include inferences about the nature of a particular set of experiences based on limited or biased evidence (Beck, 1976). Behaviorally, the depressed person may be lacking in the ability to elicit reinforcement that may reduce behaviors resulting in further loss of the potential for reinforcement (Lewinsohn, 1974).

Depression often occurs when individuals perceive they have little or no control in directing or changing their lives, which results in what Seligman (1974) refers to as learned helplessness. The helpless individual feels hopeless, gives up, and withdraws from life.

Depressed individuals often internalize responsibility and blame themselves for failure, or circumstances beyond their control that perpetuate their feelings of depression. Individuals facing traumatic circumstances prefer the company of others facing similar circumstances (Coates & Winston, 1983). The normal course of social interaction is often void of the kind of feedback, understanding, and support necessary to help the depressed individual deal effectively with traumatic events; therefore, providing a group service for individuals suffering from circumstances beyond their control can be helpful in reducing depression and enhancing growth and development.

The Depressed Client

Several research studies regarding the outcome of various treatment procedures indicate group counseling to be a viable approach for the reduction of depression. Depression-management training has been successfully used with a structured group format designed to increase participants' awareness of the sources of their depression (Lerman & Baron, 1981). Teaching individuals how to give and receive "strokes" using the transactional analysis model in a short-term group (4 weeks/2-hour sessions) was also found to be successful in decreasing depression (Fetsch & Sprinkle, 1982).

Cognitive-behavioral group counseling may be particularly useful with elderly clients who are depressed. Steuer and Hammen (1983) suggest that changes associated with aging tend to slow down the developmental stages of group work, but that this condition can be dealt with by using a behavioral approach. In predicting success with depressed clients, Steinmetz, Lewinsohn, and Antonuccio (1983) found that subjects with a variety of different depression levels improved most when they expected treatment to reduce depression, perceived mastery over symptoms, had greater reading ability, were younger, and perceived their families as more supportive.

The Depressed Client in Group

Most who have not learned to deal with serious hurtful experiences and disappointments can be helped by group counseling. They require assistance to determine what they can expect from their significant others, what others expect from them, and what new behaviors must be learned to fulfill the expectations—renegotiating these expectations, when necessary, and making requests of significant others. Frequently, these significant others unknowingly reinforce inappropriate behavior. Some also lack the skills to communicate how they feel toward the depressed, and to develop and enjoy quality companionship with them.

On the other hand, some depressed clients already have reasonably good relationships with significant others; but they have such a low opinion of themselves that they twist even these good relationships into confusion, frustration, and disappointments. Those who help must teach them to recognize and enjoy the quality relationships already available to them and, when necessary, to develop new ones. Others require assertiveness training in addition to group counseling in order to make reasonable requests of significant others and/or to stand up for themselves when the occasion calls for it.

With improved counseling services in the schools and the community-agency outreach programs, increasing numbers of children and youths will be helped to deal with their early disappointments as they occur. Elementary-school counseling programs are designed to help children and to help teachers and parents assist children. Community mental-health agencies and school adult-education programs in personal growth, parent education, and family education are designed primarily for adults. These programs are designed to help individuals develop strong personal-support systems. Nevertheless, there will be times when most persons require the help of a counselor or therapist when they become depressed.

THE LEARNING DISABLED

Kirk and Bateman (1962) defined a learning disability as follows:

> A learning disability refers to a retardation, disorder, or delayed development in one or more of the processes of speech, language, reading, writing, arithmetic, or other school subjects, resulting from a psychological handicap caused by a possible cerebral dysfunction and/or emotional or behavioral disturbances. It is not the result of mental retardation, sensory deprivation, or instructional factors (p. 73).

As for every other challenging client, the counselor must be able to detect and reflect the pain and hurt this client is experiencing. Very early in his formal education, the child with learning disabilities tends to conclude that school success will be difficult, if not impossible, and that he has less ability than his *real* potential. When, for example, a happy, confident 5-year-old was given a Stanford-Binet, his IQ score was 115. Later when he developed a serious reading problem in second grade and lost a great deal of self-confidence, his score on the same test dropped to 98. Following remedial reading instruction and a full year of school success, he was retested on the same test by the same psychologist and scored 123.

Not only do learning disabilities influence children's performance on tests and their academic expectations of themselves, but they often continue to have a negative impact on their personal and career developments as adults. They are reluctant to attempt special on-the-job training that could result in promotions, consider new employment opportunities, and accept leadership roles in community programs. When, however, they profit from remedial instruction for their learning disabilities and are provided with counseling, hard-core unemployed obtain employment, underemployed seek and obtain promotions, and adults return to college to complete preparation for much-desired professional careers.

The Learning Disabled in Group

The effectiveness of group procedure has proven successful in dealing with the multiple symptoms and problems related to children with learning disabilities. In a study comparing different therapeutic strategies in a group for learning-disabled children, the social skills group effected positive self-concept formation over other methods, such as relaxation training. However, the relaxation training group demonstrated less acting out and distractability (Amerikaner & Summerlin, 1982). In order to assist the learning-disabled child with developmental deficits on a social-emotional level, a group-counseling method using psychodrama centering around general adjustment and peer-group problems was employed. Children, in this experiment, improved the quality of their communication, attitude, and general adjustment (DuPlessis & Lochner, 1981).

Groups for parents of the learning disabled have also been used to help parents foster better adjustment in their children to the problems associated with a learning disability (Skuy & Solomon, 1980). A study by Diament and Colletti (1978) demonstrated the benefits of teaching parents basic, behavior-modification techniques for parenting. Parent groups seem especially important for the parents of learning-disabled children to provide a place where parents can share their feelings of frustration, guilt, as well as problem solve on how to provide the best learning environment at home (Kronick, 1978).

Obviously, space cannot be allocated here to deal adequately with treating learning disabilities, but counselors and therapists must be sensitive to those behaviors that suggest learning problems (Anderson, 1970; Kaczkowski & Patterson, 1975). Furthermore, every effort should be made to identify children with learning problems early and initiate appropriate treatment. Counselors should enlist children's parents', teachers', and school psychologists' assistance in identifying and correcting learning disabilities.

SUMMARY

This chapter focused on a variety of conditions that effect client emotional debilitation. Specifically, emotional conditions related to grieving, death, anxiety, hostility, depression, and learning disabilities were experienced. The purpose of exploring these states was to provide the group leader with clients in groups who are in a state of emotional crises.

A major challenge facing group counselors is learning how to help clients suffering severe emotional pain. Often, such emotional states can seem overwhelming to a leader and group members, which can lead both to feel powerless to act in helpful ways. The entire group may become paralyzed by their inability to deal with the intensity of an emotional state without the awareness and skill of an effective leader.

Developing effective helping skills as a group counselor begins with exploring why some clients' emotional states are more difficult for both a leader and members to deal with than others. Identifying the conditions that influence the emotional impacts that block the group and/or clients' progress in working through and coping with emotional crises often requires supervision. The emotional depth and breadth of a group develops as a result of its ability to accommodate to and offer assistance for a variety of client emotional conditions.

A major part of rendering assistance to individuals suffering severe emotional pain may be found in helping them identify experience and express themselves emotionally. Group members, with the assistance of the group leader, work as a team to help emotionally debilitated clients work through their emotional states, develop effective coping skills, and decide what changes they wish to make in order to effectively resolve severe life crises.

REFERENCES

Amerikaner, M., & Summerlin, M. (1982). Group counseling with learning disabled children: Effects of social skills and relaxation training on self concept and classroom behavior. *Journal of Learning Disabilities, 15*, 340–343.

Anderson, R. P. (1970). *The child with learning disabilities and guidance.* Boston: Houghton-Mifflin.

Beck, A. T. (1976). *Cognitive therapy and emotional disorders.* New York: International University Press.

Berg, C.D. (1973). Cognizance of death taboo in counseling children. *School Counselor, 21*, 28–72.

Bowlby, J. (1969). *Attachment and Loss* (Vol. 1). London: Hogarth Press.

Coates, D., & Winston, T. (1983). Counteracting the deviance of depression: Peer support groups for victims. *Journal of Social Issues, 39*, 169–194.

Cryer, L., & Beutler, L. (1980). An alternative treatment approach for rape victims. *Journal of Sex and Marital Therapy, 6*, 40–46.

Diament, C., & Colletti, G. (1978). Evaluation of behavioral group counseling for parents of learning disabled children. *Journal of Abnormal Child Psychology, 6*, 385–400.

DuPlessis, J., & Lochner, L. (1981). The effects of group psychology on the adjustment of four 12-year-old boys with learning and behavior problems. *Journal of Learning Disabilities, 14*, 209–212.

Elizabeth, P. (1983). Comparison of a psychoanalytic and a client-centered group treatment model on measures of anxiety and self-actualization. *Journal of Counseling Psychology, 30,* 425–428.

Fetsch, R., & Sprinkle, R. (1982). Stroking treatment effects on depressed males. *Transactional Analysis Journal, 12*, 213–217.

Fiedler, P. (1979). Effects of assertive training on hospitalized adolescents and young adults. *Adolescence, 14*, 523–528.

Freud, S. (1917). *Mourning and melancholia* (collected papers). London: Hogarth Press.

Gauthier, J., & Marshall, W. (1977). Grief: A cognitive-behavioral analysis. *Cognitive Therapy Research, 1*, 39–44.

Greaves, C. (1983). Death in the family: A multifamily therapy approach. *International Journal of Family Psychiatry, 4*, 247–261.

Kaczkowski, H. R., & Patterson, C. H. (1975). *Counseling and psychology in elementary schools.* Springfield, IL: Charles C Thomas.

Kirk, S. A., & Bateman, B. (1962). Diagnosis and remediation of learning disabilities. *Exceptional Children, 29*, 69–79.

Gauthier, J., & Marshall, W. (1977). Grief: A cognitive-behavioral analysis. *Cognitive Therapy Research, 1*, 39–44.

Greaves, C. (1983). Death in the family: A multifamily therapy approach. *International Journal of Family Psychiatry, 4*, 247–261.

Kaczkowski, H. R., & Patterson, C. H. (1975). *Counseling and psychology in elementary schools.* Springfield, IL: Charles C Thomas.

Kirk, S. A., & Bateman, B. (1962). Diagnosis and remediation of learning disabilities. *Exceptional Children, 29*, 69–79.

Kirschenbaum, K., & Zeanah, P. (1984). Repeated participation in a bereaved parent's group: Two case studies and implication for clinicians. *Children's Health Care, 13*, 64–70.

Kopel, K., & Mock, L. (1978). The use of group sessions for the emotional support of families of terminal patients. *Death Education, 1*, 409–422.

Kornfeld, M., & Siegel, I. (1979). Parental group therapy in the management of fatal childhood disease. *Health and Social Work, 4*, 99–118.

Kronick, D. (1978). Educational and counseling groups for parents. *Academic Therapy, 13*, 355–359.

Kübler-Ross, E. (1969). *On death and dying.* New York: Macmillan.

Lerman, C., & Baron, A. (1981). Depression management training: A structured group approach. *Personnel and Guidance Journal, 60*, 86–88.

Lewinsohn, P. M. (1974). A behavioral approach to depression. In R. J. Friedman & M. M. Katz (Eds.), *The psychology of depression* . Washington, DC: V. H. Winston & Sons.

Lindemann, E. (1944). Symptomatology and management of acute grief. *American Journal of Psychiatry, 101*, 141–148.

Maxwell, J., & Wilkerson, J. (1982). Anxiety reduction through group instruction in rational therapy. *Journal of Psychology, 112*, 135–140.

Rowen, M. (1975). A dual model of obsessional neurosis. *Journal of Consulting and Clinical Psychology, 43*, 453–459.

Roy, P., & Sumpter, H. (1983). Group support for the recently bereaved. *Health and Social Work, 8*, 230–232.

Seligman, M. E. (1975). *Helplessness.* San Francisco: W. H. Freeman.

Shaffer, C.; Shapiro, J.; Sank, L.; Lawrence, I.; & Coghlan, D. (1981). Positive changes in depression, anxiety, and assertion following individual and group cognitive behavior therapy intervention. *Cognitive Therapy and Research, 5*, 149–157.

Skuy, M., & Solomon, W. (1980). Effectiveness of students and parents in a psychoeducational intervention program for children with learning disabilities. *British Journal of Guidance and Counseling, 8*, 76–86.

Spiegel, D., & Yalom, I. (1978). A support group for dying patients. *International Journal of Group Psychotherapy, 28*, 233–245.

Steinmetz, J.; Lewinsohn, P.; & Antonuccio, D. (1983). Prediction of individual outcome in a group intervention for depression. *Journal of Consulting and Clinical Psychology, 51*, 331–337.

Steuer, J., & Hammen, C. (1983). Cognitive-behavioral group therapy for the depressed elderly: Issues and adaptation. *Cognitive Therapy and Research, 7*, 285–296.

Talland, G. A., & Clark, D. H., (1954). Evaluation of topics in therapy discussion groups. *Journal of Clinical Psychology, 10*, 131–137.

Walls, N., & Meyers, A. (1985). Outcome in group treatment for bereavement: Experimental results and recommendations for clinical practice. *International Journal of Mental Health, 13,* 126–147.

Whitaker, L., & Deikman, A. (1980). Psychotherapy of severe depression. *Psychotherapy: Theory, Research, and Practice, 17,* 85–93.

Wrobleski, A. (1985). The suicide survivor's grief group. *Omega: Journal of Death and Dying, 15,* 173–184.

10

CHALLENGING CLIENTS: THE OTHER-CONTROLLED

A number of clients are challenging to counselors as a result of their interactional style (or way of being within the group) or because of the type of concern they present within the group. Yalom (1985) described nine problem clients: "... the monopolist, the schizoid patient, the silent patient, the boring patient, the help-rejecting complainer, the righteous moralist, the psychotic patient, the narcissistic patient, and the borderline patient" (p. 375). The type of challenging client primarily dealt with in this chapter is the client who is other-controlled.

THE OTHER-CONTROLLED CLIENT

Grater (1958), in his paper "When Counseling Success Is Failure," described one variety of other-controlled client saying that this client was very sensitive to others' needs, tried hard to determine what was expected in counseling, and did it. A positive identification with the group, then, often occurs, and the client adheres to the model of the group and to the concerns of others within the group. If other clients discuss sex problems, for example, then the other-controlled also discusses sex problems. If vocational concerns are presented, then the other-controlled selects that topic as a concern. Thus, other-controlled clients discuss concerns openly, and help others feel close because they share common problems with their fellow group members. Subsequently, when counseling ends, the other-controlled is selected by fellow clients and the counselor as the one who has helped the most. In actuality, change often does occur with all the problems *except* the one that requires assistance the most: being controlled by others. There is considerable overlap between the other-controlled client and several of the categories defined by Yalom.

Other-controlled clients treasure others' acceptance so much that they discuss whatever others seem to want to discuss and are open to pressure to do whatever others prefer to do. Consequently, other-controlled clients are often used by others and resent being used, but are reluctant to express resentment because they question their own worth—in other words, doubt whether it is possible to win others' acceptance and approval any other way. Most people have some characteristics of wanting to fit in with the people with whom they associate. However, other-controlled clients allow much of their freedom—decisions, behaviors, and ideas—to be dictated by others.

Dealing with the Other-Controlled

Not all clients experiencing this issue will recognize the problem as their own. Whenever the counselor detects in the intake interview, or during counseling, that a client is unduly sensitive to others' needs and exhibits unusual desire to please others, the counselor may make a reflection such as, "You are quick to detect what others need and want very much to please them, but sometimes I'll bet it makes you a little angry when they take advantage of you. At such times, I'll bet you wish you were strong enough to stand up for your own rights and ask your friends to do just once what you'd like for them to do." As the client discusses the reflection and the importance of the feelings involved, it is important for the counselor to enlist the other group members' assistance in teaching the client to be more assertive; identify significant others with whom to learn to implement the new skills; and to practice, in role playing, specific ways of mastering her new behavioral repertoire. The counselor also should encourage the other clients to watch for instances in which the obliging client reacts submissively to them and to help her practice being assertive within the group. In group counseling, a major task is to help everyone to obtain assistance with those problems with which help is most desired. In any case, helping an other-controlled client recognize and express feelings of doubt about self-worth and resentment about being used exposes her needs to others so that they can help her deal with the needs; gives others a chance to express their positive feelings toward and their commitment to help her; and enables her to explore what she would like to do differently with whom.

Assertiveness Training

In helping other-controlled clients become more assertive, it is important to teach the behavioral skills necessary to accomplish the goals established. This requires identifying with whom the client wants to be more comfortable and assertive; situations in which it is important to use the behaviors; and circumstances in which the client has been unable to be assertive in the past. Beyond expanding the behavioral repertoire, however, it is important for the counselor to help the group assist the client in identifying the beliefs that have prevented her from being more assertive.

Even though a person may master effective interpersonal skills, without the belief that the use of those skills is acceptable, no implementation will occur. All people know how to commit crimes, but most people do not do so because of their personal belief system. The same is true of being assertive. Weiner (1985) supports accepting the group member at her present level of functioning to avoid regression to lower levels of functioning by focus on present behavior and thinking: ". . . to alter maladaptive behavior by direct teaching or modeling; and use the positive feeling engendered by small constructive steps in the group to encourage taking similar steps in one's outside life" (p. 222).

In one implementation of assertiveness training within a religious community, a pre- and a post-test of assertiveness demonstrated effective mastery of skills. A six-month follow-up, however, did not show any maintenance of the skills. When the program was revised to include attention to the socialization messages people believed ("I don't have a right to do what I want, it might insult Sister . . ."; "I would like to do . . . but people might think I am being selfish . . .") and an examination of those messages, the assertive behavior changed and was maintained at the next six-month follow-up (Horne, 1977).

TYPES OF OTHER-CONTROLLED CLIENTS

Before beginning the discussion of specific types of other-controlled clients, it is important to remember that we are describing characteristics and behaviors demonstrated by persons who are members of the group. All members of a particular group are likely to demonstrate some of the characteristics some of the time, and no particular client will demonstrate all the characteristics all of the time. It is important to remember that when doing group counseling we are working with people—with individuals who bring characteristic behaviors to a group setting—and not with stereotypes or caricatures. The categorizations described below are to give the reader an understanding of the types of behaviors that frequently have recurred within the group setting.

Silent or Withdrawn

The silent and the withdrawn may be one and the same; on the other hand, they may perceive themselves very differently, having very different reasons for remaining silent. A counselor must observe the silent one very carefully to detect how she feels about herself.

Empathic Silence

Some clients have learned to become deeply involved in interacting with others with a minimum of talking. When others express their feelings or deal with their problems, the silent ones convey empathy and support nonverbally: they experience feelings with others, learn from others, and adapt what they learn to solve their own problems. Others serve as their mouthpiece. Usually these silent ones openly reveal their problems early on in the group, so they are not looked upon with suspicion. Some clients who fall into this category recognize that their school performance or their proficiency at work is underrated because of their silence. Hence, even though they can be helped within their counseling group with minimum verbal participation, they recognize that they must improve their verbal-interaction skills in order to gain the recognition they deserve.

The Slow-Moving

Another infrequent verbal participant within a counseling group is the deliberate, slow-moving person who takes her time to figure out how she feels and what she wants to say. She also may be reluctant to interrupt others to express herself. If the counselor watches her carefully, he will note that repeatedly she nearly gets the floor then loses it to another. Merely observing that once again she has lost out is usually sufficient to sensitize other clients to her need for assistance in capturing the speaker's role. She also may need to be encouraged to express herself more assertively and to discuss underlying resistance.

Hostile Silence

Another form of silence is demonstrated by some members who cover hostility with silence. Ormont (1984) says that:

> I do not encourage such people to talk. They have good reason for their shyness. Perhaps they dread being attacked for what they might say, or they are ashamed of their angry thoughts. Whatever their motive, they do not trust logic; it is only a waste of time. . . . Probing might even make them grip their silence more tenaciously than before. Therefore, I confine myself to describing such behavior, and when the rest of the group fully recognizes the person's silence, I call it a problem. If the person sees that it is, I protect him from any possible embarrassment by turning the attention to other members, perhaps asking them to speculate about why the individual is quiet (p. 556).

Ormont goes on to say that those who are angry, aggressive, and silent flatten their affective responses through silence. They lose touch not only with their feelings of anger, but with all other feelings as well; they no longer know how they feel for they have stopped feeling. There is a fear that if they ever do become aware of their feelings and begin to express them, the outcome will be rage: they might truly harm those at whom the rage is directed or others, such as group members, who might be present when it is expressed.

By having angry, silent clients observe others in the group—those who are effective in expressing feelings without having to act out those feelings—the hostile client can learn safety within the group. She can allow the emergence of awareness of her affective state, and be able to express her feelings safely. This requires the counselor's setting the stage for the gradual expression of anger. Also, though, the counselor must make certain that the environment is safe, that other clients within the group can hear the honest, direct expression of anger without a sense of fear.

The Withdrawn

The withdrawn one tends to have a more negative self-image than any of the silent ones described above. She tends to be less confident that she can be helped by counseling or that she can say anything that really will help others. Carefully timed reflection conveys empathy and helps her reveal her problems. When she tries to express her feelings, she discovers that the other members really care and that they want to help her change. Furthermore, she discovers that they can be very patient in helping her face her problems.

Most counselors want every client to interact verbally. Some clients, especially former teachers, are made to feel uncomfortable by the withdrawn one: they are tempted to call upon her as they would a student in a class recitation. This tends to put the silent client on the spot. Fellow clients also tend to put her on the spot because they are suspicious of her. Helping her discuss precisely how she feels not only increases her readiness for change, but it increases others' acceptance of her. Participating in such interaction also provides her the practice she needs in developing her social skills.

The Client as Mere Observer

It is acknowledged that learning can occur vicariously—by observing others in the group—without actually being actively involved verbally. Clients have even reported that observing the process others went through during group sessions was therapeutic for them. Lieberman, Yalom, and Miles (1973) reported that clients can have beneficial changes in encounter group experiences by engaging in the vicarious learning of other group members. However, active participation in the group experience, as opposed to the observer role, seems to result in a more effective outcome. Coyne and Silver (1980), for example, reported that the observer role, as compared to observing plus participating, yielded negligible change and did not increase attraction to the group process. And Lundgren and Miller (1965) found that the fewer words clients spoke in group, the less change that occurred.

Scapegoat

The scapegoat is the focus of displaced aggression. Some masochistic persons set themselves up for this role. They derive pleasure from being insulted, offended, or mistreated. Other scapegoats permit such treatment in order to have relationships with others: they doubt their ability to be genuinely loved and accepted, so they would rather be a scapegoat than have no relationships at all. Some others are naive: they lack the social skills to cope with those who hurt them.

Scapegoating is a common phenomenon—which can be observed even in a group of animals. Usually one finds a scapegoat who is the victim of jokes; teased; confronted with probing questions or hurtful interpretation; or kept on the "hot seat." When these behaviors occur in a counseling group, the scapegoat may be victimized by a sadistic person who pretends to be trying to help. Since the disadvantage of putting someone on the "hot seat" and treating one client at a time have been discussed previously, it will suffice to state here that such methods tend to encourage clients to use the scapegoat as an object of their displaced aggressions.

Dealing with Scapegoating

When a counselor observes a client being used as a scapegoat, he should reflect the feelings that he feels the scapegoat is experiencing: feelings of hurt as well as those others described above. Such a reflection enables the hurt one to express how she feels and rallies support and understanding from the others. It also helps the hurter discover his impact on others while encouraging him to search for new ways of relating to others. (Sometimes when he has hurt others, the hurter will experience the role of scapegoat. Then his feelings of hurt also must be reflected.) However, this is not sufficient. Members of the group should expect, and assist, both the scapegoat and the hurter to learn new ways of relating to others. Careful structuring may be needed here, lest clients become so afraid of hurting someone that they lose their spontaneity; or, for fear of becoming hurtful themselves, they grow reluctant to put pressure on each other to learn new ways of relating. However, they can learn to distinguish between sadistic hurting and helping one another deal with hurtful material during the course of getting help.

Socializer

The socializer is the one who wants to extend the counseling relationships into social relationships outside the group. She wants her fellow clients and the counselor to be her best friends. She so thoroughly enjoys the quality of her relationships with members of her counseling group that she may wish to substitute these relationships for those with her important others. Rather than allowing this to happen, the members of her counseling group should help her perceive the counseling group for what it is: a temporary relationship in which she learns to cope with her important others and, when essential, to build new relationships with others outside her counseling group. Failure to deal openly with this problem often leads high-school and college youth to resist termination of their counseling group. It also encourages clients to socialize with fellow clients during counseling.

Socializing outside the Group

Some counselors question the extent to which a counselor can or should control socializing of members outside of the counseling group. As a consequence of his experiences in treating more-disturbed patients, Bach (1954) discussed this controversial point as follows:

> Clinical management of the natural tendency of emotionally disturbed patients to socialize with and to seek further support from each other outside the official clinical meetings is a controversial point among group therapists. Most group therapists accept their patients' socializing needs, but few make it an official part of the clinical program as we do. Classically oriented psychoanalysts see in socializing outside the therapeutic setting only obstruction to the therapeutic process (p. 114).

Pro.   Bach encourages his patients to socialize. He feels that it relieves some of the tensions that build up during group sessions and enables clients to discover that in spite of their problems, they can relate effectively to each other socially. Furthermore, he believes that they do reveal things about themselves within the relaxed social atmosphere that they may not reveal in the treatment group. He also expects his patients to bring back into their group the new material revealed during socializing. He believes that their custom of sharing and communicating all interpersonal interaction that occurred during the socializing tends to prevent misuse or acting out.

Contra.   Nevertheless, there are at least four reasons for discouraging socializing: (1) It increases chances for confidences to be broken. (2) It tends to increase acting out. (3) It encourages clients to become more dependent upon fellow clients for meaningful relationships, when instead they should learn to relate to their significant others or develop new relationships. (4) It enables them to escape from their responsibility for coping with resistance within their treatment sessions. Furthermore, socializing seems to increase drainage—the revelation of private material in social sessions rather than in therapy session.

There is also the professional dilemma of handling clients who may take advantage of other clients. The female client with a high need for socialization may be taken advantage of by a manipulative male client who encourages relationships outside of the group.

This issue of outside socialization should be dealt with as a group issue and clearly defined guidelines should be developed for the group, with an understanding of the process for addressing exceptions taken. This should encompass sexual engagement as well, since this topic has become even more prevalent in recent years.

Dependent

The majority of dependent clients feel relatively inadequate. Some feel inadequate in most situations, others in only a few. Within these situations they lack the confidence both to make decisions and to act upon them. Dependent clients have had their dependent behavior reinforced by persons who needed to have someone dependent upon them or by important others, such as parents and teachers, who did not bother to teach them, during the normal process of growing up, how to behave independently. Hence, these clients require opportunities to learn and practice independent behaviors. They also need the understanding and support that a group of peers can provide when they approach independent action and retreat from it; and when they try it, seem to fail, and then must reevaluate what they have tried, before they can develop the courage to try it again.

Using the Fiddler Game

Some profit from systematic instruction in the decision-making process, using real case materials from their own lives to practice decision making. For these occasions the use of the "fiddler game" (described in Chapter 5) also is very helpful, especially when the dependent can listen to a recording of their own struggle. For example:

> I must decide now on a college major. I am quite certain that I would like teaching English at the high-school level. I enjoy adolescents' spirit, and I can manage them, but on the other hand, what will my mother and my fiancé think about my being just a schoolteacher? Perhaps I am kidding myself, too, and I wouldn't really be as good at it as I think.

Perhaps she does require more information about her chances for success in high-school teaching, the nature of the work, the income, and the employment opportunities; but even more, she requires assistance in deciding things for herself and in asking her significant others to accept her decisions—not only to mature but to experience some real self-respect. Here her fellow clients can encourage her; help her practice presenting her case in role-playing scenes with specific significant others; and serve as a model for her during the role-reversal phases of role playing. They also can help her discover and use others as models.

Certainly good models are more powerful than advice for such a client. Such experiences encourage dependent clients to behave more independently.

The Difficulty in Dealing with the Dependent

Dependent clients are not easily helped. They have learned many effective ways of manipulating others into doing things for them. They may, for example, appear so helpless that they convince other clients and the counselor that (at least for the present) some specific advice or assistance is essential. They may also get themselves into situations in which they seem to lack any coping resources. Finally, by appealing to the strength, wisdom, and maturity of others, they may end up seducing those others into taking responsibility for them.

Usually it helps to place a dependent client in a group with someone who is trying to learn to cope with a dependent other. With role-playing scenes in which the client who is possessed by a dependent significant other expresses how negatively she feels toward that significant other, the dependent client discovers how her significant others must feel when she uses them. This also encourages her to explore why some friends have deserted her and how perhaps others, who have stuck with her, must resent her at certain times. In group counseling the counselor detects and reflects how significant others must feel toward the clients in the group and what each client must learn to do to cope with his or her own significant others. Without this confrontation with their own dependent behavior and their own recognized need for self-respect, dependent clients often are difficult to motivate to change. Usually they have surrounded themselves with some friends and relatives (and even counselors) who enjoy being needed by dependent persons.

Advice Giver

Advice giving fulfills some important unmet, and perhaps unconscious, needs of the advice giver, such as the need for recognition (Bach, 1954). It also implies and conveys mutual interest and caring (Yalom, 1975). Some clients genuinely believe that giving advice is the way to help fellow clients. Others use advice giving as a way to solicit feedback on alternative solutions that they would like to try. Advice giving also may occur when a client is experiencing resistance; she may use it to cover up her own dependency feelings; to shift focus of attention to another; or to encourage another to take some action rather than to continue to discuss material that is painful for the advice giver. Powdermaker and Frank (1953) present two additional reasons: first, to exhibit superiority to the doctor ("I can help him better than you can."); or secondly, conceal their contempt for the one who seeks advice. Freud (1933) notes an underlying sadism in the person who exhibits an overzealous desire to help another.

Symbiosis: The Advice Giver and the Advice Seeker

Yalom (1975) calls attention to the symbiotic nature of the relationship between some advice seekers and the advice giver:

> The patient who, for example, continuously pulls advice and suggestions from others only to reject it ultimately and frustrate others is well known to therapists as the "helping rejecting complainer" or the "yes, but" patient. Other patients may bid for attention and nurturance by asking for suggestions about a problem which is either insoluble or which has already been solved. Others soak up advice with an unquenchable thirst yet never reciprocate to others equally needy. Some group members are so intent on preserving a high status role in the group or a façade of cool self-sufficiency that they never ask directly for help; some are effusive in their gratitude; others never acknowledge a gift, but take it home, like a bone, to gnaw on it privately (p. 12).

> Direct advice from members occurs without exception in every therapy group. . . . Despite the fact that advice giving is common in early interactional group therapy, I can recall few instances in which a specific suggestion concerning some problem was of direct benefit to any patient (p. 11).

While being seduced by the dependent client's helplessness and/or request to be rescued, clients readily see the folly of advice giving. When the advice giver is tempted to rescue the dependent client, the counselor may be tempted to interpret the advice giver's behavior. By itself, that is rarely effective. Usually better results are obtained by reflecting the feelings of both, and encouraging the other clients' participation. For example:

> Let's all try to capture how each of you two feels and then help you [advice giver] decide what you can do to help him [advice seeker] without giving him advice. You [advice giver] are deeply touched by his helplessness and you want to rescue him and tell him what to do. And you [advice seeker] would like that. You think that those who really care about you should rescue you when you are hurting—even though it may prevent you from discovering for yourself what you could do to help yourself.

Such a response tends to stop the advice giving, encourages both parties to think about what they are doing, and encourages the other clients to help both find new, improved ways of coping with their dilemma. In trying to control others, the advice giver and the advice seeker feel controlled; but, they want to learn to assert themselves—to be real and genuine and, at the same time, considerate.

Advice Giving as Avoidance Behavior

Sometimes the advice giver cannot stand to see even a client who is dealing with his problems well (but is exhibiting a lot of pain) suffer. On such occasions, the counselor may respond to the advice giver as follows:

> When Tom suffers like that in order to convey how he feels and to decide what he must do to achieve his goals, it is too painful for you. Consequently, you suggest some things that Tom can do in order to push him quickly into some action and to spare him, and perhaps you, some pain. I wonder whether Tom has talked enough about how he feels, whether he would like to decide for himself what he would like to do, and how he feels toward you for pushing him away from his painful material that he just now developed the strength to face.

Again the primary focus of the response is to help the advice giver examine her own needs and to involve the other clients in helping her deal with the problems that motivate her to block therapeutic discussion by another.

Similarly, some beginning counselors also have trouble letting a client suffer—especially those counselors who have come out of authoritarian work assignments in which they perceived themselves as champions of the hurting and the underdog. They, too, are tempted to rescue the hurting, dependent client. On the other hand, they can be very impatient with the clients who are too quick to give advice.

OTHER CHALLENGING CLIENTS: A POSTSCRIPT

Counselors may find themselves working with challenging clients who may be challenging for reasons beyond those described above. This may include special environments or conditions under which people work. For example, counselors in a school setting in which students have been referred for disciplinary action would likely present themselves as challenging clients. Likewise, in a correctional setting, clients are likely to be quite guarded about the disclosures they are likely to make or the openness with which they will discuss their concerns. Rappaport (1982) has written:

> The prison itself stands as an edifice dedicated to punishment, not understanding. Trying to convince an inmate that he or she should trust the environment of the group, when the larger environment (the prison) is so threatening, is an almost insurmountable task. Moreover, even if the inmate overcomes the fear of peer ridicule, administrative mistrust, psychiatric stigma, "guinea pig" exploitation, and loss of time in which to participate in other, more acceptable, prison activities, there are still a multitude of intrapsychic resistances to overcome. Exposure of repressed ideas and feelings requires a patient, careful, peeling back of layers of material under gentle guidance and acceptance.

Most of these issues can be addressed during intake, and an effective initial interview will set aside most situations that may create problems.

Multicultural issues also play a role in how active or challenging clients may be. What is seen as silence or resistance by some in very quiet group members may be a reflection of a cultural norm. When this occurs, the counselor must be aware of the silence as a learned behavior and help the participant learn more-effective ways of being in the group, if appropriate. On the other hand, participants who, because of cultural differences, demonstrate attention through silence should be permitted to learn in their own styles.

SUMMARY

Every counselor must try to detect why some clients are difficult for the counselor, and to use the understanding of the impact of challenging clients to help the counselor respond in therapeutic ways. When a difficult client does not sense her impact upon others, the counselor helps her request feedback and use it to define goals and to learn new behaviors. If the counselor has difficulty in facilitating clients, supervision to help the counselor understand the problem is called for.

The other-controlled client who is so sensitive to others' needs and is so controlled by them that she has difficulty requesting assistance in learning to cope was described in this chapter. The tendency this client has to allow others to take over her life was addressed, along with measures for helping the client with the issue. The chapter also discussed the shy, silent, withdrawn, scapegoat, socializer, dependent, and advice giver. Though the latter two do have problems with others controlling them, they also tend to control their significant others.

We briefly touched upon other challenging clients: the imprisoned and the client whose challenging behavior is her culture's norm.

REFERENCES

Bach, G. R. (1954). *Intensive group psychotherapy.* New York: Ronald.

Coyne, R., & Silver, R. (1980). Direct, vicarious, and vicarious-process experiences. *Small Group Behavior, 11,* 419–429.

Freud, S. (1933). *New introductory lectures.* New York: Norton.

Grater, H. A. (1958). When counseling success is failure. *Personnel and Guidance Journal, 37,* 233–235.

Horne, A. (1977). Rational assertiveness training. Paper presented at the *Second National Conference on Rational Emotive Psychotherapy* convention, Chicago, IL.

Lieberman, M. A.; Yalom, I.; & Miles, M. (1973). *Encounter groups: First facts.* New York: Basic Books.

Lundgren, D., & Miller, D. (1965, Spring). Identity and behavioral changes in training groups. *Human Relations Training News.*

Ormont, L. J. (1984). The leader's role in dealing with aggression in groups. *International Journal of Group Psychotherapy, 34*(4), 553–572.

Powdermaker, F. B., & Frank, J. D. (1953). *Group psychotherapy.* Cambridge, MA: Harvard University Press.

Rappaport, R. G. (1982). Group therapy in prison. In M. Seligman (Ed.), *Group psychotherapy and counseling with special populations.* Baltimore: University Park Press.

Weiner, M. F. (1985). Regression in group therapy: A negative view. *International Journal of Group Psychotherapy,* 1985, *35*(2), 209–224.

Yalom, I. D. (1975). *The theory and practice of group psychotherapy.* New York: Basic Books.

Yalom, I. D. (1985). *The theory and practice of group psychotherapy* (3rd ed.). New York, Basic Books.

11

CHALLENGING CLIENTS: THE RELUCTANT

Understanding and working with reluctant clients is one of the major challenges facing the neophyte counselor; it is a continuing challenge for everyone who works with clients seeking personal help with change or being referred by others for assistance. A therapeutic alliance between the counselor and the client is based on successfully dealing with the dynamics of the client's reluctance to seek, understand, accept, and use help. Rios and Ofman (1972) believe that counseling in general is based on the contradiction of accepting the client as he is in order to assist him in changing. Ofman (1976) believes resistance is a natural part of the client's position of personal integrity. Riordan, Matheny, and Harris (1978) also believe resistance is a natural and healthy part of the client's right to be involved in his own decision making and responsibility for change.

THE RELUCTANT CLIENT

Reluctance on the part of the client is seen as fear of the unfamiliar, blended with suspicion for what some clients may perceive the counselor represents: namely, the system (such as the school) that is their adversary. Secondary gains may also influence clients' reluctance to change. Clients on welfare may be removed from financial support if they succeed in maintaining a job. Others who are reluctant may be unwilling to forego the attention they receive as a result of their personal problems. Several principles of motivation seem relevant to group counseling and the reluctant client. For example, group members are influenced by shared behavioral expectation for change and the need for maintaining consistency between what one says and does in the group. Helping others make similar changes in behavior encourages the helper to change; while more clients publicly affirm the need for change, the more likely they will behave in ways that will lead to change (Riordan et al., 1978).

227

The Causes of Reluctance

The Referred Client

Clients often become reluctant when they are coerced into seeing a counselor or therapist by a parent, spouse, teacher, friend, employer, probation officer, or judge. They are made to feel they are to blame for whatever happened at home, at school, or at work. Even when they recognize that they have problems with which they require assistance, they are reluctant to try to change; probably doubt their own ability to learn essential new behaviors; and certainly question the likelihood of being helped by the person whom they are forced to see.

To accept treatment is often perceived by such a client to mean that he accepts the blame for a problem with his significant other. At the very least, it means that he must admit to himself that he has some weakness with which he requires assistance: "Acquiescing to the counseling enterprise can become symbolic of failure by her [the reluctant client] having to internalize the notion, 'I'm inadequate.' Reluctance becomes a shield against this kind of assault on one's sense of well-being" (Vriend & Dyer, 1973, p. 242). The group-counseling client may be particularly reluctant due to the fear of losing self-esteem by exposing vulnerabilities and weaknesses in front of and to others (Gustafson & Hartman, 1978).

On the other hand, those who threaten the status quo in the establishment may be referred for counseling—not so much to help them become more self-actualizing as to protect the referrer or the establishment against their threatening demands for change. "The counselor, thus confronted, remains the institutional representative of the system, the eminently distrustful authority figure by virtue of her very role; the one who is paid to straighten out conscientious objectors" (Vriend & Dyer, 1973, p. 242).

Cultural Reluctance

Some individuals may be reluctant to confide in strangers due to cultural mores that view seeking help outside the family as a betrayal. For example, individuals from Nigerian or Asian-American cultural backgrounds may have difficulty or feel reluctant to seek outside help with personal concerns (Ipaye, 1982; Ho, 1984). Some may fear the helping process through the perception or belief that entering into a group may produce demoralization and more pain than they think they can handle. Such reluctance may, in part, be based on horror stories about what "goes on in groups." Helping reluctant clients, in this instance, may be done by teaching, clarifying, and preparing the clients to understand: how the group functions; their role; the roles members and the leaders may play; and how they can be helped by participating in the group (Lawe & Horne, 1982).

Thus, even those who do not volunteer for group counseling can be helped by it, providing that such clients are helped to express their feelings concerning the external pressure to participate; that they understand what will be expected from them in the group; that they accept these expectations; that they ask to participate; that they accept the responsibility for developing trust of the counselor and fellow clients—for convincing themselves and their counselor that they are ready for group counseling and for learning desired new behaviors.

Pressuring such clients to participate can have serious consequences for all concerned: success for them is unlikely, and they may prevent other clients from obtaining help; reluctant clients also may conclude, quite properly, that counselors do not respect others' privacy; that they can and do invade others' private world—whether or not they are wanted there. Such a complaint not only damages the counselor's relationship with reluctant clients but with other prospective clients, too. A counselor must be strong enough to help a reluctant client uncover his real reasons for avoiding counseling and still respect the client's right to decide for himself whether to accept counseling in order to learn desired new behaviors.

Dealing with the Reluctant Client

According to Riordan and his associates, counselors frequently operate with four myths that disable them when working with reluctance. The following are examples of the disabling self talk in which counselors often engage:

    1. *The client must trust me.* After having been taught all the trust-building skills, the beginning counselor in particular is sometimes immobilized by signs of distrust in the client. Such distrust is the very hallmark of the reluctant client, and counselors need help in facing distrust when appropriate or in forging on in spite of it.

    2. *I am a facilitator not a salesperson.* The reluctant client is frequently operating with survival as the only discernible goal. Without a proactive counselor the facilitated condition is more fear and evasion.

    3. *Every client can be helped,* or its opposite, *No unwilling clients can be helped.* These two extremes frustrate counselor resourcefulness on the one end and abandon responsible service delivery on the other.

    4. *I alone am responsible for what happens with this client.* Unfortunately, responsible counselor behavior is often interpreted to mean that consultation and help from others, including the client, are signs of weakness or ineptitude (Riordan et al., 1978, pp. 11–12).

A study by Paradise and Wilder (1979), designed to examine the relationship between client reluctance and counseling effectiveness, found a negative correlation between precounseling reluctance and client improvement and satisfaction with counseling services. These same authors further believe that this condition is a major counseling-process variable, in general; and, from this standpoint, all clients are seen as more or less reluctant. Future counselor trainees will most likely receive more training in this area.

The Affirmative Approach

Counselors tend not to be prepared emotionally to deal with the reluctant client: they tend to perceive the client's antitherapeutic behavior as personal rejection and to blame themselves for their client's failure to cooperate in the therapeutic process, or to become angry and frustrated with the client for failing to see the benefits of seeking help. Larrabee (1982) suggests that a process of affirmation and acceptance of the client's resistance offers the counselor an option in maintaining a facilitation position that may be conducive to exploration of the positive and negative aspects of the client's behavior without getting caught up in the quagmire of reluctance. The following are basic, affirmation-process goals set forth by Larrabee:

> The counselor's long-range goal is to assist the student in making a change only if requested, rather than to motivate a change desired by others. The counselor's immediate goal is to assist the student to become aware of both the positive and negative consequences of a particular decision or position in a manner that is personally affirming. Paradoxically, this stance often enables clients freely to examine the negative aspects of a position in an objective manner. Any change that does occur is then considered as self-determined and self-enhancing, and client defensiveness is less likely to result (1982, p. 106).

Until such a client discovers that he has a real choice concerning participation in counseling and accepts responsibility for demonstrating his own readiness and commitment to learn essential new behaviors, he is not likely to profit from counseling. Even when he decides for the present not to participate, such an approach tends to increase the chances that he will seek help from his counselor in the future and that he will explore openly the natural consequences of his failure to accept help at this time. Sometimes such a client also may be willing to make a commitment to try group counseling on a trial basis. Then the group must decide whether or not he is a sufficiently good risk to be trusted and admit him on some sort of probationary basis defined in behavioral terms.

The Confrontational Approach

Vriend and Dyer (1973) present another somewhat different, but effective, approach, which relies more on the use of confrontation and interpretation than the approach described above, which relies primarily on the use of reflection. The counselor questions the source of the reluctance: What rewards does the client receive from his obvious resistance? Is this behavior typical for this person? Despite his overt rejection of my helping efforts, can I allow him this behavior and continue to accept him as a person of worth who can be taught to benefit from counseling? Is the resistance due to my being a symbol of authority? Would he see cooperation as an admission of his own weakness? Does resistance protect him from having to admit it? These questions help the counselor to avoid the trap of projecting the client's reluctance onto herself, thus creating strong possibilities for ultimately giving up on the client.

Dealing with the reluctant behavior as it is manifested, rather than ignoring it, communicates to the client that (1) his feelings are acknowledged and understood; (2) counseling is not a process that pretends that feelings do not exist; (3) counseling does not avoid feelings; (4) the counselor has an integrated personality and is strong enough to handle resistance in any form without being personally threatened; (5) by looking at the client and his behavior openly and directly, the counselor is full of attention and respect for the importance of what is going on in him and in his world; and (6) the counselor is capable of avoiding moralization by showing the client that he is entitled to his behavior, even when it is antisocial, ineffective, and does not have the import it was generated to produce.

Reliable interpretation of silence, hostility, or excessive acquiescence tends to (1) provide the client with greater self-understanding; (2) demonstrate counselor competency and capacity as a resource for further help; (3) help the client learn the nature and causes of his own resisting behavior; (4) teach the client that counseling is not a one-sided effort in which one party does all the work; and (5) show the client that counseling does not skirt behavior just because it makes most people feel uncomfortable.

The client who encounters the accepting goal-centered counselor, committed to helping and willing to go right to work at eliminating barriers to the mutual task, can hardly maintain his pose for long. Resistance is seriously challenged when a client is asked, "Are you ready for us to do some things together to make your current life a happier one?" Or, "Can we agree to meet for three sessions and set up a goal for the end of that time?" Or, "Can we establish as a goal that you tell all you can about yourself in relation to this kind of difficulty?" (Vriend & Dyer, 1973, pp. 244–245).

FIVE SPECIFIC TYPES OF RELUCTANT CLIENTS

The Nonclient

Sethna and Harrington (1971) found that clients who did not discuss their problems openly and participate actively within the first several sessions tended to drop out or to become nonclient members—participating very little and appearing to be easily threatened. Similarly Lieberman, Yalom, and Miles' (1973) casualties did not feel safe and close to fellow clients. As casualties perceived it, their group failed to provide the support, security, and cohesiveness that most helped clients experienced. Perhaps their "dropouts" withdrew to protect themselves against attack and threat.

Negative Effects on Group Cohesion

Dropping out may result, in part, from a fear of intimacy (Stone et al., 1980) or commitment to the group beyond what the dropout believes he can manage. In a study by Holmes (1983), the suggestion is made that dropping out may be negotiated to the benefit of both the group and the perspective dropout, and that non-negotiated exits can have negative effects. One of the more negative effects of a member dropping out is that others might do the same, establishing a norm in the group that engenders quitting as a more desirable alternative to staying and helping build the group into a more satisfying experience.

Lothstein (1978) found that therapists tend to report disliking the individuals who dropped out and that the dropout tended to be hostile toward the therapist. The effects that dropouts have on the development of cohesion in a group is a major problem facing the counselor. If dissatisfied members continue without successfully resolving the issues surrounding their decision to dropout, they are likely to be a hazard to group cohesion due to negative attitudes and lack of positive participation in the group; and if they drop out without resolving their issues over leaving, the group may be further hampered by the devaluing statements made to the group by dropping out.

Positive Group Cohesion

In contrast, Lieberman, Yalom, and Miles' (1973) most-helped (high learners) experienced the pleasure of feeling close to others, of trust, and of feeling secure in seeking and giving feedback. They felt that they were quality participants: seeking help and giving it. They experienced caring and being cared for. They felt that they were encouraged to take risks and try new behaviors. They felt that they were members of cohesive groups. Consequently, they talked openly, gave others honest, considerate feedback, and felt secure in requesting feedback from others. Moreover, they developed increasing tolerance for others' views and foibles and became more self-directed and less other-directed.

In other words, the care taken to select clients and to prepare them for their responsibility as clients and as helpers described in Chapter 1 should encourage even reluctant clients to participate effectively. Even those who learn much from letting others speak for them and from observing the behavior changes in their good models could profit more by learning to speak for themselves—openly describing where they hurt, with what they require assistance, and what they must do to define and implement desired new behavior. They must practice active participation for more-effective living with co-workers, classmates, relatives, or friends; they must learn to make requests, to actively help others, and to be more assertive.

Clients who profit most from group counseling know what will be expected of them prior to deciding whether to participate in group counseling (including how to participate as clients and as helpers); have some specific behavioral goals; and are committed to discussing their problems openly and learning some desired new behaviors. They expect to participate from the beginning as active, responsible members of their groups.

Case Example

The case illustration of Ms. J. serves as an example of the nonclient. Ms. J., from the beginning of the group, sat stonelike, quiet, and appeared to be unaffected by all that took place in the group. Even when the leader attempted to draw her out, her comments and responses held nothing with which others could identify or relate; consequently, members of the group began to ignore her, as if she was not there. Eventually, this situation was brought to the group's attention by the leader asking members to process their feelings and reactions concerning Ms. J.'s nongroup-membership status. Some members felt frustrated and angry with her for taking up space, or letting them do all the work. Others felt neutral and wanted to leave her where she was: sidelined and uninvolved.

What seemed to matter the most to Ms. J., in terms of the group's response to her, was the realization that other members felt burdened by her lack of participation and resented her uninvolvement—in the sense that they took the risk to talk openly, and she seemed unwilling to risk. A combination of factors had a positive impact effecting changes in Ms. J. as a result of the feedback that she received. She was deeply moved by the feelings expressed and began to understand and accept the care that others could offer if she would allow. At first, she was confused about the desire to get to know her that other members conveyed. She did not believe that anyone would really want to know her or want to understand her—and actually caring about her seemed totally foreign to her.

Within a few sessions, and with periodic focus on Ms. J., she began to open up, reporting that all this was new to her: she had been brought up being told by her family to keep her mouth shut, that discussing personal problems in front of strangers was a stupid thing to do because others would only use such information against her. Ms. J. had a great deal of unlearning of old behaviors to do, and the focus of her work in group centered around her feelings, thoughts, and reactions to what was happening in the here-and-now of the group's experience. The goal was to help her discover her process of opening up, making contact and trusting others.

The Disruptive Client

Frequently parents, teachers, or juvenile officers seek help with disruptive clients. When this happens, the counselor must decide who is the client (and/or consultee). First, the counselor should help referrers describe the misbehaving person's disruptive behavior—including how they feel toward this person and precisely how they would like to see the person's behavior change—and cooperatively decide the extent to which they (the referrers and the counselor) wish to involve the disruptive person in achieving these desired new behaviors—including whether he will be referred for counseling and by whom. Within an institutional setting, such clients may be helped, without counseling, by various behavior-modification techniques (Azrin & Powers, 1975; Azrin & Wesolowski, 1974; Foxx & Azrin, 1972; Lobitz, 1974; Matson & Cahill, 1976; Matson & Horne, 1975; Tyler & Brown, 1967; Wells, 1962). The type of disruptive, brain-damaged children whom Werry and his associates (1966, 1967) have treated successfully by behavioral-modification techniques rarely respond to either individual or group counseling (or therapy).

What applied to reluctant clients set forth earlier in this chapter—concerning the use of counseling to force clients to comply—certainly applies to disruptive students. In the classroom, and even in prison work forces, their disruptive behavior serves two useful purposes for them: first, it attracts attention to them (something they probably have not learned to earn more honorably); and secondly, it demonstrates that no one can make them do anything that they do not want to do (of course, criminals may be forced to give up their lives to prove this point). Even when such clients can genuinely accept group counseling in order to learn desired new behaviors, the cooperation of significant others, such as parents and teachers, is essential. Best results are obtained when such clients are able to describe their desired new behaviors to their significant others and to enlist their assistance in recognizing and reinforcing their efforts to implement these new behaviors. Frequently significant others also require assistance in managing such persons. Adlerians have produced some of the best management guidelines for them (Dreikurs, 1972; Dreikurs & Grey, 1968; Dreikurs & Soltz, 1964).

Usually even adult clients of this type have difficulty postponing gratification to earn big goals; for example, the charlatan who mastered some medical skills as a military medic and practices medicine after he is discharged; or the bright bank robber who cannot wait to earn enough money to afford big cars and expensive living. Until such clients hurt enough and have decided that they probably never will achieve their most important goals by behaving as they have previously, they probably will not become good clients.

Dealing with the Disruptive

When an effective counselor is able to use the approach described at the beginning of this chapter—and these clients begin to question whether her approach will ever enable them to achieve their goals—some disruptive clients will try seriously to commit themselves to behavior changes in group counseling. Usually such a counselor is most successful when, in addition to her own idiosyncratic goals, she is able to detect and reflect the underlying needs of her clients that get them into trouble, helping them to define some behavioral goals such as: (1) earning recognition from specific significant others with specific, more readily acceptable behavior; (2) working out with specific significant others what they can expect of each other and to live out these expectations rather than trying to prove that no one can make them do what they do not want to do; and (3) defining mini-goals for each long-term goal, thereby experiencing some quick satisfaction with achievement of mini-goals. Some who are treated successfully in counseling groups also can be trained to function as peer helpers for those who cannot accept group counseling.

The Drug-Addicted Client

In defining addiction, Burnett (1979) states:

> Psychologically defined, an addiction occurs when an abuser's use of any drug becomes obsessive, compulsive, and excludes all other coping mechanisms for warding off unwanted experiences. When that drug is withdrawn, the addict becomes severely disoriented and distressed. Following the completion of the physical symptoms of withdrawal, the desire to seek out a renewed high will motivate the abuser back to the drug experience (p. 348).

With the very poor record of rehabilitation of drug addicts, schools and community agencies must give serious attention to prevention. Wherever possible young people, including addicts, should be encouraged to help plan and evaluate such programs. If these prevention programs are to be effective, Grant (1972) believes that drug educators must listen to youth; discuss openly how they feel about drug use; exhibit commitment as change agents to current glaring social injustices; and be able to help youths work constructively for social change. Moreover, most youths know quite a bit about drugs and are quick to catch authors' and teachers' half-truths and personal biases. To merely provide information alone is not sufficient (Swisher & Crawford, 1971). Youths must be given the opportunity to share findings on drugs, to compare them, and to react to the information provided. Perhaps this can best be done in classroom discussion groups of the type described by Glasser (1969) and Sonstegard and Dreikurs (1973).

Ineffectiveness of Group Therapy on Addicts

Rarely is either group counseling or group pyschotherapy effective with drug addicts. They have given up and so have their significant others given up on them. At a meeting with heroin addicts, one member who even realized that he could break the habit described his plight as follows: "I can kick the habit, but all of my friends are drug addicts. Most of the nonaddicts I know won't have anything to do with me, and I don't know how to make new friendships. I have no regular job, and I don't see much of a chance of getting a decent job." Although Krawinski, Fowler, Rotenberg, and Boyson (1972) contend that drug use is the symptom, not the the problem, nevertheless, it prevents the drug user from working on original problems.

Markoff (1969) concludes that once persons become addicted to hard drugs, there are no good rehabilitation risks. He reports that most addicts tend to be weak, immature, irresponsible people who see themselves addicted for life. Frequently they were pampered by parents who rescued them when they got into trouble, and perhaps unknowingly reinforced the unacceptable behavior by exhibiting deep caring then and only then. Perhaps these same parents have such high aspirations for them that they doubt that they can live up to the expectations; and they are too weak to deal with the problem of significant others' unreasonably high goals for them.

Synanon

Except for Synanon groups, most traditional methods for treating addicts are ineffective. Whereas a 2 percent cure rate is common for most drug programs, Gateway House (a Synanon group) reported 80 to 85 percent success (drug abstinence for the two-year, follow-up period after finishing the program) for those who completed their two-year program (Martin, 1972). These peer counseling groups have some features that are similar to the procedures for earning membership described in Chapter 1 but are much harsher: (1) Prospective members must convince a committee of current Synanon residents in an intake interview that they are committed to substitute a new, meaningful way of life for their irresponsible, selfish, stubborn, and self-pitying, drug-addicted existence (Higgins, 1972; Martin, 1972). (2) They must convince the committee that they can and will accept responsibility for themselves (arrive at appointed places on time; do their work; keep themselves clean; agree not to use drugs, fight, or smoke; and break all ties with all former associates). (3) After they are admitted, they are expected to obey the rules for the group, do their work, help others grow, and serve as good models for others.

During treatment, members are expected to discuss their problems openly and to react to each other honestly, but with compassion. Discussions focus on feelings, behavior, success, and failures. Members learn to extinguish undesirable behaviors and to reinforce desired new behaviors. Up until now, most of those treated in Synanon groups have been inpatients. The work with outpatients in mental-health centers and schools also looks promising.

Effective Group-Counseling Measures

While drug-addicted clients are difficult to work with, some group-counseling procedures have been found to be effective in dealing with the complexities of drug addiction. According to Bratter (1981), the chemically dependent are often unmotivated to change or terminate their drug-dependent behaviors, or to trust helping professionals, such as group leaders. In order to help these reluctant clients, Bratter recommends that a learning-based confrontational approach be used, in which the group leader assumes a more active role, sets limits, as well as provides support.

Part of the difficulty in working with drug-addicted clients may be found in the psychodynamics related to the role drug use plays in the client's life. Rohling (1977) believes that drugs are not used as a substitute object for unsatisfied drives, but as ideal objects capable of satisfying ego needs and narcissistic emptiness. The same author also suggests that the group milieu offers flexible yet firm boundaries; clearly defined norms that are also changeable; an open communication system where perceptions can be tested, worked through, and integrated—all of which are not typically part of the addict's primary group. Group counseling was also added as a requirement to a methadone-based, drug-treatment program resulting in a higher completion rate for the program (Khantizian & Kates, 1978).

Female drug addicts have been helped to increase their self-awareness, self-respect, and self-esteem in groups made up of only women (Wedenoja & Reed, 1982). These authors believe that drug-addicted females may feel drug-taking behaviors are linked to issues related to being a woman and not to personal failures; and that groups comprised solely of females facilitate the exploration of topics and issues that may not be addressed in a mixed group.

Extended Marathon Therapy

A marathon, extended group-therapy concept with a residential drug-treatment program using the theme "Life and Death" aimed at resistance to change was developed by Hoag and Grissen (1984). In addition to other group-counseling measures, this extended marathon group uses shock techniques, such as: having members take a tour of ghetto zones of drug and alcohol addiction, a prison, a hospital psychiatric ward, and a cemetery; environmental, spiritual, emotional, and physical death are symbolized through these experiences. Drug-treatment residents are also taken to a hospital maternity ward to present hope and new beginnings. The authors of this technique suggest that the value of their approach lies in the dramatic impact of past, present, and future consequences illustrating the need for change while stimulating the desire to change.

Dealing with the Addicted

Occasionally drug-addicted clients can be helped when they elect to join a counseling group following the type of confrontational presentation described at the beginning of this chapter. Sometimes several intake interviews are required to communicate precisely what will be expected of them; to answer their questions concerning the extent of their commitment to talk openly; to define precise behavioral goals; to assume responsibility for their own recovery and for developing meaningful relationships with significant others; and to convince themselves as well as the counselor that they are ready and committed to changing their behavior now.

If the counselor is not completely convinced on these grounds, she is ethically obligated to convey to the addict's family that she cannot help the client at this time; discuss with them the natural consequences of the addict's failure to fully accept treatment now; and discuss with them what they must do to protect the addict until he can accept treatment. When such a client detects the extent of such caring, he may accept treatment unconditionally and be treated successfully. Even then, he is most apt to be treated best with strong clients who can learn to believe in him and will have the patience to help him change. Usually his chances for help are best in a group that is made up of primarily nonaddicts—including at least one good model for him (Nye, 1973).

The Monopolist

Most group therapists and counselors agree that the monopolist is a resister and a poor treatment risk. In many ways, he behaves like a pampered child. He appears to be highly threatened whenever anyone moves in to compete with him for the limelight: he really feels inadequate and unloved. Perhaps he feels that he must control the situation because he has so little to offer as a human being. Bach (1954) believes that fear of attack and isolation accounts for monopolists' defensive overreactions and their struggles to maintain the center of the stage for themselves. Yalom (1985) believes that their compulsive speech is an attempt to deal with their anxiety. As the tension and resentment in the group increase, Yalom notes that they become increasingly anxious and speak more compulsively. Perhaps they merely want to prove that they are superior to everyone in the group, including the counselor. The monopolist is certainly skilled in capturing and holding the speaker's role. Hence, he is able to focus discussion on his preferred topics and to divert attention from the topics he dislikes.

Leader Intervention

A study done by Spinal (1984) suggests that a greater amount of leader direction is needed for groups in which members' participation is typically resistant, such as with monopolistic behavior. Leader interventions in this study focused on directing or reacting to the various processes of resistance—either on a dyadic, process, and/or task level. The leader must facilitate the personal feelings of frustration, anger, and resentment expressed by group members to the individual who monopolizes. Such facilitation is based in an understanding of the personal history and dynamics of the monopolist. On a group-process level, the leader needs to attend to the potential for group members to stereotype the monopolist, thereby locking him into a role (Bogdanoff & Elbaum, 1978). Managing monopolistic behavior is difficult for beginning counselors; and beginning therapists commonly make mistakes with these clients (Spitz et al., 1980).

Narcissism

Individuals who have the tendency to dominate, control, and manipulate others in a monopolistic manner, may also be narcissistic. The tendency of the narcissistic individual in a group is to attend sessions, but come late; expecting the group leader to be critical and hearing interventions by the leader in that regard (Nicholas, 1983). In terms of personal history, the narcissistic individual is lonely and isolated, typically aggressive and demanding, and generally hurt and angry (with anger being externalized). According to Nicholas (1983), the two themes that stand out in the history of the narcissistic behavioral pattern are: being rejected by their families; and not wanting to grow up and go to work. This same author believes that care must be taken to keep the group from attacking the narcissistic individual by setting limits on feedback; and, the therapist needs to demonstrate firmness and fairness, assuring that the narcissistic individual is treated with empathy and respect.

Dealing with Monopolistic Behavior

Usually the monopolist draws attention to himself in some way during the presentation, or when faced with threatening material during the intake interview, he speaks compulsively. It is most productive to respond to this behavior immediately:

> When you are faced with something scary or difficult, you are tempted to talk compulsively. That will interfere with you getting help in counseling. Hence, I [and your fellow clients in the group] will try to guess what you are trying to cover up or run away from and will help you discuss it. When I said _____, you changed the subject and started to talk very fast. Let's go back to that topic right now, and I will help you learn to discuss it.

It also helps to explore with him in the intake interview whether he can listen to others; share time with them; be sensitive to others' feelings and needs; encourage others to discuss openly what bothers them; and discuss openly what really bothers him. It is important for him to recognize the negative social consequences of his monopolizing behavior and to develop some specific, behavioral goals with reference to it. Generally, he requires more assistance in defining and in accepting specific behavioral goals than do most clients. Sometimes it helps in the intake interview to encourage him to describe his models; and to identify, with his assistance, the prospective clients who could serve as models and who are strong enough to interrupt his compulsive talking and to help him profit from feedback. Placing him in a group with older, more mature clients helps, too.

Probation.   Bach's (1954) recommendation that the monopolist be accepted for group treatment on a probationary basis has merit. At the opening of the first group session, he should be expected to speak first; describe his monopolizing problem; tell what he requires of fellow clients to change; and discuss some criteria that they may use to decide whether or not he be allowed to continue beyond an agreed upon probationary period. High on this list must be his ability to listen to others without interrupting and to accept and use feedback. Perhaps the most-telling feedback for him to accept is an observation and critique of a video-taped role-played session in which he observes another take his role in a role reversal. It can be further enriched by asking the monopolist to play the alter ego for the person who is trying to cope with his self-centered, controlling behavior and to supplement what she says and does. This becomes even more potent when the person who is trying to cope with the monopolist is also encouraged to use soliloquy to express the private anger, frustrations, and disappointments that she experiences in trying to get the monopolist to listen, share time, and to work on relevant therapeutic material.

Even before he gets into the group, the monopolist should be helped to examine the natural consequences of his behavior. When he can be admitted to the group on the condition that he have as a goal to change this particular behavior, he is better accepted by others and this increased acceptance enables him to accept others' efforts to cope with his nontherapeutic behavior. Without such understanding and commitment, Yalom (1985) observes that the monopolist will get feedback only in a disjunctive, explosive manner, which, in turn, elicits a defensive posture on the monopolist's part. The counselor must try to prevent this (as suggested above), or intervene early, to prevent the monopolist from committing social suicide in the group.

Case Example.   When, for example, the counselor first noticed other clients reacting negatively to Frank's monopolizing behavior, she said, "You get upset with Frank when he interrupts and takes over. It is pretty difficult for you to believe that he really wants to listen to you and help you decide what you can do when he interrupts you and talks about something else." Though he tends to be shocked and hurt when he first learns how others respond to his monopolizing in the group, he listens to their feedback providing that he has made a commitment to change prior to admission and reiterated this commitment to fellow clients at the beginning of treatment.

Fellow Clients' Input.   Fellow clients also can be taught to detect and reinforce the monopolist's developing listening and helping skills. Sometimes they also decide to set up a system for ensuring some time for everyone every session: a minimum time for the shy and reticent; a maximum for those who tend to use more than their share of time. Usually, this is enforced best by assigning each a partner: one who helps the former get the floor; and one who serves as a monitor for the latter.

Whereas the monopolist learns to share his difficulties in living up to the group's expectations of him, he appreciates their considerate efforts to help him control his monopolizing. He does not want to be perceived as a deviant within a group of fellow clients whom he respects and admires. Furthermore, learning to listen to others' problems, and experiencing success in helping them, tends to be highly satisfying and reinforcing for him. Consequently, though he is difficult to manage within a counseling group, a counseling group is probably the best place for him to learn to manage his behavior.

Acting-Out Clients

Acting out may be expressed as transference: a client may inappropriately express toward a group member feelings that he has for some important other person. Obviously, too, clients may act out with others outside their treatment group. Acting out also may be resistance: a substitute for remembering and coping with the problem within one's counseling group. Acting-out clients, according to Borriello (1979), tend to seek counseling only when they are experiencing severe crisis; must be educated to use the processes of counseling in order to avoid premature termination: group counseling is the best form of therapy for these clients.

Ziferstein and Grotjahn (1957) described a patient for whom acting out was resistance. Escaping from the pain of remembering and dealing with relevant material, she fled to the pleasure of her sexual acting out:

> Acting out is a form of activity whereby a patient unconsciously discharges repressed, warded-off impulses and relieves inner tension. Instead of remembering certain traumatic and therefore repressed experiences, the patient relives them. However, the patient is unaware of this fact, and to her, her actions seem appropriate to her present situations . . .
>
> There are people in whom the tendency to act out is prominent throughout life. There are the "acting-out" characters, who are frequently found to be oral individuals, with low tolerance for frustration or postponement of gratification, and with defects in superego and ego formation . . .
>
> Acting out is only a temporary, and not a satisfactory, solution. This analytic handling of acting out, as of any resistance, is prompt interpretation. With the help of interpretation, "acting-out" is changed into "working through."
>
> Acting out may involve the patient in realistic troubles, sometimes of a serious nature. This may complicate the treatment if the therapist reacts with anx-

iety and tries to restrain the patient, by exercising his authority rather than by understanding and interpreting. The patient may then take advantage of the therapist's anxiety and punish her by further acting out, or she may react as to a forbidding parent with castration fear or submissive compliance. The result may be a chaotic situation, aggravated in part by the countertransference of the therapist and the other group members. Most important: the therapist and the group may vicariously enjoy the patient's acting out and unconsciously encourage her, perhaps rationalizing it with the idea that it's good for the patient to develop the courage to gratify impulses, test reality, learn in the school of life, etc. In this situation the therapist and the group members are behaving like parents of delinquent children (Johnson and Szurek, 1952) who unwittingly encourage their children to act out the parents' own repressed impulses (pp. 81–83).

Case Examples

This type of encouragement to act out occurs also in groups of reasonably healthy clients.

Case 1.   An attractive college freshman joined a group of college undergraduates for assistance in relating to peers. At the first session, she revealed that she had been married and divorced the previous summer. From her description of her husband, he seemed to have considerable sex appeal; but they experienced a poor sexual adjustment, and she left him after a few weeks. She also discussed a man whom she was dating and with whom she was tempted to have intercourse. During this discussion she solicited sympathy from the group; cleverly, but subtly, attracted special attention from two of the men; and seemed to appeal for her group to condone her acting out.

   Though the members offered verbal objections to having an affair, they did condone it by their nonverbal behavior and their laughter. A well-timed reflection by the counselor, concerning her desire to have this behavior condoned and members' willingness to enjoy it vicariously, alerted everyone to what was going on so that they all could state openly what they felt. Consequently, they refused either to condone or reject her wish to act out; they conveyed that she must decide what was right for her and accept responsibility for her own behavior.

Case 2.   An 11th-grade boy (Ralph) told the members of his high-school counseling group about the way his unreasonable father nagged him. Ralph had been very open in discussing some other problems and had been very helpful to the others during the six previous sessions. Everyone, including the counselor, grew obviously angry with Ralph's father. When Ralph concluded that he would "smash him in the mouth" the next time his father nagged him, they obviously supported the idea; and no one picked up on these feelings or helped the members deal with them. Consequently, no one was surprised when Ralph had a fight with his father.

In a panel discussion, Wolf (Durkin et al., 1958) stated that acting out is always destructive and irrational but that it can be used therapeutically: "Acting out is a dramatic means of discovering persistent problems and then discovering the means to deal with them" (p. 92). In Ralph's case, the counselor did use the acting out therapeutically, but had she detected what was going on earlier, she could have helped Ralph deal with these feelings without hurting either himself or his father as he did.

Dealing with Acting-Out Clients

In the same panel discussion, Glatzer (Durkin et al., 1958) said:

> A therapist must not be involved in encouraging this blind, irrational behavior or in overstressing its possible benefits as abreaction any more than she would encourage resistance in any other form, instead of analyzing it. . . . What is needed, then, is not the opportunity to act out, to solidify the unwillingness to learn, but to stimulate understanding of its motivation and inappropriate quality so that it becomes ego-alien. Acting out seems to me like the hard core of resistance, and like all resistance it must be repeatedly worked through in order to attain what Fenichel (1945) describes as "the union with ego of what was previously warded off by it.". . .
>
> I don't think that an extended period of acting out makes it fuller or richer. It is still blind, driving behavior and it seems to me, nothing therapeutic is gained by permitting it to continue unanalyzed. Constant interpretation as soon as the therapist becomes aware that his patient is acting out and understands what she is doing (and this often gives the patient sufficient time to act out) tends to promote insight into her destructive behavior and seems to minimize its frequency. I cannot see why acting out should be permitted to remain unanalyzed any longer than it takes the therapist time to recognize it and see its significance . . .
>
> One of the advantages of immediate handling of acting out in the group situation is that a spontaneous interpretation of acting out in a fresh setting seems to have a more dynamic effect. Permitting a patient to act out, make a fool or nuisance of herself, when the therapist is aware of what is going on, may constitute a greater narcissistic injury to the patient than early interpretation and help to further encapsulate her repressed memories . . . (pp. 93–94).

We agree with most of the excellent ideas quoted above:

1. A patient should be helped to recognize the phenomenon of acting early as possible.
2. Whenever possible, it should be prevented by prompt action.
3. The acting-out patient should discover early that it is a kind of activity in which he or others can be hurt. (Whereas the authors quoted above would accomplish this by a well-timed interpretation, we would use reflection. As suggested in Chapter 1, she would teach clients to recognize and cope with this phenomenon just as they do other forms of resistance.)

4.   When acting out does occur, it can be used therapeutically within the group.

Prevention.   A counselor should not accept the notion that acting out is inevitable. Of course, it may happen sometimes, but much of it can be prevented. Perhaps, it is more easily prevented with less disturbed clients than those of the authors quoted above. A carefully timed reflection brings the material into the open where it can be dealt with. The client tempted to act out is helped to understand his motivations better, learn new and better ways of solving his problems, and discover how fellow clients react to his irresponsible behavior.

Fellow clients, in turn, often discover how they encourage and condone such behavior. Sometimes they discover that an acting-out client takes advantage of his being in treatment, using it to justify things he has wanted to do but ordinarily would not do. When the one who is or may be hurt as a consequence of a client's acting out is a member of the counseling group (or someone plays the part of the hurt one in reenacting the scene), the counselor can reflect the hurt one's feelings, and she can help both the hurt one and the hurter deal with the resulting problems. If, however, the counselor does this merely to shame the acting-out client, her response will be seen for what it is.

Role Playing.   Role playing can be used effectively to deal with acting out and to prevent it. Involving the one who is tempted to act out in describing the tempting setting; in selecting the role players from his counseling group; assigning them appropriate roles; acting out the scene; and listening to the reactions to the role playing provides him with rich feedback. Role playing also can give him practice in coping directly with such situations rather than evading them.

Although acting out can uncover repressed material to be dealt with in the treatment group, the counselor should try to prevent it whenever possible in order to protect those who may be hurt. Note also Glatzer's point that allowing a client to act out can further encapsulate repressed material, thus making it less accessible to treatment. Moreover, it is easier to help a client express and cope with his feelings for a transference object (or the real person) before he acts them out than it is to deal with the shame and embarrassment, as well as the underlying motivations, for acting out afterward.

SUMMARY

For every difficult client, the counselor must ask herself why this particular client is difficult for her; how she can use her reactions to the client to detect and reflect significant therapeutic materials; assess the extent to which her reaction is a countertransference one; help her client define precise, idiosyncratic goals; and help him develop the trust to share openly with fellow clients and to implement his own desired new behaviors.

Even reluctant clients for whom expectations and possible benefits are communicated well can learn to be good clients and be treated successfully. However, they must accept the treatment expectations; must truly want to be members of a counseling group (and without any coercion from the counselor); be committed to talk openly and to define precise behavioral goals; and exhibit genuine willingness to listen to and to help fellow clients.

REFERENCES

Azrin, N. H., & Powers, M. A. (1975). Eliminating classroom disturbances of emotionally disturbed children by positive practice procedures. *Behavior Therapy, 6,* 525–534.

Azrin, N. H., & Wesolowski, M. C. (1974). Theft reversal: An overcorrection procedure for eliminating stealing by retarded persons. *Journal of Applied Behavioral Analysis, 7,* 577–581.

Bach, G. R. (1954). *Intensive group psychotherapy.* New York: Ronald.

Bogdanoff, M., & Elbaum, P. (1978). Role lock: Dealing with monopolizers, mistrusters, isolates, "helpful Hannahs," and other assorted characters in group psychotherapy. *International Journal of Group Psychotherapy, 28,* 247–262.

Borriello, J. (1979). Group psychotherapy with acting-out patients: Specific problems and techniques. *American Journal of Psychotherapy, 33,* 521–530.

Bratter, T. (1981). Some pre-treatment group psychotherapy considerations with alcoholics and drug-addicted individuals. *Psychotherapy: Theory, Research and Practice, 18,* 508–515.

Burnett, M. (1979). Understanding and overcoming addictions. In S. Eisenberg & L. Patterson (Eds.), *Helping clients with special concerns.* Chicago: Rand McNally.

Dreikurs, R. (1972). *The challenge of child rearing.* New York: Hawthorne.

Dreikurs, R., & Grey, L. (1968). *Logical consequences: A new approach to discipline.* Des Moines, IA: Meredith.

Dreikurs, R., & Soltz, V. (1964). *Children: A challenge.* New York: Duell, Sloan, and Pierce-Meredith.

Durkin, H. E.; Galtzer, H. T.; Kadis, A. L.; Wolf, A.; & Hulse, W. C. (1958). Acting-out in group psychotherapy. *American Journal of Psychotherapy, 12,* 87–105.

Fenichel, O. (1945). *The psychoanalytic theory of neurosis.* New York: Norton.

Foxx, R. M., & Azrin, N. H. (1972). Restitution: A method of eliminating aggressive disruptive behaviors of retarded and brain damaged patients. *Behavior Research and Therapy, 10,* 15–27.

Glasser, W. (1969). *Schools without failure.* New York: Harper & Row.

Grant, R. H. (1972). Drug education: What it is and isn't. *Journal of Drug Education, 2,* 89–97.

Gustafson, J. P., & Hartman, J. J. (1978). Self-esteem in group therapy. *Contemporary Psychoanalysis, 14,* 311–329.

Higgins, A. (1972, August). Synanon is for people who never learned to live. *Dodge News Magazine,* 21–23.

Ho, M. K. (1984). Social group work with Asian/Pacific-Americans. *Social Work with Groups, 7,* 49–61.

Hoag, J., & Grissen, M. (1984). Marathon: A life and death experience. *Journal of Psychoactive Drugs, 16,* 47–50.

Holmes, P. (1983). "Dropping out" from an adolescent therapeutic group: A study of factors in the patients and their parents which may influence this process. *Journal of Adolescence, 6,* 333–346.

Ipaye, T. (1982). Introducing group counseling into Nigerian secondary schools: Report of a three-year experience. *International Journal for the Advancement of Counseling, 5,* 35–47.

Johnson, A. M., & Szurek, S. A. (1952). The genesis of anti-social acting out in children and adults. *Psychiatric Quarterly, 21,* 323–343.

Khantizian, E. J., & Kates, W. (1978). Group treatment of unwilling addicted patients: Programmatic and clinical aspects. *International Journal of Group Psychotherapy, 28,* 81–94.

Krawinski, W.; Fowler, F. S.; Rotenberg, L. A.; & Boyson, W. A. (1972). Workable community concepts in drug abuse. *Journal of Drug Education, 2,* 125–138.

Larrabee, M. (1982). Working with reluctant clients through affirmation techniques. *The Personnel and Guidance Journal, 198,* 105–109.

Lawe, C., & Horne, A. (1982). Effects of pretraining procedures for clients in counseling. *Psychological Reports.*

Lieberman, M. A.; Yalom, I. D.; & Miles, M. D. (1973). *Encounter groups: First facts.* New York: Basic Books.

Lobitz, W. C. (1974). A simple stimulus clue for controlling disruptive classroom behavior. *Journal of Abnormal Child Psychology, 2,* 143–152.

Lothstein, L. (1978). The group psychotherapy dropout phenomenon revisited. *American Journal of Psychiatry, 135,* 1492–1495.

Markoff, E. L. (1966). Synanon in drug addiction. In J. H. Masserman (Ed.), *Handbook of psychiatric therapies.* New York: Grune & Stratton.

Martin, P. M. (1972, September 20). Is God at Gateway House? *Christian Century,* 933–936.

Matson, J. L., & Cahill, T. (1976). Overcorrection: A technique for eliminating resistant behaviors. *JSAS Selected Documents in Psychology.*

Matson, J. L., & Horne, A. M. (1975). Overcorrection and extinction-reinforcement as rapid methods of eliminating the disruptive behavior of relatively normal children. Paper presented at Northcentral Association for Counselor Education, Kansas City, MO.

Nicholas, M. (1983). The narcissistic personality in group psychotherapy. *Group, 7,* 27–32.

Nye, L. S. (1973). Obtaining results through modeling. *Personnel and Guidance Journal, 51,* 380–384.

Ofman, W. V. (1976). *Affirmation and reality.* Los Angeles: Western Psychological Services.

Paradise, L., & Wilder, D. (1979). The relationship between client reluctance and counseling effectiveness. *Counselor Education and Supervision,* 35–41.

Quay, H. C., Weery, J. S., McQueen, M., & Sprague, R. L. (1962). Remediation of the conduct problem child in the special class setting. *Exceptional Children, 32,* 509–513.

Rios, R., & Ofman, W. (1972). The Chicano counseling and reality. In D. Brown & D. J. Srebalus (Eds.), *Contemporary guidance concepts and practices.* Dubuque, IA: Wm. C. Brown.

Riordan, R.; Matheny, K.; & Harris, C. (1978). Helping counselors minimize client reluctance. *Counselor Education and Supervision, 7*–13.

Rohling, G. (1977). Ego-structural approaches in the psychodynamics of addictions. *Dynamicsche Psychiatric, 10,* 17–22.

Sethna, E. R., & Harrington, J. A. (1971). A study of patients who lapsed from group psychotherapy. *British Journal of Psychiatry, 119,* 59–69.

Sonstegard, M. A., & Dreikurs, R. (1973). The Adlerian approach to group counseling children. In M. M. Ohlsen (Ed.), *Counseling children in groups: A forum.* New York: Holt, Rinehart and Winston, 1973.

Spinal, P. (1984). Group resistance and leader intervention: An international analysis. *Small Group Behavior, 15,* 417–424.

Spitz, H.; Kass, F.; & Charles, E. (1980). Common mistakes made in group psychotherapy by beginning therapists. *American Journal of Psychiatry, 139,* 1619–1621.

Swisher, J. D., & Crawford, J. L. (1971). An evaluation of a short-term drug education program. *The School Counselor, 18,* 265–272.

Stone, W.; Blaze, M.; & Bozzuto, J. (1980). Late dropouts from group psychotherapy. *American Journal of Psychotherapy, 34,* 401–413.

Tyler, V. O., & Brown, G. (1967). The use of swift, brief isolation as a group control device for institutionalized delinquents. *Behavior Research and Therapy, 5,* 1–9.

Vriend, J., & Dyer, W. W. (1973). Counseling the reluctant client. *Journal of Counseling Psychology, 20,* 240–246.

Wedenoja, M., & Reed, B. (1982). Women's groups as a form of intervention for drug dependent women. *N.I.D.A. Treatment Research Monograph Series: Treatment Services for Drug Dependent Women, 2,* 62–136.

Wells, C. G. (1962). Psychodrama and creative counseling in the elementary school. *Group Psychotherapy, 15,* 244–252.

Werry, J. S., & Wollersheim, J. P. (1967). Behavior therapy with children: A broad overview. *Journal of American Academy of Child Psychiatry, 6,* 346–370.

Yalom, I. D. (1985). *The theory and practice of group psychotherapy.* New York: Basic Books.

Ziferstein, I., & Grotjahn, M. (1957). Group dynamics of acting out in analytic group psychotherapy. *International Journal of Group Psychotherapy, 7,* 77–85.

12

COUNSELING CHILDREN IN GROUPS

Most basic principles of group counseling apply to children as well as to adolescents and adults. Nevertheless, those who counsel children must adapt their techniques to their clients' social, emotional, and intellectual development, and their previous group experiences. After a counselor has identified the group experiences with which his clients are familiar, he must *communicate the unique features of group counseling;* explaining precisely how it is like—and different from—their previous group experiences: What is unique about the topics discussed in a counseling group? How do the topics differ from those talked about in classroom discussions? How can they learn to become better listeners—and why should they? How can they tell when they need help in figuring out how to introduce a painful topic? What does keeping confidences mean? Perhaps the counselor must take greater care than he does with adolescents and adults to ensure that children know what is expected of them, and how they may ask for assistance when they do not know what to say or how to say it. On the other hand, they do tend to trust the counselor more readily than adolescents do—especially when their parents and teachers have been briefed and endorse counseling.

DEALING WITH CHILDREN

To communicate effectively with children, a counselor must listen empathically; understand his clients' language development; make reflections of recognition and clarification; and be sensitive to their search for words—which will enable them to communicate their worries and concerns and share their dreams and successes. When appropriate, he must teach them the vocabulary they require to discuss their pain, define desired new behaviors, and enlist fellow clients' and significant others' assistance in implementing the new behaviors. For example, when her counselor concluded that Dana was having difficulty communicating

248

her feelings, he said: "You feel lonely."—trying to convey to Dana that she lacked intimate, satisfying relationships. Dana said, "I am with lots of people here and at home." Then the counselor defined lonely as he was using it, and Dana responded as follows: "If that is what lonely means, I am lonely." Thus, the counselor taught Dana the meaning of a word that she required to communicate her pain, and did it in a manner that did not embarrass her or pressure her to verbalize material that could better have been communicated with use of play media or activities (dolls also could have been used to convey these same feelings). Morever, teaching vocabulary in this manner facilitates development of a fascination with learning new vocabulary; it also can carry over into classroom instruction. Children thrive on the kind of undivided attention they experience in an effective counseling group and in learning to express themselves with increasing clarity and forcefulness.

Preparing Children for Group Counseling

Laying It All Out

Preparation for participation in group counseling begins with a description of the process, expectations of clients, and what can be done to increase chances for successful outcomes (presentations). For parents and teachers, the counselor stresses the importance of them learning to listen to their children, encouraging children to celebrate their successes, and learning to reinforce their *children's successes in implementing their desired new behaviors*. During the first few counseling sessions with the children, the counselor watches for and reinforces good client behaviors (such as, discussing pain openly; defining precise goals; and implementing new behaviors outside counseling) and good helper behaviors (such as, listening empathically; giving undivided attention; exhibiting confidence in the speaker's chances for successful results; learning to be encouraging rather than discouraging or criticizing; and learning to reinforce new behaviors). It is not sufficient for the counselor to say that a given behavior is good; clients need to be told precisely what it was that they did that made their behavior productive as a client or as a helper. The counselor communicates with each child on her level of language development without condescension; and he avoids parents' and teachers' tendencies to criticize rather than to encourage.

Verbal Participation

When children are adequately prepared prior to their first group session, they will be able to participate verbally (Ohlsen, 1973). For example, Jeffries (1973) observed that though inner-city children may not use correct English, they can communicate verbally. Sonstegard and Dreikurs (1973) rely heavily on verbal communication. They use verbal techniques to help each child discover her own real goals; determine whether or not she is pursuing her goals in ways that enhance success or failure; and, when appropriate, define new goals—helping her discover her mistaken goals so that she may replace them with goals that produce better consequences. Ellis (1973) believes that children can be helped to ferret out why they feel and behave as they do and to learn new behaviors to replace their unproductive ones. Hawes (1973) concluded that children can participate in class discussions that help them discover the relevance of school for improving daily life, manage their environment, and accelerate language development.

On the other hand, Gazda (1973) and Glass (1973) were the two contributors who most question children's ability to interact verbally in a counseling group. Prior to the third grade, Glass uses projective tests to uncover therapeutic material. Gazda questions the use of verbal techniques below age nine and makes only limited use of verbal techniques until age thirteen.

Group Adjustments

The size of a counseling group and the length of sessions must be adjusted to clients' attention span, their ability to sustain interest in a fellow client's problems, and their general social maturity. Ohlsen and Gazda (1965) concluded that their fifth-grade clients were sensitive to fellow clients' feelings and needs, but they required formal instruction in both client and helper roles to profit most from group counseling. Even without formal training, clients improved these skills during the course of treatment. Ohlsen and Gazda believe that much of the clients' restless, distracting, and competing behaviors could have been prevented by teaching them to perform as clients *and* as helpers. They also concluded that better results could have been achieved in smaller groups (five or six instead of seven or eight) and for shorter counseling sessions (40–45 minutes instead of 60). Perhaps most upper-grade children should be scheduled for even shorter periods (30–35 minutes) twice a week. Primary-school-aged children should be scheduled for only 25–30 minute sessions three times a week.

Children's Problems

Children require the assistance of significant others in achieving independence; learning to relate to peers, developing confidence in themselves; coping with their ever-changing physical development; forming basic values; and mastering new knowledge and ways of thinking. Today's children in particular require assistance in adjusting to change and stress (Gardner, 1975; Thompson & Rudolph, 1983). Furthermore, children have become unwillingly and unknowingly victims of our fast-paced, pressure-cooker society (Gumaer, 1984). Our child clients, and our practica students' and interns' clients, also have discussed loneliness, grieving, school phobias, and drug use; concerns about their abilities to succeed in certain school subjects, especially arithmetic and reading; conflicts with family, friends, and classmates; and their life goals. It appears that many upper-grade, elementary-school children, especially the very bright, are more interested in beginning to explore career goals than most counselors realize. Group counseling and classroom discussion groups help children begin exploring their ambitions and dreams; to discover their own similiarities and differences; to enlarge their repertoire of human relation skills; and to adapt to ever-enlarging environment.

The Child as Client

Children who profit most from group counseling volunteer for counseling; are committed *to discuss what genuinely concerns them;* are committed to learn new behaviors; are interested in helping fellow clients learn new behaviors; and believe that their counselor and parents (and even their teachers) have confidence in their ability to learn and implement new behaviors. These children also believe that the counselor is committed to helping them define and implement *their own goals* rather than others' goals for them. Furthermore, this growth is enhanced, and better maintained, when the children believe that they can count on their significant others' support, encouragement, and reinforcement. Rarely is it advisable for a counselor to include in a group only one type of client, such as discipline cases or gifted underachievers. Usually the latter can be treated most effectively with some other children who have accepted their superior mental ability and are motivated to achieve, but have other problems with which the underachiever can provide assistance.

CHILDREN'S NEEDS

Scholars tend to agree on children's needs. Both for helping children define counseling goals and for helping parents and teachers facilitate normal development, the counselor must understand children's needs. Thus, these needs are reviewed to help counselors take cognizance of them in initiating group counseling, developing classroom discussion groups, and organizing consultation for parents and teachers.

Self-Acceptance

Self-acceptance is nurtured in healthy families (Satir, 1972). Early in her life, a self-accepting child discovers that she is usually accepted by her family and friends; this acceptance by significant others facilitates her acceptance of others and herself. She discovers she can master some skills and develop some relationships with minimal effort, but that others require considerably more effort. She also discovers that for still others, either she lacks the required abilities and aptitudes or has learning disabilities that must be corrected before she can achieve them. In any case, it helps to have her significant others exhibit confidence in her ability to cope with the problems she meets; when she questions her ability to cope, they provide quality support rather than a rescue service. Thus, she discovers that she can influence her own chances for success when she is willing to invest the time and effort required to correct the deficiencies. Furthermore, she learns that she does not have to be perfect to accept herself and to be accepted by significant others.

When, on the other hand, a child is reared in a home in which she is not accepted, she tends not to accept herself. Even when, for example, she earns recognition in school, she may not be able to accept it. She must be taught to accept it and be reinforced for accepting it. These can be learned in group counseling and classroom discussion groups in which classmates develop compassion for her plight and reinforce her acceptance of self. Getting her parents to enroll in parent education and/or counseling groups with other more nurturing parents helps her parents capture her pain, learn to exhibit more caring for her, and reinforce self-acceptance when it occurs.

Acceptance by Significant Others

Acceptance by significant others facilitates acceptance of self. Everyone needs acceptance by and recognition from signficant others. Gardner (1975) illustrates this point:

> Meaningful relationships with others are the stuff of life. More than anything else they enrich us; without them, we become shells—mere imitations of living individuals. From the moment we are born until the time of our death we need others—necessary times for solitude notwithstanding. The child in treatment has generally suffered some difficulties in his ability to form and gain gratifications from his involvement with others. Hopefully, therapy can help him to do so. But I cannot imagine its being successful in this regard if a meaningful relationship hasn't been accomplished between the therapist and his patient (p. 16).

A counselor can help parents and teachers discover from whom each child requires recognition in particular, at a given time, and for what. He also can teach them to use encouragement and to reinforce desired behaviors rather than to use criticism and discouraging tactics to extinguish undesirable behaviors.

When a child enters school, her list of persons from whom she seeks recognition is extended beyond her family and a few friends: to a teacher and some classmates. Eventually, she learns to please even some whom she does not like in order to earn the recognition that she feels she needs to achieve certain goals. As a consultant to the teacher, a counselor can often help her provide needed recognition to children who may have trouble earning it in typical classroom activities. Moreover, for ghetto children, it is important to help both teachers and parents motivate them to earn recognition for academic performance.

Love

Loving and learning to accept love are learned in nurturing homes (Satir, 1972). Everyone wants to love and to feel loved, but many cannot accept and enjoy the intimacy they desire. Both parents and teachers often require assistance in satisfying this need. Parent education and/or counseling groups are often required to help parents learn to request, accept, and enjoy the intimacy that they desire and to help them develop within their homes the atmosphere in which children can learn to give and accept love. With competent consultants many teachers can learn to use magic shop (Carpenter & Sandberg, 1973), magic circle (Ball, 1972), DUSO (Dinkmeyer, 1972), and classroom discussions to help children learn to accept and give love.

Moral Values

Developing moral values is primarily the parents' responsibility, but some parents fail their children here. Fortunately, increasing numbers of parents are seeking assistance from counselors, parent education centers, churches, and adult-education centers to fulfill this responsibility. Value-clarification techniques have been used successfully by counselors for such programs. Classroom discussions have been used to encourage children to discuss lifestyle decisions, to help them identify the choices open to them, and to enlist their family's assistance in forming moral values.

Motivating parents to take adequate time to discuss moral values; to share their own struggles in deciding what is right and wrong; to model the values they claim to accept; and to request their children's assistance and reinforcement of desired new behaviors facilitates their children's moral development. Such openness and sincerity also facilitate children's respect for their parents and portray their parents as mature, caring adults. Children's participation in defining limits and reinforcing them through the use of techniques, such as family council, helps children put moral values into practice.

Sex Roles

Sex roles are learned in the home and reinforced in school. Increasingly, special programs are being offered to help single parents discover ways in which they can help each child identify and use models selectively—consciously copying only the model's good behaviors. Big Sister and Big Brother programs also have been used very effectively in such programs.

On the other hand, we encourage elementary-school counselors to introduce career discussion groups for parents and classroom discussions for children to reduce sex-biased choice of careers. In addition to presenting what is involved in career planning, such discussions encourage children to consider the careers that *they genuinely believe* will provide them the most personal satisfactions and challenges—even those that previously have been restricted to persons of the opposite sex.

Career Interests

Career interests develop much earlier than many parents and teachers realize, and these interests should be nurtured. Parents and teachers, as well as counselors, should listen to children and help them clarify their questions about themselves as well as the occupations for which they require more information. Moreoever, such contacts afford the adult contacted with the opportunity to teach children how to use information in decision making. Demonstrating these processes with children is essential for parents participating in parent discussion groups and for teachers leading classroom discussions on career development.

Physical Health

Physical and health needs are primarily the parents' responsibility, but public health, schools, and health maintenance programs also are making significant contributions to helping children satisfy these needs. In particular, these programs are helping teachers detect child abuse and neglect, diet deficiencies, contagious diseases, and children's general poor health. We have known for a long while that it is difficult to motivate tired undernourished children. Now we realize that nutritional deficiencies can cause distress, even mental illness, and behavioral problems (Gumaer, 1984; Long, 1982).

The type of seminars provided for teachers by Moustakas (1966) and the parent-education groups described by Sonstegard and Dreikurs (1973) prepare teachers and parents to detect and answer children's questions concerning their physical and sexual development. Competent counselors have found value-clarification techniques helpful in leading parent and teacher discussion groups designed to examine their own values and to clarify those that they would like to instill in their children.

Physical and Emotional Changes

Physical and emotional changes arouse anxiety and a wide range of questions in children—especially during latency and in early adolescence. They often worry about their skin condition, sexual development, physical attractiveness, and size. Many are unduly concerned about being different, and tend to look upon differences as deficiencies. Some children also worry about what they can expect from themselves scholastically, socially, and athletically. It is very important for each to have someone to whom she can turn for help in answering her questions about herself. A competent counselor can fulfill this need as well as to help parents and teachers do it better, too. Because we believe that many children who are helped with these problems in counseling groups can, upon completion of group counseling, be taught to help classmates answer these questions, we encourage elementary-school counselors to select clients for a group out of one teacher's classroom. Then upon dealing adequately with a developmental task, these children can be prepared to help the counselor and teacher lead classroom discussions designed to answer these types of questions for classmates.

Basic Learning Skills

Mastering basic learning skills enhances school success, motivation to learn, and self-acceptance. Counselors can facilitate mastery of basic skills by serving as a consultant to parents and teachers. They *can help parents and teachers* decide what they have a right to expect from each child; detect and correct learning disabilities; appraise school progress; reinforce academic performance; stimulate intellectual curiosity, and identify and help develop promising talents.

INTRODUCING GROUP COUNSELING FOR CHILDREN INTO THE COMMUNITY

Most professionals who provide group counseling for children today are employed as elementary-school counselors. The primary exception is Adlerian Family Education Centers which offer a variety of group treatments: the family; the children's group; the parents' group; and the community group. Furthermore, Sonstegard and Dreikurs (1973) endorsed the idea of elementary-school counselors developing these family education centers in their schools as well as in community agencies.

The Children's Group Counselor

Since the middle 1960s, there has been a marked increase in the number of carefully selected and prepared counselors who are employed in elementary schools. There also has been an increase in the number of competent counselors and counseling psychologists who have been employed by mental-health centers and by physicians in family practice to counsel children. Increasingly these counselors have had practica and internships in which they were supervised in counseling children; but, even today, few have completed adequate didactic preparation in child development, learning disabilities, social psychology, group dynamics, and group counseling or have been supervised counseling children in groups. Nevertheless, some counselors have developed competencies to counsel children in groups. Use of carefully selected consultants and peer supervision often have contributed to the development of these professionals' competencies.

Wherever counselors of children are employed, they must be able to win the trust and cooperation of their clients' parents and teachers. These significant others can help identify the problems for which a child requires treatment while learning to reinforce the child's desired new behaviors. Increasingly, children's counselors are asking their clients' entire family, and occasionally even significant others such as teachers, to participate in family counseling (Horne & Ohlsen, 1982). Because teachers' cooperation and assistance is so important in treating children, some community agencies are employing elementary counselors to function as liaison persons with schools as well as to counsel children.

Elementary-School Counselors

Counselors employed in elementary schools have a natural contact with parents and teachers and can enlist the school principal's assistance to schedule parents' and teachers' meetings in which the counselor describes group counseling and answers their questions concerning their children's participation (presentation). At the first such meeting for teachers, for example, a counselor describes his entire program including classroom discussions, consultation with teachers and parents, and group counseling. He also explains why he would like to be invited periodically into their classrooms to make presentations to children—especially when he is planning to initiate group counseling and classroom discussion groups. With reference to consultation, it is important for him to stress the mutual nature of the consulting process—cooperating to help each other understand children and to facilitate their normal development. Such meetings also provide the counselor with the opportunity to introduce the idea of parents' and teachers' discussion groups in which the counselor can draw upon his knowledge of developmental psychology to help parents and teachers understand their children's behavior, exchange ideas, and encourage them to apply what they learn to facilitate children's development (Moustakas, 1966).

Those teachers who invite the counselor to make classroom presentations give the counselor a chance to meet the children and convey what will be expected of them in counseling groups; how they can recognize what really worries and upsets them; what others like themselves (especially those of their age and grade) have discussed in their groups; and how the children have been helped by counseling. The counselor also explains how they can get themselves ready for counseling; how they will define their goals for counseling; how they can be helped to implement their new behaviors; how they can learn to help fellow clients; and what they will be expected to do between counseling sessions. The counselor also explains what is unique about the counseling relationship and how it differs from other similar relationships. Finally, children are encouraged to ask any questions they have about group counseling, and other counseling services, too.

The Child's Input

Important as it is to solicit teachers' and parents' assistance, the single best source of information about the child *is* the child. There is no substitute for the information that can be gleaned from a child by observing and interviewing her. To understand a child, the counselor must give her his undivided attention and teach her to tell him how she perceives: her world, her own needs, her problems, and her behavior. Furthermore, counselors are just beginning to realize the extent to which even a young child, when confronted by the natural consequences of her self-defeating behaviors, can accept responsibility for learning her own desired new behaviors and for helping her peers learn their new behaviors.

When children are treated in such a manner and are prepared for counseling as suggested above, they often seek counseling *on their own* before either their parents or teachers recognize their children's need for counseling. We also have found that helping these self-referred children enables us to reach, and prepare for treatment, parents who heretofore have not requested counseling for themselves. Furthermore, Axline (1964) believes that truly deep and effective treatment of a disturbed child can improve the parents' mental health.

PLAY MEDIA

One of the adaptations counselors of children make is to use play media to help children communicate the pain, the self-defeating behaviors, the developmental tasks, the crises, and the unfinished business with which they require assistance. Bosdell (1973) believes that play enables a child to convey varied shades and nuances of meaning that adults convey with modifiers and slang expressions. Moreover, Bosdell believes that play provides a child with more emotional release and expressive potency than merely telling a counselor how she, the child, feels; but, it can be enhanced with words, too. Bosdell states:

> . . . the totality of the meaning is frequently enhanced by the addition of verbal comments. These verbal comments, which are frequently supplementary to the play, may for many children coexist as a necessary part of the activity. Indeed, it is sometimes difficult to determine whether the child's play explains the words and verbal messages he is sending or whether the words amplify and give substance to the play activity. As the counselor works with a child or a group of children, one of his first tasks is to identify and to be sensitive to the idiosyncratic usage of play and words of each child within the group. Understanding the ways in which various children communicate helps the counselor

to proceed with the therapeutic work of clarification, reflection, interpretation, and confrontation as it suits the style of the particular counselor. There seems to be a natural evolvement in the play group which tells the counselor when it is best to participate, to remain silent, or to help a child explore some aspect of himself with the group.

Play, the natural medium of child expression and conversation, does not replace verbalizations. For the child with expressive difficulties, it may serve the same function as preverbalizations. For most children and the counselor the interview becomes a living segment of life where play and words coexist for a totality of meaning that neither could achieve alone (1973, pp. 28–29).

Models for Play Therapy

Moustakas (1959) believes that a child soon discovers that in the playroom she has unique status: she can express her anger and fear; be critical and resentful; or act silly, carefree, or joyous. She can act out her dreams and ambitions. She can make her own decisions. She can be herself. She has the freedom to do what she wants to do and be what she wants to be.

Bosdell (1973) believes that these same advantages (plus some additional ones) can also be achieved in a group:

> . . . For children, the group experience with play media available provides a situation where the child can express himself, feel what he is feeling, and can direct his own life. Feedback from his peers as well as from the counselor provides an instant reality check. The group provides a setting in which children can explore standards and ways of relating to one another and to the environment (p. 32).

Axline (1947) outlined eight principles to follow in use of play media:

1. Good rapport must be established with each client as soon as possible.
2. The counselor must accept the child as she is.
3. He develops a relationship with each child that encourages her to express her feelings.
4. He must detect the child's feelings and mirror them back to her in a manner that helps her understand her behavior.
5. He maintains respect for each client, conveys confidence in her ability to solve her problems, and gives her responsibility for implementing her own new behaviors.
6. The client is encouraged to lead the way and the counselor to follow and facilitate the therapeutic behavior.
7. The counselor does not hurry the process; he recognizes that new learning is a gradual process.
8. The counselor establishes only those limits that are essential to anchor the treatment to reality.

In other words, Axline provides less structure than we outlined at the beginning of this chapter.

Though Glasser (1969) seems to stress structure a little more, perhaps his definition of human needs agrees with Axline's play-therapy model. The need to feel worthwhile in one's own eyes as well as in others' eyes is one of man's two basic needs. The other is to love and be loved. Glasser believes that a person is free to do whatever is necessary to fulfill these needs and achieve her goals so long as she takes cognizance of others' needs, too.

Case Examples

Case 1

Brenda (a fifth-grader in a group with four classmates) had difficulty communicating the way she felt when her parents argued and fought; her counselor suggested that she use puppets or dolls to show what happened the previous evening when her father came home drunk. After some discussion with fellow clients, she selected four dolls to show what happened; she spontaneously produced very revealing dialogue among the four family members. After seven or eight minutes she stopped and said, "I think Grandma [father's mother] is as worried about Dad's drinking as I am. What could I say to her to get her to help me?" This question resulted in a discussion about her grandmother, how she gets along with her father, and whether her father would listen to his mother anyway. Finally, Brenda decided to ask the grandmother to talk to her son before trying to bring the matter of his drinking up in family council. After Brenda reported on that session, one of the children asked her whether she would like to use the dolls again to practice presenting her family with the idea of her family coming to see the counselor for at least one session.

Thus, in addition to using play media to help children communicate their feelings—and accept, manage, and learn to enjoy them—play techniques can be used instead of role playing to help these young clients prepare to cope with difficult interpersonal situations. Using a family of dolls in this manner also enables a child to step back, and as an observer of her own challenging situation, develop the courage and self-confidence to take productive action.

Case 2

Play also enables fellow clients and the counselor to discover problems of which the client herself seems not to be aware: Jill had played with a telephone in the playroom several times. One day the counselor and two clients observed her pretending to talk to a friend—discussing openly a painful event that she had never discussed in the group. This opened the way for her to bring it up in the group and discuss it.

Case 3

Most children require only clay, finger paints, crayons, charcoal, paper, puppets, a variety of dolls, doll clothes, building blocks, and a playhouse. These are the materials that an elementary-school counselor used with a group of five second-graders all from the same classroom. The group consisted of a boy who requested help in dealing with his abusive father, a girl who was a good student but not satisfied with her academic performance and, three disruptive children (a girl and two boys).

At the beginning of treatment, the three boys usually played with clay and finger paints and talked only when called upon. As each child played with his or her medium, the counselor moved about responding to one child's product and feelings, then to another's, and encouraged them to interact with each other. Sometimes he encouraged them to share with the entire group—a sort of show-and-tell. Gradually, they moved from such individual play to increasingly sharing their worries and concerns more openly and revealing with whom or what they required assistance. As they played out family and school scenes with dolls, puppets, and the playhouse they gradually learned, with the counselor's help and encouragement, to speak for their characters and to reveal their unfinished business, self-defeating behaviors, and the developmental tasks with which they required help.

One boy (Tim) portrayed a scene in which a boy was being scolded for refusing to read aloud for others. When the other clients discovered that he could not read the material, they suffered with him, exhibiting empathy and compassion. The counselor said, "You wish you could let Tim know that you care about how he feels—how it hurts to be scolded for something you can't do." All of the other four said "yes." "Perhaps after the four of you have huddled and decided what you would like to say to Tim, you could select a doll to speak to him for you." Tim listened very carefully while they developed the script for the doll. Besides conveying compassion and caring (which Tim seemed to detect), their responses, and the counselor's clarifying comments, helped Tim discover what he could read and how he could seek help to improve his reading. From that point forward, they began interacting more openly with each other.

The Use of Unstructured Play

Unstructured play in a play-therapy room in which children are provided a variety of media can be very revealing. When a counselor decides that he needs projective data, he should formulate the questions for which he requires answers such as: What are my hunches concerning this particular child's unmet needs, unfinished business, or self-defeating behaviors? What should I look for to confirm or disprove each particular hunch or hypothesis? What can I do to guard against biased observations? Why do I feel I need to observe this particular child in this unstructured play? On the other hand, beginning treatment with completely unstructured play can create expectations (and/or group norms) that interfere with the development of therapeutic relationships in a group. Finally, the counselor must, at least in his own mind, clearly differentiate between merely playing with children or really using play media therapeutically.

Two of the most convincing advocates for play therapy for children are Axline (1947, 1964) and Moustakas (1959, 1974). Their techniques can be readily adapted for counseling children in groups. Moustakas strongly endorses play therapy for healthy children as well as those who require remedial care. He feels that too few children experience the undivided attention of a significant adult who listens, watches, recognizes their genuine feelings, helps them express their feelings, and accepts them.

ROLE PLAYING

Role playing can be used to help a child confront a significant other with whom she has unfinished business; to decide whose assistance she requires to complete that unfinished business; and how to enlist those persons' assistance. Sometimes a counselor can facilitate this process by using early recollections (Mosak, 1958) to identify the problem scene and the relevant characters in it.

The Use of Role Playing

Case 2 (revisited)

After witnessing Tim's play scene, the counselor decided that Tim's reading difficulty was triggered, possibly, by some earlier traumatic experience. He shared this hunch with the group and instructed Tim as follows: "Close your eyes, think about a scary early memory in learning to read that you can recall vividly. You remember it so clearly that it makes your heart begin to pound even now. Perhaps the rest of you would like to do that, too, for other learning problems as well as with reading."

Then after several moments of silence, he said, "By now you know, Tim, that you can trust me and these classmates. Describe the hurtful incident, the situation in which it occurred, and tell us what made it so scary or embarrassing." Tim cried as he told about an incident that occurred near the end of grade one while his father and grandfather were babysitting him. His grandfather picked up his reader and asked him to read aloud. Tim knew he was not a good reader, but he didn't want his grandfather and father to know it. He panicked when he stumbled over several words and ran from the room.

With the preparation described below, his group members helped him select the three role players to reenact the scene in which he played his grandfather's role. After they processed the scene in role reversal, they replayed the scene with Tim playing his own role. This helped Tim decide with whom he had what unfinished business and whose assistance he would require to complete it. It also helped him develop the interpersonal skills to talk with his father and his counselor about the painful incident.

The Roles in Role Playing

The Client as Director

When a client agrees to use role playing she is usually taught to function as director. She describes the problem situation to be presented, does the casting and staging, and prepares actors for their roles. If roles are left unfilled, the counselor encourages clients to suggest clients to fill the roles. As part of the preparation, many counselors encourage the group to begin with the director playing the part of the other principal character in the scene and assigning someone else her role. Thus, she portrays the character with whom she has the most difficult unfinished business. During the critique of the recording of the role-played scene, she discovers new perceptions of herself and that particular significant other, and what she can do to complete her unfinished business (called *processing the role-played scene*).

During the processing of the recording of the role-played scene, the director obtains specific assistance in deciding what to do next. Sometimes she recognizes that she needs to practice more before she feels sufficiently confident to implement the desired new behaviors. The director also knows that she can stop the interaction whenever she does not know how to proceed; she has obtained the help she needed; she wants to process the part completed; or she wants to advise a fellow client on the way he is playing his character's role.

The Counselor as Coach

Though he keeps his participation to a minimum, the counselor uses reflections to help characters express the feelings they need to communicate that represent their characters well. The counselor also may teach clients to use soliloquy to convey feelings that their characters harbor but do not believe they would be able to express directly to relevant persons at that particular time. Some counselors like to put a mask with a character's name on each player, and take the masks off after the scene is played to "de-role"—to convey that each player is no longer that particular significant other in the director's life.

The Fellow Client as Actor and Audience

Basically each character participates in an impromptu play for which she is briefed and given an opportunity to clarify her character's role and feelings prior to playing the scene. She is even taught to use soliloquy to clarify those feelings during the course of role playing the scene. The other role players profit from experiencing each other's pain and discovering how they coped with it. Those who profit least are the observers. When, however, the counselor teaches them to assume alter-ego roles and speak lines that a character is unwilling or unable to express, they become more involved and profit more from the role playing and the processing of it.

CLASSROOM DISCUSSIONS

When a school counselor makes presentations to teachers and fields their questions as suggested earlier, he lays the groundwork for helping teachers introduce classroom discussions. For best results the counselor describes the process, answers teachers' questions, and volunteers to demonstrate the process for those who exhibit interest. Then he enlists these teachers' assistance in critiquing recordings of the demonstrations and encourages volunteers to lead discussions for their pupils. Following the first discussions, he offers to help each critique the session (and eventually to let other teachers sit in on the critiques). Finally, he serves as a consultant when invited by a teacher.

The Uses of Classroom Discussion

Such classroom discussions have been conducted to help children manage specific developmental tasks; to accept and manage their emotions; to deal with crises; to learn to be tutors; to begin to explore career and social goals (and/or lifestyle decisions); and to improve their classroom learning climate. For example, Wells (1962) described a second-grade classroom situation in which a disruptive child (Michael) was helped. The children were asked to try and catch Michael doing something helpful, to remember precisely what he did to whom, and to report it to the teacher at the end of each half-day session. The teacher incorporated these into a note which Michael then delivered to the principal. Once children learn to reinforce desired behaviors, they can learn the advantages of encouraging behaviors over discouraging ones.

Helping Children of the Divorced

Pfeifer and Abrams (1984) conduct successful discussion groups for children of divorced parents. Kelly and Wallerstein (1980) and Slavson and Schiffer (1975) also endorse such groups. These groups are a natural forum in which children learn to share the pain associated with their parents' divorce, discover that others are experiencing similar pain, and learn from a respected, adult discussion leader (teacher, counselor, or consultant to the school) that their feelings are to be expected. Furthermore, they learn that they can do some things to help alleviate the isolation and loneliness that most experience during their parents' divorce and adjustment to a new life. They learn to express their angry feelings to the absent parent and to stop thinking of themselves as bad for having these feelings.

Enhancing Skills

Anderson and Bauer (1985) make a good case for intimacy skill training for children. Based upon their review of the research, they developed exercises to teach participants to listen and to share. They found that sharing a secret with another person enhanced openness in that relationship.

Shaw (1986) urges school counselors to develop programs that enhance competence; professionals should spend more time on prevention and facilitating normal development, and thereby reduce the need for remedial treatment. He cites research that indicates that it is possible to cut down on the amount and severity of disabilities arising from psychological distress. Moreover, the schools seem to be the best place to initiate these broad preventive efforts because the program can be incorporated into the schools' existing programs, reach most children, and make better use of school personnel.

Wilson (1986) is genuinely concerned because remedial articles are receiving a disproportionate amount of the space in the primary journal for elementary school counselors. She would like to see elementary-school counselors devote more of their time to enhancing normal development and to early detection of children's problems.

Leading a Discussion Session

Those who lead such classroom discussions must realize precisely how these discussions differ from teaching lessons, such as arithmetic or English. First of all, it is a special 20–30 minute session set aside, perhaps once a week, to discuss topics not normally discussed in other classes. Usually such discussions are valued highly because the topics are selected by the pupils to meet special needs of many, if not all, pupils. Children also are given the opportunity to ask the questions for which they feel they need information but are reluctant to ask their relatives and/or friends. Rather than merely answering their questions, the discussion leader encourages pupils to explore from whom and from what resources they could turn for their answers. Frequently, the leader will ask several volunteers to cooperate in helping the one who asked the question to find the information and report back to the class. Finally, the leader helps the children decide how to use the information, and why different children use the same information to reach different conclusions.

Gumaer (1984) contends that children learn about themselves by interacting with peers and listening to their feedback. They learn that there are times when they must conform and cooperate, and that there are other times and places where they are appreciated for being original and creative. They learn how they are alike and different from others, and that it is all right to be unique. Thus, a climate is created in which children learn to accept one another's differences as differences rather than as deficiencies. Even when the discussion leader is the regular classroom teacher, he seems to be more pupil-centered than he is when he teaches his regular classes. He is more sensitive to pupils' feelings, exhibits more caring, encourages them to discuss their feelings more openly, and tries harder to discover relevance in each child's contributions.

Discussion Tools

Ojemann and his colleagues at Iowa were among the first to develop materials for elementary teachers' use (Ojemann, Hawkins, & Chowning, 1961). Magic Circle (Ball, 1972), and DUSO (Dinkmeyer, 1972) are useful materials to help children understand, accept, and manage their feelings. Moustakas (1966) developed some excellent materials to help teachers facilitate mental-health programs in the classroom. He teaches teachers to become more authentic—to recognize the uniqueness of each learner and to confirm him. He perceives the classroom as a human relations laboratory in which authentic life emerges by respecting differences; cherishing the child as a person; accepting honest expression of feelings; and encouraging the development of each pupil's interests and talents.

CONSULTING TEACHERS AND PARENTS

First, what is unique about the consultation process? How does it differ from counseling and supervising? Gumaer (1984) states that counseling is an interchange in which a counselor helps a client with a problem that the client is experiencing. The focus is entirely on the client's problem. Like counseling, the development of a good relationship is important in consulting, but the primary focus of the interaction in consultation is to help the consultee treat or manage or teach a third person(s). Finally, the effective supervisor also cares about the supervisee and is committed to help him learn to function better; but, in addition, the supervisor has the authority and the responsibility for evaluating the supervisee's performance as an employee. For consultation with a school's professional staff, the consultant helps consultees assess their strengths, diagnoses their difficulties, and uses their strengths to resolve their problems. Gallassich (1986) states that consultants are experts who possess specialized knowledge that enables them to help consultees solve problems in some aspects of their work.

Mannino and Shore (1985) define nine commonalities of consultation:

1. The service is designed to help the consultee counsel, manage, or teach another person(s).
2. An open, trusting relationship between the consultant and the consultee is essential.
3. Consultee and consultant have equal status.
4. The consultee should have an active status in the process. The consultant must guard against making the consultee dependent.
5. The consultee has the right to reject the recommendations and suggestions made by the consultant.
6. Participation by the consultee is voluntary.
7. Information shared is confidential.
8. The consultation focuses upon work-related problems.
9. Every consultation should provide the consultee with remedial assistance in solving her presenting problems and help her generalize her new learnings to similar problems that she may face in the future. In other words, it is a temporary relationship designed to prepare the consultee to function increasingly better on her own.

The Counselor/Parent/Teacher Relationship

When a counselor developes the type of relationship with parents and teachers described earlier in this chapter and enlists their assistance in helping him understand his clients, he makes himself available for consultation. He advances and reinforces their competencies for furthering their children's social, emotional, moral, intellectual, and career development. When either seeks a counselor's assistance, he must help that adult describe the child with whom she requires assistance; decide what behaviors she would like to replace with what precise, more-productive behaviors; decide whose assistance will be required to achieve the desired changes; and decide what reinforcers may be used to implement and maintain the desired new behaviors. Sometimes when a teacher is the consultee, the counselor must help that teacher assess the child's impact on classmates and on the teacher herself, their impact on the child, and what the rest of them can do to reinforce the child's desired new behaviors. Frequently, the counselor must observe a child at work in the classroom, and even within the home, to obtain adequate data to help the consultee. In the instance of consulting a teacher, the following have been found to be important:

1. The teacher concludes that the counselor (consultant) is genuinely interested in her as well as her pupils.
2. The teacher realizes that the counselor will treat confidentially the information and hypotheses they share.
3. The counselor will not be expected to evaluate the teacher for raises, promotions, or tenure.

4. The teacher believes that she can discover her weaknesses and failures and request the counselor's assistance in correcting them.
5. The teacher is not pressured to seek consultation.
6. The teacher recognizes the counselor's sincere need for her assistance as well as his willingness to serve as consultant. It is a partnership designed to enhance her pupils' social, moral, emotional, intellectual, and career development.

The Counselor as Liaison Officer

Increasingly, elementary-school counselors and agency counselors who serve as liaison officers to schools are learning to function as consultants to parents and teachers. They are resource personnel in human growth and development. They help parents and teachers decide what quality of work they can expect from a given child, what her special interests and talents are, and how these may be developed. They also help parents and teachers identify the needs, feelings, and behaviors that require special attention. When a child exhibits undesirable behavior, they help the counselor identify the behavior that needs to be replaced, define the new, more-productive behavior to be learned, and decide how the desired new behaviors may be reinforced. Usually, the counselor has to take the initiative in developing such a relationship. When, for example, a counselor seeks a teacher's assistance, he increases the odds that the particular teacher will seek consultation from him. Though much of this kind of consultation will be done on an individual basis, it can be done in groups. A good example is Moustakas' (1966) work with teachers. He models as he leads discussion groups for teachers.

Developing Parent Education Groups

Not all whose assistance is required by the counselor agree to consultation. Some do not care, or perhaps they do not believe that this particular child can be helped. Others question the counselor's sincerity and/or competency to help the pupil. For example, when a child attempted suicide, the principal asked the counselor to help him talk to the child's parents. Both professionals were shocked with the parents' indifference. They said it was just an attention-getting device. It was not until the principal and counselor sought the county state's attorney's assistance to protect the child that the parents' cooperation was achieved to arrange for treatment for the child, and to have that treatment coordinate with school services. In such a case, the consultee must be convinced that consultation is essential, that the source of help is sincere and competent, and that the consultants will do whatever is required to protect the best interest of the child.

West, Sonstegard, and Hagerman (1980) reported on a project in which they helped the staff develop a program, led three groups (functioning as models), and helped the staff select and prepare tutors. In other words, they became working partners in initiating a new program.

Adlerians often use this type of involvement in their parent education groups (Sonstegard & Dreikurs, 1973). They encourage school counselors to develop parent education programs in their schools, too. Though Adlerians work with much larger groups of parents, we prefer to work with five or six couples who have sought assistance with children of approximately the same age: pre-school, primary-school age, upper elementary-school grades, junior high school or middle school, or senior high school. Though many parents of senior-high-school-aged children have given up on learning to help them, even they can be helped. We provide them with material to read, and encourage them to pick out ideas that they desire assistance in implementing. They decide which ideas to try first, share their successes, and try to learn from their failures in implementing their desired new behaviors. Usually some of the couples elect to join a couple's counseling group in which they can discuss their personal pain more openly, decide what new behaviors must be learned (goals), and implement their new behaviors with assistance and reinforcement of spouse and children (Horne & Ohlsen, 1982).

Since parents of younger children are more apt to believe that their children can still be helped, they tend to accept the counselor's consultation services more readily than parents of older children. In any case, both parents and teachers of elementary-school children seem to accept the notion that the counselor is a consultant to teachers and parents as well as a counselor for children. Moreover, they expect elementary-school counselors to be competent to help them diagnose their children's learning problems and to find remedial services to correct the problems.

SUMMARY

Those who counsel children in groups must adapt their methods to their clients' social, emotional, and intellectual development and the children's previous experiences in groups. Though most children can participate verbally, counselors of children must recognize when to teach them the words they require to function effectively in a group and when to use play media and role playing to facilitate the therapeutic process.

The size of the group, the length of the counseling session, and the frequency with which the group meets must be adapted to the children's attention span, their ability to sustain interest in fellow clients' problems, and their general social maturity. Children tend to be very open in learning to be good clients and good helpers, to trust the counselor more readily than adolescents or adults, but tend to require more-detailed structuring. How quickly they adapt to the group tends to be a function of how clearly the counselor has communicated the unique nature of the counseling group and prepared them to be good helpers as well as good clients.

A knowledge of their children's (or pupils') unique needs and the developmental tasks helps parents (teachers) further normal growth and development. Increasingly school counselors and community agency personnel are offering community and school programs to help parents and teachers understand children's needs and apply the knowledge to help their children. Those counselors who are employed in schools counsel parents as well as children, consult parents and teachers, and coordinate pupil personnel services within their school buildings.

Important as it is for counselors to win parents' and teachers' cooperation in treating children, the single best source of information about a child is the child herself. Confronted with the natural consequences of self-defeating behaviors, most children can accept considerable responsibility for learning desired new behaviors. When children understand the counseling services available to them in schools, many request counseling on their own before either parents or teachers recognize their need for the services. Moreover, treating children successfully can encourage parents to seek counseling for themselves.

REFERENCES

Anderson, W. P., & Bauer, B. (1985). Support for intimacy skills groups from research in social psychology. *Journal of Counseling and Development, 64,* 269–273.

Axline, V. (1947). *Play therapy.* New York: Basic Books.

Axline, V. (1964). *Dibs: In search of self.* Boston: Houghton Mifflin.

Ball, G. (1972). *Magic circle at school.* LaMesa, CA: Human Development Training Institute.

Bosdell, B. G. (1973). Counseling children with play media. In M. M. Ohlsen (Ed.), *Counseling children in groups: A forum* (pp. 25–45). New York: Holt, Rinehart and Winston.

Carpenter, P., & Sandberg S. (1973). The things inside: Psychodrama with delinquent adolescents. *Psychotherapy: Research and Practice, 10,* 245–247.

Dinkmeyer, D. (1972). *DUSO D-1C and D-2C kits.* Circle Pines, MN: American Guidance Services.

Ellis, A. (1973). Emotional education at the living school. In M. M. Ohlsen (Ed.), *Counseling children in groups: A forum* (pp. 79–93). New York: Holt, Rinehart and Winston.

Gallassich, J. (1985). Toward a meta-theory of consultation. *The Counseling Psychologist, 13,* 336–354.

Gardner, R. A. (1975). *Psychotherapeutic approaches to the resistant client.* New York: Jason Aronson.

Gazda, G. M. (1973). Group procedures with children. In M. M. Ohlsen (Ed.), *Counseling children in groups: A forum* (pp. 117–145). New York: Holt, Rinehart and Winston.

Glass, S. C. (1973). Practical considerations in group counseling. In M. M. Ohlsen (Ed.), *Counseling children in groups: A forum* (pp. 170–182). New York: Holt, Rinehart and Winston.

Glasser, W. (1969). *Schools without failure*. New York: Harper & Row.

Gumaer, J. (1984). *Counseling and therapy for children*. New York: Free Press.

Hawes, R. M. (1973). Getting along in the classroom. In M. M. Ohlsen (Ed.), *Counseling children in groups: A forum* (pp. 183–203). New York: Holt, Rinehart and Winston.

Horne, A. M., & Ohlsen, M. M. (1982). *Family counseling and therapy*. Itasca, IL: F. E. Peacock.

Jefferies, D. (1973). Counseling ghetto children in groups. In M. M. Ohlsen (Ed.), *Counseling children in groups: A forum* . New York: Holt, Rinehart and Winston.

Kelly, J., & Wallerstein, J. (1980). The divorced child in school. *National Elementary Principal, 59*, 51–58.

Long, T. (1982). Counselors, nutrition, and mental health. *Personnel and Guidance Journal. 60*, 389–392.

Mannino, F. V., & Shore, M. F. (1985). Understanding consultation: Some orienting dimensions. *The Counseling Psychologist, 13*, 363–367.

Mosak, H. (1958). Early recollections as a projective technique. *Journal of Projective Techniques, 22*, 302–311.

Moustakas, C. E. (1959). *Psychotherapy with children*. New York: Harper & Row.

Moustakas, C. E. (1966). *The authentic teacher: Sensitivity and awareness in the classroom*. Cambridge, MA: H. A. Doyle.

Moustakas, C. E. (1974). *Children in play therapy*. New York: Ballantine.

Ohlsen, M. M. (Ed.). (1973). *Counseling children in groups: A forum*. New York: Holt, Rinehart and Winston.

Ohlsen, M. M., & Gazda, G. M. (1965). Counseling underachieving bright pupils. *Education, 86*, 78–81.

Ojemann, R. H.; Hawkins, A.; & Chowning, K. (1961). *A teaching program in human behavior and mental health*. Iowa City: University of Iowa Press.

Pfeifer, G., & Abrams, L. (1984). School-based discussion groups for children of divorced: A pilot program. *Group, 8*, 22–28.

Satir, V. (1972). *Peoplemaking*. Palo Alto, CA: Science and Behavior Books.

Shaw, M. C. (1986). The prevention of learning and interpersonal problems. *Journal of Counseling and Development, 64*, 624–627.

Slavson, S. R., & Schiffer, M. (1975). *Group psychotherapy for children*. New York: International Universities Press.

Sonstegard, M. A., & Dreikurs, R. (1973). The Adlerian approach to group counseling of children. In M. M. Ohlsen (Ed.), *Counseling children in groups: A forum* (pp. 47–77). New York: Holt, Rinehart and Winston.

Thompson, C. L., & Rudolph, L. B. (1983). *Counseling children*. Monterey, CA: Brooks/Coles.

Wells, C. G. (1962). Psychodrama and creative counseling in the elementary schools. *Group Psychotherapy, 15*, 244–252.

West, J.; Sonstegard, M.; & Hagerman, H. (1980). A study of counseling and consulting in Appalachia. *Elementary School Guidance and Counseling, 15*, 5–13.

Wilson, N. S. (1986). Developmental versus remedial guidance: An examination of the articles in *Elementary school guidance and counseling*—volumes 8–18. *Elementary School Guidance and Counseling, 20*, 208–214.

13

COUNSELING ADOLESCENTS IN GROUPS

Adolescents are engrossed in their search for identity, in establishing themselves in adult roles, and in achieving their independence. At the same time, they are trapped by dependence. They do not want to give up their parents' financial support or help in establishing themselves in adult roles, but they resent assistance because they associate assistance with control. Many adolescents also openly admit that they want and value parents' and relatives' emotional support and guidance. Yet, at times, they would prefer adult friendships and adult consultations that would allow them to request information, feedback, and even advice—but with the mutual understanding that, as adults themselves, they are free to accept or reject their consultant's advice. They would appreciate adult relationships with parents; in transactional-analysis terms (Steiner, 1974); adult-to-adult transactions rather than child-to-parent or parent-to-child transactions.

McCandless (1970) believes that many adolescent problems involve frustrations in achieving major goals: status, adequate sexual adjustment, and self- and socially fulfilling values and morals; and that rapid social changes and relaxation of moral values have complicated adolescents' lives even more than they have adults':

> Status may be more highly valued for boys, sociality for girls. Both are probably more important in the long run than sex although the importance of sexuality is likely to be underplayed within the core, middle-class culture. While often neglected by scholars, an individual's moral values development is likely to be more important than anything else in determining the quality of his life. These four major goals are achieved in all life settings, whether family, school, community groups, or job.
>
> The point that needs greatest emphasis in a psychology of adolescence is that a drive-change theory predicts that the period is one in which great personal change can occur. Such change can be malign or benign, and it is society's responsibility to maximize the latter while minimizing the former (p. 36).

ADOLESCENT NEEDS

A Review of the Literature

Adolescents are trying to determine who they are; what they would like to do; what they can do; and how they can develop the will and self-confidence to do it. At the same time, they are changing their reference group from family to peers. Because of rapidly changing times, and peers encouraging one another to be independent, adolescents question many of their parents' values. According to Cole and Hall (1964), the social and maturational goals of adolescence are (1) achieving social poise; (2) self-control; (3) constructive expression of emotions; and (4) self-acceptance of sociability.

Unlike Hall (1904), who described adolescence as a period of storm and stress, Hurlock (1967) cited Gesell, Ilg, and Ames' (1956) findings to support the notion that the period could better be described as a period of heightened emotionality. Ausubel (1954) characterized adolescence as a period for testing the adequacy of the personality structure laid down during childhood. Ackerman (1955) believed adolescents tend to be extraordinarily sensitive to others' judgment of their worth. Being caught between the twin horns of conformity and defiance explains their hair-trigger irritability.

Nowhere is their rawness and their need to prove themselves more vivid than in their relationships between the sexes. Each is acutely aware of the other, is highly sensitive to the other, and lacks the confidence of the more experienced, mature adult. They do tend to get excited more easily and are more easily threatened than mature adults. Significant others in the lives of adolescents (parents, teachers, employers) often vacillate, treating the adolescent as a child one moment, as an adult the next. Also, these important persons in the adolescent's life often are attempting to fulfill their own unmet needs. Adolescents often lack the self-confidence and interpersonal skills to react maturely to these situations.

On the other hand, Ausubel (1954) found that although personality defects appear to be more glaring during this period, they tend to be only transitory disturbances. Even when the personality defects are more basic, he concluded that the appearance of the most serious personality disorders occur after, rather than during, adolescence. Except for those who experienced markedly deviant sexual development, Hurlock (1967) concluded that most learn to cope with the problems with which they are confronted as adolescents. Adolescents often give their parents and teachers a difficult time, thereby causing these adults to wonder whether they will ever find themselves; Kirkpatrick (1952) agreed that most do, and without any permanent scars.

Garrison's (1965) review of the research on adolescents suggested that much of adolescents' anger results from frustration of some goal-seeking activity. Adolescents feel that they are pressured to work for others' goals for them, that they are not allowed to make their own important decisions, and that they are expected to work for goals that are not appropriate for them. On these occasions they often feel that their significant others bully them. Lacking the verbal and social skills to cope with these limitations, they tend to strike back in the only way they know how; and this frequently comes across as aggression.

Adolescents want to be participating members of society (Ayer & Corman, 1952). Their interest in local, national, and world affairs has long been fostered by high-school and college teachers, and it has been greatly increased by television. Adolescents are more concerned about social problems than most adults realize. They appreciate support and encouragement from significant adults when they try to solve social problems (and under these circumstances they will listen to adults' suggestions). They thrive on genuine opportunities to solve social problems and on recognition for real accomplishments. On the other hand, when adults ignore obvious social problems, they tend to become disappointed, disillusioned, and even cynical with adults' complacency (Neidt & Fritz, 1950). Some adolescents feel that they must protest with demonstrations, strikes, and even riots to get adults' attention and to bring about desired changes. Others give up and withdraw by ignoring or running away from significant adults, by turning to drugs, by quitting school, or by staying in school but withdrawing from the learning process.

Achieving Independence

Much as adolescents want their independence from parents, there are times when they feel very dependent upon them. They are ambivalent about their financial dependence; they resent it, and at the same time, they are reluctant to relinquish it. When they want to lean on adults they must know they can count on them. For example, they are willing to comply with parents' rules as a way of coping with peer pressure to do something that they do not want to do anyway, and perhaps feel is wrong to do. They feel more secure when they realize that their parents have the will to enforce limits when they do not feel able to do so for themselves.

Some adolescents feel that no one has ever tried to teach them to behave independently. Others feel that they are forced to rebel to escape from their parents' control. Though, at some times, most adolescents rebel to avoid conformity, the rebellious tend to conform as much as conformists. The difference is that they are controlled by peers rather than by their family's values and traditions. Sometimes the rebellious are used by unprincipled demagogues who may approximate their own age, but more likely are adults who pretend to understand them in order to use them.

Rebellion

When rebellion serves no purpose except to fight conformity or to revolt against the establishment and its traditions, it is an unhealthy reaction to authority.

Healthy rebellion arises out of love for something—a recognition that something must be changed and a commitment to change that which is wrong. Healthy rebels have goals and do not rebel for the sake of rebellion, but for a goal. In other words, they think and consider the consequences. Furthermore, they want to participate in the planning and the implementing of specific changes, and most are willing to accept adults' assistance.

Unfortunately, many adults seem to assume that adolescents must rebel to earn their independence; hence parents must learn to tolerate it. When parents, teachers, and employers learn to empathize with adolescents; listen to them when they want to talk openly; respect adolescents' ideas; and enlist their assistance in solving problems and in defining meaningful limits and enforcing them (and changing limits as the adolescents are able to function more responsibly), many of the heartaches and conflicts with which adolescents (and their parents) are confronted in their growing up can be resolved without rebellion. Gold and Petronio (1980) in their extensive review of research with delinquent adolescents identified two therapeutic ingredients that are consistently found in effective treatment programs: warm, accepting relationships with adults; and enhancement of adolescent self-image as a autonomous individual.

Accepting Assistance

Adolescents can accept from strong, understanding adults the assistance that they require to meet their increasing responsibilities. They are searching for meaning in their daily lives (here and now), in their communities, as well as in their schools and homes. They cherish meaningful group experiences with peers in student government, leadership training, personal growth groups, and in counseling groups. Competent counselors, whom they perceive as unequivocally trustworthy confidantes, are required to provide them with counseling and to provide their parents with child-rearing education.

MEETING ADOLESCENTS' NEEDS IN GROUPS

The adolescent's needs may be stated as general goals for group counseling as follows:

1. Search for identity by defining meaningful goals for various facets of life.
2. Increase understanding of their interests, abilities, and aptitudes.
3. Improving skills for identifying opportunities and for evaluating them in terms of their own interests, abilities, and aptitudes.
4. Increasing interpersonal skills and self-confidence to recognize and solve their problems.
5. Improving interpersonal skills and self-confidence to recognize when decisions are required, how to make them, and how to implement them.

6. Increasing sensitivity to others' needs and improving skills for helping others satisfy their needs.
7. Improving communication skills for conveying their real feelings directly to relevant persons, and with considerations for their feelings.
8. Independence to examine what they believe, to make their own decisions, to take reasonable risks, to make mistakes, and to learn from their mistakes.
9. Improving interpersonal skills to deal with authority figures in a mature manner; for example, employers, police, government officials as well as parents and teachers.
10. Meaningful participation in developing and maintaining limits on their own behavior.
11. Growing knowledge and skills for coping with their physical and emotional changes associated with maturation.
12. Improving skills to learn and live new roles.

Yalom (1970) identified what he believes are curative factors in group psychotherapy. These factors are a tentative list of mechanisms and conditions of groups that are believed to promote behavior change. The factors are: altruism; group cohesiveness; universality; interpersonal learning (input and output); guidance; catharsis; identification; family reenactment; insight; instillation of hope; and existential awareness. Yalom's factors refer to group work in general, and to working with adults in particular. In an attempt to identify which of the factors were also relevant for adolescents, Corder, Whiteside, and Haizlip (1981) conducted a study of curative factors in group therapy with adolescents. They found that adults and adolescents show very similar patterns of perceptions of curative factors in group work. In order of importance, the factors chosen by adolescents as most helpful, according to Corder et al. (1981, p. 348) are:

- *catharsis* (Learning to express my feelings.)
- *existential factors* (Learning that I must take ultimate responsibility for the way I live my life.)
- *interpersonal learning* (input) (Other members honestly telling me what they think of me.)
- *family reenactment* (Being in the group was, in a sense, like being in a big family, only this time, a more-accepting and understanding family.)
- *group cohesiveness* (Belonging to a group of people who understand and accept me.)
- *interpersonal learning* (output) (The group is giving me an opportunity to learn to approach others.)
- *universality* (Seeing I was just as well off as others.)
- *altruism* (Helping others and being important in their lives.)

Dealing with Adolescents' Needs

Group counseling contributes to the fulfillment of some of the adolescent's special needs. In this chapter, we address several ways in which this occurs. Incorporated are the curative factors adolescents identified in the study by Corder et al. (1981).

Search for Identity

A central theme for adolescents is their search for identity. They want to know who they are, what they can become. Most adolescents know many things about themselves, and they know that they are important to some people. At the same time, they have many doubts about themselves (often more than they think most other adolescents have, and certainly more than the adults they know and admire had when they were adolescents). For some, these feelings can be dispelled by good reading material on adolescent psychology and by voluntary discussion groups; but neither of these can provide the warm, accepting atmosphere that a college freshman portrayed in describing her group-counseling experiences as a high-school senior (five girls and a young male counselor):

> As the weeks passed, I learned to talk about more facets of me and to make more daring decisions. The relationship I had with the girls was unique because, for one, I could talk about the real me with no fear of being attacked . . .
>
> We all talked about our abilities to express emotion, about our role as women in a working world, and about our work as students. I was more concerned than other girls about my role as a career woman. I wanted a career and a home . . .
>
> We all found ourselves growing up in the group . . . we had gained self-confidence regarding social situations and our abilities to achieve our goals. We were more sure of accomplishing our goals because we had learned to set realistic goals. Our confidence in social situations was inspired by the open, honest relationship we had in the group. Finally we had taken on some decision-making responsibility in the group; we were treated like adults there, so we wanted to act like adults (L. Ohlsen, 1966, pp. 401–402).

Within such a group (especially with both sexes present), adolescents discover that they are special. They also discover that other teenagers whom they admire and respect have problems, some perhaps more serious than their own. Furthermore, in spite of their faults, they really accept each other, and they are committed to help each member learn to relate to important others outside the counseling group as well as to relate richly to those within their group. Experiencing such genuine acceptance strengthens them giving them the self-confidence and the courage to face up to their problems and to solve them.

Increased Understanding

The increased understanding of special interests, abilities, and aptitudes should have begun prior to adolescence. Very early in life, understanding parents and teachers should have helped adolescents discover what they can rightly expect from themselves. Even when this has been done well, adolescents tend to face many questions about their interests, abilities, and aptitudes that will require thorough self-appraisal with the individual assistance of a competent counselor, and often with some special testing—carefully interpreted by a counselor for the individual. Possessing this kind of information, adolescents are better able to explore their real selves with fellow clients: sharing their positive feelings about strengths; explaining why they cannot accept and use certain strengths; revealing their areas of doubt; and wondering to what extent their weaknesses will block certain plans. Fellow clients' ability to empathize and to accept each other provides the support they all need to face up to their weaknesses, correct them if they can with reasonable effort or accept them and adapt their plans accordingly.

Gathering Information

Improving skills in obtaining adequate information about options and environment is a problem for everyone, but especially for adolescents. Who should go to college? What does one need to know to choose a college? How can one get ready for scholarship and admission-testing programs? What can one do to increase chances for getting off to a good start in college or on a job? What problems do young people meet on their first job? How may they cope better with them? How does one get a job? How can one make the most of opportunities? How can one best meet a girl or boy whom one would like to date? How can one decide when he is really in love?

Teaching basic communication skills to both youngsters and parents has been emphasized by researchers addressing counseling approaches with adolescents (Buntman & Saris, 1979; Guerney, 1979). Persons (1966) found that group counseling with delinquent adolescents that had an emphasis on cognitive-behavioral techniques was especially effective in increasing socially acceptable interactions and effective skills for gathering information.

Though adolescents may sometimes appear to be flippant, they are seriously concerned to learn more about their opportunities and to improve their understanding of their environment. Many of them are naive and they know it, and they are embarrassed about it. Many of their questions can be answered by directed reading, especially when they are given an opportunity to discuss and clarify what they have learned in small voluntary discussion groups or in counseling groups where they feel it is safe to ask their questions and say what they think. Within the safe atmosphere of a counseling group, they also enhance their own self-respect by helping others. Rarely do today's adolescents feel as genuinely needed and appreciated as they do in counseling groups.

Discerning Information

Improved skill in assimilating and appraising information about one's opportunities can be acquired in the ways just discussed. However, one must also learn where to find validating information and how to make decisions. When adolescents fail, they can profit from the assistance of fellow clients in appraising their decisions and actions and in planning for new ones. Failure alone teaches adolescents nothing except how one can be hurt. With the assistance of accepting others (especially peers), though, they can discover why they failed and how to approach the problem again; discuss openly how they were hurt and why they may be reluctant to try again; but also discover that they must try again. Where the problem involves new or threatening relationships, they can even practice their new approaches by role playing the encounter.

Understanding teachers also can do much to help youth assimilate and appraise information. They can look for and take note of instances in which youths displayed good judgment in class discussion and in written work. They can also try to limit their discouraging behavior, trying to help young people learn from their mistakes rather than merely criticizing them. A conscientious teacher appreciates the assistance of an accepting counselor in learning to play a supportive role more effectively.

Confidence

Increasing interpersonal skills and confidence in their ability to recognize and solve their own and other adolescents' problems develops in a counseling group. When adolescents discover that other teenagers have problems, are willing to deal openly with them, and can solve them, they develop more confidence in themselves and the treatment process. Good models have a tremendous impact on adolescents and can teach them how to relate openly and to help others. Ackerman (1955) found that adolescents catch on quickly to the notion of reaching behind mere talk to respond to genuine feelings. They learn how to pick up on real feelings revealed by such nonverbal behavior as body posturing, facial expressions, and motor behavior. Ackerman also found that he could foster the use of these nonverbal cues by sharing his bases for his interpretations.

Sensitivity to Others

Improving sensitivity to others' needs and improved skills for helping others are developed in a counseling group. Adolescents also learn, in ways just discussed, to communicate their real feelings and needs. A family conference can be used effectively to further this process. If, even after role playing a scene in a counseling group, adolescents do not feel adequate to face and deal with family conflicts, the counselor can arrange a family conference in which adolescents are given an opportunity to reveal how they feel about their parents (and usually they feel much more positive toward the parents than adolescents have let them know), how they have hurt in the home, and what they would like from the parents. Usually the most important wants are much more acceptable than the parents had realized.

During such a family conference the counselor helps the other members listen to the adolescent express feelings and requests. The counselor also helps the adolescent listen to family members as they discuss their feelings, thereby increasing the client's sensitivity to others' needs. Finally, the counselor helps the family to agree at least on some tentative solutions, often by helping them establish a family council, providing them with a technique for dealing with family problems and for helping adolescents improve communication skills. Such a structure also enables adolescents to help parents function more effectively as parents, accepting and fulfilling their roles as models for their children.

The family council is a very effective method for helping parents and adolescents talk together. The family council involves having family members gather weekly to discuss family issues and to work out goals, expectations, family guidelines, and issues that develop among the members. The council is democratic and is conducted in such a way that all members are heard and understood. Often, counselors will need to prepare families for having family councils, for the model of cooperation and empathic understanding of the council probably is not endemic to the operating style of the family.

Relationships

Improving relationship skills learned in such meaningful groups as family councils, classroom discussions, voluntary discussion groups, and counseling groups can be used to improve social skills. Merle M. Ohlsen (1974) described meaningful programs that have been developed in agencies and schools. The relationship model developed by Guerney (1979) is especially applicable to helping adolescents learn effective relationships skills, as is Goldstein, Sprafkin, Gershaw, & Klein's (1980) model for teaching adolescents skills. Other skill-specific groups are also very appropriate for counselors to lead for adolescents, including groups specifically designed to teach such abilities as assertion training, job-seeking skills, study skills, and other groups with a limited goal.

Independence

Independent behavior can be observed, practiced, and reinforced in a counseling group. With this atmosphere, adolescents discover that their ideas are respected; that they as well as others do foolish things in trying to achieve independence; and that their fellow clients can provide helpful feedback and suggestions for improving their behavior. They also learn, by role playing as well as talking, to communicate feelings directly to relevant persons and to be assertive, yet considerate, in communicating directly with authority figures, such as employers and police as well as parents and teachers.

Important as these experiences are for adolescents, perhaps even more can be accomplished in separate discussion groups for parents and teachers. In such groups, the adults learn to accept adolescents and their responsibilities for them when they discover for themselves, not only from reading but also from observing adolescents and talking frankly with them: (1) what really bothers the adolescents with whom they are involved; (2) how they feel and how much they really want acceptance, understanding, and assistance in coping with their new selves; (3) how much they appreciate assistance in developing independence in preference to fighting for it; (4) what it means to adolescents to be respected, to have their ideas seriously considered and, at least, sometimes accepted; (5) the extent to which they will try to get along with authority figures who try to empathize with them; and (6) the extent to which they use important adults as models—copying bad characteristics as well as good ones. However, it still will not be easy for adults to help adolescents learn to be independent, because most of the adults' models have used authoritarian approaches in trying to cope with adolescents. Beleaguered adults also recognize and appreciate the type of consultant's assistance provided in discussion groups.

Setting Limits

The rationale has already been presented for giving adolescents an opportunity to participate in developing and maintaining limits for their own behavior. Obviously, it helps teach them to accept the responsibilities that accompany increased independence. Equally crucial are the experiences that develop meaningful values and reasonable expectations and provide good models. When important others failed to provide such essential positive influence, Gadpaille (1959) noted from his experiences in treating delinquent adolescents that:

> The great majority of such adolescents I have interviewed came from such disrupted and rejecting homes that they were never able to feel their needs could or would be fulfilled by their parents. There was no real benefit to be gained by "being good" and conforming to the demands of their parents, and the resentment of this state of affairs spread to include all authority. The only way to get what they wanted was to take it by force, considering only themselves. Since this learned pattern is associated with considerable pleasure-impulse gratification, they become fixated on it.
>
> It should be stressed here that the delinquent population from which the observations of this communication are drawn is, I think, a typical one. Most of these adolescents were not the products of criminal subcultural groups or of rigid, punitive societies. They were primarily products of homes in which social values were, at least, verbally stressed, but were stressed without adequate parental reward for adherence to those values (p. 277).

These important others who should have helped these adolescents develop meaningful values and served as models for them in their daily lives are phonies, and hence adolescents rejected both the people and their values. Adolescents need models who try to live the values they preach. However, youths' models need not be perfect. In fact, many good models have their greatest impact when they discuss with adolescents the significance of their values for themselves; reveal the problems they are facing in trying to be the kind of adults they would like to be; and enlist the adolescents' assistance in reinforcing the behavior they are trying to learn to practice. Adults important in adolescents' lives must also possess the strength to enforce the limits that adolescents have helped to define. Unfortunately, many authority figures do not possess the strength, the knowledge of adolescents, the human-relations skills, and the confidence in their adolescent wards to fulfill these roles. Many are afraid to do what is necessary lest the adolescent challenge their authority or reject them and their love.

Within an effective counseling group, adolescents discover fellow clients who are good models. They also discover their peers' models and how these models have shaped their fellow clients' behavior. Good books, especially biographies, also can provide powerful models for youths. Once they discover the value of such models, they often suggest relevant books for each other. They observe their peers' search for reasonable compatibility between real selves and ideal selves; they help others change their attitudes and behaviors; and they help them learn to convey their new selves to important others outside their counseling group. Eventually, they conclude that they can achieve these goals, too. Observing others solve their problems increases adolescents' confidence in their ability to solve their own problems.

Maturation

Growing knowledge and skills to understand and to cope with physical and emotional changes is achieved in group counseling for the very reasons stated above. In this meaningful relationship with admired and trusted peers, adolescents can learn to discuss their new feelings, how to cope with these feelings, and others' expectations of them (for example, what a date expects). They discover that they can talk about their concerns about their size, personal grooming, condition of skin, appetite, health, sexual development, social development, and attractiveness to the opposite (or same) sex.

Counselors also can enhance normal development by preparing teachers and parents to answer adolescents' questions. In discussion groups, a counselor can help teachers and parents discuss, and role play coping with, such communication problems as (1) their own discomfort and embarrassment with adolescents' questions; (2) their sensitivity to adolescents' emotional readiness for the information; (3) their intelligent use of good reading material to answer their questions and to open up topics for discussion; (4) their good sense to stop when they have answered questions to the adolescent's satisfaction; (5) their ability to accept questions seriously, no matter how naive or irrelevant they may find them; (6) their ability to answer questions now rather than answer the related questions that they wished someone had answered for them; (7) their own maturity to recognize and admit when they lack adequate information to answer questions; and (8) their ability to recognize and help discuss the feelings behind these questions and, when appropriate, to refer adolescents for assistance that they have not been able to give.

Improving skills to learn and live new roles ties in directly with the previous paragraphs. Fulfilling this need also relates directly to adolescents' search for identity, increased understanding of themselves, and improved social skills. To discover that others are struggling with familiar problems makes their own more acceptable; seeing others learn to cope with their problems is encouraging; and helping them increases their respect for themselves. Thus group counseling is especially appropriate for adolescents. It enables them to satisfy some of their strongest needs, especially in providing real assistance to peers while obtaining assistance from them.

SPECIAL CONSIDERATIONS FOR ADOLESCENTS

Adolescents are often brought to counseling and therapy under duress. They are made to feel that they are to blame for whatever happened at school, at home, or at work. Even when they elect to seek help on their own, they often harbor some misgivings about it because of the way they have been blamed by significant adults. Therefore, the counselor must be very sensitive to adolescents' underlying feelings and doubts; to detect and reflect their unique feelings; to answer nondefensively their questions about expectations; and to help them formulate precise, behavioral goals. Unless school counselors are very careful, they can come across as defending authority figures at school, at home, or at work, thereby markedly reducing their chances of being accepted as trustworthy helpers. On the other hand, their task in not to defend the adolescent's actions; but to help the adolescent function more effectively.

Group Structuring for Adolescents

For junior and senior high-school groups, counselors tend to be more active than they normally are for groups of college students and adults. Although they appreciate the opportunity to help define working relationships and to take an active role in developing and in maintaining a therapeutic climate, adolescents seem to have less tolerance for ambiguity than college students and adults. Adolescents want to know precisely what they are getting into, what will be expected of them, and how it will help them. Therefore, the counselor's presentation should include examples of problems that adolescents have discussed in groups (including some that are obviously the problems of prestigious youth), how they were helped, and how fellow clients as well as the counselor contributed to their growth. Clearly stated expectations, nondefensive counselor responses to clients' efforts to clarify them, and a working atmosphere in which they believe that they can shape the structure are all important to adolescents.

They also appreciate an informal setting with space so that they can shove the chairs back and sit on the floor and/or use movement and exercises. The drama of relating genuinely to each other and trying to be themselves is enticing and exciting for adolescents. It encourages them to respond most openly and helpfully. They are intrigued with counselors' helping behaviors and the way they teach clients to be helpers as well as clients. They learn readily from models. As they grasp and integrate what is expected of them, the counselor gradually becomes less active. Rosenthal (1971) explains:

> Because of the adolescent's emotional volatility, his propensity to quickly transform feeling and impulse into action, and his exquisite developmental sensitivity to anxiety and discomfort, it is necessary to help him put into language, as early as possible, his ambivalent feelings toward the group. The verbal expression of negative affect toward the group is the best guarantee against precipitous withdrawal. The group therapist can alert the group to a disgruntled and potentially withdrawing member by asking, "Do you think John is planning to return next week?" On a group level, the extension of opportunities to evaluate the group experience and the therapist's performance are fruitful. A question such as, "How do you feel this group is going or not going?" is fertile on several levels; it elicits unspoken negative feelings and demonstrates that the therapist's ego can sustain their criticism (p. 358).

We agree with Rosenthal's general suggestion, but prefer to use a reflection rather than the type of questioning with which he used to surface the adolescent client's volatile feelings. For example, "John, you seem to be so upset with us that you are wondering whether you want to return for our next session"; or "John, you aren't completely satisfied with this session so far today. Perhaps it would help to replay the tape in order to give you a chance to point out to me, and to your fellow clients, where we missed something with which you wanted help, or tried to help, but weren't effective. It also would be useful to have you point out where you wanted to talk about something, but you were kind of afraid or embarrassed to do so." Similar responses also can be used to surface impulses to act out and to encourage clients to cope with such feelings prior to acting out.

Group Attractiveness

Given adolescents' peer orientation and their need to be acceptable to peers, the attractiveness of the group is more important to adolescents than to most clients. Its attractiveness is further increased by the fact that everyone who volunteers is not admitted: that each client is selected with care to maximize the chances for obtaining the best possible combination of clients for success. Moreover, a presentation that stresses the responsibility of clients to decide whether to participate, to take responsibility for getting ready for counseling, and for convincing the counselor that they are ready to talk openly and to learn new behaviors seems to convey both responsibility and caring to adolescents: "We want you in our group. Are you ready? Can you make the necessary commitments to learn your desired new behaviors?''

The selection process for adolescent clients is very important. Clients must be attractive to others in the group. Attractiveness has been defined in earlier chapters, but bears repeating. Attractiveness for group membership can occur on a variety of levels, but includes: (1) willingness to talk openly and directly about concerns; (2) a desire to establish clear goals that are capable of being achieved; (3) a commitment to assist others in learning new ways of managing problems; and (4) an agreement to maintain respect for others by maintaining confidentiality.

Other areas of attractiveness may include status within the school (as with student leaders or athletes) or the community. Attractiveness also may take the form of similar problems to other group members, problems that are significantly different from others, or a reputation for having learned to effectively manage other concerns and a willingness to continue working on new issues as a way of growing. The counselor must guard against identifying participants who are attractive only to the counselor but who may lack credibility for other students. Group counseling is not an elitist activity; this is particularly true among adolescents who are especially sensitive to cliques and special-status groupings.

Developing New Relationships

Inasmuch as acceptance by peers is so crucial for adolescents, the presentation notes precisely how group counseling helps clients to improve their relationships with significant others and to develop new relationships—even with those with whom they have been reluctant to do so. In the intake interview the counselor is encouraged to help prospective group members explore with whom they would like to be placed and with whom they would prefer not to be placed. Moreover, role playing is introduced early in the therapeutic process in order to help clients improve their relationships with specific persons and to practice meeting specific developmental tasks, especially those pertaining to functioning in relevant adult roles.

In addition to helping adolescents practice building and/or improving relationships with specific persons through role playing, a number of relationship-building techniques can be used profitably with adolescents: human potential lab exercises for teaching them to give positive feedback; breaking into and out of a group for dealing with membership needs; intimacy exercises; touching experiences; and an approach-avoidance exercise. Since the last two can be used to help adolescents express their feelings toward peers of the opposite sex and to manage their related fears and insecurity, their use with adolescents is discussed further here. Although adolescents' expression of these intense feelings is enhanced by an informal atmosphere and the use of nonverbal techniques (Olsson & Myers, 1972), these exercises can be used more effectively when the purposes of each exercise, and the clients' participation in it, are spelled out carefully prior to its use.

Touching

Touching exercises are helpful when, for example, the counselor detects "skin hunger." Clients are assisted in discussing their need, wish, or desire to touch and be touched, and usually clients discover that others share this need—that even most adults have not learned to satisfy this need satisfactorily. By discussing the topic, clients may still be afraid, but it is now tolerable fear. They come to accept it as a normal desire for which they can learn appropriate and considerate responses, and practice them in their counseling group.

Frequently the counselor defines, with the assistance of the group, some specific situations with which most members of the group would like to learn to cope. Then the counselor selects from volunteers members who do the prescribed touching (described in the situations they developed cooperatively); share their feelings as they approach and touch each other (and use soliloquy to express those feelings that they do not feel able to express directly); and learn from the feedback that they are given during subsequent discussions. The counselor reinforces risk taking and successful touching experiences; and when members fail, helps them decide what they are willing to attempt next. The counselor also teaches fellow clients to provide encouragement and support for the next trial efforts. Thus, with sensitive consideration for individual's rights, the group uses the exercises to desensitize clients to touching as well as to practice appropriate touching.

The issue of touch with adolescents is very important. All people have a need to touch and to be touched. Basic research has demonstrated that infants who do not have the opportunity to be touched, caressed, held, do not mature as healthily as babies who do, and, in extreme cases, infant death can occur as a result of lack of touch. Recent research examining differences in families with well-behaved boys as compared to families with aggressive boys found that the families did not differ in the amount of touch among family members, but there were significant differences in whether the touches were affection touches or control touches, with functional families using more affection and aggressive families using more controlling touches. Also, functional families understood what was meant by touches much more so than did dysfunctional families (James, 1986).

Teenagers need to touch and to be touched, but their developmental stage of life causes touch to be more difficult. Some adolescents feel uncomfortable with their developing sexuality and confuse touching with being sexual: they do not understand the difference between *sexual* and *sensual*. Parents often are confused by the same issue, and withdraw from touching their children as they reach puberty, at times giving children a message that touch is bad or wrong. Yet adolescents need touch and reach out for it—at times through physical activities (school athletics), at other times through dating. Our experience with adolescent girls in groups is that sometimes they agree to sexual advances among male peers not because of a desire for sex, but to be touched, held, caressed, and cared for. Teaching adolescents appropriate ways of receiving the touch they need can be a valuable contribution of counselors, though counselors must be prepared to defend the practice if necessary.

The Approach–Avoidance Exercise

The approach–avoidance exercise consists of two volunteers looking at each other and walking toward each other; sharing their feelings as they approach (and using soliloquy to express those feelings that they are unable to express directly); touching each other as they meet; and discussing their experiences, including the feedback from observers. Best results tend to be achieved when the exercise has been preceded by the touching exercises. Furthermore, the counselor usually finds that it is profitable to help participants review what they learned from the touching exercises: for example, that others want to learn to deal directly with each other; to express their real feelings to others; and without threatening or hurting, to touch significant others, too.

This is something that can be learned; however the partner in the scene must be as interested in learning to be close to significant others as the primary client is; the partner is committed to help the primary client and does not laugh at the primary client even when a dumb mistake is made; and that mistakes will not be told to others. In other words, the primary client is provided with safe practice situations. After clients have utilized the technique successfully they often attempt a variation of it to practice expressing positive feelings to significant others and to practice making requests of such persons. Adolescents have a great need to prove themselves to opposite-sex peers, and consequently they often find it difficult to express tender feelings to opposite-sex peers; nevertheless, they recognize quickly that the counseling group is a place where they can develop these skills.

Building Confidence

Although adolescents often act as though they are confident, and even spurn significant adults' efforts to protect them from their needlessly careless behaviors, they admit readily in a safe counseling group that they are not very confident, and that they need to practice (role play) dealing with peers as well as their significant adults. The counselor helps them explore with whom they want to learn to do what, and in doing so conveys empathy and understanding of their real inner needs. Thus, clearly stated behavioral idiosyncratic goals increase the security and attractiveness of a counseling group. Role playing facilitates these essential learnings, alerts clients to developmental tasks with which they require assistance, and enables them to discover that others whom they accept and admire are struggling with similar problems. Frequently, even adolescents who have demonstrated the commitment for membership in a counseling group may have difficulty owning a problem as their own until they have helped another in role playing to cope with a similar problem. Use of role reversal, accompanied by tape recordings of the role-played scene (and preferably video recordings), enables clients to understand better their impact on others, and helps clients grasp what others must experience as they try to relate to one another.

As suggested earlier, some clients require a session with parents and/or the entire family in which the counselor helps clients communicate how they really feel toward the parents, how the parents have hurt them, and what they require of family members to implement desired new behaviors. At such sessions, parents tend to be deeply touched when they discover that the adolescent does still care about them and genuinely wants their help in implementing desired new behaviors. Moreover, the adolescent is often touched deeply when listening (and perhaps for the first time) to family members deal with many of the same issues. Rosenthal (1971) explains:

> It is important, if not imperative, for the group therapist to discuss with group members the question of how the inevitable approaches and contacts from parents should be handled. Parental phone calls requesting information on a member's group functioning or the unsolicited transmission of information which the member is not yet ready to share with the group create potentially thorny problems for group leaders of adolescent groups. The therapist's early willingness to consult with the group on this matter not only gives him practical operational guidelines with individual members but also enhances group self-esteem and aids in creating a climate of trust and respect (pp. 360–361).

Since quality membership in an attractive group of peers is valued so highly by adolescents, the counselor's presentation stresses the quality of membership in group counseling, clients' responsibilities for obtaining it, and specific new types of behaviors learned by clients. They are impressed too by the genuine opportunities provided in group counseling to help peers. Hodgman and Stewart (1972) strengthen this feeling by involving previously successfully treated outpatients in a community mental-health center in screening clients for groups.

Accepting Responsibility

This counseling model's emphasis on each client's acceptance of responsibility for getting ready for counseling and for defining precise behavioral goals helps to satisfy adolescents' need for independence and enhances their feeling of security in their group. They accept their responsibility for learning to trust. They also are comforted by the emphasis on their learning new behaviors rather than on making basic personality changes.

Meaningful *participation* in developing and in maintaining therapeutic norms is essential for all clients, but for adolescents it is crucial. Since discovering others' as well as their own growth is so satisfying to them, they require clearly stated criteria for evaluating fellow clients as well as their own growth:

ADOLESCENT: I want to learn how to talk with my dad about my career choices—to learn a way of letting him know I must make my own decisions about my work.

COUNSELOR: How will you know when you have accomplished this?

ADOLESCENT: I have given a lot of thought to what I want to do. When I can sit down with him, tell him what I've decided, and have me be able to not be so upset that I yell and scream. I'd like for him to be able to hear me, too, but there's no assurance of that. But I do want to practice how to say what I need to say, and then learn to accept the outcome, no matter what it is.

On the other hand, the counselor must be careful lest adolescent clients resist termination of a wonderful, accepting relationship. Rather than to seemingly attack them with a penetrating interpretation, better results seem to be achieved with a reflection such as: "You really like each other, and even though most of you have achieved your goals, you are reluctant to say your goodbyes." Termination exercises that focus on growth one or two sessions before termination also help them accept termination when it seems to be indicated:

Perhaps each of us could think about which goals have been achieved; what is still left to do; what each of you think the others have achieved, and what they have left to do. After we have discussed these, perhaps we will be able to decide how much more time we will require and be able to figure out how to say our goodbyes to each other.

Obviously, adolescents thrive upon responsibility for their own growth. Frequently, however, they require instruction in decision making, assertion training, conflict resolution, and need the opportunity to practice these skills in their counseling group prior to implementing them with significant others. Clients can be involved in such a manner that they accept responsibility for their own growth.

For adolescent clients, the counselor also must watch for and reinforce their development and maintenance of a therapeutic interaction among themselves. This last point is true for all clients, but adolescents require it more than most, and it certainly helps prevent clients banding together against the counselor (group resistance) in ways that have concerned some therapists (Hauserman, Zweback, & Plotkin, 1972; Redl, 1948; Slavson, 1957).

Openness

Openness is contagious in a group of adolescents. Although most adolescents find that it is easier to discuss their problems with a group of peers than alone with a counselor, being given responsibility for getting themselves ready for counseling further strengthens this openness. Both the meaningful participation in defining precise behavioral goals and the emphasis that the model places upon learning new behaviors enhances adolescents' feelings of security and willingness to be open with fellow clients. Furthermore, membership in an attractive group of motivated peers provides the adolescent client with much needed, good peer models for self-disclosure, for developing behavioral goals, for discovering and celebrating growth, and for soliciting and using feedback required to implement new behaviors outside the group.

Finally, helping adolescents learn new behaviors and implementing them is not sufficient. Best results are achieved when adolescents learn to share their goals; to solicit encouragement and reinforcement from significant others; to communicate their new selves to significant others; and to request assistance in maintenance of new behaviors. When the counselor detects an adolescent's discouragement because significant others continue to treat him as he used to be, and unknowingly reinforce rejected old behaviors, the counselor can alert the entire group to this problem with a reflection such as: "You get pretty discouraged when you try so hard to change, and your mom continues to distrust you for what you used to be. I guess you need help in conveying to her precisely how you have changed, how she hurts you and makes you want to give up when she continues to be critical of you, and what instead you require of her to further your growth." Such a reflection usually surfaces several clients' need for such assistance and encourages all of them to discuss precisely how they have changed, how they may best communicate their new selves to their significant others, and how they may solicit reinforcement for their continuing growth.

PEER HELPERS

A popular trend is to augment the services of professionals in community agencies, schools, and colleges with the services of paraprofessionals and peer helpers. They are often used effectively in crisis centers to prevent suicides and to assist drug addicts. Furthermore, there is evidence to support use of paraprofessionals (Carkhuff, 1969; Lamb & Clark, 1974; Pyle & Snyder, 1971) and of peer helpers (Carkhuff, 1968; Ohlsen, 1974; Tucker & Cantor, 1975).

Confrontational Models

From his review of the research on treating drug addicts, Ohlsen (1974) concluded that groups using a high-confrontation model designed to tear away defenses and excuses provide some of the most effective treatment for drug addicts, including alcoholics. This peer-counseling technique has been used primarily with the institutionalized or with outpatients in programs such as community drug and alcohol treatment programs. Ohlsen encourages counselors in other settings to help youths adapt the confrontation model for club-type groups that would meet for an hour a day, five days a week. Obviously, the success of such groups would be enhanced by participation of successfully treated former members who have lived in a setting using the confrontation model.

Combining Confrontation and Support

A group-counseling approach combining confrontration methods with empathic support in an inpatient setting has been described by Leaman (1983). The program emphasized peer involvement in helping other group members, confrontation of excuse-giving and defensiveness, and a major emphasis on behavioral/structured approaches for helping group members acquire interpersonal skills. The format of the group sessions included an adaptation of Ivey's (1973) microcounseling techniques. Ivey's microcounseling approach has been used for training counselors and paraprofessionals and is readily adaptable to helping adolescents learn effective interpersonal process skills.

Skill-Building

Another model developed for helping adolescents learn effective problem-solving and interpersonal skill methods is presented in *Skill Streaming the Adolescent* (Goldstein, Sprafkin, Gershaw, & Klein, 1980). This program is highly structured, skills-specific for helping participants learn communication, assertiveness, and problem-solving skills. The program includes audio modeling tapes for use with students in counseling groups, as well as readings for counselors and participants.

Peer helpers also are being used successfully with children and adults. Mowrer (1973) endorsed their use to aid the emotionally disturbed as well as to enrich the quality of life for normal, healthy adults.

Peer Relationships

Hamburg and Varenhorst (1972) have developed a very carefully designed program to train peer helpers to provide very specific services for secondary-school students. Varenhorst (1983) has written *Real Friends*, a book for adolescents to teach them effective relationship skills and problem-solving methods. The book has been used both as reading for adolescents interested in learning more effective interpersonal skills, and also to train peer counselors to help fellow students in school. The book presents clearly defined methods for managing adolescent life-development stages effectively, though not without some pain.

Peer Counselors

Effective peer-counseling programs have been developed for schools and community agencies. The selection process for peer counselors is very important, for they must be attractive to peers and demonstrate good leadership skills. They must also participate in training on issues such as problem solving, relationship skills, and most particularly, confidentiality and trust. Our experience with peer leaders in schools has been that they have been able to provide a valuable resource to other students and have provided support and greater credibility to the counseling department of the schools in which they have worked.

Peer Counselor Limitations

We have found, at times, that some students, particularly those from different socioeconomic groups, have had reservations about working with peer counselors in school settings. After being paired together, however, the reservations have quickly disappeared as the peer counselors demonstrated their concern and willingness to be available, supportive, and helpful with problems. Careful coordination with adult counselors is important to be certain that peer counselors do not extend their offerings of help into areas in which they do not have the skills, strengths, or abilities to be of professional help. This would include particularly dangerous areas such as suicide.

Residential Peer Counseling

Biehn (1972) describes her experiences in helping college students housed on one floor in a dormitory to create a therapeutic community. Living with them, she helped them to determine what and how they wanted to learn; develop a structure for learning to accept the responsibility for learning; cope with the conflict within their group; and develop the skills that they required to help each other develop socially and emotionally as well as intellectually. She found that as she learned to be truly herself and less concerned about being the counselor, she became a better helper and trainer of helpers.

Case Examples

Perhaps two of the writers' experiences can be used to illustrate how adolescent peer helpers can be used. Both types of clients tend to be difficult to help, especially when the counseling groups are made up entirely of either type.

Case 1

In the first instance gifted, underachieving ninth-graders were invited to tutor—and generally encourage—gifted, underachieving seventh-graders. Soon the helpers requested assistance in doing tutoring. Informal seminars with eight to a group were organized for this purpose. The seminar leaders possessed a reasonably good background in learning disabilities and study skills, and were very effective counselors of groups. The tutors were encouraged to request specific help with specific seventh-graders, to discuss their feelings toward their helpees, to practice their desired new helping behaviors in their seminar, and to share their successes and failures. As they learned to empathize with these seventh-graders, to encourage them, to help them seek encouragement from significant others, and to feel better about themselves as a consequence of providing significant help for others, their own school achievement improved markedly, and perhaps more than it would have had the counselors organized a counseling group for them.

Case 2

A second group of helpers were institutionalized delinquent males. After several attempts to develop a productive group-counseling program, an effective counseling group was finally developed. As these clients terminated their group, they reviewed precisely how the group had helped them. When they had finished the counselor said, "You have demonstrated that you can help each other. There are many others in this institution who also need help but don't know how to request it or would be ashamed to admit it; I wonder how we could reach them. I wonder whether each of you know of such fellows whom you would be willing to help if I were to help you learn how to do it." This generated a discussion on such clients. Each identified at least one such person whom he would like to help individually. Then a seminar was planned for them.

The first session was devoted to helping them plan and practice their approach to their helpees. Thereafter the sessions were used primarily for their sharing successes, examining failures, and identifying new approaches. Those who were most successful in working with their clients helped them to define specific desired new behaviors. About half of their clients were helped individually and enough clients were identified and referred for two more effective counseling groups.

SUMMARY

Adolescents are engrossed in their search for identity, in establishing themselves in adult roles, and in achieving their independence. At the same time, they are changing their referent group from family to peers. On the other hand, most parents still have a great deal of influence on adolescents.

Perhaps the two most important elements provided in a counseling group are genuine acceptance and encouragement offered by peers who are committed to help them; and a trustworthy adult who seems to trust and respect adolescents. Such a safe, therapeutic group encourages adolescents to talk openly; to seek essential information about themselves and the opportunities open to them; to appraise the information and feedback they obtain; to develop an essential repertoire of social and human relations skills; to formulate essential life goals; to become more aware of significant others' needs; to learn to satisfy their own needs and help their significant others satisfy their needs, too; to learn to live with the increasing number of adult roles; and to develop the confidence, skills, and ego strength to cope with life problems as they meet them.

Most of the ideas presented in the previous chapters apply to adolescents as well as to adults. Since adolescents are often brought to counseling under duress and made to feel that they are to blame for whatever went wrong at home, school, or work, the counselor must be very sensitive and attuned to these feelings, help clients discuss them, and convey that the counselor's task is not to prove who is wrong; but instead, it is to help the adolescent function more effectively. Furthermore, adolescents are impressed more than most clients with the reasons why clients are selected with such care for each group; why they must accept responsibility for getting themselves ready for counseling and proving their readiness; and why they must define precise behavioral goals and growth criteria.

Many adolescent problems result from significant others' failure to try to empathize with them, to understand their unique needs, and to help them fulfill these needs during this period of rapid maturation. Therefore some of the counselor's time should be devoted to helping significant others further adolescents' wholesome development. Though individual consultations with significant others are essential too, much can be accomplished through group consultation with significant others such as parents and teachers, and with peer counseling.

REFERENCES

Ackerman, N. W. (1955). Group psychotherapy with a mixed group of adolescents. *International Journal of Group Psychotherapy, 5,* 249–260.

Ausubel, D. P. (1954). *Theory and problems of adolescent development.* New York: Grune & Stratton.

Ayer, F. L., & Corman, B. R. (1952). Laboratory practices develop citizenship concepts of high school students. *Social Education, 16,* 215–216.

Biehn, J. (1972). Community as counselor. *Personnel and Guidance Journal, 50,* 730–734.

Buntman, P., & Saris, E. (1979). *How to live with your teenager.* Pasadena, CA: Birch Tree Press.

Carkhuff, R. R. (1968). Differential functions of lay and professional helpers. *Journal of Counseling Psychology, 15,* 117–126.

Carkhuff, R. R. (1969). *Helping and human relations: A primer for lay and professional helpers* (Vol. 1). New York: Holt, Rinehart and Winston.

Cole, L., & Hall, I. (1964). *Psychology of adolescence.* New York: Holt, Rinehart and Winston.

Corder, B.; Whiteside, L.; & Haizlip, T. (1981). A study of the curative factors in group psychotherapy with adolescents. *International Journal of Group Psychotherapy, 31,* 345–354.

Gadpaille, W. J. (1959). Observations on the sequence of resistances in groups of adolescent delinquents. *International Journal of Group Psychotherapy, 9,* 275–286.

Garrison, K. C. (1965). *Psychology of adolescence.* Englewood Cliffs, NJ: Prentice-Hall.

Gesell, A.; Ilg, F. L.; & Ames, L. B. (1956). *Youth: The years from ten to sixteen.* New York: Harper & Row.

Gold, M., & Petronio, R. (1980). Delinquent behavior in adolescence. In J. Adelson (Ed.), *Handbook of adolescent psychology* (pp. 495–535). New York: John Wiley & Sons.

Goldstein, A.; Sprafkin, R.; Gershaw, N. J.; & Klein, P. (1980). *Skillstreaming the adolescent: A structured learning approach to teaching prosocial skills.* Champaign, IL: Research Press.

Guerney, B. (1979). *Relationship enhancement.* San Francisco: Jossey Bass.

Hall, G. S. (1904). *Adolescence.* New York: Appleton.

Hamburg, B., & Varenhorst, B. (1972). Peer counseling in the secondary schools. *American Journal of Orthopsychiatry, 42,* 566–581.

Hauserman, N.; Zweback, S.; & Plotkin, A. (1972). Use of concrete reinforcement to facilitate verbal initiations in adolescent group therapy. *Journal of Consulting and Clinical Psychology, 38,* 90–96.

Hodgman, C. H., & Stewart, W. H. (1972). The adolescent screening group. *International Journal of Group Psychotherapy, 22,* 177–185.

Hurlock, E. B. (1967). *Adolescent development.* New York: McGraw-Hill.

James, L. (1987). Study of the differences in touch patterns between functional and dysfunctional families. Unpublished doctoral dissertation, Indiana State University.

Ivey, A. E. (1973). Microcounseling: The counselor as trainer. *The Personnel and Guidance Journal, 51,* 311–336.

Kirkpatrick, M. E. (1952). The mental hygiene of adolescents in the Anglo-American culture. *Mental Hygiene, 36,* 394–403.

Lamb, D. H., & Clark, R. J. (1974). Professional versus paraprofessional approaches to orientation and subsequent counseling contacts. *Journal of Counseling Psychology, 21,* 61–65.

Leaman, D. (1983). Group counseling to improve communication skills of adolescents. *Journal for Specialists in Group Work, 8,* 144–150.

McCandless, B. R. (1970). *Adolescents: Behavior and development.* Hinsdale, IL: Dryden.

Mowrer, O. H. (1973). Group counseling in the elementary school: The professional versus peer-group model. In M. M. Ohlsen (Ed.), *Counseling children in groups: A forum* (pp. 243–269). New York: Holt, Rinehart and Winston.

Neidt, C. O., & Fritz, M. F. (1950). Relation of cynicism to certain student characteristics. *Educational and Psychological Measurement, 10,* 712–718.

Ohlsen, L. (1966). A student's perception of group counseling. *Clearing House, 40,* 401–403.

Ohlsen, M. M. (1974). *Guidance services in the modern school.* New York: Harcourt.

Olsson, P., & Myers, I. (1972). Nonverbal techniques in an adolescent group. *International Journal of Group Psychotherapy, 22,* 186–191.

Persons, R. (1966). Psychological and behavioral change in delinquents following psychotherapy. *Journal of Clinical Psychology, 22,* 337–340.

Pyle, R., & Snyder, F. (1971). Students as paraprofessional counselors at community colleges. *Journal of College Student Personnel, 12,* 259–262.

Redl, F. (1948). Resistance in therapy groups. *Human Relations, 1,* 307–313.

Rosenthal, L. (1971). Some dynamics of resistance and therapy management in adolescent group therapy. *Psychoanalytic Review, 58,* 353–366.

Slavson, S. R. (1957). Are there group dynamics in therapy groups? *International Journal of Group Psychotherapy, 7,* 131–134.

Steiner, C. (1974). *Scripts people live.* New York: Grove.

Tucker, S. J., & Cantor, P. C. (1975). Personality and status profiles of peer counselors and suicide attempters. *Journal of Counseling Psychology, 22,* 423–430.

Varenhorst, B. (1983). *Real Friends.* Englewood Cliffs, NJ: Prentice-Hall.

Yalom, I. (1970). *Theory and practice of group psychotherapy.* New York: Basic Books.

14

COUNSELING ADULTS IN GROUPS

Counselors are increasingly being called upon to develop proficiencies and skills for assisting adults who face developmental issues and concerns (Wortley & Amatea, 1982). A major part of developing proficiencies for assisting adults in counseling groups is based in understanding the developmental issues, stages, phases, and cycles that are characteristic of the adult life span. This chapter provides a brief overview of adult developmental theory; issues involved in the adult life span; and strategies for working with adults in groups. For the purpose of this chapter, *adulthood* is defined as that period of time between 20–65 years old.

ADULT DEVELOPMENTAL THEORY: A BRIEF OVERVIEW

Erikson's Stage Theory

Viewing adult development as passing through a series of stages involving growth and crises, through which individuals develop various senses of themselves, is one of the basic models of human development (Erikson, 1963). Accordingly, Erikson divides adulthood into a series of psychosocial stages that human beings pass through. The extent to which the individual successfully meets the demands and issues relevant to a particular stage sets up the basis for successful progress to the next stage. Likewise, a failure, limitation, or block that inhibits and hinders development at a particular stage further complicates future development. Successful aging equals resolving crucial issues at the various stages of life. The adult stages characteristic of the Eriksonian model include: identity versus role confusion; intimacy versus isolation; generativity versus stagnation; and ego integrity versus despair.

Identity versus Role Confusion

In identity versus role confusion, the young adult learns to play several roles through the ability to integrate various identities. The ego has developed an inner stability. On the other hand, role confusion may occur if the individual overidentifies to the point of loss of identity with groups, heroes, and cliques. Identity problems may also occur if the individual feels rejected by others, which may foster doubt regarding esteem and self-worth. Much of what may be going on at this stage of development has been covered in the chapter on working with adolescents in groups, and therefore will not be included here.

Intimacy versus Isolation

With the search for identity completed, the individual moves on to the relationship stage and moves toward intimate contact with others. The essence of this stage is developing the ability and capacity for love and work. Problems at this stage may result when the individual develops difficulty in bonding with others to form friendships and love relationships. An inability to develop support systems by learning how to give to and take from others may result. Nurturance, caring, and intimate contact are hindered when the individual experiences difficulties in regulating her psychological distance from others in a way that allows for a sense of safety, comfort, and love, as well as trusting, sharing, and loving in return.

The ability to invest in and identify with a career is also a major part of one's identity and self-concept. The stresses involved in developing and maintaining a career, family relationships, and friendships are subject to problems in the event that the individual isolates herself, withdraws, and avoids intimate contact.

Generativity versus Stagnation

According to Erikson (1963) generativity encompasses the evolution of human development in teaching, instituting, and learning. Erikson believes that generativity reflects the need one has to be needed, as well as the need one has for encouragement. The interplay between the younger and older generation is based on the need to guide, teach, and encourage the younger, more immature to be more productive and creative. Problems at this stage are often a result of regressing to self-indulgence and an inability to find support in others. Excessive self-love resulting from feeling a lack of faith and trust in others to give aid, care, and love is a core issue involved in feeling a sense of stagnation.

Ego Integrity versus Despair

Culmination of the previous stages unfolds in ego integrity. This stage of life involves the essence of self-acceptance; one's life takes on the quality of an inner sense of meaning and order as one comes to accept and honor their personal dignity. Difficulties develop at this stage when the individual views her life with despair for not having taken opportunities or lived more fully. Often the individual has not resolved unfinished business with significant others in their lives, consequently remorse and regret foster a further despair that life has gone by leaving no second chance. Ego integrity, on the other hand, celebrates one's emotional integration of fellowship, involvement, and acceptance of the responsibility of leadership. In Erikson's (1963) words, adult integrity comes full circle with infantile trust that "healthy children will not fear life if their elders have integrity enough not to fear death" (p. 269).

Life-Cycle Theory

Bernice Neugarten (1979) disagrees with the views of life stage theorists like Erikson. She argues that the timing of life events is becoming less regular; that age is losing its customary social meaning; that psychological themes are recurrent, appearing and reappearing in new forms that do not follow a fixed order; that intrapsychic processes change slowly with age and not in a stepwise fashion; and finally, that future trends are toward a more fluid life cycle and age-irrelevant society. Life-cycle theorists (Neugarten, 1979; Lowenthal, 1975; Vaillant, 1977) do not believe that adult developmental issues are a result of childhood issues. Instead, they believe psychological change is continuous throughout life. Vaillant (1977), for example, emphasizes the process of adaptation over time, believing that an adaptation style emerges as a result of how one learns to adapt to life which leads to maturation. Such maturation is dependent on development from within instead of being contingent on changes in the interpersonal environment.

While stage theorists contend that individuals go through discrete stages in a chronological fashion, life-cycle theorists caution against the presumption that regularities or dramatic transitions define what is normal; and that if one has not experienced them, they are off track. Life-cycle changes influence perceptual changes in self-concept and identity, but do not necessarily result in crisis. Death of a spouse may not produce a crisis if it's expected and timely. Life-cycle theorists believe the fluid life cycle is marked by the disappearance of transitional timetables and replaced by the idea that life-cycle development involves an increasing number of role transitions (Neugarten, 1979).

Mental-health professionals will most likely be faced with helping individuals cope with a number of issues related to life-cycle change. For example, counselors may be involved in helping individuals adjust to role changes resulting from life becoming more varied and fluid, with transition becoming more irregular, and age norms less limiting.

Levinson's Life-Cycle Theory

Daniel Levinson suggests that we know more about the pre-adult years than we do about adulthood, and that a developmental approach is needed to study adulthood. Levinson and his associates' (1978) theoretical formulations follow Jungian theory which holds the entire life cycle as important to psychic development, especially the second half of one's life and adult development, which is in contrast with Jung's mentor, Sigmund Freud. Freud's emphasis on early childhood as crucial to the psychic development of the adult was too limiting for Jung to accept. Instead, Jung held that social institutions, religion, culture, and mythology influenced human development. Levinson bases his life-cycle theories of adulthood in the Jungian principle of individuation (Levinson et al., 1978) which Jung described as a process involving a regulating center within the self that brings about a constant extension and maturing of the personality (Jung et al., 1968). Individuation is essentially a process of self-development, involving a constant integration and synthesis of information and experiences coming from both conscious and unconscious forces. This process of individuation requires a willingness to trust in the unconscious as a valuable source of information.

Seasons

In using the term *life cycle*, Levinson suggests that one's life course has a particular character and follows a basic sequence (Levinson et al., 1978). The idea of a life cycle implies that a process is involved from a starting point to an ending point, like a journey. The journeys we take in our lives follow underlying patterns with endless cultural and individual variations that interact with the time and place of a particular event. Time and place constitute what Levinson refers to as a "season" of one's life. Accordingly, each season is different from the preceding one and those that follow, but there are common themes. The metaphor of a "season" defines the life course in terms of having a shape and form that evolve in a dynamic fashion. Change occurs in each season, and a transition is required to shift to the next season. Each season is unique and important and needs to be understood in its own context. Each season adds its unique contribution to the whole life course and is valued, from that standpoint, on its own merit.

Four Eras

Levinson believes, based on his research, that there are four distinct eras in the life cycle (childhood and adolescence; early adulthood; middle adulthood; and late adulthood) each lasting approximately twenty years. The same author also characterizes eras like acts in a play, or major divisions in a novel which are an overview of the life cycle as a whole. Moving from one era to another is a process that takes approximately four to five years, and changes the major fabric of one's life. The mid-life transition (40–45 years old) is an example of a transition of one era to another. Perhaps the notion of "mid-life crisis" associated with this period is an illustration of its substantial developmental importance in the life cycle. Levinson believes that the transition linking early adulthood to middle adulthood may be the most dramatic of all life-cycle transitions (Levinson et al., 1978).

Life Structure

Study of the developmental process needs to consider both the individual and the society as they interact to influence developmental periods. The structural pattern of an individual's life is a result of the interplay between self and society. Levinson terms this "life structure." He believes the course of adult psychosocial development is dependent on the life structures that are built during the transitional phases of an era. Transitions in the life cycle, as mentioned earlier, are like bridges or zones that demarcate changes of major proportion in one's life. Transitional periods are required to terminate the past and to start the future. Life structure is said to be successful to the extent that it functions for both the society one lives in and one's self-concept. Life structures provide both gains and losses for both the self and society. In addition to the concept of life structures, Levinson defines specific events that occur in one's life that have major impact, trauma, potential benefit, as "marker events." Such events cause marked change in one's life.

ISSUES INVOLVED IN ADULT LIFE

Developmental issues are also issues of adulthood. Adults continuously experience transitions, and psychic growth does not end at adolescence (Schlossberg, 1981). Group counseling with adults is essentially a process of using group facilitation to help adult group members deal with transitions relevant to their life-cycle changes. Helping members adapt to events that necessitate changes in the assumptions about themselves and their world, as well as the effects of these changes in terms of behaviors and relationships with others, can be effectively dealt with in groups (Budman, Michael, & Wisneski, 1980).

Transition

We define *transition* as an event-causing change in assumption about self and world with subsequent effects on behavior and relationship with others. According to Schlossberg (1981) it is not the transition that is important, but how the transition fits with the stage of the individual's life, the situational circumstances facing the individual, and the individual's particular style of adjustment. Schlossberg (1981) also develops a model for analyzing human adaptation to transition in which she analyzes the effects of a transition in terms of the perceptions the individual holds regarding the transition; the circumstantial condition of the environment both before and after the transition; and the characteristics of the individual—all of which affect how one might adapt to a transition. The magnitude of a transition may be assessed partially by several factors. For example, one's perceptions regarding the transition may be affected by the timing of a particular event in terms of age appropriateness or whether the event involved in the transition is gradual or sudden; and how effective a support system the individual in transition has is crucial to successful adaptations.

Individual factors of transition involve several abilities. The ability to maintain a coherent and consistent self-image, positive self-esteem, self-worth, constructively interacting with the world, and the ability to be introspective, all correlate positively with adaptation during transition. The sex role and identity of an individual may also play an important part in one's ability to adapt to life transitions. The capacity for intimacy and mutuality in relationships make it easier for females to obtain support than for males who tend to withdraw (Schlossberg, 1981). However, middle age is a period of high risk for both sexes because they are more likely to experience negative instead of positive stresses and to be overwhelmed by them (Lowenthal & Chiriboga, 1975).

Life transitions are influenced by the nature of life in a highly industrialized and urbanized society: for example, greater mobility, increased rate of job change, reeducating for technical advancement, more leisure time, sex-role identity changes, among others. All of the previously stated can yield opportunities for growth or lead to despair and decline. As Hobson (1981) states:

> A transition simultaneously carries the needs of our yesterdays, hopes and fears of our futures, the pressing sensations of the present which is our confirmation of being alive. There is danger and there is opportunity, ecstasy and despair, development and stagnation, but above all there is movement. Nothing and no one stays the same. Nature abhors a vacuum and stability. A stable state is merely a stopping point on a journey from one place to another. Stop too long and your journey is ended. Stay and enjoy but with the realization that more is to come. We may not be able to stop the journey, but we can fly the plane (p. 39).

Dealing with Transition in Group

A well-developed support system suggests that group counseling may be a helpful format for providing individuals undergoing major transitions in their lives with the support they need in order to adapt more effectively.

Group counseling seems especially well suited to helping individuals assess and develop the necessary coping skills for managing their life transitions. Brammer and Abrego (1981) outline some of the key issues involved in developing basic coping skills appropriate for managing transitions. Helping individuals identify and mobilize their personal style of responding to change, accept transition as a normal part of life, and recognize specific problems presented by the nature of a particular transition, as well as the role of feeling as important to the resolution and adaptation of a transition, are important skills for beginning to deal with a transition. Helping individuals identify their emotional needs and express them in a way that allows the person to feel supported and cared for during a transitional period is ideally dealt with in a group of individuals with similar life transitions. Essentially, group formats can be used to teach skills to adults going through transitions to develop new perspectives regarding transitions and to learn new skills for coping with the changes involved in making a transition (Brammer & Abrego, 1981).

Individuals seek assistance from mental-health professionals for a variety of reasons. Some requests are stigmatized and carry with them labels that may be construed by the individual requesting assistance as negative and foreboding; making such requests difficult to say the least. However, seeking assistance with transitional issues of life seems to carry with it a message of normality, ("We all struggle with these issues."), which allows individuals the freedom to share their concerns openly. Brammer and Abrego (1981) indicate this by their work with groups for managing transition.

Homogeneous Age Groups

Budman, Michael, and Wisneski (1980) found short-term, process-oriented groups with a population of life-phase-homogeneous group members to be an effective use of group counseling. The therapeutic forces (Yalom, 1975) seem to pull together around developmental issues, and similarity of life stage appears to override other differences (diagnosis), resulting in the strong and rapid development of cohesion. This study seems especially valuable to the practitioner because of its findings regarding the interaction between developmental issues and leadership function.

Young Adults Group

In the young adults group (20–30 years), members presented issues such as assertiveness; and relationship concerns, with complaints of inabilities to form intimate lasting relationships; or problems resulting from withdrawal and isolation, such as loneliness, sadness, and despair. The developmental issues typical to this age group are intimacy versus isolation (Erikson, 1963). *Intimacy* is defined by Budman et al. (1980) as the ability to be open and trusting and loving with others. Intimacy is also the ability to bond with others. This study found that a basic problem that interferes with the pursuit of intimacy is the tendency to give up, withdraw, and become intellectual. The authors suggest that these groups be closed instead of open-ended where members may leave when they feel they have accomplished their goals for being in the group. The leadership function used emphasized the here-and-now interpersonal focus to assist members in dealing with one another in a more-emotional and intimate way, instead of withdrawing and becoming intellectual which tends to distance members from each other. The primary role of the leader is to facilitate interaction in the here and now illustrated by the initiating structural question: "Who are we, and why are we here?"

Mid-Life Group

The mid-life group's (35–50 years) presenting issues tended toward viewing personal distress as connected to an event or circumstance acute in their lives, especially loss or disappointment in a relationship (death of loved one, separation, divorce, physical impairment). This group also dealt with professional and relationship assessment that involved an examination of where each member had come to professionally and interpersonally. Aging was also a common issue that involved experiencing fear of aging or death as vague discomfort with the future and a sense that time was running out and options were limited. Bonding seemed to occur around the existential and real issues of loneliness. A basic problem for this group was that intimacy had been established but allowed to fade. Individuals admitted to the middle-aged group had the capacity to give and receive love, value social interactions, but had let their lives become barren, routinized, and isolated.

The format for this group was open ended; members during a 15-week period were rotated with two members being added with four to six older members. The group issues centered around the finality of time, the reality and necessity of separation and loss, the possibilities of forming new relationships, utilization of old social skills, and risking vulnerability in the need to trust and share with others. A rich aspect of this group's potential centered around the theme of generativity in that veteran members were willing and able to teach and encourage newer members in the process of building group culture. Members in this group were ready to relate and were open to each other. Members tended to not rely on the leader to show them the way or cure them as in the young adults group. Members seemed to be able to use the group effectively without becoming dependent.

Post Mid-Life Group

The issues involved in the post mid-life group (50–60 years) centered around presenting problems from members such as depression or depressive anxiety which often relates to recent life changes such as death of spouse, separation, divorce, or financial loss. The key element seemed to be a sense of loss. The issues in this group were grieving or mourning one's sense of loss. Members tended to be reflective with underlying hope for future serenity. The focus of this group was on the notion that life is short and on making the best of what is left.

The leadership function was largely determined by the needs of group members. Members tended to rely on themselves and interact freely with each other without structure from the leader to prompt such behavior. The focus by members was on the here-and-now with an emphasis on problem solving and discussion of practical solutions to real-life problems. The therapist functioned primarily as an organizer, catalyst, and a provider of a sense of constancy and cohesiveness. The format was open and members could attend up to thirty sessions during a year but generally used the group as both they and the therapist felt appropriate. Members were informed at the beginning of the group about the nature of the structure of the group, and group members evidenced no problem with this format. Due to the relative short-term nature of this group, issues of personal mortality were not brought up or dealt with by the group or therapist.

This study (Budman et. al., 1980) illustrates that over the adult life cycle, people reduce their idealization for the leader. A major focus is on the leader, especially initially, in the young adults group, while the focus is considerably less in the mid-life group, and nearly absent in the post mid-life group.

WORKING WITH ADULT DEVELOPMENTAL ISSUES IN STRUCTURED GROUPS

Structured groups represent a useful means for helping individuals resolve critical issues involved in life transitions (Drum & Knott, 1977). Adulthood, according to the same authors, represents a need for a developmental format for structural groups. The structured-group format seems appropriately suited to the demands of an ever-changing society with an accelerating pace which requires the development of coping skills.

According to Drum and Knott (1977) there are three types of structural groups: life-skills groups, life-theme groups, and life-transitions groups, all having an educational–experiential problem-solving format.

Life-Skills Groups

The life-skills groups have the objective and purpose of helping individuals develop the skills necessary to enhance the quality of life and to enable them to adapt to the demands of life. The structural elements of these groups include systematic procedures and techniques employed by the leader and designed to facilitate the development of effective and interpersonal skills. Examples of such groups include assertiveness training groups, anxiety and stress-management groups, and interpersonal effectiveness groups.

Clients in life-skills groups are selected and screened in terms of their ability and need to profit from the group, and members are screened out if they run the risk of having negative side effects as a consequence of their participation. The emphasis of these structured groups is not on teaching people tricks or gimmicks to get by with interpersonally, but instead to encourage members to develop an awareness and responsibility to their own growth and development. Members of such groups are taught the rationale for the use of such skills as well as given an opportunity to practice their skills and receive feedback from group members regarding the effectiveness of their behaviors; consequently an atmosphere of mutual sharing, trusting, and a sense of cohesion is valued and developed in the group. Each session of the group is a unit that fits sequentially into the overall objectives of the group. Generally, these groups last from four to eight sessions (Drum & Knott, 1977).

The leader in these groups behaves very much like that described in the behavioral format illustrated in Chapter 2. Essentially, the leader is active, directive, models appropriate behavior, and is technically proficient in all the skills relevant to the objective of the group. Drum and Knott (1977) suggest that cofacilitation be used with the majority of life-skills groups.

Life-Theme Groups

The life-theme groups deal with key developmental issues or stages and are aimed at helping the individuals resolve crucial issues such as sexual identity, desire for intimacy, and sense of loss or loneliness. The groups' objective is to provide people with a framework for understanding their beliefs, assumptions, and values regarding the course of action they are taking or have taken in their lives. These objectives are accomplished by helping members examine the nature of their relationships, their professional and career identities, and the blocks they have that limit further growth and development. Resolution of crucial issues with an emphasis on living more fully in the here-and-now by letting go and finishing business with the past is the significant characteristic of these groups. The life-theme groups may range, according to Drum and Knott's model, from one to six hours. Examples of these groups include: values clarification groups, male/female consciousness-raising groups, as well as groups for creating a more satisfying personal lifestyle, self-esteem, and so on.

The leadership functions change somewhat in comparison to the life-skills group format. These groups are highly structured but at the same time have a humanistic–existential perspective. The leader is less directive, facilitates exercises designed to help members examine elements of a life theme, and encourages discussions and interactions among members to foster identification with the group and a sense of cohesion.

Life-Transition Groups

The life-transition groups described by Drum and Knotts (1977) embody the philosophy and basic thesis of Schlossberg (1981) regarding the definition and process of transitions. The basic purpose of a life-transitions group is to assist people in dealing with the issues involved in major life transitions, such as death of a spouse, divorce, retirement, children moving away from home, among others. The need for support during these periods of life is vitally important to the well-being of the individual and the successful resolution of the transition. Life-transition groups offer the individual an external resource that provides a place to check out perceptions, test reality, receive support and encouragement for change, as well as a place to observe and model the behavior of others struggling with similar transitional issues.

The amount of structure and leadership varies with the nature of the circumstances involved in the transitions shared by the group. Helping individuals assess their personal assets and liabilities and develop new coping skills as well as relearn old skills is a major part of the "taking stock" aspect inherent in a life transition. Life-transition groups last between four to ten sessions according to the structural models of Drum and Knott (1977). The leader is much more group centered in this structured approach than the other two groups previously mentioned. Structural aspects are integrated into the supportive group process to facilitate appropriate skill development and problem-solving ability.

MARRIAGE COUNSELING IN GROUPS

When couples seek marriage counseling in groups, they are selected with the same care described in Chapter 1. Prior to the first group-counseling session with four or five couples, the counselor schedules an intake interview with each couple. She listens first to one then the other describe briefly what each believes their primary marriage and/or family problems are. Then she encourages, and teaches, each to discuss his or her own shortcomings, feelings of inadequacy, and faults that interfere with one or the other's being a productive, lovable adult and good marriage partner. When, for example, the wife speaks first, the counselor not only listens very empathically and responsively but also she teaches the husband to be his partner's helper—to be a good listener, to detect and reflect back his recognition of her experience, to guess what new behaviors she might like to learn, and to offer quality support while she is implementing these new behaviors. In other words, right from the first contact, the counselor teaches the wife to discuss her own pain rather than to complain, or argue, or criticize, and hurt her husband (Ohlsen, 1979; Horne & Ohlsen, 1982). Next the counselor talks to each separately in order to help them practice discussing their own fears and pain openly, to define precise behavioral goals, and to make the commitment to implement their desired new behaviors in a reciprocal way. Finally, the counselor meets with the two of them together again to share their personal goals, formulate their goals as a couple, decide whether they are willing to contract for marriage counseling, and answer any questions they may have concerning what will be expected of them in counseling, what they can expect from the other clients, and the counselor's ability to help them in a couple's group.

Functioning as the counselor's helper increases the husband's sensitivity to his wife's needs and pain and his commitment to help her, while decreasing his need for revenge and winning in a power struggle. It also encourages him to negotiate for increased intimacy, to learn new skills for managing conflict, and to improve communication with his wife. Gradually husband and wife discover that each must accept responsibility for defining and learning his or her own desired new behaviors—that one can change only oneself. Each also learns to solicit the spouse's encouragement and reinforcement, to use the spouse's support, to seek his or her council in learning from mistakes, and to celebrate their successes together.

Thus, each client is prepared to begin group counseling by discussing his or her own real pain, by defining specific goals, by listening to others' feedback, by implementing new behaviors, and by accepting help from fellow clients—especially the spouse. Nevertheless, there will be times when a husband (or wife) will have difficulty listening to his spouse. He may be tempted to complain or edit what she says. When this occurs, the counselor may interrupt him and ask other members to explain how criticism tends to hurt one's spouse, wastes time, and tends to result in his or her discontinuing counseling without getting help. When, however, a spouse senses a problem that he feels calls for the other to learn specific new behaviors, he is encouraged to ask whether or not she would be willing to consider adding this particular item to her list of goals. In such an instance, the counselor helps her decide whether or not she can accept these new goals and encourages her to explore the natural consequences of refusing her husband's request. Such an instance also enables the counselor to help the other couples as well as this one to discover the difference between a request and a demand.

While the wife is talking, as in the above example, the counselor reinforces not only the husband's but other clients' good helper and client behaviors as well. Especially in early group sessions, she points out such good behaviors, notes what precisely made them productive, and also notes specific ways in which unproductive efforts could have been improved with minor changes. Video recordings, and playing back of a portion of a session to cite a specific instance can be very helpful in teaching these desired behaviors. Moreover, encouraging clients to do the same for her also helps the counselor improve her treatment skills.

Selecting clients with care and teaching them to assume responsibility for defining their personal goals and for implementing their desired new behaviors makes couples groups more attractive and increases clients' hope for successful results. Instilling such hope for success is crucial (Yalom, 1985). No less important is the counselor's confidence in herself and the techniques she uses.

Though acceptance by fellow clients tends not to be as unconditional as the counselor's acceptance, it is communicated. Moreover, those who discuss their real pain early tend to be admired for exhibiting such openness and making a commitment to learn new behaviors. However, the counselor should note this admiration and help fellow clients communicating it to the ones who took that risk early in the life of their group. It also is important that the counselor help each discover that fellow clients have self-defeating behaviors, unfinished business, need for information about themselves and/or the situation, and poorly managed developmental tasks, passages, and crises similar to his or her own. Noting these similarities among clients' problems increases affiliation feelings and increases clients' motivation to help each other (Powdermaker & Frank, 1953).

Many clients must be taught to locate and use sources of self-help on topics such as parenting, sexual adjustment, requesting and negotiating for desired intimacy, assertiveness, conflict management, cooperative decision making, and cooperative career planning. Usually special sessions are scheduled between regular counseling sessions to meet the needs of particular couples. However, other couples in the group are usually admitted on their request. These special sessions are usually devoted to clients sharing their new learnings from their self-help readings, discussing what they can and cannot accept, deciding which to implement first, and deciding what they must learn before they will be able to apply their new learnings. Role playing is often used to help clients develop the self-confidence and the interpersonal skills required to implement their desired new behaviors.

When husband and wife are treated together, each learns to empathize, communicate, and share more spontaneously with the other. Each feels safer with the other. Each learns to enlist the partner's help in recognizing developing conflict, in resolving it, in discussing what each expects from the other, in negotiating their different expectations, in giving and accepting love, in enjoying intimacy, and in sharing their dreams. Furthermore, they learn to do these things in the presence of other couples who can detect when they get caught up in their unproductive games, are able to give them frank, considerate feedback, and can even pressure them to implement new, more productive, behaviors. Within such a group they also discover others with problems similar to their own who have at least begun to function better than they have, and therefore can serve as models. With the help of their counselor and fellow clients, they discover that they do not have to be victims—that they can help each other take charge and manage their lives. They also can learn the difference between a support group and a rescue service, and how to develop and profit from good support groups. As clients learn to present themselves as they genuinely are, they usually discover that their real selves are better accepted by their fellow clients than the façades they previously presented to others. Learning to be more genuine usually enables them to request, accept, and enjoy greater intimacy with their spouses.

FAMILY COUNSELING

Though we counsel families in various settings and use a variety of approaches (Horne & Ohlsen, 1982), the best example of application of the techniques endorsed in this book focuses upon teaching the parents in couples groups to become increasingly self-actualized mature adults. Within the type of group counseling described in the previous section, we help couples develop, with their children's assistance, an emotional climate within their family that facilitates their children's and their own social, emotional, moral, career, and intellectual development. For example, parents learn to teach their children to:

- Recognize developmental tasks and learn the behaviors required to cope with each
- Discover and use their unique abilities, aptitudes, interests, and values
- Accept increasing responsibility for themselves
- Participate in defining and maintaining guidelines for daily living
- Give and accept love—including developing, enjoying, and maintaining satisfying personal relationships
- Increase their encouraging behaviors and decrease their discouraging ones
- Recognize early signs of conflict and learn to cope with it
- Recognize when decisions need to be made, make them, and implement them

Thus, parents learn to become patient, considerate, loving teachers as well as good marriage partners.

When the primary treatment is to be group counseling for the parents who seek family counseling, the entire family for each couple is scheduled for an intake interview. First the counselor talks to the entire family, enlisting every member's help in determining what each believes the family's problems are and what new behaviors each must learn to function better as a healthy family unit. Then the parents are seen individually to help parents to individually define precise behavioral goals for each child and the other parent. The children are seen together, with each being given the option for an individual session, to discuss what is bothering them, to define personal goals, and to enlist their assistance in helping themselves improve the quality of their family life. Finally, the entire family is seen again as a unit to share what each thinks they have learned, discuss individual goals and enlist others' assistance in implementing new behaviors, assess each one's commitment to learn new behaviors and reinforce others' efforts to learn, and determine whether the family will contract for counseling.

Rarely are both husband and wife equally committed to counseling. Sometimes a child, especially during adolescence, is reluctant to discuss his pain openly, to define behavioral goals, to make the commitment to learn new behaviors, and to reinforce the parents' success in implementing new behaviors. When such reluctance is discovered, an additional intake interview is scheduled.

First, such a child needs to explore what he feels is safe to discuss, what risks are involved in cooperating, and what he will gain by cooperating fully. No matter who the reluctant one is, the child must be helped by the counselor to discuss the natural consequences of refusing to participate or of participating only half-heartedly, and developing the courage to be an enthusiastic participant. Even when he concludes that he genuinely wants to help improve the quality of his family life, he may require special assistance in learning to participate effectively. When the reluctant one is a parent, the couple may be admitted to the couple's group on some specified probation status. When the reluctant one is a child, he may be treated in individual counseling, or more extra family sessions may be scheduled to increase the odds for good results for the family.

During the course of couples counseling the counselor schedules family sessions for couples as needed. On such occasions, the counselor schedules a special family session for the hour just before the couple's regular session. For these sessions the counselor follows essentially an Adlerian model (Dreikurs, 1972). Prior to the family session, parents are requested to prepare their children for the session by asking each to identify family problems with which they would like assistance and to suggest what new behaviors should be learned by whom to improve family life. Moreover, sometime during the first session, the counselor usually describes the family council and explains how this particular family may be able to use it. Unless someone in the family strongly objects, this session is observed by the other couples in the parents' group. Following the family session, the other couples encourage the family members to discuss what they learned from the session, give each member considerate feedback, and help each decide what new behavior he or she requires to succeed. Finally, the observers help the family decide how they can tell when they require another family session in order to help the parents function as leaders in implementing these new behaviors. Whether family members recognize the need for it or not, the counselor should teach them and their observers to reinforce desired new behaviors (to use encouraging behaviors for this purpose rather than discouraging ones such as criticism, ignoring, or withholding love) and to celebrate their successes.

In our ever-changing mobile culture, many parents no longer have the support system provided by extended family and long-term friendships, and they do not know how to develop quickly such a support system. Increasingly couples are recognizing that parenting requires more caring, maturity, commitment, time, knowledge, patience, and skills than they possess. Consequently, they are turning to the type of couples groups described here for counseling. They recognize that they need more than an adult education course in parent education.

When working with families, it is important to understand what the problems are that are being addressed by the family, an area covered by the intake interview. If parenting issues seem to be the primary focus, attention is directed toward identifying whether the problem is one of excesses (temper tantrums) or deficits (not completing chores) and how the behavior is maintained within the family system.

A program designed specifically to help families with child management problems is *Troubled Families: A Treatment Program* by Fleischman, Horne, and Arthur (1983). *Troubled Families* describes the steps necessary for a counselor to help families change the dysfunctional interactions that have been going on within the family structure. The steps include:

- *Setting Up for Success.* During the setting-up phase of treatment, counselors teach parents effective ways of identifying areas of conflict and ways to prevent the conflict from developing in the first place. Included are (1) ways to structure the environment to prevent problems (for example, providing snacks for children after picking them up from school and before going to the grocery store); (2) establishing agreed-upon routines; (3) learning to give effective and clearly understood commands or instructions ("I want you to take the trash out by 6:00); (4) showing care, respect, and love; (5) improving spousal relationships; (6) coordinating parental roles; and (7) providing for parent growth and good feelings.
- *Self-Control.* Parents who lack effective self-control are unrealistic if they expect their children to have a skill the parents themselves do not have. Self-control skills are taught to both parents and children.
- *Discipline.* Specific noncorporal disciplinary methods are taught to parents. These include (1) withholding attention; (2) Grandma's law ("you can't have ice cream until you eat the peas"); (3) time out; (4) natural and logical consequences; (5) extra work assignments; and (6) removing privileges.
- *Social and Positive Interactions.* It is even more important that parents learn effective positive interaction skills than it is to learn the disciplinary methods. Once parents are able to provide the circumstances described under "Setting Up for Success," use self-control, and provide positive social interactions, most disciplinary problems disappear.
- *Communication Skills.* Effective communication within the family by all members is stressed as a way of managing conflict.
- *Generalization.* Once people are interacting within the home in a manner desired, then the counselor helps the family members, particularly the children, generalize the new behaviors outside the home and to other problem areas.

The treatment program has been demonstrated to be very effective for helping families change, and families are able to demonstrate maintenance of the change. Further, the change has been able to generalize from the home to the school (Sayger, 1986).

One chapter of *Troubled Families* is devoted to describing how to use the treatment program within a group setting. The program has recently been evaluated in a group format and has been found to be effective for helping families change disruptive and dysfunctional behavior patterns; the result is that families have found their family life more enjoyable and pleasant (Reid, 1988).

In treating families in which the primary focus is on marital conflict rather than child management problems, a much greater emphasis is placed on helping couples understand that all marital behavior is interdependent, as described by these three elements (Jolliff & Horne, 1986):

1. *Mutuality.* Behavior is a two-way process. Both spouses behave in ways that are reinforcing as well as punishing.
2. *Reciprocity.* Within couples' relationships, rewarding and punishing behaviors are exchanged at approximately equal rates.
3. *Circularity.* A person is likely to receive from the spouse the same behavior that is given: pleasantness leads to pleasant interactions; nastiness leads to nastiness.

Counseling couples involves helping each partner understand his or her responsibility for change and helping each to accept responsibility for taking the first step to change his or her personal behavior; one can never begin by attempting to change the other. The counselor must use the group format to teach members how to focus attention on how they want to be for themselves, not how they want to change the other. Richard Stuart (1980) has identified five relationship change principles that represent the foundation of helping couples change:

1. Personal responsibility. Both partners must assume responsibility for change.
2. Change first. Each partner must agree to be the first to make change rather than wait on the spouse.
3. Act "as if." Each partner must act "as if" the other spouse will also change.
4. Change in small steps.
5. Change behaviors first. Affective, feeling changes will follow.

Marriage counseling in groups follows the model presented throughout this text and includes presenting a rationale for what is done, explains steps to be taken and the importance of what is being done, models the behavior for couples, has couples rehearse the new behavior, and provides homework for practice. These steps are most efficiently done within a group setting, but even more important, group resources provide for more effective learning of the skills. Additionally, group members are highly effective at identifying when one spouse or couple is not making effective change, and they can be more confronting in an acceptable way than the counselor can in many cases.

SUMMARY

The increasing life span, improved quality of life for the aging, increasing percentage of middle-aged adults in society, occupational specialization, and changing sex roles, are some of the more-important psychosocial issues facing adulthood in the 1980s. Adults face new challenges in development. For example, the quality of one's career, in terms of status, identity, and meaning will change as society increases in average age. Relationships between human beings in the pursuit to find intimacy and love, promises to pose new issues and concerns centering around the change in sex roles, as well as have subsequent impact on the family. As women expand their roles outside of the family, men will have more time to involve themselves in forming mentoring and fathering relationships (Levinson, 1978). The transitions in lifestyle development influenced by the psychosocial changes in our culture and society, make the process of individuation an important part of adult development. Integration of polarities such as young/old, male/female, and attachment/separation, according to Levinson et al. (1978), is essential to our cultural, social, and personal evolution.

Helping individuals find solutions to specific problems they face in adapting to life transitions, helping individuals develop the necessary skills and abilities to integrate polarities, and helping individuals cope with major life change, are major challenges and responsibilities confronting mental-health professionals in the 1980s. This chapter served as an introduction and brief overview to what may be a new frontier for the counselor.

REFERENCES

Brammer, L., & Abrego, P. (1981). Intervention strategies for coping with transitions. *The Counseling Psychologist, 9* (2), 19–36.

Budman, S. H.; Michael, J.; & Wisneski, M. J. (1980). Short-term group psychotherapy: An adult developmental model. *International Journal of Group Therapy, 30,* 63–76.

Dreikurs, R. (1972). *The challenge of child rearing.* New York: Hawthorne.

Drum, D. J., & Knott, E. J. (1977). *Structured groups for facilitating development: Acquiring life skills, resolving life themes, and making life transitions.* New York: Human Sciences Press.

Erikson, E. H. (1963). *Childhood and society.* New York: W.W. Norton.

Fleischman, M.; Horne, M.; & Arthur, J. (1983). *Troubled families.* Champaign, IL: Research Press.

Hobson, B. (1981). Response to the papers by Schlossberg, Brammer, and Abrego. *Counseling Psychologist, 9,* 36–39.

Horne, A., & Ohlsen, M. M. (1982). *Family counseling and therapy.* Itasca, IL: Peacock.

Jolliff, D., & Horne, H. (1986). Social learning family therapy. *Individual Psychology, 42,* 567–582.

Jung, C. G.; VonFranz, M. L.; Henderson, J. L.; Jacobi, J.; & Jaffe, A. (1968). *Man and his symbols.* New York: Dell.

Levinson, D. J.; Darrow, C. N.; Klein, E. B.; Levinson, M. H.; & McKee, B. (1978). *The seasons of a man's life.* New York: Alfred Knopf.

Lowenthal, M. F. (1975). Psychological variations across the adult life course: Frontiers for research and policy. *Gerontologist, 15,* 6–12.

Lowenthal, M. F., & Chiriboga, D. (1975). Response to stress. In M. F. Lowenthal; M. Thurnher; & D. Chiriboga, *Four stages of life: A comparative study of men and women facing transitions.* San Francisco: Jossey Bass.

Neugarten, L. (1979). Time, age and the life cycle. *The American Journal of Psychiatry, 136,* 887–894.

Ohlsen, M. M. (1979). *Marriage counseling in groups.* Champaign, IL: Research Press.

Powdermaker, F. B., & Frank, J. D. (1953). *Group psychotherapy.* Cambridge: Harvard University Press.

Reid, A. (1988) Social learning therapy for families with aggressive boys: Individual versus parent-group treatment. Unpublished doctoral dissertation, Indiana State University, Terre Haute.

Sayger, T. (1986). The maintenance of treatment effects for families of aggressive boys participating in social learning family therapy. Unpublished doctoral dissertation, Indiana State University, Terre Haute.

Schlossberg, N. K. (1981). A model for analyzing human adaptation to transition. *Counseling Psychologist, 9,* 2–18.

Vaillant, G. E. (1977). *Adaptation to life.* Boston: Little, Brown.

Wortley, D. B., & Ametea, E. S. (1982). Mapping adult life changes: A conceptual framework for organizing adult developmental theory. *Personnel and Guidance Journal, 60,* 476–482.

Yalom, I. D. (1985). *The theory and practice of group psychology.* New York: Basic Books.

15

WORKING WITH STRUCTURED GROUPS

A particular model of group counseling has been presented in this book. The model may be seen as quite structured compared to some group procedures. Compared to T-groups or sensitivity training, the model presented here would be seen as providing considerable structure in terms of descriptions of the group to potential members, intake, procedures for conducting the group, and termination guidelines. Leaderless groups would similarly be considered much less structured than the model we have presented. On the other hand, many groups offered in our schools, colleges, community counseling centers, and employment sites often provide much more structure than the model presented here.

THE NATURE OF STRUCTURED GROUPS

Structured groups have been developed to meet specific needs of clients. In college or university settings, for example, the needs of students are many and one way of serving students is to provide a group model that will focus on specific topics for several students at once. Structured groups are developed to meet specific needs of participants by helping them develop specific skills, address certain life transitions, or address specific issues or themes relevant to the lives of those who join the group. The specific topic of the group varies, but there is a focus on providing participating members with new skills, or with helping members address a specific topic relevant to their lives.

Gazda (1984) has identified the structured group as an important element in group work. In his *Group Counseling: A Developmental Approach*, Gazda distinguished between the interview counseling group and the more structured, developmental life-skills training group. He noted that structured groups were a variation on traditional group guidance with influence from the behavioral counseling and the skills-training movement.   He grouped them in a prevent-ative growth-engendering remedial category along with group counseling, T-groups, organizational development groups, and encounter groups. Gazda de-voted a chapter to presenting a rationale and a system for developmental life-skills training.

The Elements of Structuring Groups

There are a number of elements of structured groups which overlap with other group models, but which are always found in structured groups. These include components related to effective learning.

Defining the Problem.   The structured group leader defines the problem or theme to be addressed by the group. During the intake interview or group presentation the leader carefully spells out the purpose of the group, the specific skill to be learned, and the importance of that skill to the lives of persons interested in changing.

Assessing Current Level.   The counselor is interested in how well the client may be functioning before beginning the program. For marital enrichment, for example, the counselor may assess marital satisfaction. For assertiveness training, the counselor is likely to assess skills both on paper-and-pencil invento-ries and on practice sessions. For weight-management programs, the counselor will probably request members to track their weight from the very beginning of the group.

Explaining the Importance of the Learning.   While some group approaches do not explain why what they do is important, a structured-group leader is going to provide a rationale for learning that takes place in the group.

Teaching.   Teaching may take a variety of styles and approaches, but the expectation in structured groups is that people can learn new skills through being taught how to do what they need to do more effectively. Teaching often takes on the following characteristics:

- *Direct instruction.*
- *Modeling.* In this the leader or a group member models the skill to be learned in an effective manner to show how the skill should look or feel to participants. Frequently one can expect to see an exaggeration of a poorly performed skill, followed by a demonstration of the skill performed effec-tively.
- *Role playing.* Participants have an opportunity to practice what they have seen modeled.
- *Feedback.* Members provide feedback, and frequently the counselor ar-ranges for audio or video feedback of how well the member has been able

to learn the skill and provides for additional practice, revising areas that need improvement.

- *Transfer of training.* Since the goal of structured-group learning experiences is to learn to live more effectively out of the group, the counselor provides the opportunity to generalize skills outside the group.
- *Evaluation of change.* The structured-group counselor is very likely to provide some form of assessment of how much change has occurred during the group learning experience.

Structure and Structuring

Day and Sparacio (1980) defined structure and structuring as follows:

> *Structure* in counseling is defined as a joint understanding between the counselor and client regarding the characteristics, conditions, procedures, and parameters of counseling. *Structuring* refers to the interactional process by which *structure* is reached. *Structuring* is the means by which the counselor and client together define the guidelines that govern the counseling process, possibly involving such activities as informing, proposing, suggesting, recommending, negotiating, stipulating, contracting, and compromising. (p. 246).

These authors perceptively pointed out that even when neglected by the counselor, structure is present in all counseling situations. Rather than letting structure evolve in a haphazard manner, the counselor should develop it. This development should be explicit so that the counselor and the client have similar perceptions of the structure. Structure should be a means to achieving counseling goals rather than an impediment. That is, structure must be flexible. They explained that when structure is developed by the counselor, it serves facilitative, therapeutic, and protective functions. It is important to note that these authors included limits and guidelines for structure and structuring. Among the limits and guidelines Day and Sparacio (1980, pp. 248–249) established are:

1. Structure should be negotiated or requested, not coerced. Clients should be given the opportunity to respond and react to structure as well as to be able to modify it.
2. Structure, particularly restrictions and limitations, should not be applied for punitive reasons or in a punitive manner.
3. The counselor should be aware of his or her rationale for structuring and should explain the reasons at the time of structuring or be prepared to provide rationale in response to the client's request for explanation.
4. The counselor should be guided by the client's readiness for structure and by the context of the relationship and process.
5. Too much or a too-rigid structure can be constraining for both the client and the counselor.
6. Ill-timed, lengthy, or insensitive structuring can result in client frustration or resistance, and can interrupt the continuity of the therapeutic process.

7. Unnecessary and purposeless recitation of rules and guidelines can imply that the counselor is more concerned with procedure than with helpfulness. In fact, a compulsive approach to structuring can be indicative of low levels of counselor self-assurance.
8. The counselor must relate structure to the client's emotional, cognitive, and behavioral predisposition.
9. Structuring can "imply that the relationship will continue with this particular client. It may turn out that the counselor will decide not to work with this client, or that the client may not be suitable for this counselor.
10. Structure cannot replace or substitute for therapeutic competence. Structure is not a panacea. It is not the total solution to building a productive therapeutic relationship. Structure is complementary and supplementary to human relations, communications, diagnostic, and intervention skills.

The structured group, then, can be very useful for clients and can be an effective medium for conducting group work for the counselor. The limitations cited, though, must be observed in order to provide the most effective learning experience for all concerned. Several additional issues need to be addressed by the structured-group counselor.

Member Selection.   As with the group model we have described, an intake interview is recommended for counselors using a structured-group approach. It is important that the counselor be able to identify why people are interested in being in a group and whether the particular model being offered will meet the needs of the client. While the counselor will be unable to screen all persons who do not belong in a particular type of group, she will have a much more effective group as a result of identifying those most likely to benefit. The individual interview is particularly important for helping the counselor understand what appeals to the client about the particular group, and the counselor may be able to discern from this information that another therapeutic experience might be more helpful than what is being offered. A student, for example, who wants to be in a career exploration group in order to gather data to convince her father that she should be allowed to withdraw from school would probably benefit from a group with a different emphasis, or from individual counseling. Similarly, a couple who want to participate in a marital-enrichment group in order to stop their constant arguing is not likely to experience success: a couples group would be more appropriate. And a person who signs up for a weight-management group in order to get a spouse to quit criticizing will need to be in an alternative experience.

Confidentiality.   Generally, confidentiality is not as important an issue with a structured group because all people are coming to attend to a specific issue, learn a specific skill, or participate in some similar, structured learning experience. For that reason, some structured-group leaders do not discuss confidentiality or address it as an issue. The counselor still needs to be aware that participation in a group, regardless of the structure, is a very important undertaking and one that is not to be taken lightly. Therefore, the confidentiality issue should be addressed during intake and during the initial meeting with the group. At that point, bounds should be established for what information is to be shared with the group and what information group members may share outside of the group.

Leader Observations.   As with all group work one of the functions of the group leader is to observe the process as well as the individual issues being discussed. Co-leaders are very helpful for this purpose, allowing one of the leaders to attend primarily to the individual presenting, while the co-leader can observe group processes and identify issues that develop. With either a single leader or with co-leaders, it is important to be aware of the pacing of the group to see what impact the group topic may be having on participants.

Pacing.   Leader observations are very important to make certain the pacing of the group is appropriate. Sometimes, because of the nature of the group or the make-up of the participants, modifications in the group may be necessary. The counselor can pace the group work to the slowest members at times, as in relaxation training. When teaching group members relaxation training, the slowest member of the group generally determines the pacing; and, faster members seldom are disturbed by the situation because the relaxation feels good, and the extended opportunity to practice is acceptable to them. On the other hand, for some other activities, if some members lag considerably behind other participants, then the counselor should consider either breaking the group into two smaller groups or providing additional "booster" sessions for those having more difficulty. This has been necessary, for example, with some participants in a cognitively oriented, assertiveness training group where a few members had considerably more difficulty grasping the concepts presented until several reme-dial sessions were held.

Ethical Issues.   There are some special ethical issues related to structured groups. Counselors often identify whether persons interested in the group lack the skills that will be taught in the group, which is an important activity for the counselor. There is also, though, a need to try and understand what has perpetuated the absence of the skill or the failure to resolve a theme in the client's life prior to this point. It is necessary to know why the client has elected to seek change at this time, regardless of how structured the group might be.

An example of the importance of this issue may be found in assertiveness training groups. If people have been nonassertive for a number of years, something has maintained that behavior. What has changed now that will provide support for the change? If there is no support for the change within the living system of the person, there is little likelihood that the change will be sustained unless the counselor works with the client to develop a specific, change maintenance program. This has been found to be an issue, for example, with women who enter assertiveness training groups because they are interested in changing their life circumstances, but may have spouses or employers (perhaps other family members, even friends) who do not support the assertive behavior and, in fact, work to undermine the changes brought about by the group.

Ethically, the counselor needs to review with potential members what the positive outcomes may be as a result of participating in a structured group; but, also, there should be a review of possible harmful effects to the person. This may include pressure or even outright anger from others who do not value the changes. Since structured groups have a common theme and orientation, many counselors have overlooked this important topic.

Individual Issues. In the counseling model presented in this book, it is expected that group members will each have their individual issues that are developed during the intake interview and that are discussed with the entire group. With structured groups, though, there is a common theme or common skill to be attended to by all members of the group. Once the group has begun, however, counselors often find that while there may be a common need to learn skills, the precipitating factors may vary considerably and may strongly influence the degree to which people learn the skills being presented.

In a parenting group, for example, it may become apparent that some members are present because they need to brush up on skills such as communication and effective discipline. Others may have never known the skills and may be quite skill deficient in many areas of parenting. Then others may be there because a spouse insisted that they come to learn to handle the child better, even though their child problems may be related more to marital issues than to inadequate knowledge of parenting. Still others may be in the group because of a self-concept issue in which they feel so inadequate in so many areas of their lives that they are unable to be effective at anything, including parenting.

In a group such as this, the counselor may have a common theme, but there is great variation in group members' expectations, openness to change, and resources for effecting the change. In this situation the counselor must be open to understanding the individual issues that each member brings to the group and be aware that the success of the group will be determined by how effectively she can handle the specific expectations and needs of its members.

Structured Experiences

One approach to structured groups has been developed by University Associates and represents a way of approaching specific tasks to be accomplished in an organized and structured manner. According to J. William Pfeiffer (1983), structured experiences are designed for experience-based learning. For Pfeiffer, structured-group experiences offer "fresh ways to help us focus awareness and enhance our understanding of the world in which we live" (p. iii). Dr. Pfeiffer and his colleagues at University Associates have been publishing collections of structured experiences for human relations training since 1969, when Volume I appeared. Each volume contains 24 structured experiences. The following titles of structured experiences demonstrate the range from the simple and less affectively involved:

Synonyms: Sharing Perceptions between Groups
News Bulletin: Focusing the Group
Bricks: Creative Problem Solving
All Iowans Are Naive: Breaking Cultural Stereotypes

to the more complex with increased affective generation:

Matrix: Balancing Personal Needs
Values and Decisions: Checking for Congruence
The Promotion: Value Clarification
Training Philosophies: A Personal Assessment

In Volume IX, Pfeiffer (1983) noted: "Based on an experiential model, structured experiences are inductive rather than deductive, providing *direct* rather than vicarious learnings. Thus, participants *discover* meaning for themselves and *validate* their own experience" (p. 1). Pfeiffer's experiential learning model consists of five steps that occur in a cycle: experiencing (the "activity" phase); publishing (sharing reactions and observations); processing (discussing patterns and dynamics); generalizing (developing principles); and applying (planning how to use the learning). *The Structured Experience Kit* contains structured experiences from all volumes of the *Handbook* and all volumes of the *Annual.* Each experience in the kit has been rated according to: how much affect is likely to be generated; how structurely complex the design is; and how difficult the activity is to process.

Although Pfeiffer's work has been of greatest interest to the industrial/organizational area, structured experiences are used in a wide variety of settings (Cerio, 1979; Drum & Knott, 1977).

Structure is present in all counseling situations. What differs is the amount of control exercised by the counselor or facilitator, and the congruence of expectations between the counselor and the client. Pfeiffer's structured experiences are actually quite open-ended with a process emphasis. Structure for Pfeiffer is a technique designed to stimulate process, as explained by his experiential learning model. In this sense, the groups utilizing these structured-group experiences are much less structured than structured groups. The goals of such groups are much more broadly defined (for example, increased awareness) than the precise goals of structured groups (for example, increased parenting skills). While the object of interest in groups utilizing structured experiences is group process, in structured groups it is the development of personal awareness and skills.

EIGHT SPECIFIC TYPES OF STRUCTURED GROUPS

A Structured Group on Structured Groups

Russell and Easton (1979) described a class that used a structured model to teach the design, leadership, and evaluation of structured groups. The class was designed to be a model structured-group experience for a counselor-education curriculum, and was limited to ten members with a duration of 16 two-and-a-half hour sessions.

Session I (Group Rapport and Course Goals) was devoted to helping students focus on their goals for the course and to take responsibility for their learning. A structured exercise was conducted in which the class negotiated specific goals, means to reach those goals, and criteria to assess goal attainment.

Session II (Contrasting Structured and Unstructured Groups) began with a simulation of an encounter group. This was followed by a short lecture in which encounter groups and open-ended methodologies were compared with structured groups. Structured groups were defined and key elements outlined.

In Session III (How to Design a Structured Workshop) the leader (professor) outlined a sequence for designing a group workshop and demonstrated the sequence by evolving a rough design of a workshop on the board by using a topic suggested by the class. Some of the proposed exercises were conducted.

Session IV (Design of the Practice Workshop) consisted of an extended exercise in which class members conducted a needs assessment, proposed a specific topic, and arrived at general goals for their own practice workshop.

Session V (Design Refinement and Leadership Lecture) was a continuation of work by the group on the practice workshop. Each member chose one workshop segment to refine, supply materials for, and lead. Didactic instruction was given with regard to the structured leadership role.

Session IV (Refinement of Design) addressed any continuity and design problems of the practice workshop. The class then conducted the practice workshop during nonclass hours. It was videotaped and then viewed during Session VII.

Session VII (Video Playback of Leadership) provided fertile ground for discussion:

> The discussion included facilitating and distracting nonverbal postures, defensive or self-conscious leader behaviors, comfort with silence, handling latecomers, coffee and restroom breaks, when to interrupt and stop a task, appropriate processing styles, frustration of the leader's membership needs, inserting hidden agendas, monitoring of energy and fatigue levels, the effect of leader's voice quality, and the amount and function of humor (Russell & Easton, 1979, p. 428).

Sessions VIII through XVI (Students' Individual Workshop Presentations) were devoted to the presentation of workshops designed by individual students. Each student prepared a leader outline, a set of leader instructions, and worksheets for the members. The workshop was then carried out in the class.

In commenting on their practical skill-building approach to group leadership training, these authors noted, "The class shared the advantages of the structured model, which include a high degree of acceptance by the members, the lack of feeling of personal intrusion, and consensus that the course as advertised and conducted met the goals of the students" (p. 428). Their idea of instructing the course using the model or format being taught was clever and theoretically consistent with the structured-group model.

Depression Management Training (DMT)

Lerman and Baron (1981) proposed a structured group on depression management in order "to present an intensive, interactive experience to participants who have or anticipate having problems in handling recurrent, episodic depression" (p. 86). The choice of structured-group methodology was further explained as follows:

> Structured group design is a hybrid of formal didactic presentation along with individual and small group experiential learning processes. While sharing of experiences or personal situations is often encouraged, structured groups differ from therapy or encounter groups in that specific problem resolution is not the primary goal. In the case of DMT, the intent is increased awareness and knowledge of the nature of depression as well as the acquisition of skills in more effective coping with or, preferably, prevention of dysfunctional depressive experiences (p. 87).

Five assumptions underlie DMT. The first, that depression is multifactorial in etiology, draws upon the work of Richard Lazarus (1983) on stress. DMT was designed to pinpoint these sources. The second addresses the idiosyncratic nature of depression. DMT helps identify individual vulnerabilities and response styles to depression. The third involves the widespread potential for depression across many aspects of daily living. DMT is proactive and encourages an "active mastery" philosophy. Fourth, these authors hold that the most effective intervention is the multimodal or broad-spectrum approach of Arnold Lazarus (1981). Concomitantly, DMT includes a wide variety of cognitive, affective, behavioral, and interpersonal learning components. Finally, because it is aimed at helping people with recurrent depression, DMT provides conceptual and behavioral skills for a lifelong learning process. The goal of DMT is the reduction, not the elimination, of depression in the individual's life situation.

The Effectiveness of DMT

The DMT structured-group experience consists of six two-hour weekly sessions with groups of 10 to 12 participants. Lerman and Baron (1981) recommended that the group be led by two professionals who have experience with depressed individuals. They provided detailed guidelines for the selection of leaders and participants for DMT. They outlined each of the six sessions with regard to the didactic portion, group exercises, individualizing the interventions, and homework.

To these authors' credit, they offered data with regard to the evaluation of DMT. Participants have overwhelmingly judged DMT to be successful in helping them meet personal goals. The great majority also found the activities and materials useful. Pre- and post-measures on a test of depression level yielded tenuous results on the slightly positive side. Overall, the authors reported that preliminary data suggest increases "in awareness of (a) sources of depression, (b) coping techniques, and (c) the facilitative effects of group support on the management of depression" (p. 88). Lerman and Baron believe that this program provides the participant "with new awarenesses and skills to cope more effectively with the depression inherent in their daily living" (p. 88).

Skill-Streaming the Adolescent

Goldstein, Sprafkin, Gershaw, and Klein (1982) offered a group skill-training approach, called structured learning, in order to teach adolescents social skills, planning skills, skills for dealing with feelings, skill alternatives to aggression, and skills for responding effectively with stress. Goldstein and his colleagues argued that the three largest categories of behavior disorders (aggression, withdrawal, and immaturity) represent adolescents with skill deficiencies. They claim:

> Each type may be described in terms of both the presence of a repertoire of dysfunctional and often antisocial behavior and of the absence of a repertoire of prosocial or developmentally appropriate behaviors. It is our belief that a training program oriented toward the explicit teaching of prosocial skills can remediate many of these skill deficits" (1980, p. 5).

The authors also noted that any adolescent experiencing the need for assistance over a developmental hurdle is appropriate for this kind of structured group.

Structured Learning

Structured learning grew out of the psychoeducational training movement of which the broad goal is skill competence—which, in turn, leads to effective and satisfying daily living. The four components of structured learning are modeling, role playing, performance feedback, and transfer of training. In this case, structured learning is being applied to adolescents with behavior disorders. Goldstein and his colleagues provided detailed discussion with regard to matters of organization and trainer preparation. Perhaps most importantly, they offered a step-by-step procedural accounting of the modeling, role play, performance feedback, and transfer training sequence. They noted that the optimally sized group for the structured-learning group consists of five to eight adolescents (trainees) plus two trainers; however, the authors provided instructions for how to carry out the approach in larger groups.

Detailed outlines of the group sessions were provided including the behavioral steps for 50 structured-learning skills, falling into six content areas. A 50-item, structured-learning skill checklist was included in these authors' book. This checklist can be used a number of ways: as a pre- and post-test, as a self-rating technique and as a diagnostic tool for the trainer, among others. An initial session transcript was also included as a learning aid for those interested in this approach. The book is replete with concrete examples of how to carry out this approach. For example, a chapter was devoted to vignettes that describe how to identify problem behaviors and how to manage them within a structured-learning group.

A Structured Group Dealing with Test Anxiety

Cognitive/relaxation therapy and study-skills training are found to be effective in reducing self-reported anxiety and improving the academic performance of test-anxious students. In a study by Kenneth M. Dendato and Don Diener (1986) forty-five test-anxious students were randomly assigned to one of four treatment conditions: (1) relaxation/cognitive therapy; (2) study-skills training; (3) a combination of relaxation/cognitive therapy and study-skills training; or (4) no treatment. Data were collected pre- and post-treatment on self-reported state anxiety and classroom examination performance. The combination treatment groups demonstrated both reduced anxiety and improved performance relative to the other groups.

Basing the structured group on the premise that poor academic performance is a function of both anxiety *and* poor study habits, they offered a treatment approach combining study-skills training, relaxation training, and cognitive therapy. The relaxation/cognitive aspects were designed to deal with both the affective and worry components of test anxiety; and the study-skills training dealt with teaching efficient study habits and test-taking strategies.

Group members were assigned to receive six one-hour sessions of treatment scheduled once weekly. During each of the first four sessions, the group focused on relaxation/cognitive therapy. Thirty minutes of deep muscle relaxation that involved having subjects tense and relax various muscle groups while observing state differences (Morris, 1980) were followed by rational-emotive (RET) psychotherapy (Ellis, 1973) in which irrational thoughts and beliefs relative to examinations were identified and challenged. Group pressure was used to examine and challenge irrational beliefs and replace them with rational thinking. Groups examined how irrational beliefs could lead to dysfunctional feelings such as worthlessness and anxiety, and to maladaptive action such as dropping out of school. The substitution of rational thoughts, such as accepting the need to spend more time studying, was practiced both in group and in homework situations.

Additionally, stress-reduction relaxation techniques were practiced outside the group and, by the fourth session, abbreviated to deep breathing coupled with the cognitive cue, "I am calm." Subjects were encouraged to practice during all anxiety-provoking situations. The final two sessions focused on study skills modeled after procedures developed by Talley and Henning (1981) and Langan (1978). Lecture and group discussion concerning goal setting, time management, and note-taking strategies were augmented by homework assignments designed to facilitate practice.

It has been suggested by Dendato and Diener that as a result of following this course of group treatment, test-anxious students can improve academic performance. Effective test-taking skills enhance the reduction of worry and anxiety.

Parent Training Groups

The Adlerian Models

Parent training groups have been important for generations. One of the major contributions that Alfred Adler made was to the development of child guidance centers and to parent education as an important component of social living. A number of helpful structured programs have developed from his early leadership, including the book by his students and collaborators, R. Dreikurs and V. Soltz, *Children: The Challenge* (1964). The book was used for many years as a text for parenting groups. More recently, still within the Adlerian orientation, Dinkmeyer and McKay (1976) have developed *Systematic Training in Effective Parenting: STEP* which is a structured program for parent education classes. The classes have a lay orientation in that they have been developed from the beginning with the idea that leaders will be other parents or interested persons who have developed skills that can be shared with other parents. The STEP program provides considerable support for parenting groups, including a detailed leader's manual, a workbook for participants, audio tapes to provide group examples and lessons, and charts that depict points being made by the leader and the audio tapes. More recently, other programs have been developed that incorporate videotapes to provide a visual stimulus to the work.

The Behavioral Models

Some parenting problems require a more intensive intervention than is provided from lay-led groups. In the 1960s and 1970s, behavior modification became the treatment of choice for a number of childhood disorders. Generally, the treatment scenario included a professional helper and the problematic child. Emphasis was placed on the use of operant conditioning principles to effect positive behavioral change. While beneficial effects were often noted, generalization and long-term changes did not materialize consistently.

To ameliorate this situation, clinicians then included not only the identified children in their training but also the parents of these children. Therefore, instead of focusing primarily on the children having the behavioral difficulties, clinicians turned their attention to the parents. A number of parent training programs then began to appear, some of which demonstrated significant therapeutic gains for the involved families. Patterson and his associates (Patterson, 1969; Patterson, Cobb, & Ray, 1973; Patterson, Ray, & Shaw, 1969) using a social-learning orientation, have been extremely successful in effecting positive behavioral change in families through the training of parents as social change agents.

Structured-Group Programs

At this point in time, clinicians have taken yet one more step forward by focusing on the training of parents in structured groups. Behrens (1970) demonstrated that parents trained in groups are just as effective in effecting positive behavioral changes in their children as parents trained separately. He concluded that both training programs were equally successful in terms of gain scores, but the amount of time saved by the group method was extremely significant. Other benefits of group parent training over individual parent training may be reduced cost and greater social support.

Systematic Parent Training   One such parent training model often utilized with groups is systematic parent training (S.P.T.) (Miller, 1975). From an educational approach, S.P.T. attempts to train parents in effective parenting skills. Miller asserts that it is essential, at first, to have the parents provide baseline measures of the targeted behaviors. Such data is considered essential so that treatment effects can be validly assessed.

Next, intervention techniques are taught to the parents that can then be utilized in the home environment. With each training session, the parents learn more about ways of increasing desirable behaviors and decreasing undesirable behaviors. Emphasis is on accurate data collection throughout the duration of the training sessions so that the parents will have unbiased records of the success of their interventions.

Miller encourages rigorous post-treatment follow-up to investigate generalization and maintenance of results. At a minimum, he feels that a six-month follow-up is essential with further follow-up encouraged. He notes that, unfortunately, with few exceptions, studies to date have failed to realize maintenance of positive treatment effects.

Programs for Parents of Disruptive Children

Parent training in groups is appropriate for a majority of parents who experience child-rearing difficulties. However, it is not a substitute for child, marital, or family therapy. With more serious individual or familial disturbances, group parent training should not be the treatment of choice.

A program that has been established for helping families with disruptive children has been described by Fleischman, Horne, and Arthur (1983) in their book *Troubled Families*. They provide a chapter that explains how to use their model with parents in a group setting. Topics covered in the model include:

1. *Understanding children's behavior*. Why children behave as they do, how behavior is learned and maintained, and how family systems contribute to the stability of the behavior.
2. *Defining desired changes and setting goals for improvement*.
3. *Setting up for success*. In this phase parents are taught how to set themselves up for success instead of failure. Specifics include learning how to give clear commands ("I want you to take out the garbage now."); use good eye contact; and treat the child as they would a neighbor (friendly, not as an enemy). Included in the setting-up stage is helping parents identify ways to strengthen the marital relationship (if there is a two-parent family), and ways to promote parental self-growth.
4. *Learning self-control skills*. It is assumed that parents who lack self-control will not be able to teach their children to have any better control. The self-control model presented is determined by parent abilities. Some parents who seem able to understand the concepts are provided instruction in cognitive self talk and how to improve their skills at producing effective thinking. Other parents are taught a modified reality therapy program ("What is my problem; what am I doing; is it helping me; what can I do differently?"). Then parents are taught brief relaxation and stress-management skills.
5. *Disciplinary skills*. In this next area of attention, most parents already know what not to do. This stage identifies several effective ways of working with children. Particularly emphasized is natural and logical consequences.
6. *Reinforcement skills*. Once parents know how to discipline effectively, attention is directed toward reinforcement skills, particularly emphasizing social skills parents need to be effective with their children.
7. *Communication skills*. These skills are taught to parents to teach them to relate more effectively with their children and learn to avoid many of the behaviors that lead to conflict.
8. *Generalization of skills*. This next topic, generalization, includes how to work effectively as a parent in public settings (stores, restaurants, and so on), and how to impact the behavior of the child's school performance.

One of the positive characteristics of the Fleischman, Horne, and Arthur (1983) program is that treatment and follow-up data have been collected. The data available indicate that the program is effective for helping approximately 75 percent of the families who participate to effect change that lasts a year after treatment (Sayger, 1986).

Marriage Counseling Groups

Gershenfeld (1985) identifies three broad categories of marriage counseling groups: mutual support groups, educational workshops, and marriage-enrichment groups. With a mutual support group, there is no professional leader, no required fee, and the criterion for membership is a basic situation or problem. With educational workshops, also known as microlabs, the group program is designed by a professional leader and the group focus is on a specific educational objective as identified by the leader (e.g., budgeting). There is a fee charged to participants.

Marriage-Enrichment Groups

With marriage-enrichment groups, there may be a professional leader or a facilitator trained in the program method. Such groups are usually church- or community-sponsored and require a nominal fee. The objective of marriage-enrichment programs is not to treat dysfunctional marriages but, rather, to make currently satisfactory marriages even stronger. Hof and Miller (1981) see the aim of marriage enrichment as assisting couples to achieve the following goals: (1) to increase each spouse's self-awareness and the awareness of his or her partner, especially regarding the positive aspects, strengths, and growth potential of the individuals and the marriage; (2) to increase exploration and self-disclosure of the partners' thoughts and feelings; (3) to increase mutual empathy and intimacy; and (4) to develop and encourage the use of skills needed by the partners for effective communication, problem solving, and conflict resolution.

Marriage enrichment can take place in a variety of formal or informal settings. The two most common formats are the intensive weekend program (from two to five days) and the multiweek program. With the weekend program, couples have the advantage of being able to take an intensive look at their relationship away from the usual pressures of life. Hof and Miller note that there is a need for follow-up and support groups to facilitate the couple's reentry into the "real world." The multiweek program offers couples the advantage of spaced learning with its related benefits, but the lack of intensity can reduce the benefits gleaned.

As marriage-enrichment groups are so new, there is not yet much research support documenting their effectiveness. The book *Working with Couples for Marriage Enrichment* by Diana Garland (1978) is an excellent resource for a full description of contemporary marriage enrichment and a discussion of ways to measure program effectiveness.

Stress Inoculation Training

In his clinical guide for stress inoculation training (SIT), a cognitive-behavioral treatment procedure, Donald Meichenbaum (1985) stated that the object of his book was "to provide an integrative framework for a better understanding and critique of current efforts designed to reduce and prevent maladaptive stress reactions" (p. ix). Though the specific training operations depend on the population treated, there are, of course, common elements. "SIT combines elements of didactic teaching, Socratic discussion, cognitive restructuring, problem solving and relaxation training, behavioral and imaginal rehearsal, self-monitoring, self-instruction and self-reinforcement, and efforts at environmental change" (p. 21).

SIT has been widely applied in behavioral medicine and health psychology. It has also been used with a number of high-stress occupational groups such as nurses, other medical staff, police officers, teachers, and athletes. On a more limited basis, it has been offered as an intervention for victims of major stressful life events. SIT has been used for treatment and prevention—with individuals, couples, and groups—and in clinical and nonclinical settings. Meichenbaum noted that SIT is in the early stage of development and invited further systematic evaluation. He carefully outlined the conceptual model underlying SIT and offered clear and concrete guidelines for developing and carrying out stress reduction and prevention programs.

The Three Phases of SIT

Although the length of training varies greatly depending on the target population, it often consists of 12 to 15 sessions, plus booster and follow-up sessions faded over a 6-to-12 month period. The initial one-sixth to one-third of SIT training consists of the conceptualization phase. The objectives of this first phase are to:

1. Establish a collaborative relationship with the client and with significant others where appropriate (e.g., spouse),
2. Discuss the client's stress-related problems and symptoms, focusing on a situational analysis,
3. Collect information in the form of interviews, questionnaires, self-monitoring procedures, imagery-based techniques, and behavioral assessments,
4. Assess the client's expectations with regard to effectiveness of the training program and formulate treatment plans, establishing short, intermediate, and long-term goals,

5. Educate the client about the transactional nature of stress and coping, and consider the role that cognitions and emotions play in engendering and maintaining stress,
6. Offer a conceptual model or reconceptualization of the client's stress reactions,
7. Anticipate and subsume possible client resistance and reasons for treatment nonadherence (Meichenbaum, 1985, p. 27).

Meichenbaum offers specific measures for the trainer to take in order to achieve these objectives. Special attention is paid to number six, the reconceptualization process, which concludes the first phase of SIT. During the reconceptualization process, the trainer helps the individual reconceptualize stress in more benign terms.

The second phase is the skills-acquisition and rehearsal phase. Coping techniques presented include relaxation training, cognitive restructuring, problem-solving training, and the training of coping self statements. Again, Meichenbaum offers specific techniques and accompanying clinical guidelines needed to implement these training procedures.

The third phase is the application and follow-through phase. This is the generalization phase, and Meichenbaum emphasizes that nothing during this phase should be left to chance. Practice is gradually moved from the training sessions to the everyday environment. He explains techniques (and corresponding guidelines) such as imagery and behavioral rehearsal, modeling, role playing, and graduated *in vivo* practice. Booster sessions, follow-up, and follow-through interventions are explained.

Anyone considering developing a structured group in which the SIT model is utilized would be well advised to consult Meichenbaum's (1985) book as well as related research articles. For example, his references include over one hundred citations in which specific problems or populations have been addressed by SIT or SIT techniques.

A Structured Assertiveness-Training Group

A structured assertion group, according to Arthur J. Lange and Patricia Jakubowski (1978), can focus on cognitive restructuring and behavior rehearsal best if the group is limited to seven to ten participants. Using two opposite-sex leaders (trainers) serves to increase modeling of assertive behavior as well as the depth of this modeling. Six to nine two-hour sessions seem to optimally meet the needs of the participants.

The authors note that screening of this group is essential to set up for success. Would-be participants showing signs of apathy, manipulative behavior, resistant dysfunctional behavior, or other psychological dysfunction that might best be dealt with prior to the assertion group could be invited to explore other avenues first. They recommend screening applicants to determine candidates' expectations and need. Above all, "it is important that the prospective group member be seeking the *process* of assertion training as well as the outcomes since other groups and other procedures might be preferred and lead to similar outcomes" (p. 199). Therefore, an adequate overview of the group process should accompany the screening session. Appropriately skilled leaders, with an awareness of psychological dynamics, should undertake the group. Professional supervision is recommended. Each session is exercise-oriented in order to maximize the acquisition of the basic skills of assertiveness.

Session 1. Session 1 is basically a mini-lecture describing each of the six or more sessions: highlighting the nature of exercises, cognitive restructuring, and behavior rehearsal; defining assertive versus aggressive versus nonassertive behavior; and discussing what may reasonably be expected from being in the group. Group confidentiality and notification of planned absences are discussed. Next, positive assertion exercises (such as "yes/no exercise," giving and receiving compliments, and social conversations) precede the homework assignment. The positive experience increases the likelihood of successful experiences later on. Processing effective behaviors seen in the participants develops a supportive atmosphere.

Session 2. Session 2 focuses first on a discussion of homework and incidents that participants feel they handled assertively or not. Next, a discrimination exercise with a discussion of types of assertive responses and an exercise in identifying personal rights are conducted. During this session participants begin to see how their belief systems regarding personal rights directly effect their choice of responses. Cognitive assessment of beliefs and actions is thus begun. Finally, homework is assigned.

Session 3. In Session 3, following the regular discussion of the week's homework and critical situations, the group conducts a "rational-emotive principles" exercise and a "rational self-analysis" exercise. The session culminates in a discussion of cognitive restructuring "where participants discover their negative self-statements, recognize their relationship to their behavior, and make plans to alter them with the help of the trainer's cognitive intervention techniques" (Lange & Jakubowski, 1978, p. 205). Behavior rehearsal is coupled successfully with cognitive restructuring. Homework follows.

Session 4. Session 4 starts out with a discussion of homework and critical situations, moves to a "making and refusing request" exercise and finishes with a "dealing with persistent persons" exercise. Homework follows.

Session 5. In Session 5, besides processing the past week's homework and incidents and issuing new assignments, a "small group behavior rehearsal line" exercise and a "defining one's own behavior" exercise are employed. Acting on personal rights is the focus of these exercises, and practice is considered essential.

Sessions 6–9.   For the remaining sessions, in addition ot the usual opening and closing procedures, cognitive restructuring and behavior rehearsal procedures are used as volunteers work on personal situations. Groups are ended in positive, reinforcing ways, encouraging outside support for assertive behavior and positive self statements. The general thrust is that of reinforcing for the cognitive-behavioral work.

The use of videotape, interpersonal recall, and other group-processing techniques enable the individual participant to concentrate on thoughts, feelings, and internal dialogue during critical exercises. A wider range of behaviors can thus be more easily learned.

The authors recommend a follow-up session, not only to collect post-treatment information, but to futher reinforce gains made during the training. Participants interested in advanced assertiveness groups can explore such possibilities.

SUMMARY

Structured groups have often been ignored or given only cursory attention in textbooks on group counseling (see, for example, Corey, 1985). This is somewhat baffling since these same sources also report the growing popularity of structured groups. Structured groups offer many advantages to both the leader and the participant (Day & Sparacio, 1980; Russell & Easton, 1979). As the sample structured groups examined in the chapter illustrate, the range of topics and target populations is great. The design of structured groups also makes them amenable to conducting outcome studies. Why then have they been given such cursory treatment? Perhaps for a number of reasons. First, counseling groups, with their more open-ended format, tend to be more stimulating for leaders and participants, but with this increased stimulation comes increased risk. More open-ended formats offer more open-ended goals and perhaps more potential for greater change, but such formats also offer the potential for vague goals and little change. Accountability seems more likely in the structured group since the goals of the leader and of the participant are more likely to be explicit and congruent.

This chapter was not meant to advocate structured groups over other interventions. To the contrary, the crux of the matter seems to lie in the selection criteria. That is, we believe that the point has been reached where some sort of clinical consensus is possible in identifying which potential participant is appropriate for what kind of intervention, including group interventions.

REFERENCES

Behrens, E. M. (1970). Individual versus group training of parents in behavior modification techniques. Unpublished master's thesis. University of Utah.

Cerio, J. E. (1979). Structured experiences with the educational growth group. *Personnel and Guidance Journal, 57,* 398–401.

Corey, G. (1985). *Theory and practice of group counseling* (2nd ed.). Monterey, CA: Brooks/Cole.

Day, R. W., & Sparacio, R. T. (1980). Structuring the counseling process. *Personnel and Guidance Journal, 59,* 246–249.

Dendato, K. M., & Diener, D. (1986). Effectiveness of cognitive/relaxation therapy and study-skills training in reducing self-reported anxiety and improving the academic performance of test-anxious students. *Journal of Counseling Psychology, 33,* 131–135.

Dinkmeyer, D., & McKay, G. (1976). *Systematic training for effective parenting.* Circle Pines, MN: American Guidance Service.

Dreikurs, R., & Soltz, V. (1964). *Children: The Challenge.* New York: Duell, Sloan & Pearce-Meredith Press.

Drum, D. J., & Knott, J. E. (1977). *Structured groups for facilitating development: Acquiring life skills, resolving life themes, and making life transitions.* New York: Human Services Press.

Ellis, A. (1973). *Humanistic psychotherapy.* New York: McGraw-Hill.

Fleischman, M.; Horne, A.; & Arthur, J. (1983). *Troubled Families: A treatment program.* Champaign, IL: Research Press.

Garland, D. R. (1978). *Couples communication and negotiation skills.* New York: Family Service Assoication of America.

Gazda, G. M. (1984). *Group Counseling: A developmental approach* (3rd ed.). Boston: Allyn/Bacon.

Gershenfeld, M. K. (1985). A group is a group is a group: Working with couples in groups. In D. C. Goldberg (Ed.), *Contemporary marriage: Special issues in couples therapy* (pp. 374–419). Homewood, IL: Dorsey Press.

Goldstein, A. P.; Sprafkin, R. P.; Gershaw, N.J.; & Klein, P. (1982). *Skill-Streaming the Adolescent.* Champaign, IL: Research Press.

Hof, L., & Miller, W. R. (1981). *Marriage enrichment: Philosophy, process, and program.* Bowie, MD: Brady.

Langan, J. (1978). *Reading and study skills.* New York: McGraw-Hill.

Lange, A. J., & Jakubowski, P. (1978). *Responsible assertive behavior: Cognitive/behavioral procedures for trainers.* Champaign, IL: Research Press.

Lazarus, A. A. (1981). *The practice of multimodal therapy.* New York: McGraw Hill.

Lazarus, R. S. (1983). The costs and benefits of denial. In S. Breznitz (Ed.), *The denial of stress.* New York: International Universities Press.

Lerman, C. A., & Baron, A., Jr. (1981). Depression management training: A structured group approach. *Personnel and Guidance Journal, 60,* 86–88.

Meichenbaum, D. (1985). *Stress inoculation training.* New York: Pergamon.

Miller, W. H. (1975). *Systematic parent training: Procedures, cases, and issues.* Champaign, IL: Research Press.

Morris, R. J. (1980). Fear reduction methods. In F. H. Kanfer & A. P. Goldstein (Eds.) *Helping people change: A textbook of methods* (2nd ed.) (pp. 248–293). New York: Pergamon Press.

Patterson, G. R. (1969). Behavorial techniques based upon social learning: An additional base for developing behavior modification technologies. In C. M. Frank (Ed.), *Behavior therapy: Appraisal and status* (pp. 341–374). New York: McGraw-Hill.

Patterson, G. R.; Cobb, J. A.; & Ray, R. S. (1973). A social engineering technology for retraining the families of aggressive boys. In H. E. Adams & I. P. Unikel (Eds.), *Issues and trends in behavior therapy* (pp. 139–210). Springfield, IL: Charles C Thomas.

Patterson, G. R.; Ray, R. S.; & Shaw, D. A. (1969). Direct intervention in families of deviant children. *Oregon Research Institute Research Bulletin* (Vol. 8).

Pfeiffer, J. W. (1983). *A handbook of structured experiences for human relations training.* San Diego, CA: University Associates.

Russell, J. M., & Easton, J. (1979). Teaching the design, leadership, and evaluation of structured groups. *Personnel and Guidance Journal, 57,* 426–429.

Sayger, T. (1986). The maintenance and treatment effects for families of aggressive boys participating in social learning family therapy. Unpublished doctoral dissertation, Indiana State University, Terre Haute.

Talley, J. E., & Henning, L. H. (1981). *Study skills.* Springfield, IL: Charles C Thomas.

16

APPRAISAL OF GROUP COUNSELING

Recently there has been a marked increase in the use of group procedures. With this increase has come the development of interesting and promising innovations by competent leaders of groups on one hand and poorly conceived procedures developed by unqualified leaders on the other. Both types have often failed to describe adequately the treatment process, to indicate precisely what is expected of participants, or to communicate who is most apt to be helped by the treatment and under what conditions. Leaders must provide prospective participants with this type of information for them to decide whether they can be helped in groups and by what treatment. Leaders also must screen participants and help them define reasonable, achievable goals.

Most critics of group work have focused their attack on encounter, sensitivity, and marathon groups rather than on counseling or psychotherapy groups. Hartley, Roback, and Abramowitz (1976) report that evaluations vary from Rogers' (1968) "most significant social intervention of this century" to Maliver's (1973) "a multi-million dollar business—a callous exploitation and a sham of group therapy."

The charismatic pull of encounter groups is attracting an increasing number of persons who are ill-suited for interpersonal confrontation and for whom thorough treatment may be appropriate. This situation has intensified mental-health professionals' expression of concern about possible psychonoxious effects on encounter groups. Such diverse organizations as citizen groups, the U.S. Congress, and national organizations of psychiatrists and psychologists have also voiced alarm at the growing faith vested in spokesmen for the encounter cult. In contrast, many encounter leaders deny the existence of undue risk to participants (Hartley et al., 1976, p. 247).

Anyone following the history of modern psychotherapy cannot fail to be impressed by the depth and vehemence of feeling attending introduction of new theories and techniques, the acrimony of the ensuing debates, and the powerful

337

emotional reactions generated in professional and lay circles alike (Strupp, 1973a, p. 115).

The heavy barrage of the mid 1970s against the encounter movement in group work cast the entire process of encounter groups as hazardous and ineffective (Lieberman et al., 1973). More recent literature has found benefits and effectiveness in the use of encounter groups. Russell (1978) suggests that the psychotherapeutic benefits of caring, emotional stimulation, or "group intensity" (characteristic of encounter) are common psychotherapeutic elements for therapy groups and encounter groups. Furthermore, this same study, based on a reanalysis of the Lieberman data, found either no difference between encounter and therapy groups or a slight advantage in effectiveness for the encounter group method. Perhaps overgeneralizations regarding encounter groups led by careless, untrained leaders, misguided in their zealous efforts to create growth experiences in their groups, have overshadowed the benefits of the process of encounter. The needs on which the encounter group movement was based are as important now as they were then. Future research to determine the efficacy of encounter methods for specific needs and clientele is undoubtedly necessary to protect the clients' welfare.

Even though they are not as apt to feel the sting of public criticism, counselors and therapists must be able to define their treatment more clearly than they have previously (and tell precisely how it differs from other similar techniques); describe their expectations of participants; and characterize the type of clients for whom the treatment is most appropriate (and for whom it may be hurtful). The group movement is attracting clients, but it is also encouraging more clients to question their prospective counselor (or therapist) concerning its worth. Recent emphasis on accountability and increasing competition for tax dollars has caused administrators in public institutions to call for improved evaluation of services.

For school counselors, Kefauver and Hand (1941) stress the importance of counselors' soliciting periodic feedback from students, staff, and parents. Similarly, Dressel (1961) concludes that decision makers, whether they are conscious of it or not, judge the worth of a product, an idea, or a service. When professionals fail to define specific criteria and to collect essential data for evaluating their services, Dressel believes that they run the risk of being evaluated unknowingly on the basis of prejudice, tradition, or rationalization rather than on the worth of the idea, the service, or the product.

Increasingly, counselors are learning to help their clients, at the beginning of counseling, to define specific goals in terms of observable or measurable changes in behavior, interpersonal skills, feelings or attitudes. Even the counselor who does not believe that he has the skills or time to do systematic research, but does help his clients develop precise goals, can assess outcomes of counseling and solicit systematic appraisal from clients and their significant others. When, for example, a kindergarten girl told her counselor that she was worried about her three-year-old brother becoming her mother's favorite child, the counselor helped her define the following counseling goals (and the criteria for assessing each is listed parenthetically): (1) to tell her mother she was afraid that, when she was not home all day, her mother would learn to like her brother more (to report back to her counselor on whether or not she told her mother and what happened); (2) to tell her mother how much she loves her (to report back when she did it and what happened); and (3) to request time alone with her mother every day to do something special (to report back how many days each week she succeeded).

The counselor's notes showed these three outcomes: (1) her mother listened to her and hugged her; (2) the mother called the counselor to tell especially what item 2 (above) meant to her; and (3) the mother began at once to spend some time, at least once every day, alone with the girl. Even such specific case notes can be used effectively to convince administrators, clients' significant others, and colleagues that specific treatments do help clients.

Important as the type of case notes described above are, they are not sufficient. The counselor must determine how efficacious his treatment methods are for whom and under what circumstances. In order to meet the ethical standards of his profession, he must ask himself in selecting each client for a group: Is this a client whom I can help best by this method? During the course of treatment he must continue to ask himself this same question. After terminating treatment, he must ask: Who was helped most by this technique? Who failed to profit from it? Who was hurt by it? What information about these clients might have enabled me to predict who would have been hurt or helped? In what specific ways did my behavior contribute to or interfere with each client's growth?

In other words, an investigator must ask more precise questions than "Was group counseling effective?" or "Did group counseling really change clients' attitudes and behaviors?" Instead, an investigator must ask: For whom was this particular group counseling effective, and under what kinds of circumstances? Were some counselors more effective than others? How did the successful counselors differ from the others? What professional preparation and experience are required to provide it? Who profited most from it? Who may be hurt by it? How was readiness for counseling assessed? To what extent were clients committed to change their behavior and to help fellow clients change their behavior? To what extent were they convinced that they could be helped, and that their fellow clients could be helped? To what degree did clients participate in defining their treatment goals and accept these goals as reasonable for them- selves? To what extent did the actual treatment focus upon each one's own idiosyncratic goals? To what degree was the counselor able to develop a therapeutic relationship with each client, to help each to relate therapeutically to the others, and to help each accept responsibility for developing and maintaining a therapeutic climate within the group? Were adequate criteria developed to appraise techniques used to appraise each client's growth in terms of relevant criteria for her? Was the research design adequate to fulfill the researcher's purposes? Did he use appropriate statistical methods?

Obviously it is difficult for researchers to meet all of these conditions in appraising outcomes of group counseling. When one considers the practitioner's commitment to service, the limited time and financial support available to him for research, and the difficulties involved in appraising counseling outcomes, one can readily understand why some practitioners avoid systematic appraisal, and why some who attempt it overlook avoidable errors in their research design. Though no study even approaches perfection, counselors must improve their techniques for appraisal of clients' growth. They must also design better studies for formal appraisal of group counseling, conducted for specific clients under specified conditions by adequately described treatment methods and counselors. Within its limited space, this chapter tries to identify the most-serious problems involved and offers some practical suggestions for solving them. Relevant outcome studies also are reviewed briefly. For readers who work in a school setting and would be interested in soliciting systematic feedback on counseling services from teachers, parents, and students, Ohlsen (1974) describes a cooperative self-study procedure.

DEFINITION OF THE PROBLEM

Stating a research problem clearly and developing a rationale for it is a slow and painstaking process. Conducting a research project generally involves developing a method for answering the following questions: What is the question (or the research problem)? Why is it worth investigating? From whom will I collect what data?

If, indeed, the idea proves to be a good one, eventually the investigator must also be able to incorporate into a proposal the answers to questions such as: What is the central problem? Does the proposal focus primary attention on the central problem? Has the study been delimited sufficiently to answer the central research question? Are hypotheses stated clearly? Can adequate data be collected to test essential hypotheses? Will the order in which the data are collected influence subjects' responses? What pilot studies are required to clarify the treatment; to appraise the competencies and the commitments of the treaters with reference to each treatment; and to solicit feedback from similar subjects with reference to each of the selected criterion measures? Is it perfectly clear which are the dependent and which are the independent variables? How will the data be analyzed? Are the hypotheses stated in clear, testable language? Do the hypotheses indicate clearly a logical statistical test? Does the investigator defend adequately his use of these statistical analyses with these data? Does the investigator seem to be prepared to explain either significant or nonsignificant findings? What are practical implications of each significant (or failure to obtain significant) finding? How may each be accounted for?

Though clearly stated answers to these questions are important in obtaining support from a funding agency, such answers are even more important for the investigator; they ensure that the investigator understands precisely what he has contracted to do prior to beginning the research.

Fortunately, some counselors *are* beginning to ask important questions and formulating carefully stated hypotheses to evaluate the impact of clearly defined treatments provided by competent professionals on clearly described subjects in specific settings. Others could do significant research with the help of competent research consultants who are committed and able to help the potential researcher define his research problem. However, even some well-funded agencies have failed to produce good research because they employ uninvolved research specialists as consultants who do not listen to the researcher or help him develop his own research (and either they force him to do a study that appeals to them, or they leave him feeling even more unsure of his research competencies). In order for research to have meaning for the practitioners in an agency—and for them to try genuinely to apply it—they must participate in the formulating of the research, help carry it out, and feel safe in asking questions about the results.

Finally, in defining a research problem there is no substitute for a thorough review of the related research. It can help the investigator: (1) clarify and sharpen the statement of his problem; (2) identify and separate interacting variables; (3) clarify the unique features of the treatment process; (4) discover problems that may occur in appraising or supervising the competencies of the treaters; (5) discover variables to be controlled or observed carefully during treatment; (6) clarify hypotheses to be tested; (7) discover methods for evaluating change in subjects; and (8) identify new, improved statistical methods for analyzing his data. Every beginning graduate student should know this; but, even many experienced researchers fail to do it carefully, or they have it done by inexperienced assistants who merely identify results, missing the subtle design errors that could have been detected by sophisticated researchers and corrected rather than repeated again.

THE TREATMENT PROCESS

In order to generalize another's findings and apply them to his own situation or to replicate a study, a counselor must know the answers to the following questions: What are the primary features of the treatment? Precisely how does it differ from other similar treatments? What unique professional skills must the treater possess in order to provide it? What did the investigator do to ensure mastery and use of these skills during the course of the experiment? Who were the clients? Was there anything special or unique about them? Was there anything about the setting in which the treatment was administered that should be considered in applying it in other settings?

Unfortunately, researchers often fail to provide the answers to such questions. Furthermore, they often use the term *group counseling* to label very different treatments. However, when the relevant elements in their studies have been described in sufficient detail, a reader can determine for herself whether any of the findings can be applied to her situation.

For purposes of discussion in this chapter, it is assumed that the counselor has mastered at least the facilitative behaviors described in Chapter 2, that he understands the unique features of group counseling described in Chapter 1, and that he can provide the crucial elements in the helping process reviewed in Chapter 1. When, therefore, the writer reviews outcome studies, he asks himself whether they could possibly apply to these kinds of counselors doing group counseling.

THE COUNSELOR

Rarely have researchers adequately described the counselors (and psychotherapists) used in their studies. For example, in one study, well designed in most of its aspects, the researcher compared the efficacy of the same counselors providing individual and group counseling for a specific type of client, but failed to describe the professional competencies of the counselors. Correspondence with the researcher revealed that the counselors were trainees who had had formal course work and supervised practicum in individual counseling, but neither course work nor practicum in group counseling. In other words, their minimal professional preparations and inadequate professional experience made them questionable performers in individual counseling and completely unprepared to provide group counseling. Neither those treated in individual and group counseling improved significantly more than the control subjects. Had those treated individually improved significantly more than those treated in groups, readers would have assumed that individual counseling was superior for that particular type of client when treated within that particular setting. Obviously, such a conclusion would have been unwarranted.

The counselor is an important variable in the therapeutic process. When he presents himself for professional preparation he must be screened carefully and humanely. His preparation must help him develop the essential competencies to facilitate behavior change while simultaneously encouraging him to continue his professional growth on the job. When the counselor does not develop these essential helping skills during professional preparation—and accept responsibility for their continued growth—the profession must be prepared to discipline him. Clients can be hurt as well as helped by treatment (Bergin & Garfield, 1971; Carkhuff & Berenson, 1967; Truax & Carkhuff, 1964). Those who prepare counselors and therapists must select carefully for training to develop counselors and therapists of the client/counselor types 4 and 5 (defined below) in Carkhuff and Berenson's (1967) five-point scale:

1. Describes the severely disturbed client who is essentially immune to human encounter; and the retarding therapist.

2. Describes the distressed client who distorts reality but lives in the world of reality; and the moderately retarding therapist.
3. Describes the situationally distressed client who functions moderately well; and the minimally facilitative therapist.
4. Describes the more potent client who relates effectively and has a positive influence on others; and the therapist who facilitates change in those he tries to help.
5. Describes the person (both client and counselor) who is involved in a lifelong search for self-actualization for others as well as himself.

Using this scale, Carkhuff and Berenson reported that their typical client was slightly lower than 2, with a range between 1 and 3, and that counselors and therapists varied in their facilitating functioning from 1 to 4, with a mean of approximately 2.

> At the highest levels, these facilitators communicate an accurately empathic understanding of the deeper as well as the superficial feelings of the second person(s); they are freely and deeply themselves in a nonexploitative relationship; they communicate a very deep respect for the second person's worth as a person and his rights as a free individual; and they are helpful in guiding the discussion to personally relevant feelings and experiences in specific and concrete terms (p. 45).

There are far too many counselors who do not possess the professional competencies to help their clients and patients. Those who provide professional preparation for counselors and psychotherapists must appraise their programs with care and develop new improved programs, especially improved in-service programs for practitioners. They must search for the answers to questions such as: How may we improve our screening and selective admission–retention techniques in order to identify the good prospects early and encourage them (and identify the poor prospects and help them define new more appropriate goals)? On the basis of research findings concerning which techniques are most effective with whom (and which are rarely effective in bringing about behavior change), what should be taught to prospective treaters? What crucial questions must be answered on treatment techniques? How may students in training, recent graduates, and employers of recent graduates be involved in appraising preparation programs, including early human-relations skill training, personal therapy, and practicum and intern experiences as well as didactic preparation? What may be done to encourage the staff to do cooperative field studies with practitioners and trainees in field placements? What can be done to encourage and to reinforce continued growth in the field as practitioners?

A treatment can be fairly appraised only when it is provided by competent counselors, and various treatments can be compared only when counselors accept each method's worth, are committed to provide the treatment under specified conditions, and feel confident to provide each effectively. It is to be hoped that increasing research will be done in the field by experienced, competent counselors and therapists.

GOALS FOR GROUP COUNSELING

Failure to define specific goals for counseling in precise measurable or observable terms for each client is one of the most serious weaknesses of the research designed to appraise counseling outcomes. Such goals are necessary in order to define precise criteria for selecting or developing instruments and observational techniques to appraise changes in clients. Without such behavioral goals, researchers are tempted to use whatever evaluation techniques are readily available; and, consequently, they often use vague, general measures that cannot be defended as relevant, reliable, or valid. Specific goals also help clients understand and recognize the specific ways in which they change during, and subsequent to, counseling; such discoveries tend to reinforce further growth.

Paritzky and Magoon (1982) have developed a method for assessing the level of attainment of specific outcome goals for clients identified prior to group counseling. These authors suggest that "the mere setting of goals was motivation to begin making changes in their lives" (p. 384), and that individuals felt more in control of the processes involved in change as a result of clearly defined and measurable goals.

Hill (1975) contends that all too frequently when specific behavioral goals are not defined at the beginning of treatment, neither clients nor counselor has any real idea upon termination whether or not the treatment was helpful. She believes that clearly stated goals enable them to decide which problem areas require attention, to develop strategies for change, and to make necessary commitments for change.

Seligman (1975) believes that the helplessness of the depressed is learned behavior. He also believes that depressed patients can be helped to develop goals and be guided through specific situations in which they learn to exert progressively greater control over their environment. As the depressed patients discover that they can have some impact on the forces in their lives, their depression dissipates. Assertiveness training also helps such clients.

Broad knowledge of one's clients (gleaned from observation of them, listening to them) and review of the literature about clients in their particular stage of life helps the counselor understand his clients and detect the therapeutic material upon which he can help them define behavioral goals. More and more counselors are accepting their clients' reasons for seeking counseling; helping them translate these reasons into specific goals stated in terms of specific behaviors, attitudes, or skills; and helping them develop new goals during treatment. When such goals are developed cooperatively, they encourage client growth. Obviously, doing is much more difficult than merely discussing, but effective counselors *are* learning to do.

From the point of view of the funding agency as well as the researcher, specific treatment goals are important, too. Meade's (1972) appraisal of Ford Foundation projects revealed that the most successful school-improvement projects were those for which specific goals were carefully defined prior to funding; another crucial factor was good, continuing leadership by a committed project director.

CRITERIA

After specific goals have been defined for each client in behavioral terms, the counselor helps each decide how she will recognize when she has achieved them. These goals can then be used to select or develop criterion measures to appraise changes in clients.

When one examines the literature by practitioners, one is impressed with their commitment to help their clients with their distressing problems, with their concern about helping clients achieve their own goals, and with their practical suggestions for helping clients; but, when it comes to appraising outcomes of counseling, they tend to accept very general, vague criteria for appraising clients' growth (for example, improved interpersonal functioning or increased self-acceptance). Frequently, failure to obtain significant growth can be traced to use of vague, general criteria. According to Bergin and Lambert (1978), self-report methods that are situational to the client's change processes may yield outcome data that are more relevant in terms of the client's state condition. Edwards and Cronbach (1952) argue against global criteria too:

> Some investigators have tried to keep broad measures and yet stay within conventional statistics by pouring their data into a single overall index of adjustment. This is not recommended, for such an index blurs together the strengths and weaknesses of each method and provides no guide for improvement. . . . In therapy an overall index is not a good criterion if progress of a patient away from anxiety is concealed by negative scores assigned for an increase in expressed aggression (p. 56).

As the counselor examines the behavioral goals for each client he must not only ask, "What data must I collect to assess each client's growth?" but "Is there a likelihood that some clients may be hurt as well as helped by this technique?" and "Are individuals apt to move in opposite directions on the same criterion measures; and if, therefore, we combine the data for these clients, will they cancel out each other's growth?" When the latter possibilities occur, the counselor must try to identify these two types of clients, observe them during treatment, and analyze their responses to criterion measures separately.

For the last question (in which the researcher is suspicious that clients' movement on criterion measures may be in opposite directions, canceling out each other's growth) signed numbers must be used to prevent the canceling out of opposite change. If, for example, a counselor treats in the same counseling groups underconforming and overconforming clients (and increase in test scores indicates increased conformity), then signed numbers could be used to convert the negative change in overconforming clients' scores into positive change, thereby preventing their negative (but appropriate) movement from canceling out the positive movement of underconformers. Inasmuch as the worth of counseling must be appraised in terms of its impact upon individual clients, perhaps the counselor should help clients define significant growth for each prior to counseling. When, for example, George, a very bright tenth-grader, asked to join a counseling group to improve his grades and his relationships with teachers and parents, the counselor helped him decide how he (and his parents and teachers) would know when he had achieved these relationship goals. With reference to grades, he had a GPA of 3.4 the previous semester. He decided that he could raise it to a 4.5 (on a five-point scale). After eight or nine weeks, George decided that he should revise his GPA goal to 4.0 to enable him to spend more time on a physics project and to do some special reading in psychology and literature. When two of his fellow clients raised a question about a similar change in GPA goal, George argued against it on the grounds that they required scholarships in order to finance their college education. Had the counselor used change in mean GPAs as a primary criterion measure rather than achievement of the client's goal, the change would have posed a threat to the client's chances for success.

When prior to treatment a counselor helps clients decide what would be judged to be significantly changed behavior with reference to each of their idiosyncratic goals, then all the researcher must do is compare the number of instances in which experimental subjects achieved their goals with the number of instances in which control subjects (or clients treated by other methods) achieved theirs. Although there is no way to prove that these achievements are of equal worth, this approach does take account of individual clients' needs; makes them responsible for helping to decide what would be significantly improved behavior; involves them in both the treatment and the appraisal process; and conveys respect for their personal judgments.

CRITERION MEASURES

Even after researchers have helped clients define goals and criteria for appraising change in behavioral terms, they must select or develop measures that detect and appraise the exact nature of each client's growth or negative movement. When the researcher fails to follow these steps, he may be tempted to make some of the errors discussed earlier: (1) to use whatever appraisal measures are readily available; (2) to collect the same data on all subjects even when they are pertinent for only part of the research subjects (for example, using improvement in GPA for all subjects when it can be defended as relevant for half or less); (3)

to overlook use of signed numbers for subjects for whom the researcher can predict movement in opposite directions; and (4) to use vague, global measures to assess precise behavioral change. In selecting criterion measures, researchers also frequently make two other common errors: First, they select criterion measures that are insensitive to change; secondly, they use measures that they cannot defend as either reliable or valid.

Bereiter (1962) contends that although standards for test construction tend to produce stable measures of status and mastery of concepts, skills, and knowledge, such measures tend to be insensitive to the differential changes that guidance and counseling services tend to produce. If, therefore, such changes are to be detected and appraised, criterion measures must focus on change rather than on status.

Without reasonably good reliability, an instrument cannot be valid. Although researchers could establish reliability on their criterion measures more readily than validity, far too many do not bother to do so. Jensen, Coles, and Nestor (1955) make a case for four methods for guidance workers who are concerned with demonstrating the reliability of their instruments: internal consistency, stability, equivalence, and agreement between two or more raters. With increasing emphasis upon observation of behavior outside the treatment setting by significant others and judges, the last of the four takes on increased importance. Although computations of correlation coefficients among raters' scores are still most often used, this writer's experience suggests that percentage of agreement between pairs of judges' ratings on each decision is a more severe test of reliability. Forgy and Black (1954) conclude that agreement between experts' responses to criterion measures was sufficient evidence of content validity. In addition to reliability, Jensen, Coles and Nestor (1955) also argue for the use of construct validity for such instruments.

Leary (1957) provides a system that we will use to discuss the common types of instruments used to appraise counseling outcomes. His five levels of personality are determined by the following sources of data:

1. public communication level (impact on others)
2. conscious description (self-report) level
3. autistic, projective-fantasy, preconscious-symbolization level
4. unexpressed unconscious level
5. ego level

The last two levels have no practical value for researchers at this time. Level-1 appraisals are usually labeled as external measures of change. Typically sociometric tests, behavior inventories, Q-sorts, and checklists are used to obtain data from significant others such as classmates, friends, teachers, siblings, parents, and employers (and occasionally trained judges). In marriage counseling, for example, the best data concerning clients' growth seem to be provided in response to Q-sorts or behavior inventories which are developed out of the goal and criterion statements for the members of each group and responded to by fellow clients and spouses. Self-reports generally agree less with expert judges than either of the Q-sorts or behavior inventories, and counselors generally overestimate clients' growth. Except for Hilkey's (1975) findings in which inmates in a federal prison rated their own growth as greater than their counselors' rated growth, counselors (and therapists) tend to exaggerate clients' growth. Sethna and Harrington's (1971) therapists' ratings of their patients' improvement also was less than what the patients reported for themselves.

With self-referred clients, Horenstein, Houston, and Holmes (1973) question whether counselors' or therapists' opinions should be used to evaluate outcomes. They believe that clients know better than they can articulate why they came for assistance and whether they were helped. Their findings on the therapists' inaccurate perceptions of clients' problems certainly helps make the case for therapists using reflections to check out their perceptions of clients' problems and to involve clients in helping them develop precise behavioral goals early in the treatment process.

> Therapeutic progress of 41 clients was assessed by the clients, their therapists, and two independent judges. The clients' evaluations were unrelated to their therapists' evaluations, but they were highly related to the evaluations made by independent judges. Further analyses suggested that the disagreements between clients and therapists stemmed from the therapists' inaccuracy in perceiving clients' problems and the therapists' tendency to overestimate the progress of therapy relative to clients and independent judges (Horenstein et al., 1973, p. 149).

Even though they run the risk of biasing their reports from significant others, Broedel, Ohlsen, Proff, and Southard (1960) strongly encourage clients to share their treatment goals with relevant significant others and to solicit from them systematic reinforcements of desired new behaviors. Otherwise, these very persons either may not notice the desired new behaviors when they are exhibited (and the hard-working client will feel let down and disappointed); or, worse still, they will unknowingly reinforce the undesirable behaviors that the clients are trying to extinguish or replace.

> The fulcrum for therapeutic change is the affective relationship which becomes the vehicle for therapeutic change. Through the medium of that relationship the therapist exercises his power as a better socializer and change agent. Thus, therapy seeks to effect a better (more adaptive) balance between the need for self-expression, self-fulfillment, and freedom, on the one hand, and the demands for self-control, socialization, conformity, and self-discipline, on the other (Strupp, 1973b, 3. 117).

> The criteria of improvement most helpful for our purposes and used in this study were those evolved by Hartley and Rosenbaum (1963). They were derived from the responses of 81 psychotherapists to questionnaires in which they had to indicate their criteria for judging improvement. These criteria were

(a) improved interpersonal functioning in and out of therapy group, (b) ability to cope with and adapt to a variety of experiences, (c) self-acceptance, self-confidence, self-reliance, (d) insight, self-awareness, and (e) symptom reduction (Sethna & Harrington, 1971, p. 652).

Rickard (1965) also endorses the involvement of significant others in the treatment and evaluation of its outcomes. In order to minimize biased reporting, he trains his judges to solicit appraisal information on the basis of precise criteria:

> It seems feasible to select a board of judges, not necessarily psychologists, who might interview important figures in the patient's life, examine case material, and interview the patient more precisely to identify stable, sensitive, relevant behavior to be changed. After psychotherapy or the experimental treatment, the same judges without knowledge of which patients were experimental Ss, would again examine sources of evidence which would bear upon whether the behavior had, in effect, changed. Rickard and Brown (1960) have demonstrated that judges may show a high degree of agreement as to whether or not a specific behavior changes as therapy progresses. An additional function of the judges would be to consider the stability of the behavioral change over time (p. 65).

Horenstein et al. (1973) obtained interjudge reliabilities of clients' behavior: .92 and .97 pretherapy and .97 and .98 post-therapy.

Meehl (1959) recommends that the type of data obtained from others described by Rickard be recorded on a standard form for more effective statistical treatment. He prefers to have observers and interviewers use the Q-sort for recording their findings. The writer prefers to use a behavior inventory whose items consist of precise, behavioral descriptions that were developed out of the goal statements for the members of the counseling group. Observers (or interviewers) are required to indicate for each item the degree to which the behavioral description describes each subject (and without knowing which subjects were treated and which were the controls). Where a criterion involves an event that can be observed and counted, such as the number of times each week a student completes his homework on time, it should be reported as a specific number so that it can be compared with the relevant behavior during the baseline period.

Even though Broedel et al.'s (1960) clients complained that significant others often failed to notice and reinforce desired new behaviors, they found that parents and trained observers did detect and report significant changes on a behavior inventory. Very likely, even better results would have been obtained had the items in the inventory been designed especially for these clients and developed out of their behavioral goals. Unless significant others can detect and describe the desired new behaviors, they will tend to discount the worth of counseling, and certainly will not be able to reinforce the desired changes.

Most investigators who attempt to evaluate the worth of counseling solicit appraisals from clients' significant others and trained observers (Level 1) and from self-reports (Level 2). In addition to behavior inventories, Q-sorts, semantic differentials, sociometric tests, and checklists, which are used for both Levels 1 and 2, clients are administered personality tests and asked to write autobiographies. In general, Berg (1952) noted that the major virtue of all rating scales is their convenience, accessibility, and capacity to provide quickly a comprehensive estimate of adjustment not readily available by other methods. Unfortunately, such devices are often thrown together carelessly and little effort is made to establish reliability and validity. Such carelessness must not be tolerated.

Earlier, the limited worth of vague, general measures such as personality tests was discussed. Ohlsen (1974) concludes that there is no solid supporting evidence for the use of personality inventories to help clients identify or accept specific problems, to define goals for counseling, or to help their counselors appraise the outcomes of counseling. Although Pattison (1965) also criticizes all global measures of change in clients, he concludes that personality tests are especially disappointing for appraising outcomes of counseling and psychotherapy. Paul (1967) points out that subjective measures are notorious for their lack of reliability and validity and that personality inventories in particular hold little promise for appraising the outcomes of counseling and psychotherapy.

When a counselor has established a good relationship with clients, they are tempted to report what they think their counselors wants to happen. On the other hand, when clients do not volunteer for counseling and never fully accept its worth or develop a good relationship with their counselor, some may deny even the precise, behavioral changes that a trained observer detects. Nevertheless, when most clients are given the opportunity to describe their own growth in terms of specific changes in behavior, their reports tend to agree with independent judges (Horenstein et al., 1973). In any case, counselors cannot afford to ignore clients' evaluations of their services. Their evaluation determines to some extent the support for these services. Furthermore, even young clients can give valuable feedback that can be obtained only from them.

Limited data for appraising outcomes of counseling are obtained from Level-3 data (autistic, projective fantasy, or preconscious views). Leary (1957) used primarily TAT and Rorschach to obtain these data. Just as content analysis can be used to determine whether or not clients actually discuss the topics related to their goals or identify from their reports on successes and failures and how they were helped, it also can be used to obtain answers to specific questions from projective tests (which clinicians can use to complete behavior inventories and Q-sorts). If for example, a client's goal pertained to increased acceptance of self, one would expect her to describe the identification figure with considerably more positive affect during post-testing on the TAT than she did during pretesting. Moreover, when Wigell and Ohlsen (1962) did a content analysis of the first several sessions for groups of underachieving adolescents, they discovered that these clients discussed authority figures with significantly more frequent use of negative affect than either ambivalent or positive affect. During the last several sessions, they discussed this same topic with significantly less negative affect. When the counselor is able to schedule several follow-up sessions (usually 60 to 90 days following termination), content analysis can be used to determine whether gains identified in post-testing were maintained. During the follow-up sessions, clients are encouraged to discuss the problems for which they sought help. They also may be encouraged to discuss: what they accomplished or how they were hurt; with whom they learned to do what; what is left to be done; whose help is required to learn these new behaviors; and how that assistance may be requested.

RESEARCH SUBJECTS

When a researcher has defined the prescribed treatment for whom, under what conditions, and by whom, he should have a basic criteria for selecting research subjects. He must ask: What is my population? How may I best sample it in order to be able to generalize? In order to use the desired statistical analysis, what must I consider in selecting my sample? How large a sample will I require in order to appraise adequately this technique, under these circumstances, and especially with these evaluation techniques? What control subjects do I require? What are my obligations to controls? What can I do to encourage (and ensure) that controls not seek some other treatment while they are serving as control? What must I do to ensure that all data are obtained on all subjects (including follow-up data)?

Although most researchers seem to accept the need for control subjects and use some technique for randomly assigning subjects into experimental and control groups, they often fail to determine whether by chance the groups differed prior to treatment. Moreover, they must monitor the behavior of control subjects to ensure that they do not seek treatment elsewhere while they are serving as control subjects. When researchers have made a convincing presentation and screened prospective clients carefully, they tend to accept treatment, and often seek it during the control period.

Bergin (1963) concludes that one reason why experimental subjects have, at times, failed to improve significantly more than their controls is that controls had obtained treatment, too. Consequently, researchers must investigate the daily life experiences of both control and experimental subjects in order to identify influential experiences other than counseling that could have influenced behavior change. For this reason, the researcher should also explain to controls how chance determined which were treated first, convey continuing interest in them, and tell clients precisely when their treatment will begin. Researchers also should seriously consider budgeting to pay all for post-treatment and follow-up testing; it markedly enhances cooperation.

With careful planning the control subjects can be treated later and have their scores during treatment compared with their scores during the control period. This design ensures treatment for controls as well as experimental subjects (thereby improving cooperation with institutions as well as with research subjects), increases the number of experimental subjects, and ensures that at least part of the experimental subjects are like control subjects. On the other hand, this method does not permit the investigator to obtain follow-up data on these subjects as control subjects. After they are tested at the beginning and end of the control period, they are given the prescribed treatment (and the post-testing for the control period also serves as pretesting for the treatment period). Whether the investigator uses subjects as their own controls or uses only other subjects as controls, some clients who have accepted the need for specific treatment must be forced to postpone treatment, and this tends to reduce their readiness for treatment.

Three methods are commonly used to select control subjects who are comparable to experimental subjects: (1) select subjects, test them, have them wait the length of the treatment period, and serve as their own controls (as suggested above for part of the experimental subjects); (2) match experimental and control subjects on the basis of relevant variables; and (3) statistical controls (for example, analysis of covariance). Prior to deciding which sampling as well as statistical analysis he will use, the researcher must determine which will enable him to test his hypotheses. If, for example, he decides to match experimental and control subjects, then certain statistical tests that require random sampling cannot be used. When he draws a large sample, however, he may be able to divide the experimental and control groups by use of random number techniques, and feel reasonably certain that they are similar. Nevertheless, he may wish to use appropriate statistical analyses to determine whether or not chance can account for observed differences in experimental and control subjects' scores prior to treatment.

Some scholars have developed long-term cooperative working relationships with school systems and community agencies for training centers. Such cooperative relationships have been especially effective in providing student teaching in public schools. The writers believe that similar, cooperative continuing relationships could provide a pool of research subjects for the evaluation of counseling services. Although university researchers have usually taken the initiative for short-term projects, guidance directors should be encouraged to initiate such continuing working relationships.

For individual projects, the guidance director must try to assess the researcher's acceptance by the cooperating school staff and his ability to state clearly what he expects to do, why it needs to be done, and how the results may be used to improve the particular service involved. The guidance director also should try to assess the researcher's commitment to help cooperating school staff implement the findings of the research. When these conditions have been met, cooperating school personnel achieve genuine satisfaction from helping solve professional problems; research scholars are encouraged to do research in the practitioners' work setting; school personnel obtain assistance in appraising their services; and the research findings tend to be more readily accepted and used by practitioners.

Where university training centers have been developed to provide clients for practice and internships and have earned a reputation for good service to schools and community agencies, a wide variety of clients tend to be referred to these centers (which could open the way for using these centers for cooperative research as well as for service and training). From such a large pool of clients, a researcher can identify appropriate clients, treat them as they become available, and markedly increase the number of subjects available over a period of time for a particular project. When the particular type of clients that are needed for a project are described carefully, counselors in cooperating institutions will help identify and refer them for the project, too. In addition to obtaining a large pool of appropriate clients, this approach tends to have the further advantage of clients coming to the project knowing what is expected and accepting the need for treatment.

STATISTICAL ANALYSES OF DATA

The process begins with identifying the questions for which the researcher is seeking information. After he decides what the research questions are, he can develop his hypotheses and select the essential statistical analyses to test his hypotheses. Early in the process, he must review the assumptions that he makes when he reviews each of the possible ways of analyzing his data and determine which must be met. He also must be certain that he has collected his data in a form that lends itself to his statistical analysis.

Two of the most common mistakes researchers make in selecting statistical procedures are: first, the use of statistical tests for which the basic assumptions for their use have not been met; secondly, a consultant's assistance with statistical analyses of the data is sought after the data have been collected. When consultants are employed during the planning stage, the researcher can obtain help in stating hypotheses more clearly; in collecting essential data to test his hypotheses; in arranging to have at least some instruments machine-scored; and in selecting or writing a computer program (and in scheduling his computer analysis of data). Such arrangements not only save precious time but such assistance encourages some who are unsure of the quantitative skills to do research.

With better-qualified counselors, the need to compare several alternative treatment methods, and the sophisticated computer program that can be made available to counselors, researchers are able to tackle much more complicated problems: To what extent is the effectiveness of a technique a function of the type of clients treated, of the circumstances under which the treatment is administered (including elements such as type of clients combined, place of treatment, length of counseling session, number of times per week, and so on), and of the competency level of treaters? What elements within the group seem to have the greatest impact on the counselor and clients? Do counselors and clients who are members of effective groups play different roles than they do in ineffective groups? How do those clients who profit most from group counseling differ from those who profit least from counseling? Are some methods more productive for certain types of clients, or possibly, when provided by a certain type of counselor? Several of the above questions would require a three-dimensional analysis of variance. Others would require a factorial design as suggested by Edwards and Cronbach (1952). Cohn (1967) and his team of researchers strongly encouraged researchers to use multivariate statistical methods to investigate process and outcome variables simultaneously.

Edwards and Cronbach (1952) conclude that those who appraise outcomes of counseling must be sufficiently suspicious and tough-minded to recognize proven fact and sensitive enough not to discard unproven ideas for which their experiments were not powerful enough to detect significant results:

> If this tender-minded soul is gullible, believing in what has met no significance test, he will end up with a science stuffed with superstitions. But if he holds these yet-unproven ideas in the air, as notions which may guide him in the next experiment or the treatment of the next patient, he is more likely to be correct than the man who casts the idea from his mind as soon as one experiment fails to provide significant confirmation (p. 57).

A SUMMARY OF LITERATURE APPRAISING GROUP COUNSELING

This section is a review of selected literature related to group counseling. The discussion of findings is designed to introduce the counselor in training to the nature and implications of group counseling in order to foster an integration between research findings and the actual practice of group counseling. The assumption is that sound professional practice of group counseling is based in empirical research findings. However, a study by Wolfgang and Pierson (1977) that explored the relationship between current group-counseling practices and what was suggested by research literature found that 75% ($N = 122$) of those surveyed reported that research literature had no relevance or minimal relevance to clinical practice.

Coche and Dies (1981) report similar findings regarding the belief on the part of practitioners that outcome research for group counseling is not relevant. Perhaps findings such as these are due in part to the global nature of outcome research. As has been previously stated, such research lacks in clarity and specificity and therefore has little to offer in terms of upgrading the quality of service. Nevertheless, the practitioner is still faced with the problem of developing and improving the quality of service, which is ultimately linked to sound research findings. With these thoughts in mind, the following outcome research is reviewed.

RESULTS OF STUDIES WITH CHILDREN

Even though it involves too few subjects, Davis' (1948) study is reviewed here because it is one of the better, early studies for which relevant criterion measures were used. She counseled nine first-grade children in two groups twice a week for ten weeks. She photographed her subjects periodically during free play and obtained pretreatment, post-treatment, and follow-up sociometric testing to appraise changes in classmates' social acceptance of clients. She concluded that their social acceptance was improved.

Barcai, Umbarger, Pierce, and Chamberlain (1973) compared the effects of three group treatments on low socioeconomic fourth- and fifth-graders: (1) group counseling (which was cognitively oriented); (2) group remediation; and (3) art activity. They concluded that activities that reward the use of language and focus on specific interventions were the more effective methods. They also concluded that teachers' personality, expectations, and attitudes may enhance or retard the impact of an intervention.

Crow (1971) compared the effects of three types of group counseling with varying degrees of structure. She provided each group of sixth-graders with group counseling once a week for 45 minutes for 12 weeks. Although she obtained no significant differences among treatment groups, the combined clients for all three treatments made significantly greater growth than her control subjects on all but one of the criterion measures (improved grades). On one variable, improved self-concept, boys exhibited significantly greater growth than girls. No follow-up data were obtained.

Although they used a small number of subjects (and usually GPA tends to be difficult to improve by short-term treatment), Deffenbacher and Kemper (1974) found that counseled sixth-graders suffering from text anxiety improved their grades significantly more than control subjects. They used group desensitization with two groups of sixth-graders for 40–45 minutes once a week—one group for five weeks and the other for six.

Hansen, Niland, and Zani (1969) investigated the effectiveness of model reinforcement and reinforcement group counseling with elementary-school children using sociometric status as a criterion. They compared three combinations of clients, each consisting of 18 subjects: (1) low-sociometric-status students counseled with those of high-sociometric status; (2) low-sociometric students counseling by themselves; and (3) a control group that met for an activity period. All groups met twice a week for four weeks (usually considered too short a period). This discussion focused on learning to get along with others. The counselors consciously reinforced desired behaviors. Low-sociometric-status students in the model reinforcement groups made significantly more gain in social acceptance than did those counseled without models and the controls. Moreover, the gains were maintained in the two-month follow-up.

Hinds and Roehlke (1970) appraised the effectiveness of a learning theory approach to group counseling with third-, fourth-, and fifth-graders who were referred by classroom teachers as disruptors of learning. They used co-counselors (the authors) for 20 sessions over a 10-week period. Prior to counseling, a base rate for disruptive behaviors was established. Counselors used systematic reinforcement in groups to shape each client's behavior and to extinguish disruptive behaviors. When each group earned the desired points, they selected the game they played. Perhaps the same results could have been obtained had the counselors functioned as consultants and helped the classroom teachers learn to be behavior modifiers. Nevertheless, like the previous study reviewed above, this is a good example of a well-designed study in which competent counselors provided the treatment and obtained significant results.

Kelly and Mathews (1971) adapted Glasser's (1969) classroom-meeting model for group counseling. Even though they seemed to have designed their study with care, they failed to obtain significant results. Possibly their limited experience with the model, their small sample, their limited treatment period, and their criterion measures account for their negative results. Perhaps also, some children who have adapted well to school and who desire counseling for other reasons could be combined with this type of child to improve the chances for success in the group. In any case, the study should be repeated with the suggested changes.

Kern and Kirby (1971) compared the effects of a counselor-centered, group-counseling procedure with one in which trained peer helpers were used to assist the counselor. Groups of five to eight fifth- and sixth-graders met for 50-minute periods once a week for nine weeks. In those groups in which peer helpers were used, clients exhibited significantly greater improvement on personality measures than did either the controls or the ones treated in counselor-centered groups. These results should encourage counselors to invite (and even train) clients to serve as helpers as well as clients. Unfortunately, no follow-up data were collected to determine whether gains were maintained.

Omizo, Cubberly, and Omizo, (1985) conducted a study to determine the effects of a rational-emotive, education counseling group on self-concept and locus of control. Sixty learning-disabled children between the ages of 8–11 were randomly assigned to control and experimental conditions. Group counseling consisted of one-hour sessions lasting for 12 weeks. A univariate and discriminate analysis of the data was conducted, and the findings indicate that rational-emotive education groups are effective in enhancing some aspects of self-concept and increasing internal locus of control for learning-disabled children.

Mayer, Kranzler, and Matthes (1967) compared changes in pupil-teacher relationships for two types of groups: one was given a combination of individual and group counseling; and the other participated in teacher-led guidance groups.

Both were compared with controls. They found that counseling enhanced pupil-teacher relationships in the more pupil-centered classrooms, but that it had less apparent effect in the more teacher-centered classrooms. With a larger sample and more-experienced counselors, perhaps stronger results would have been obtained.

Moulin (1970) assessed the effects of client-centered group counseling with play media on intelligence, achievement, and psycholinguistic abilities of under-achieving first, second, and third graders (largely black and educationally deprived children). Significant changes were noted following treatment for nonlanguage sections of the mental test and for the psycholinguistic ability test.

Novick (1965) compared the results obtained for good and poor prospects treated as outpatients by individual and group counseling in a community mental-health center. Groups varied in size from three to five. Clients were behavior problem cases. Observers rated each client on 19 behavioral characteristics (such as bullying, cheating at school, and so on) at three different intervals: precounseling; after 10 sessions; and after 20 sessions. No significant changes were noted after 10 sessions, but significant changes were noted after 20 sessions. Good prospects responded to treatment better than poor prospects. Chance could account for any differences in scores for those treated individually and in groups. This last point is also supported by Meltzoff and Kornreich's (1970) review of the research on psychotherapy.

Ohlsen and Gazda (1965) appraised the impact of group counseling upon bright, underachieving fifth graders. Twenty-two students were counseled twice a week for eight weeks in groups of five or six. Compared to their controls, they increased congruence between perceptions of self and ideal self; increased acceptance of peers; markedly decreased instances of psychosomatic illnesses such as asthma attacks, stomach cramps, and headaches; but failed to improve their grades, achievement test scores, acceptance of self, and behavior inventory scores. Perhaps selection of more highly committed clients with clearly defined behavioral goals and the use of a behavior inventory based upon their goals would have increased their chances for greater success.

Randolph and Saba (1973) designed a study to compare the relative effectiveness of four group experiences for off-task fifth- and sixth-grade pupils: (1) modeling; (2) modeling with behavioral consultation; (3) control (no attention); and (4) a placebo (they were provided with a career-development experience). Four groups of six each received group counseling. The precise nature of the treatment for each was described exceptionally well. Both treatments improved on-task behaviors significantly better than either control. For grade point average, only the modeling with consultation group improved significantly over first controls, but not second controls (placebo). Neither treatment group improved attitude toward school more than controls.

Sonstegard (1961) found that group counseling for fifth-grade under-achievers improved reading achievement, classroom behavior, and work habits when parents and teachers also were actively involved in the treatment program.

Twardosz and his associates (1983) designed a study that illustrates specific and concrete measures that characterize and describe behavior change in detail. One group consisted of children identified as social isolates and developmentally disabled were exposed to affective activities designed to desensitize individuals to touch. The second group involved a program designed to encourage expression of affection. Teachers were also stimulated to be more affectionate. Results suggest that the previously stated methods are effective interventions for socially isolated preschool children, especially when both handicapped and nonhandicapped children are placed together.

Tosi, Swanson, and MacLean (1970) appraised the impact of social reinforcements in group counseling on verbal output of nonverbalizing sixth-graders and concluded that the treatment changed behavior. They also observed that clients and teachers learned to reinforce desired new behaviors. In a similar study, Tosi, Upshaw, Lande, and Waldron (1971) found that systematic reinforcement was the more effective of their two reinforcement models.

Clark and Seals (1984) enhanced social skills for coping with ridicule by using an Adlerian-based group process for children who had been ridiculed and abused by other children. The authors believe that ridicule constitutes a form of abuse eventually leading to lowered interpersonal competency and self-concept. The group treatment procedure involved three separate phases: (1) the relationship phase, which encouraged members to share their experience of being ridiculed; (2) reorientation phase, which consisted of cognitive and perceptual restructuring; and (3) the accomplishment phase, which taught effective coping skills for ridicule.

In a study by Tiktin and Cobb (1983) a group paradigm was used with children 7–12 years old ($N = 42$) whose parents were either getting a divorce or were separated. The paradigm consisted of a parent-child assessment system, a set of group activities and games for the children, and concurrent sessions including parents. Results witnessed an observable decline in tantrums, anger outbursts, and withdrawal behavior plus the improvement of problem-solving skills; and subjects increased expression of appropriate affect to parents.

In a study by Zimpfer and Waltman (1982), seventy 12–17-year-olds with behavior and learning problems in nine schools were exposed to a client-centered group approach. This approach was aimed at identifying problem areas, venting emotions, and developing problem-solving skills. Measures on self-concept, social relationships, and dogmatism were taken; and findings indicate that both the counselor and group composition are significantly related to subjects' value for the group, how they interacted, and how much self-image changed.

Berry and his associates (1980) designed a matching study using twenty-four 6–9-year-olds defined as having disruptive classroom behaviors. Subjects were matched on IQ ($\bar{x} = 109$), age, and sex and were assigned to a self-concept focused group or to a behavior modification-based group approach. Pre- and post-measurements were taken on self-esteem and disruptive behavior. Results found that the self-concept group had more change on behavior measures than the behavior-modification group approach. Self-esteem was not significantly affected by either approach.

Based upon their review of the research concerning counseling children in groups, Howard and Zimpfer (1972) concluded that group counseling is effective, but that group approaches with parents and teachers appear to be even more promising. Inasmuch as many children's problems develop prior to school enrollment and during primary grades, they urge elementary-school counselors to devote more of their time to primary-school children and their parents and teachers. They concluded that group counseling with children improved affective learning, sociometric status, attitudes toward school, and reading performance; but that it often failed to improve grades. With reference to achievement, the writers believe that in order to improve grades, the counselor must focus more therapeutic attention on improved achievement; help clients to assess the degree to which they want to improve their grades and for whom, and (for those who accept the need to improve their grades) to define precise behavioral goals related to improved achievement; place underachievers with achieving clients who are worried about good achievement; obtain remedial instruction for those who require it (and possibly by peer teaching, especially by fellow clients); and enlist parents' and teachers' encouragement and reinforcement of desired new behaviors.

In general, positive results were obtained in these cited studies, but perhaps better results would have been obtained had the researchers helped counselors identify and focus upon the problems that brought the children to counseling, involved the children in defining specific, behavioral goals, and appraised outcomes in terms of clients' idiosyncratic goals. Increased use of role playing probably also would have helped clients learn to behave more effectively with specific target persons. Possibly, clients should have been helped to communicate their desired new behaviors to significant others, especially parents and teachers, and to enlist their assistance in reinforcing desired new behaviors. The most carefully designed studies in which highly competent persons served as counselors produced the best results.

RESULTS OF STUDIES WITH ADOLESCENTS

Chapter 13 makes a psychological case for the use of group counseling with adolescents. During the past decade there has been a marked growth in its use. There also has been an increase in research designed to appraise its efficacy for adolescents.

Bates (1968) investigated clients treated by two methods: (1) weekly meetings for a class period for thirteen weeks; and (2) continuous-session meetings during school hours for two consecutive days. The 36 students who were treated by each method were divided into three groups for counseling. Except for the responses to the Rotter sentence-completion test (for which their responses improved over those of the controls), the marathon groups failed to exhibit any significant change over controls. For the regular counseling groups, changes over controls were obtained with reference to school attendance, citizenship, vocational choice, acceptance of self, and acceptance of others. They also maintained their GPA whereas the GPAs of those treated by marathon and controls deteriorated. Bates concluded that treatment over a longer time provided the continuing reinforcement that is required to sustain change.

Benson and Blocher (1967) appraised the effectiveness of developmental group counseling for low-achieving, tenth-grade boys. This technique is primarily concerned with helping clients master developmental tasks and develop a more adequate repertoire of coping behaviors. In spite of their small N (12 students treated in two groups), their counseled students improved their grades, decreased discipline referrals, improved feelings of adequacy, and persisted in school better than controls.

Broedel et al.'s (1960) gifted, underachieving ninth-grade clients were provided group counseling twice a week for eight weeks. Their counseled clients improved significantly more than their controls with reference to achievement test scores; acceptance of self and others; ability to relate to peers, siblings, and parents; but failed to improve their GPAs significantly. Follow-up data in 15–18 months indicated that they maintained their growth. Three-year follow-up also indicated that the treated underachievers tended to improve their grades slightly, whereas the general trend for bright students was for grades to decrease gradually. More careful selection of clients and greater care in helping them develop precise behavioral goals probably would have increased these gains.

Bush (1971) did the first of four studies designed to appraise the efficacy of the model of group counseling described in Chapter 1. His primary concern was division of time among clients during each session. Bartell (1972) appraised the effect of the intake interview on client outcomes. Hilkey (1975) assessed the impact of videotape training in client and helper roles on counseling outcomes. Generally, all three concluded that group counseling was effective, but that no one of these elements by itself had a significant effect on outcome—especially in the latter two instances. They concluded that though the element that each studied influenced the quality of interaction during the first few sessions, competent counselors were able to compensate for the fact that it was not provided. However, at first, counselors felt more comfortable with the clients who had completed careful intake interviews or had been trained as clients and as helpers by the videotape.

De Esch (1974) counseled disruptive secondary-school students and obtained significant changes with reference to decreased, deviant sign scores on the Tennessee Self-Concept Scale, improvement in GPAs, and decreased referrals to the principal's office for disruptive classroom behavior. He also noted that on several variables, controls also improved their performance. De Esch concluded that the carefully conducted intake interviews, in which specific behavioral goals were established, enabled controls to decide how they wanted to change and to develop the commitment to do it. Davis and Sanborn (1973) also demonstrated that counselors, who help high-school students develop specification contacts and encourage them to take responsibility, can produce change with brief contacts.

A study designed by Henry and Kilmann (1979) compared two basic procedures for group counseling (behavioral/directive against client-centered/nondirective) across three levels of participation: voluntary, semi-voluntary, and nonvoluntary. Subjects were high-school seniors. Results indicate that voluntary subjects with clear counseling goals made greater gains than the other nonvoluntary client-centered subjects. Academic achievement, change in attitude, behavior, and vocational decision making were used as outcome criteria.

Catron (1966) appraised the impact of group counseling by co-counselors in training upon thirteen groups of high-school students. Though the clients' stated purpose was educational-vocational planning, they exhibited much more interest in discussing (and were permitted to discuss) parent–child relationships, variation in quality of their teachers, peer relationships, and social attitudes. In addition to helping them discuss their feelings related to personal problems, counselors helped them surface underlying feelings concerning decision making. Catron's clients improved significantly perception of self, but exhibited no significant changes in either ideal person or ordinary others.

Clements (1966) evaluated the efficacy of group counseling to reduce anxiety of college-bound, high-school seniors. Counseling sessions (six while in high school, and additional ones for those who volunteered as college freshmen) focused on attitudes, fears, and aspirations. The counseled students exhibited significantly less anxiety both prior to college entrance and after beginning college.

Finney and Van Dalsem (1969) used GPAs and scores from California Study Methods Survey to compare results from underachieving, high-school tenth-graders who were counseled for four semesters and from similar students who were not counseled. Although the counseled students did not perform significantly better on the above two criteria, they were rated by teachers as more cooperative in class, and they were absent less; but, they were not referred to the office less for poor deportment.

Mayer (1982) evaluated the effects of using adolescents with conduct problems as tutors for educable, mentally retarded students who were 8–10 years old. Subjects in this study were 18 high-school-aged students considered to be emotionally disturbed. Adolescent tutors were randomly assigned to one of three experimental conditions. Experimental treatment group 1 consisted of providing cross-age tutoring; experimental group 2 received peer tutoring; and experimental group 3 received group counseling. Measures were taken before, during, after, and a follow-up measurement 10 weeks later. Outcome criteria of increased academic performance, decreased absenteeism, and decreased disciplinary referrals was found to be significant for subjects exposed to the provision of cross-aged tutoring group.

Rosenstock and McLaughlin (1982) conducted a study investigating the efficacy of a treatment strategy defined as "The Positive Group" for troubled adolescents. This technique requires adolescents to learn to make positive statements about themselves and other group members. Essentially, this strategy teaches group members to give and receive support. The results of this strategy were found to be effective with a wide range of adolescent clientele for enhancing self-image, social skills, and the development of leadership potential. The findings in this study were based on clinical observations and anecdotal records collected by the staff. This study could have been improved by using more precise measures of idiosyncratic charges among group members.

Gilliland's (1968) black high-school students who were counseled for a year in group improved more than controls with reference to vocabulary, reading, English usage, vocational maturity, and occupational aspirations. Hansen, Zimpfer, and Easterling (1967) investigated the relationship between changes in self-concept and therapeutic climate in their counseling groups (six groups of 8–9 in six high schools). They found that students' perceptions of the relationship was important to achieving increased congruence between real and ideal self-concept.

Hansen and Sanders (1973) identified extreme cases of "overshooting" and "undershooting" unrealistic vocational choices and compared the impact of individual and group counseling on eleventh- and twelfth-graders. Chance could account for any observed differences between those treated and their controls, but they obtained a significant interaction. The "overshooters" who were counseled in groups and the "undershooters" who were counseled individually developed more realistic choices.

Jesness (1975) conducted a very carefully designed study for the treatment of delinquent boys, aged 15–17, in two institutions. Clients were randomly assigned to one of two similar institutions differing only in the treatment provided: behavior modification in one; transactional analysis in the other. In addition to the twice weekly, small, group-therapy sessions for the latter, large community meetings were held two or three times a week. TA principles also were applied daily in coping with the delinquents' management. With reference to parole criteria, the two techniques were equally effective. However, each treatment generated some specific advantages. Behavioral programs resulted in greater gains noted on specific observer ratings, whereas TA programs resulted in greater changes in attitudinal and self-report appraisals. Moreover, the data showed that delinquents in both programs' recidivism rates for the experimental period were significantly lower than the base rate for the year prior to the research project.

Krumboltz and Thoresen (1964) assessed the effect of both individual and group behavioral counseling on volunteer eleventh-graders from six high schools near Stanford University. Two types of treatment were used on both individual and group basis: reinforcement counseling (for information-seeking behavior);

and model-reinforcement counseling. They also provided for a special control for the Hawthorne effect. Individual and group counseling were both effective, but males who received model-reinforcement counseling were stimulated more by the group than by the individual setting. Model-reinforcement counseling was generally more effective for males than females. However, the model was a male, hence it may have been easier for the male students to identify with him. This is another unusually well-designed study.

With group counseling, Lodato, Sokoloff, and Schwartz (1964) modified the attitudes of slow learners: three groups from grades 7 and 8; one from grades 4 and 5; and two groups from grade 3. On the basis of teachers' ratings, they improved students' attitudes toward learning and authority figures, school attendance, and teachers' tolerance of students.

McCarthy (1959) divided 24 bright, underachieving ninth-grade boys into four groups (two experimental and two controls) and provided six one-hour treatment sessions in which subjects' attention was focused on disguised case materials based on the boys' own problems. The clients' task was to try to diagnose the reasons for failure and to plan ways of helping these boys. Though they were not told that these were their own problems, they became defensive when their own case materials were discussed, and perhaps insufficient attention was given to helping them discuss these feelings. In any case, significant changes were not obtained.

Mezzano (1967) discovered a statistically significant relationship between investment in group counseling and improvement in GPA. His subjects were low-motivated, high-school students (18 received individual and group counseling, 18 received group counseling only, and 28 served as controls).

Sarason and Ganzer (1973) investigated the relative effectiveness of two group methods: one relied on modeling and required subjects to imitate roles that they observed their models perform; and the other employed structured discussion of the same material, but without modeling or imitation. Both types (groups of four or five) were attended by two models or discussion leaders. There were 64 subjects for each type of group: $15\frac{1}{2}$–18 years old with a mean IQ of 95. Modeling appeared to be superior to discussion only. The study also makes a case for the practice of interpersonal skills in role playing advocated in Chapter 12 and the use of videotapes for feedback.

Smith and Evans (1973) compared results achieved with experimental group guidance with individual counseling to facilitate vocational development. Significantly better results were obtained by those treated by group procedures than controls and individually counseled.

Thoresen and Krumboltz (1967) investigated the relationship between counselor reinforcement of certain responses and specific behaviors with volunteers from six high schools near Stanford University. Model reinforcement produced significantly more information-seeking behaviors than reinforcement alone did.

RESULTS WITH COLLEGE STUDENTS AND ADULTS

In the final group of selected studies, investigators primarily used college students; but, a few used reasonably healthy, out-of-school adults as research subjects.

Abramowitz, Abramowitz, Roback, and Jackson (1974) used 26 mildly distressed college students to evaluate the differential effectiveness of directive and nondirective group therapies with internally controlled clients (those who believe that the events that occur in their lives are results of their own initiatives) and externally controlled clients (those who believe that events in their lives are determined largely by luck or powerful outside forces). They found that internally controlled clients were more responsive to the nondirective therapy whereas externally controlled clients tended to be more responsive to directive therapy.

Brown (1969) tried to determine whether the degree of structure had differential impact on high- and low-anxious students. He found that high-anxious, underachieving college students benefited more from an unstructured approach than low-anxious, underachieving students. Furthermore, he recommended less structure for high-anxious and more structure for low-anxious students, even in remedial courses such as study-skill courses.

Chestnut (1965) evaluated the effect of structured and unstructured group counseling for gifted college underachievers. Whereas those assigned to the unstructured group were permitted to discuss whatever originated spontaneously in their group, the counselor for the structured group encouraged clients to discuss, and to develop skills for coping with, the genesis of poor achievement. By the end of treatment, only those in the structured group had improved grades significantly more than their controls. At the three-month follow-up, their grades were still significantly better than those of the unstructured group.

Kivlighan, McGovern, and Cerazzini (1984) conducted a study using an interpersonal process model of group counseling with a university student population ($N = 31$). This study was designed to test the effects of providing information on the phases of group. The content of the information given students pertained to anger or intimacy and was either given at the stage appropriate to such information or mismatched with a stage. The two stages of group development focused on in this study were either "storming" or "norming." Results indicate that information relevant to a particular stage of group development produced less anxiety in dealing with intimate behavior, more appropriate expressions of intimacy, increased congruence between self-ratings and ratings by other group members regarding interpersonal behavior, and less interpersonal rigidity in general.

Dickenson and Truax (1966) assessed the efficacy of time-limited group counseling for underachieving college freshmen. By comparison with their controls, counseled students tended to earn passing grades and to improve their

GPAs more than noncounseled students. Furthermore, those clients who experienced relatively high levels of therapeutic conditions (accurate empathy, unconditional positive regard, and genuineness) showed the greatest improvement.

Gazda and Ohlsen (1961) appraised the effects of group counseling on four groups of prospective counselors (34 clients). By comparison with their controls, those counseled improved significantly their manifest needs in the predicted direction: increased autonomy and decreased abasement and succorance for all four groups, but other changes for only two groups; increased heterosexuality for two groups and decreased nurturance for two groups. Changes assessed by the picture-story test and the behavior inventory failed to achieve significant results for either post-testing or follow-up. When, however, the interviewer (in a 14-month follow-up) requested clients to describe specific ways in which they had been helped or hurt, all but two clients were able to describe some specific ways in which they had been helped.

Gilbreath (1967) reported on a study in which he assessed changes in underachieving, first- and second-year college males. Two counselors participated in the group-counseling projects; each counseled two groups by the high-authority, leader-structured method. Those counseled by the leader-structured method experienced a higher rate of increase in GPAs and greater ego strength than did either the group-structured clients or the controls. At the three-month follow-up, the leader-structured group's rate of increase in GPAs was not significantly greater than that for those counseled by the group-structured method. Furthermore, the investigator concluded that his dependent clients improved GPAs in leadership-structured groups but not in group-structured groups. By contrast, his independent clients seemed to improve GPAs more in group-centered groups than in leader-centered groups.

Gorlow, Hoch, and Teleschow (1952) counseled 17 graduate students in three groups twice weekly for 18–20 sessions. After prospective clients volunteered, the counselors used an intake interview to determine whether or not they were deeply concerned about some problem on which they were willing to work. After counseling, all clients perceived themselves and their fellow clients in a more favorable light. The investigators also developed a reliable method for dividing clients into two groups: most-profited and least-profited. Most-profited clients exhibited a significant decrease in negative behavior and increase in positive behavior, whereas no significant change was noted in the behavior of least-profited clients.

Graff, MacLean, and Loving (1971) compared results obtained by reactive-inhibition and reciprocal-inhibition therapies for anxious college freshmen with results obtained from similar clients who participated in a neutral discussion group. They obtained significant gains with both methods. Furthermore, their gains were maintained in the eight-week follow-up.

Lieberman, Yalom, and Miles (1973) completed the most carefully designed and conducted study. They compared ten treatment methods for which, in most instances, two top advocates for each system were chosen to lead a group. For two systems, no leaders were required: Synanon and Bell-and-Howell Peer Tape. Each system and the way the group functions are described in detail in Chapter 2 of their book. Of those completing the groups, 50–70 percent (depending on the method of evaluation) experienced some positive change; 61 percent thought that they had learned a great deal. For those who changed positively, three out of four maintained their gains. All in all, experimental-control differences were modest, but probably meaningful and positive. For almost 80 percent of both participants and controls, specific positive changes were noted by their significant others. In general, these researchers concluded that their encounter groups were less effective than the results for psychotherapy reported by Bergin and Garfield (1971). Moreover, results for a technique varied markedly with different leaders: For one leader, a technique proved to be one of the best; whereas with another, it proved to be one of the poorest (least gains for clients and most casualties).

An outcome study using three different group methods for dealing with bereavement was conducted by Walls and Meyers (1984). Subjects were 38 females aged 30–65, widowed for three to twenty-five months, who were assigned to one of three treatment conditions. Treatment conditions consisted of a cognitive restructuring group, a behavioral skills group, a self-help group, and a delayed-treatment control group. Pre- and post-measurements were conducted on depression and amount of life events experienced as pleasant. Results revealed that subjects who remained in treatment were much older ($\bar{x} = 54.7$ years old) than dropouts ($\bar{x} = 47.6$ years old). No significant differences were found among treatment methods. However, the cognitive restructuring group demonstrated a marked reduction in depression and social anxiety, but reported fewer incidents of enjoyable and pleasant activities.

A study by Flowers (1978), involving frequency and intensity of positive and negative feedback for college students ($N = 9$) in group counseling with two therapists, found that negative feedback on the part of the therapist to the client increased the frequency of interactions between clients as compared with interactions between group members and therapists. When therapists gave more negative feedback of lower intensity, clients reported feeling more satisfaction with the group experience and trusted group members significantly more than when therapists gave primarily positive feedback. When the therapist increased the intensity of negative feedback to clients, they reported less satisfaction with the group experience and reported trusting fellow group members less, but continued the same frequency of member-to-member interactions. This study has limited generalizability due to its small number of subjects. However, it exemplifies the kind of study regarding specific processes that practitioners may find valuable.

Ofman (1965) tried to appraise the impact of group counseling on college students. Owing to the design of the experiment and the statistical methods used, it is difficult to assess the impact of counseling. The investigator's study should alert future researchers to some of the differences between experimental subjects and those who are selected as controls. He made a good case for a baseline group and for researchers' making a greater effort to control motivational factors. At the beginning of his study, there were no significant differences between volunteers in his treatment and control groups, but his subjects in the baseline group earned significantly higher GPAs than the volunteers. By the end of the experiment, his treated subjects had improved their grades sufficiently so that there was no longer a significant difference in GPAs between treated and baseline subjects. Furthermore, his treated subjects earned significantly higher GPAs at the end of his experiment than did his control group.

Roth, Mauksch, and Peiser (1967) provided group counseling for bright, underachieving undergraduates (52 counseled in groups of 7–12, and 52 controls). Counseling groups met twice a week for approximately one hour. The investigators concluded that these students do poorly in order to avoid risk taking and to maintain a dependent relationship with their family. Hence, the counselor tried to provide help with both study skills and these dynamics. Those counseled improved their GPAs more than their controls, and the follow-up appraisal revealed that they maintained their gains.

Spielberger, Weitz, and Denny (1962) evaluated the effectiveness of group counseling for anxious college freshmen. Volunteers who were provided group counseling showed greater improvement in GPAs than did the controls, who volunteered for group counseling but were not provided it. The investigators also found a significant relationship between the number of sessions clients attended and the improvement in their GPAs (a Pearson r of .63). From their analysis of MMPI scores, they concluded that high attenders may be tentatively described as active-repressive, middle attenders as passive-rebellious, and low attenders as passive-withdrawn and ruminative. In their later study, Spielberger and Weitz (1964) appear to have added subjects from another group of freshmen and to have made additional analyses of their data. Besides finding additional support for the findings reported above, they found proportionately fewer severe under-achievers among the anxious than among the nonanxious underachievers; failure dropout rate for anxious volunteers in 1959 was less than for nonanxious students; and failure dropout rate in 1960 was lower for anxious volunteers and anxious nonvolunteers than for nonanxious students. Spielberger and Weitz' (1964) rationale for providing counseling at the very beginning of college for these students is quoted below:

> There is little evidence, however, that personality problems are direct and immediate causes of poor academic performance. It seems more likely that, in response to the pressures of college life, students with personality problems are predisposed to develop maladaptive study habits and attitudes which, in turn, interfere with the learning process and lead to underachievement. For college students identified as having personality problems, preventive measures imple-

mented at the beginning of the freshman year would come at a time when the potential for serious maladaptive behavior is heightened by new environmental stresses (p. 1).

Tavormina (1975) evaluated the relative effectiveness of behavioral counseling and reflective group counseling with mothers of mentally retarded children. Compared to his waiting-list controls, clients in both treatment groups improved significantly, but those treated by the behavioral technique made significantly greater growth.

Teahan (1966) evaluated the effects of group psychotherapy on first-semester college sophomores who were in the top quarter of their high-school class, but were not successful as freshmen. Because he believed that certain aspects of their personality interfered with college success, the counselor focused attention on personal and emotional problems. He obtained significant improvement in GPAs. Those whose GPAs improved described their fathers as more dominating and ignoring than those whose grades did not improve. Those who improved most also tended to obtain high Ma scores on MMPI. The high F scores on MMPI suggest, the investigator concluded, that those most helped were more ready to discuss their personal problems, and their Si scores suggest that they were drawn into the group to satisfy their need for social interaction.

Thelen and Harris (1968) identified and contacted by letter 127 under-achievers: 52 did not respond; 38 responded and completed the 16 PF, but were not interested in group psychotherapy; and 37 completed the test and volunteered for group psychotherapy. The latter were divided randomly into treatment subjects and controls—with dropouts, these became $C = 13$ and $E = 19$ (four counseling groups). Those counseled improved their grades. The investigators concluded that those helped had less apprehension about treatment, were more self-accepting and accepted the notion of obtaining assistance. Those who volunteered for group psychotherapy have the most to gain from it and the most to lose from not obtaining it.

The primary focus of Wetzel, Kinney, Beavers, Harvey, and Urbanuk's (1976) treatment was to help patients each develop their own effective and satisfying means to get out of the hospital and stay out. From the beginning, the staff emphasized development of specific target behaviors for each, establishment of priorities, rapid pursuit of target behaviors, and short-term treatment. Inasmuch as Veteran Administration patients were released as soon as they achieved their goals, there was rapid turnover in membership. The outcomes appear to be promising, but the results were based upon informal questionnaire follow-up from patients after discharge. Nevertheless, their treatment seems to be promising; hence it should be evaluated more carefully.

GENERALIZATIONS ABOUT RESEARCH OUTCOMES

During the past decade, the research on outcomes of counseling as well as the helping skills of counselors and therapists have improved markedly, especially in group counseling; but, all the helping professions must learn to cooperate more effectively in order to protect the public from unscrupulous persons who offer professional services that they are unqualified to provide, especially in various group techniques. The helping professionals also must screen prospective helpers with greater care, improve the quality of professional preparation, and encourage practitioners to grow on the job. Much also must be done to help liaison workers and referrers, such as teachers and clergy, to provide quality support and encouragement and use peer-helping techniques, but without attempting to provide therapeutic service for which they are not qualified. The professionals must recognize that even qualified helpers can hurt as well as help certain clients under certain circumstances (Bergin & Garfield, 1971; Lieberman, Yalom, & Miles, 1973).

Meltzoff and Kornreich (1970) also concluded that the quality of research has improved:

> From every point of view (design, sampling, criteria, nature of controls, data analysis), the quality of research has improved along with the quantity.
> . . . Among the adequate studies, 84% showed positive effects of psychotherapy that were statistically significant. Similarly 75% of the questionable studies reported significant results (p. 174).

> The weight of experimental evidence is sufficient to enable us to reject the null hypothesis. Far more often than not, psychotherapy in a wide variety of types and with a broad range of disorders has been demonstrated under control conditions to be accompanied by positive changes in adjustment that can significantly exceed those that can be accounted for by passage of time alone (p. 175).

> There is little existing evidence of any systematic differences in efficacy between group and individual therapy. Studies that purport to show advantages of combination of the two methods are not sufficiently conclusive, either in design or analyses, to permit such conclusions (p. 183).

Strupp (1973b) draws a similar conclusion:

> During the past 30 years the quantity as well as quality of research contributions has grown, and there is every reason to believe that the coming decades will see intensification of this effort (p. 734).

> New treatment methods in this area, it may be observed, do not arise from the efforts of researchers or as the result of experimentation in the laboratory; instead, they emerge in response to social needs that are met by the ingenuity or inventiveness of charismatic therapists whose individual temperament and

philosophy of life are thoroughly intertwined with the therapeutic approach they espouse (p. 794).

> From everything that has been said, it follows that significant increments in knowledge, at least within the therapeutic framework, are likely to come from intensive study of individual cases in which disciplined observation is complemented by, and takes account of, the complex interaction of variables, a task that cannot be accomplished by statistical manipulations, although certain statistical techniques may be helpful in other respects (p. 799).

Inasmuch as there is clear evidence that individuals can be hurt as well as helped, practitioners as well as researchers must continue to look for the answer to the questions: Who was helped and hurt by this method, with whom, under what conditions, and with what kind of a treater? It also means that researchers must develop better criterion measures (an area in which the profession is seriously deficient at this time) to assess change and use multivariate statistical analysis to examine the interaction of process variables and outcome variables. Finally, since the treater is such an important variable in process (Grunebaum, 1975; Lieberman, Yalom, & Miles, 1973; Truax & Carkhuff, 1964), researchers must do everything possible to produce selection techniques that will enable them to select and prepare the best possible helpers. Furthermore, when they appraise a technique, they must make every effort to ensure that they have chosen treaters who accept it and are committed to using it effectively to help a particular set of subjects under a particular set of circumstances.

SUMMARY

Both the quality and quantity of outcome studies have improved in the last decade. Moreover, investigations are asking increasingly difficult questions. It is no longer sufficient to ask: "Was group counseling effective?" Today researchers are asking: "For whom was group counseling effective; with what quality level of leadership; with what type of clients; and what types of problems; and under what circumstances?" Increasingly, researchers are encouraged to use multivariate analyses to investigate process and outcome variables simultaneously.

Research questions and hypotheses must be formulated with greater care. Such careful planning identifies weaknesses that can be corrected prior to beginning the research, helps to ensure that the investigator collects the data required to test his hypotheses with statistical methods chosen, and helps to ensure that a well-designed plan is followed. If research consultants are to be used they should be involved early in order to improve the design; to select the best possible criterion measures; to ensure that proper methods are used to select research subjects and controls; to collect the data in manageable form; and to analyze the results appropriately.

These common weaknesses of outcome studies were discussed: (1) Researchers commonly fail to define and defend a clearly stated, researchable problem. (2) The treatment process is not defined with sufficient care and detail for another to replicate the study or even to determine whether similar results were obtained. (3) Treaters often are trainees with minimal experience and training. In order for methods to be compared, researchers must use treaters who are competent to provide the designated treatment(s), and where the experiment calls for the same treaters to use more than one technique, they must be equally competent in each and feel equally committed to provide quality service with each. (4) Researchers often fail to help each client define specific behavioral goals in precise measurable or observable terms. (5) Without adequate treatment goals, it is very difficult to define adequate criteria to appraise outcomes. (6) Even after researchers have helped their clients to define behavioral goals and clear criteria, they still must select or develop adequate criterion measures (and unfortunately they often use poor criterion measures). (7) Research subjects and control subjects are not selected with sufficient care (and often the sample is too small). (8) In addition to selecting appropriate statistical methods required to test the hypotheses, the researcher often fails to take necessary precautions to ensure that data were collected and subjects were sampled in a manner to justify the use of desired statistical analyses. (9) It is not sufficient to demonstrate that desired changes occurred during treatment. Follow-up studies are essential to determine whether gains achieved were maintained. Suggestions for coping with each of these weaknesses were discussed.

During the last decade research has improved, but many of the weaknesses described above still have not been adequately corrected. Nevertheless, perhaps the most serious problem with which the helping professions are faced today is improving the competencies of the helpers. Increasingly, however, researchers are selecting competent treaters to provide the prescribed treatment; helping clients to define meaningful, relevant, behavioral goals; helping them define criteria to appraise outcomes; selecting improved criterion measures; and obtaining better results than previously. The best designed studies conducted by the most competent professionals are obtaining the best results. Although clients may be hurt as well as helped, there is supporting evidence that competent professionals can help clients in groups.

References

Abramowitz, C. V.; Abramowitz, S. I.; Roback, H. B.; & Jackson, C. (1974). Differential effectiveness of directive and nondirective group therapies as a function of client internal–external control. *Journal of Consulting and Clinical Psychology, 42,* 849–853.

Barcai, A.; Unbarger, C.; Pierce, T.; & Chamberlain, P. (1973). A comparison of three group approaches to underachieving children. *American of Journal of Orthopsychiatry, 43,* 133–141.

Bartell, W. (1972). The effect of the intake interview on client-perceived outcomes of group counseling. Unpublished doctoral dissertation, Indiana State University, Terre Haute.

Bates, M. (1966). A test of group counseling. *Personnel and Guidance Journal, 46,* 749–573.

Benson, R. L., & Blocher, D. H. (1967). Evaluation of developmental counseling with groups of low achievers in high school setting. *The School Counselor, 14,* 215–220.

Bereiter, C. (1962). Use of tests to measure change. *Personnel and Guidance Journal, 41,* 6–ll.

Berg, I. A. (1952). Measures before and after therapy. *Journal of Clinical Psychology, 8,* 46–50.

Bergin, A. E. (1963). The effects of psychotherapy: Negative results revisited. *Journal of Counseling Psychology, 10,* 244–249.

Bergin, A. E., & Garfield, S. L. (1971). *Handbook for psychotherapy and behavior change.* New York: Wiley.

Bergin, A. E., & Lambert, M. J. (1978). The evaluation of therapeutic outcomes. In Bergin & S. L. Garfield (Eds.), *Handbook of psychotherapy and behavior change: An empirical analysis* (2nd ed.). New York: John Wiley & Sons.

Berry, K.; Turone, R.; Richard, J.; Hardt, P. (1980). Comparison of group therapy and behavioral modification with children. *Psychological Reports, 46,* 975–978.

Broedel, J.; Ohlsen, M.; Proff, F.; & Southard, C. (1960). The effects of group counseling on gifted underachieving adolescents. *Journal of Counseling Psychology, 7,* 163–170.

Brown, R. D. (1969). Effects of structured and unstructured group counseling with high- and low-anxious college underachievers. *Journal of Counseling Psychology, 16,* 209–214.

Bush, J. (1971). The effects of fixed and random actor interaction on individual goal attainment in group counseling. Unpublished doctoral dissertation, Indiana State University, Terre Haute.

Carkhuff, R. R., & Berenson, B. G. (1967). *Beyond counseling and therapy.* New York: Holt, Rinehart and Winston.

Catron, D. W. (1966). Educational-vocational group counseling: The effects on perceptions of self and others. *Journal of Counseling Psychology, 13,* 202–207.

Chestnut, W. J. (1965). The effects of structured and unstructured group counseling on male college students' underachievement. *Journal of Counseling Psychology, 24,* 388–394.

Clark, A., & Seals, J. (1984). Group counseling for ridiculed children. *Journal for Specialists in Group Work, 9,* 157–162.

Clements, B. E. (1966). Transitional adolescents, anxiety and group counseling. *Personal and Guidance Journal, 45,* 67–71.

Coche, E., & Dies, R. (1981). Integrating research findings into the practice of group psychotherapy. *Psychotherapy Theory, Research and Practice. 18,* 410–416.

Cohn, B. (1967). *Guidelines for future research on group counseling in the public school setting.* Washington, DC: American Personnel and Guidance Association.

Crow, M. L. (1971). A comparison of three group counseling techniques with sixth graders. *Elementary School Guidance and Counseling, 6,* 37–42.

Davis, J. L., & Sanborn, M.P. (1973). Getting student action on guidance goals. *Journal of Counseling Psychology, 20,* 209–213.

Davis, R. G. (1948). Group therapy and social acceptance in first grade. *Elementary School Journal,* 219–223.

De Esch, J. B. (1974). The use of Ohlsen's model of group counseling with secondary students identified as being disruptive to the educational process. Unpublished doctoral dissertation, Indiana State University, Terre Haute.

Deffenbacher, J. L., & Kemper, C. C. (1974). Counseling test-anxious sixth graders. *Elementary School Guidance and Counseling, 9,* 22–29.

Dickenson, W. A., & Truax, C. B. (1966). Group counseling with college under-achievers. *Personnel and Guidance Journal, 45,* 243–247.

Dressel, P. L. (Ed.) (1961). *Evaluation in higher education.* Boston: Houghton Mifflin.

Edwards, A. L., & Cronbach, L. J. Experimental design for research in psychotherapy. *Journal of Clinical Psychology, 8,* 51–59.

Finney, B. C., & Van Dalsem, E. (1969). Group counseling for gifted underachieving high school students. *Journal of Counseling Psychology, 16,* 87–94.

Forgy, E. W., & Black, J. D. (1954). A follow-up after three years of clients counseled by two methods. *Journal of Counseling Psychology, 1,* 1–8.

Flowers, J. (1978). The effect of therapist support and encounter on the percentage of client-client interactions in group therapy. *Journal of Community Psychology, 6,* 69–73.

Gazda, G. M., & Ohlsen, M. M. (1961). The effects of short-term group counseling on prospective counselors. *Personnel and Guidance Journal, 39,* 634–638.

Gilbreath, S. H. (1967). Group counseling, dependence, and college male achievement. *Journal of Counseling Psychology, 14,* 449–453.

Gilliland, B. E. (1968). Small group counseling with negro adolescents in a public high school. *Journal of Counseling Psychology, 15,* 147–152.

Glasser, W. (1969). *Schools without failure.* New York: Harper & Row.

Gorlow, L.; Hoch, E.; & Teleschow, E. (1952). *The nature of nondirective group psychotherapy.* New York: Bureau of Publications, Teachers College, Columbia University.

Graff, R.; MacLean, G. D.; & Loving, A. (1971). Group reactive inhibition and reciprocal inhibition therapies with anxious college students. *Journal of Counseling Psychology, 18,* 431–436.

Grunebaum, H. (1975). A soft-hearted review of hard-nosed research on groups. *Group Psychotherapy, 25,* 185–199.

Hansen, J. C.; Niland, T. M.; & Zani, L. P. (1969). Model reinforcement in group counseling with elementary school children. *Personnel and Guidance Journal, 47,* 741–744.

Hansen, J. C.; Zimpfer, D. G.; & Easterling, R. E. (1967). A study of the relationships in multiple counseling. *Journal of Educational Research, 60,* 461–462.

Hansen, J. T., & Sanders, D. L. (1973). Differential effects of individual and group counseling on realism of vocational choice. *Journal of Counseling Psychology, 20,* 541–544.

Hartley, D.; Roback, H. B.; & Abramowitz, S. I. (1976). Deterioration in encounter groups. *American Psychologist, 31,* 247–255.

Hartley, E., & Rosenbaum, M. (1963). Criteria used by group psychotherapists for judging improvement in patients. *International Journal of Group Psychotherapy, 13,* 80–83.

Henry, S., & Kilmann, P. (1979). Student counseling groups in senior high school settings: An evaluation of outcome. *Journal of School Psychology, 17,* 27–46.

Hilkey, J. H. (1975). The effects of video-tape pretraining and guided performance on the process and outcomes of group counseling. Unpublished doctoral dissertation, Indiana State University, Terre Haute.

Hill, C. (1975). A process approach for establishing counseling goals and outcomes. *Personnel and Guidance Journal, 53,* 571–573.

Hinds, W. C., & Roehlke, H. J. (1970). A learning theory approach to group counseling with elementary school children. *Journal of Counseling Psychology, 17,* 49–55.

Horenstein, D.; Houston, B. K.; & Holmes, D. S. (1973). Clients', therapists', and judges' evaluations of psychotherapy. *Journal of Counseling Psychology, 20,* 149–153.

Howard, W., & Zimpfer, D. G. (1972). The findings of research on group approaches in elementary guidance and counseling. *Elementary School Guidance and Counseling, 6,* 163–169.

Jensen, B. T.; Coles, G.; & Nestor, B. (1955). The criterion problem in guidance research. *Journal of Counseling Psychology, 2,* 58–61.

Jesness, C. F. (1975). Comparative effectiveness of behavior modification and transactional analysis programs for delinquents. *Journal of Counseling and Clinical Psychology, 43,* 758–779.

Kefauver, G. N., & Hand, H. C. (1971). *Appraising guidance services in secondary schools.* New York: Macmillan.

Kelly, E. W., & Mathews, D. B. (1971). Group counseling with discipline problem children at elementary school level. *The School Counselor, 18,* 273–278.

Kern, R., & Kirby, J. H. (1971). Utilizing peer helper influence in group counseling. *Elementary School Guidance and Counseling, 6,* 70–75.

Kivlighan, D.; McGovern, T.; & Cerazzini, J. (1984). Effects of content and timing of structuring interventions on group process and outcome. *Journal of Counseling Psychology, 31,* 363–370.

Krumboltz, J. D., & Thoresen, C. E. (1964). The effects of behavioral counseling in group and individual settings on information-seeking behavior. *Journal of Counseling Psychology, 11,* 324–333.

Leary, T. (1957). *Interpersonal diagnosis of personality.* New York: Ronald.

Lieberman, M. A., Yalom, I. D., & Miles, M. D. (1973). *Encounter groups: First facts.* New York: Basic Books.

Lodato, F. J.; Sokoloff, M. A.; & Schwartz, L. J. (1964). Group counseling as a method of modifying attitudes in slow learners. *School Counselor, 12,* 27–29.

Maliver, B. L. (1973). *The encounter game.* New York: Stein & Day.

Mayer, C. (1982). Behavioral effects of using conduct problem adolescents as cross-age tutors. *Psychology in the Schools, 19*(3), 360–366.

Mayer, G., Kranzler, G. D., & Matthes, W. (1967). Elementary school guidance and peer relations. *Personnel and Guidance Journal, 46,* 360–365.

McCarthy, M. V. (1959). *The effectiveness of a modified counseling procedure in promoting learning among bright underachieving adolescents* (Research Project No. SAE-6401). Washington, DC: Department of Health, Education and Welfare.

Meade, E. J. (1972). *A foundation goes to school.* New York: Ford Foundation.

Meehl, P. E. (1959). Some ruminations on the validation of clinical procedures. *Canadian Journal of Psychology, 13,* 102–128.

Meltzoff, J., & Kornreich, M. (1970). *Research in psychotherapy.* New York: Atherton.

Mezzano, J. A. (1967). A consideration for group counselors: Degree of investment. *School Counselor, 14,* 167–169.

Moulin, E. K. (1970). The effects of client-centered group counseling using play media on the intelligence, achievement, and psycholinguistic abilities of underachieving primary school children. *Elementary School Guidance and Counseling, 5,* 85–89.

Novick, J. I. (1965). Comparison of short-term group and individual psychotherapy in effecting changes in nondesirable behavior children. *International Journal of Group Psychotherapy, 15,* 366–373.

Ofman, W. (1965). Evaluation of a group counseling procedure. *Journal of Counseling Psychology, 11,* 152–159.

Ohlsen, M. M. (1974). *Guidance services in the modern school.* New York: Harcourt.

Ohlsen, M. M., & Gazda, G. M. (1965). Counseling underachieving bright pupils. *Education, 86,* 78–81.

Omizo, M., Cubberly, W., Omizo, S. (1985). The effects of rational-emotive education groups on self-concept and locus of control among learning disabled children. *Exceptional Child, 32,* 13–19.

Paritzky, R., & Magoon, T. (1982). Goal attainment scaling models for assessing group counseling. *Personnel and Guidance Journal, 60,* 281–384.

Pattison, E. M. (1965). Evaluation studies of group psychotherapy. *International Journal of Group Psychotherapy, 15,* 382–393.

Paul, G. L. (1967). Strategy of outcome research in psychotherapy. *Journal of Consulting Psychology, 31,* 109–118.

Randolph, D. L., & Saba, R. G. (1973). Changing behavior through modeling and consultation. *Elementary School Guidance and Counseling,* 98–106.

Rickard, H. C. (1965). Tailored criteria of change in psychotherapy. *Journal of General Psychology, 72,* 63–68.

Rickard, H. C., & Brown, E. C. (1960). Evaluation of a psychotherapy case in terms of change in a relevant behavior. *Journal of Clinical Psychology, 16,* 93.

Rogers, C. R. (1968). Interpersonal relationships: Year 2000. *Journal of Applied Behavioral Science, 4,* 265–280.

Rosenstock, H., & McLaughlin, M. (1982). Positive group efficacy in adolescent treatment. *Journal of Clinical Psychiatry, 43,* 58–61.

Roth, R. M., Mauksch, H. O., & Peiser, K. (1967). The non-achievement syndrome, group therapy, and achievement change. *Personnel and Guidance Journal, 46,* 393–398.

Russell, E. (1978). The facts about encounter groups: First facts. *Journal of Clinical Psychology, 34,* 130–137.

Sarason, I. G., & Ganzer, V. J. (1973). Modeling and group discussion in the rehabilitation of juvenile delinquents. *Journal of Counseling Psychology, 20,* 442–449.

Seligman, M. E. (1975). *On depression, development and death.* San Francisco: Freeman.

Sethna, E. R., & Harrington, J. A. (1971) Evaluation of group psychotherapy. *British Journal of Psychiatry, 118,* 641–658.

Smith, R. D., & Evans, J. R. (1973). Comparison of experimental group guidance and individual counseling as facilitators of vocational development. *Journal of Counseling Psychology, 20,* 202–208.

Sonstegard, M. (1961). Group counseling methods with parents of elementary school children as related to pupil growth and development (mimeographed report). State College of Iowa.

Spielberger, C. O.; Weitz, H.; & Denny, J. P. (1962). Group counseling and academic performance of anxious college freshmen. *Journal of Counseling Psychology, 9,* 195–204.

Spielberger, C. O., & Weitz, H. (1964). *Improving academic performance of anxious college freshmen* (Psychological Monograph No. 590). Washington, DC: American Psychological Association.

Strupp, H. H. (1973a). The experimental group and the psychotherapeutic enterprise. *International Journal of Group Psychotherapy, 23,* 115–124.

Strupp, H. H. (1973b). *Psychotherapy: Clinical research and theoretical issues.* New York: Jason Aronson.

Tavormina, J. B. (1975). Relative effects of behavioral and reflective group counseling with parents of mentally retarded children. *Journal of Consulting and Clinical Psychology, 43,* 22–31.

Teahan, J. E. (1966). Effect of group psychotherapy on academic low achievers. *International Journal of Group Psychotherapy, 16,* 78–85.

Thelen, M. H., & Harris, C. S. (1968). Personality of college underachievers who improve with group psychotherapy. *Personnel and Guidance Journal, 46,* 561–566.

Thoresen, C. E., & Krumboltz, J. D. (1967). Relationship of counselor reinforcement of selected responses to external behavior. *Journal of Counseling Psychology, 14,* 260–266.

Tiktin, E. A., & Cobb, C. (1983). Treating post-divorce adjustment in latency age children: A focused group paradigm. *Social Work with Groups, 1983, Sum. Vol. 6 (2),* 53–66.

Tosi, D.; Swanson, C.; & MacLean, P. (1970). Group counseling with nonverbalizing elementary school children. *Elementary School Guidance and Counseling, 4,* 260–266.

Tosi, D.; Upshaw, K.; Lande, A.; & Waldron, M. A. (1971). Group counseling with nonverbalizing students. *Journal of Counseling Psychology, 18,* 437–440.

Truax, C. B., & Carkhuff, R. R. (1964). The old and new theory and research in counseling and psychotherapy. *Personnel and Guidance Journal, 42,* 860–866.

Twardosz, S.; Nordquist, V.; Simon, R.; & Bofkin, D. (1983). The effect of group affection activities on the interaction of socially isolated children. *Analysis and Intervention in Development Disabilities, 3,* 311–338.

Walls, N., & Meyers, A. (1984). Outcome in group treatments for bereavement: Experimental results and recommendations for clinical practice. *International Journal of Mental Health, 13,* 126–147.

Wetzel, M. C.; Kinney, J. M.; Beavers, M. E.; Harvey, R. T.; & Urbanuk, G. W. (1976). Action laboratory: Behavior group therapy in a traditional context. *International Journal of Group Psychotherapy, 26,* 59–70.

Wigell, W. W., & Ohlsen, M. M. (1962). To what extent is affect a function of topic and referent in group counseling? *American Journal of Orthopsychiatry, 32,* 728–735.

Wolfgang, A., & Pierson, D. (1977). The relationship of group research and current practices in counseling on therapy in Metro Toronto. *Canadian Counselor, 11,* 185–191.

Zimpfer, D., & Waltman, D. (1982). Correlates of effectiveness in group counseling. *Small Group Behavior, 13,* 275–290.

17

PROFESSIONAL PREPARATION AND ETHICAL GUIDELINES

THE COUNSELOR

The counselor is an approachable, committed person who has mastered essential helping skills. Those who are involved in training professional group counselors face common issues with those who prepare other professionals: (1) selecting good prospects for professional training; (2) determining what is to be taught and the manner in which it is to be presented; (3) deciding how to organize professional material into instructional units; (4) developing a plan for appraising the progress of students' learning; and (5) facilitating students' development of a professional identity and affiliation within the profession.

STUDENT SELECTION

Not all persons have the characteristics to become effective counselors, nor do all counselors have the characteristics to become effective when working in a group setting. Since there are more people interested in entering training programs than there are positions available, persons involved in the training process must develop skills for identifying those who offer the most promise for becoming effective in the field. Counselors prefer to help people achieve their goals rather than act as gatekeepers for the profession. On the other hand, admitting poor risks and ignoring their early unsuccessful efforts in helping others is not being kind nor is it professionally responsible. The more time, effort, and money the poor prospect invests before being removed from a program (or admits that he

378

or she does not have the potential to be an effective counselor and self-selects out), the greater the loss of resources and sense of self-respect.

Screening Procedures

A number of screening procedures have been used, including undergraduate grade-point average, Graduate Record Examination scores, Miller Analogy Test scores, and other objective inventories such as the MMPI, the 16-PF, and Edward's Personal Preference Inventory. Some programs have used counseling-related measures, such as Carkhuff's (1969) scales, counselor responses to videotapes (Carr et al., 1972), and an intake interview similar to the one used to screen clients for participation in group counseling. Overall, what has been found is that students who have demonstrated higher achievement in the form of grades and standardized instruments do better than students who show lower ability; students who have higher skills in identifying and providing effective human relationship conditions on Carkhuff's scales or videotaped interviews perform better, in general, in counseling programs, than those who score lower.

At the same time, counselor educators must be careful to not exclude persons who have a high level of commitment and interest, but who may not score as well on standardized evaluation procedures. Persons from minority or handicapped backgrounds, for example, may have good potential to learn effective counseling skills while not being able to demonstrate an ability to score high on standardized inventories. Thus, counselor training programs should be willing to take the time and energy to identify the potential of applicants for programs even though the process may not be as easy as it would be for other programs.

PROGRAM CONTENT

Counselor training programs are becoming more specific in identifying what the content of educational experiences should be, and a number of standards have been developed for evaluating and certifying counselor training offerings. For group-counselor training, the Association for Specialists in Group Work (ASGW) has developed a listing of standards that approved programs should include in training. ASGW's *Professional Standards for Training of Group Counselors* (1983) represents the minimum cognitive and applied competencies that ASGW has identified for the preparation of group counselors. The categories described in the ASGW standards are:

Knowledge practice areas with survey item(s) under each

Major theoretical approaches
    Understand current models and theories
    Theories of interpersonal relations
    Theories and models of group counseling

Group dynamics principles
    Understand small group dynamics and process
    Group dynamics content

Personal characteristics of group leaders
    Understand group leadership and intervention
    Develop specific leader skills/competencies
    Leadership style
    Group intervention techniques

Ethical problems and considerations in groups
    Ethics and professional issues

Research in group counseling

Major group work modes
    Special types of groups

Process components of group work
    Practical considerations
    Group process (interaction, stages, etc.)
    Design a group work program

Facilitative and debilitative member roles
    Problems and process issues in groups
    Dealing with problem group members

Advantages/disadvantages of group counseling
    Evaluation and assessment

Clinical practice areas with survey item(s) under each

Critique of group tapes
    Videotaping
    Audiotaped/videotaped samples

Observation
    Demonstration/observation of group counseling
    Films or other media

Participation as a client
    Personal growth experience
    Self-directed group experience
    Laboratory, T-group experience

Lead with a partner
    Co-leading groups

Lead alone
    Leadership of in-class group
    Leadership of an outside group

Fieldwork or internship

Basic Conditions for Training

Yalom (1985) identified four major components essential to training in group therapy: (1) observing experienced group therapists at work; (2) close clinical supervision during one's first groups; (3) a personal group experience; (4) a personal psychotherapeutic or self-exploratory experience. The guidelines spelled out by ASGW have the characteristics that Yalom identified.

Capuzzi and Muffett (1980) suggested that programs that train group counselors should include graduate-level course work, one-to-one counseling experiences, self-awareness training, skills in interpersonal relationships, and supervised experiences.

Stockton (1980) reported that four areas of group work identified most in the literature on group counseling including didactic skills and knowledge, individual counseling skills, knowledge of group dynamics, and good personal adjustment.

Huhn, Zimpfer, Waltman, and Williamson (1985) conducted an extensive survey of programs that provide professional preparation for group counseling. They identified that there are 475 counselor education programs but only 157 of those have faculty who are members of both the ASGW and the Association for Counselor Education and Supervision (ACES). They suggest that there should be some examination as to why so few group and counselor education trainers belong to the two groups. In their review Huhn et al. identified training content areas, by percentages, for programs involved in training group counselings. Further, they sampled the texts, the techniques, and assessment procedures for the programs.

Experiential Components

Several reviews of programs that provide training for group counselors have provided additional support for the experiential learning component of the program ASGW has adopted. Lechowicz and Gazda (1975), for example, found that experts in group counseling rated experiential objectives highest on a list of 179 behavioral objectives. And Dies (1974) reported that psychologists, psychiatrists, and social workers rated programs that contained experiential components higher than those lacking such components. Jacobs, Brown, and Randolph (1974) found that professionals prefer practical components, such as experiences for trainees, while Smith (1976) found close supervision to be very important.

Lecture/Didactic Components

While an emphasis on practical and experiential activities has been identified, a review of training programs that actually prepare group counselors found that the teaching method most commonly used was the lecture/discussion method (Zimpfer, Waltman, Williamson, & Huhn, 1985). Zimpfer et al. reported that

95% of the training programs they surveyed used the lecture/discussion for student teaching, while fewer than 70% reported actual leading of groups, using supervision, or permitting observation as teaching methods. Zimpfer et al. report that "programs place relatively lower emphasis on clinical practice than on the knowledge domain" (p. 139).

Practicum Component

Even recognizing the low emphasis placed upon the experiential and practical aspects of group counseling, the standards of ASGW are minimal in requirements for training counselors. There is a recommendation of at least 80 clock hours to be given to the various experiential activities, but this time can include evaluating tapes of sessions and observing groups, as well as leading them. Zimpfer et al. recommend that to achieve adequate learning of group counseling skills will require 300–400 hours (three to four courses), rather than 80 hours suggested by ASGW. And since the majority of programs do not even achieve the recommended 80 hours, training seems to be inadequate given the standards established by group-counseling leaders. With fewer than two-thirds of programs training group counselors requiring their students to lead a group, it is unlikely that beginning counselors will develop sufficient skills to be able to operate at even the minimal level of expertise given the current training situation. Indeed, in the original development of training standards for ASGW, Kottler (1981) specified 225 as the preferred rate of clinical practice and 460 hours as the ideal rate.

Zimpfer et al. (1985) further found in their survey of training programs for group counselors that the average number of group trainers on a faculty was 2.3 with more than one-third of all group programs having only one faculty member who was a group-counselor educator. The average number of courses being offered in training programs was 2.2, with 64% of programs offering two or fewer courses for all training levels combined. Zimpfer et al. therefore concluded that "it is doubtful whether preparation programs presently have the resources or commitment to meet their standards adequately" (p. 139). Therefore, continuing education following completion of basic training appears to be imperative. This, too, presents a problem: The current ASGW standards dropped the recommendation of ongoing professional development as a standard. And the Zimpfer study reported that only 18% of the programs surveyed offered in-service work for ongoing learning experiences of those in the field.

Entry Standards

Professional preparation is designed to enable those who do group counseling to master essential professional knowledge and facilitative behaviors. The ASGW standards are concerned with the philosophy and objectives of a program; the way in which a program should be developed; its staff competencies; the quality of instruction; its program of studies; its supervised experiences; and the methods used by the staff to select, retain, endorse, and place students. The minimum one-year graduate program includes philosophy and principles of counseling; use of appraisal and measurement techniques; statistics and research methods (including data-processing and computer utilization); career development; counseling theory and practice; group-counseling procedures; professional relationship and ethics; coordinations and administration of counseling services; and supervised experiences in all essential components of the counselors' work. Most professional organizations now endorse a minimum two-year graduate program for counselors. Usually, it includes some preparation in group-counseling techniques.

Ohlsen's Program

For carefully screened, practicing counselors who had completed at least the minimum one-year graduate program and were endorsed by counseling practicum supervision, Ohlsen (1975) described a twelve-semester-hour program that has been designed to prepare successful, practicing counselors to do group counseling. The program, while preceding the ASGW guidelines, is consistent with the training expectations spelled out by ASGW.

Group Dynamics Laboratory. Group dynamics laboratory is designed to increase students' sensitivity and improve their interpersonal skills. Intensive, small group experiences—including, perhaps, an off-campus weekend retreat—are supplemented by skill-building activities to promote increased knowledge of group dynamics theory and to encourage enrollees to explore the relevance of their knowledge for their personal as well as their professional lives.

Group Counseling. The group-counseling course includes considerable reading in the professional journals as well as in textbooks. This text covers the basic topics of the course. Class discussions focus on clarifying and implementing ideas. Case materials, recordings, and demonstrations are often used.

Group-Counseling Practicum. Each enrollee describes group counseling for prospective clients, conducts intake interviews, and selects the best combination of clients for two counseling groups, with the assistance of a supervisor and a feedback partner (a fellow enrollee selected by the practicum student). Besides weekly supervision by both the supervisor and the feedback partner, the student is supervised twice during the term by guest supervisors. Moreover, every enrollee is expected to come to practicum prepared to present a critique of recorded sessions and to solicit feedback on particular parts of the session. Although audio recordings are usually used for supervision, enrollees are expected to submit periodically a video recording of their counseling sessions.

Participation as a Client in a Counseling Group. Students select their counselor from those available each term, schedule their intake interview, and demonstrate their readiness for group counseling. In other words, procedures described in Chapter 1 are followed. Perhaps the counselors devote a more than usual amount of attention to the extent of the client's interest in having experience as a client, its potential benefits, and the commitment to talk openly about what bothers him. Care must be taken to protect the confidentiality of students while at the same time providing them an experiential learning experience.

For this program a follow-up evaluation was developed to solicit trainees' appraisal of each component of the program. Their responses clearly indicated that the program improved their counseling skills and their personal adjustment (Ohlsen, 1975).

Evaluating Group Counselor Preparation

Most graduate professional programs appraise enrollees' mastery of professional knowledge. It is more difficult to evaluate their mastery of helping skills. It is even more difficult to evaluate the extent to which enrollees implement their new professional knowledge and skills. Nevertheless, those who prepare counselors must assess the impact of their programs on student attitudes, values, professional skills, and on their commitment to implement their new knowledge and skills on the job. An adequate evaluation of counselor's preparation includes periodic appraisal of knowledge and skills by carefully constructed achievement and performance tests during preparation; periodic interviews with enrollees during preparation to appraise their progress, to identify problems with which they would like assistance, and to help them identify resources for assistance; end-of-preparation appraisal to evaluate adequacy of various components of the program, working relationships, teaching materials, facilities, and the degree to which program objectives were achieved; and follow-up visits to each student's place of employment, if possible. Perhaps the follow-up visits are the most important of all. The visit provides feedback on the value of specific components of the training program from a practitioner's perspective. Furthermore, when counselor's know that they are going to be visited on the job, they tend to be more highly motivated to implement their new helping skills and to be more innovative—knowing that they can count on support and consultation help from the follow-up visitor.

There can be no substitute for staff members in the training programs who are enthusiastic about their profession; who possess good helping skills and keep up-to-date; who can teach; who are allocated adequate time to supervise; who have the knowledge and courage to screen applicants; who know how to encourage students and can motivate them to learn; who care about their students; and who can do research that contributes to improving helping skills.

Evaluating Programs

Students selecting training in group counseling should investigate the extent to which the programs to which they are applying meet at least the minimal standards established by ASGW, including the experiential and supervised experiences. For programs that do not meet the minimal requirements and that do not provide an opportunity to lead groups under supervision as part of the learning experience, students should inquire as to why the minimal level of training is not met. Furthermore, applicants should inquire as to whether the persons teaching group classes and practica are, in fact, trained in group work themselves and have experience that will be relevant to students. Also, students should inquire as to whether faculty belong to ASGW and/or other relevant group organizations. Faculty who are not active in their professional organizations, at least through membership maintenance, are unlikely to be current in their knowledge and familiarity of the field.

Appraising Progress

Zimpfer et al. (1985) in their survey of group-counselor training programs found that the most common methods for evaluating student progress was class participation (85%), written examinations (80%), term papers (59%), self ratings (39%), and ratings by other trainees (37%). For assessing skills, Zimpfer et al. reported that 79% of the programs relied upon *in vivo* observation and feedback by the supervisor.

The most commonly used assessment methods in the training programs surveyed were paper-and-pencil type measures. These are not likely to be the most effective way to measure the current state of abilities or skills. Since Zimpfer et al. reported that fewer than two-thirds of the programs actually had students conducting groups, it is understandable why programs use paper-and-pencil evaluations. They probably have insufficient assessment opportunity to assess skills and have to rely upon written evaluations.

Counselor Certification

Increasingly those who prepare counselors are being asked to endorse graduates of their programs for certification or licensing. Certainly, they learn many things about these prospective professionals in teaching and supervising them in practice and internships that are not assessed on the usual licensing examination. Whether or not formal examinations are required by the state for certification or licensing, this practice makes those who prepare counselors accept responsibility for their "products." Perhaps this procedure also will encourage counselor educators to screen candidates more carefully and assess their growth during training with greater care. Carkhuff (1972) advises:

A technology allows us to grow. The choice is ours. We can continue to live like fools producing unmotivated counselors with 13% success rates or motivated counselors with 25% success rates or even 50% or 67% success rates. Or we can demand of ourselves and the counselors we train a level of skill acquisition necessary for success rates closer to 100%. And in those instances where we fall shy of our goal, we can determine the reason why. We can choose, as our helpees, between the resisting growth and growing. When we choose for ourselves we choose for mankind. If we cannot choose to grow, then there is no future for us, our profession, or our world (p. 29).

Student Evaluation

Assessment of student progress and ability should occur as a regular part of each course. Program faculty should also have a process for evaluating each student on a regular basis in order to be able to provide the student with feedback about performance and likelihood of success in the training program. Faculty have a professional obligation to provide students with direct and honest evaluations of the student's level of skill attainment and whether the faculty see the student being able to function effectively as a counselor. The task of faculty is not to select a body of students who will mirror exactly their background and training (traditionally male, white, middle-class orientation), but rather one that will identify capable students from a variety of backgrounds. There should be a special emphasis on facilitating the learning opportunities of students from lower socioeconomic backgrounds, from minority racial groups, and for students with handicapping conditions. Students with special conditions often do not do as well on standardized measures as do middle-class majority students. For that reason, counselor educators must pay special attention to ways in which the group-counseling processes may be taught to students, and used by those students, in a professional and responsible manner. For example, blind students can learn group-counseling skills and can be very effective, particularly when working with a co-counselor to facilitate awareness of nonverbals within the group.

To work with students from minority backgrounds in a counseling program requires that faculty clearly identify what the characteristics are that contribute to effective students in counseling and to identify how minority students may be helped to be as successful as possible without compromising the work of the counselor.

Professional Identity

Members' services and the conditions under which those services can be provided are defined by the profession. Entry into a profession is usually controlled by the profession, and is based upon a common body of professional knowledge and skills specified by a commission named by the leaders in the profession. Therefore, professional schools and colleges must try to admit to the program only those who would benefit from professional preparation and qualify for a license upon completion of the program. Further, faculty must represent the profession by being involved and by modeling the behaviors that students will be expected to demonstrate as members of the profession. Also, faculty will most likely be recommending students to the profession in the form of providing letters of recommendation to membership committees and to state or national certification or regulatory offices.

Professional Recognition

Standards of professional performance are also determined by the profession. Therefore, only a qualified member can evaluate a practitioner's performance for salary increases, promotions, or tenure. For many school counselors, this has been a problem because educators who are not qualified as counselors have been allowed to define their responsibilities and evaluate their performance. Consequently, other professionals question the professional status of such counselors.

Those who provide leadership for various group procedures have a similar problem in community agencies. Persons from other disciplines (and sometimes without adequate professional preparation) present themselves as qualified to lead various types of groups. Usually, the unqualified, irresponsible leaders do not belong to any professional organization. Consequently, no professional group tends to accept responsibility for screening, for licensing, or for appraising the quality of these unqualified leaders' services, or for ensuring that they function ethically. When there is no one to protect the client's welfare, the odds are greatest that clients will be hurt rather than helped.

Professional Certification

Fortunately, a number of professional organizations have developed guidelines for counseling procedures to protect the public, to communicate that there are competent professionals doing group work, and to offer support for their qualified leaders of groups. These organizations include the American Group Psychotherapy Association, the American Association for Counseling and Development, the American Mental-Health Counselors Association, the American Rehabilitation Counseling Association, the Association for Specialists in Group Work, the International Association of Applied Social Psychologists, the National Board of Certified Counselors, the National Training Laboratories, and University and College Counseling Center Directors.

These organizations have little impact, though, without members. Therefore, practicing counselors must identify relevant groups and become members, and they must also work to have colleagues and other professionals become members. Organizations generally have some censoring role for evaluating professionals who are not working within ethical or professional guidelines. The organizations, though, generally have little impact beyond the membership of the particular organization, and so it is important that people identify with and develop a professional relationship with relevant organizations.

Continued Professional Development

Associated with professional practice is a need for a commitment to ongoing professional training. The kind of person the counselor is determines both the counseling style and the motivation for continuing growth. The counselor must strive to be the best possible, while being aware of shortcomings and areas that need strengthening. Counselors need to ask themselves regularly about their progress and their effectiveness, using questions such as these:

- Can and will clients talk openly about the problems that worry and upset them?
- Do I believe that my clients can define precisely the new behaviors they desire and are committed to implement?
- Do I believe that my clients possess the potential for learning their desired new behaviors?
- What have I done to enhance each client to accept responsibility for learning new behaviors? to teach clients to recognize and reinforce each other's independent, responsible behaviors?
- What do I do when I feel I know what is best for a client and he is tempted to do something else?
- What do I do when a client appeals to my need for power and control?
- What have I done to enhance each client's learning to function increasingly independently? How do I really feel when a dependent client no longer seems to need me . . . or admire me?

True professionals make the most of their opportunities for personal and professional development during graduate education and continue their growth on the job. Employers who are interested in providing good counseling services employ competent counselors who have the potential for growth, intellectual curiosity, and the commitment to grow and provide them with the type of supervision that enhances growth.

Continued Professional Training

Even where good supervision is provided, the professional counselor must take initiative to ensure continuing professional growth. This growth may occur through attending conferences, conventions, and workshops. Several professional organizations offer training workshops prior to or following annual conventions. A number of them also provide for regional training workshops. Further, most states have state counseling organizations that both sponsor outside workshop presenters and also offer presentations workshops/conventions that feature local presenters. Within a given community counselors may establish an organization to meet monthly or quarterly. In one region, counselors meet one morning a week for breakfast and one person is responsible for each session to present some new information or a new method or technique. The group is comprised of counselors from public schools, but has become sufficiently popular that agency counselors and several counselor educators have joined in for the weekly meetings.

Professional growth is an obligation that the counselor owes to the clients being served and also to herself. Professional growth provides for the opportunity to continue learning and growing; and without that experience, counselors can begin to wither and die, both professionally and personally. So counselors do owe it to themselves to stay active in order to be healthy, contributing persons.

Continued Skill Evaluations

Counselors must believe in themselves and the methods they use, feel supported by colleagues and supervisors, and realize to whom they can turn for assistance when it is needed. Counselors need to develop at least one trusted colleague with whom they can discuss cases, solicit feedback on ideas, and criticize audio and video recordings. Best results are obtained when counselors and their colleagues use some guidelines for critiquing a session. A six-column worksheet on which the counselor records the following data has been helpful for many: (1) the significant feelings expressed by each client; (2) responses, if any, that the counselor made to each feeling; (3) alternate or, perhaps, more productive responses that could have been made; (4) possible behavioral goals for each feeling; (5) mini-goals or immediate actions that the client could take to implement the goals; and (6) feelings experienced by the counselor at that moment in the interaction.

When following the process, counselors are encouraged to listen to a taped session, complete as many of the columns as possible, and note specific spots where they would like colleagues' assistance prior to meeting with them. Beginners often request assistance in completing columns 1, 2, and 3. If, however, the counselor is to help clients learn new behaviors, she must also give attention to columns 4 and 5. To discover where one's personal needs may be interfering with effectiveness as a counselor, the counselor must direct attention to column 6. The worksheet can be used to help the counselor identify significant new therapeutic material (column 1); to improve responses to therapeutic material (columns 2 and 3); to help clients formulate new goals and clarify old ones (column 4); to help clients decide where to initiate new behaviors (column 5); and to be open about the counselor's own feelings and needs and to use them therapeutically (column 6). The worksheet can also be used to ask why a given client is causing the counselor to feel and react as she does, and to ask how to use the responses to better understand and respond to that client.

Such experiences with trusted colleagues help provide the basic support system that everyone requires for personal and professional growth. It provides encouragement and feedback when it is needed. It encourages professionals to implement new practices; to define precise new professional goals; to discover and develop new, improved criteria for appraising their professional services; and to explore new and improved ways of serving their clients.

Continuing Supervision

Good supervision enhances continuing growth on the job. Best results tend to be achieved when the supervisor looks upon supervision as a leadership rather than as a regulatory function. The former stresses support, encouragement, and reinforcement of desired new behaviors; whereas the latter stresses judgment, criticism, and enforcement of policies. Counselors must believe that their supervisor respects them, genuinely wants to help them, and is competent to do so. Besides exhibiting caring for them, a supervisor can aid them best by helping them define specific behavioral goals, recognize and build upon their own professional strengths, and develop a support system for themselves (both a group of colleagues such as described above and a support system of friends and relatives for an enriched personal life).

Under such circumstances, counselors feel sufficiently secure to request assistance and to discuss openly specific incidents for which they desire help. They can recall how they felt about the troublesome incidents; admit their mistakes; suggest what they would like to say or do the next time a similar situation occurs; and select from the supervisor's suggestions those they can adapt to their lifestyle. With a favorable psychological climate and the precise kind of feedback provided by a device like the worksheet described earlier, a counselor can discover her own deficiencies and uncover ways of correcting them. Although the very best counseling programs do provide good supervision and a climate in which growth is encouraged, every professional counselor must accept responsibility for her own growth, even when the local situation does not encourage it.

ETHICAL PRINCIPLES OF GROUP WORK

A number of organizations have written about the ethical guidelines involved when working in groups. These include the American Association for Counseling and Development, the Association for Specialists in Group Work, the American Psychological Association, the National Association of Social Workers, the American Mental-Health Counselors Association, the American Association for Marriage and Family Therapy, American Group Psychotherapy Association, and the International Association of Applied Social Scientists. In order to function effectively as a group counselor, the professional counselor must have a thorough grounding in the ethical principles that govern the profession. It is expected that the training program a student completes will have a course on professional practice, a professional seminar, or a course specifically devoted to ethics; and that from this course will come a clear understanding of professional practice and appropriate ethical behavior. The following discussion provides some clarification of topics that may provide ethical dilemmas for practicing counselors.

Counselor Self-knowledge

A first assumption for developing an ethical stance is to know oneself. This involves having each counselor address the question: "What needs of mine are being met through my work?" All people have emotional and psychological needs. In some fields, there is no attempt to examine the importance of the needs for the persons who practice in that field. In counseling, however, this is very important. The process should begin early in the graduate program by having each student address the question of what needs will be met in providing counseling. While most students are able to identify ways in which they will be able to help others, few students enter training fully aware of their own needs.

Individual needs can be studied and understood more fully from a variety of ways. First, in class it is important to have that issue be addressed. A person who is not aware of her own needs is not going to be particularly respondent to the needs of others. Also, a person who is so closed to her own experiencing of life is not likely to be open to others, nor to be aware of the impact that person may have on another.

Since counselors may use the counseling process to help fulfill emotional needs, it is important to be aware of what those needs are. This can be a topic covered in sensitivity training groups, or even in counseling groups in which students participate. It would be an important criteria for the training committee to be aware of and to use in evaluating who should be allowed to continue in the program versus those who should not continue.

The basic function of the group is to serve the needs of the group members. A person who is unable to attend first to the members of the group is ethically bound to seek supervision and/or counseling in order to help become more available to group members.

Community and Legal Standards

The group counselor must not only be open to the experiences of the members of the group, but must also be aware of community standards, legal limitations to work, and state laws governing the practice of group counseling. A number of resources have been prepared recently specifically addressing legal and ethical guidelines for counselors, including *Ethical and Legal Issues in Counseling and Psychotherapy* by Van Hoose and Kottler (1977); *Law and Ethics in Counseling* by Hummel, Talbutt, and Alexander (1985); *The Counselor and the Law* by Hopkins and Anderson, (1985); *Ethical, Legal and Professional Issues in the Practice of Marriage and Family Therapy* by Huber and Baruth (1987); *The*

Law and the Practice of Human Services by Woody; *Issues and Ethics in the Helping Profession* by Corey, Corey, and Callanan (1984) and *Ethics in Psychology* by Keith-Spiegel and Koocher (1985).

In addition to these resources, which provide information about the legal and ethical practices of counseling, counselors must be familiar with the state and local laws governing the practice of counseling. This can be learned by contacting state departments of education, state psychology boards, and becoming involved in state associations such as the state division of AACD and ASGW as well as the state psychology board. Other professional resources include attorneys who work for particular organizations such as community mental-health centers, school boards, and other organizations.

Beyond the legal guidelines that must be addressed, counselors should be aware of the cultural norms operating. Familiarity with community standards can be obtained by talking with other counselors, school teachers and administrators, community mental-health workers, and local clergy. A number of counselors, while not violating any law, have found their practice in jeopardy as a result of not being familiar with local norms.

Specific Ethical Issues for Groups

Information about the Group

Clients who join a group should do so with full information about the group. This information will generally be learned through the counselor's presentation to a class or larger group in which the purpose of the group is explained, as well as what people can expect if they agree to participate. In addition to the information that has been provided in other chapters, particularly the description in Chapter 1 of the presentation, the counselor should prepare a self-disclosure statement that would provide participants with information about the counselor. This information should include:

- name
- educational background
- licenses or certificates related to the work
- specific training in group work
- experiences in group work
- theoretical orientation or model from which the counselor operates
- expected length of the group in hours and weeks
- other information that might be relevant to people deciding whether to participate

Once people have decided that they are interested in participating in the group, more-extensive information should be shared, including any information that would influence participation. This would include: any research that would be conducted related to the group; whether any observers would be watching the group through observation mirrors; whether (and what type) of recordings might be made; rules and guidelines for the group, including confidentiality, not hurting others in the group, respect of privacy, and related issues.

Voluntary Membership

A second issue is voluntary membership in the group. Since the purpose of group counseling is to help people who want to make some changes in their behavior or their life circumstances, the group is not designed for people who are there involuntarily. When the group presentation is made, it should be stressed that participation is available to those who are interested, but that it is not a requirement or a mandatory experience. Some persons who initially are not voluntary may be included in the group if they change their position from resistant to active participant. An example would be in a school setting: If an assistant principal insists that a student come for counseling, the counselor can explain the advantages of being in the group and describe how the group might work with the student to help him figure out ways to get along with teachers and other students more effectively. If, however, the student insists that he does not want the experience and refuses to participate, he should not be put in the group. He has a right not to be a member; and the counselor should respect the student's right to experience the consequences of his behavior.

Case Example.   In a family therapy project underway by one of the authors (Horne), parents are invited to participate in group counseling. Some parents do not want the experience, and so the counselor explains to them that they do not have to participate. But the parents will hear something like this:

> I can understand that being in the parents' group is somewhat scary: You haven't done anything like this before. I also can see how you are a little angry even being here; as I understand, this wasn't your idea and you don't like being told by the school to come here. I'll tell you what. I don't like you having to be here either, to be forced to come down here. What I'll do, if you are interested, is work with you in the group. You do the exercises we go over in the group and in exchange for the participation, I'll see if I can't get the school off your back, see if I can get your son back in school right away. No guarantees, of course, but we've had some really good success in the past in helping parents get the school off their back, being more cooperative. Would you like to try this with me?

Terminating

Once group members have agreed to participate, they are allowed to drop out at any time. They are required, though, to come to the counselor and explain in person why they are dropping out. This is presented this way:

> You may leave the group at any point. There are a couple of requirements that I have, though, and we need to understand these and agree to them before starting. First, you may withdraw from the group for whatever reasons you have. But you must come and tell me; you can't just drop out by not showing up. This is to be certain that if you decide to stop coming and there are unfinished issues or if you have a problem with either me or the group, that I can make a referral for you to another counselor or another group experience. I am obliged to not have you hurt by the experience; if you are, I would want to know so that you can have help at once. The other requirement is that you would need to discuss your leaving with me and preferably with the group. If you can't share with the group, then you need to share with me so that I can explain to the group why you aren't going to be participating any more.

Understanding Risks

Any form of growth can lead to possible hurt or risk of damaging relationships. It may be that growth on the part of one person causes problems for someone else; and as counselors, we are ethically bound to let participants know that detrimental circumstances may occur. For example, in counseling with women who wish to become more assertive, it is important to discuss the ramifications of their becoming more assertive on their other relationships.

A husband, for example, may not want the changes, and a employer may not value the change at all. Children who have taken advantage of the nonassertive mother, and other relatives who have enjoyed the advantages of the lack of assertiveness, have much to lose. This is not to say that the client should not become assertive. On the contrary, it is most likely important for her to become more in control of her own life. But there will definitely be consequences for the change; and the counselor needs to discuss the possible advantages, and disadvantages, inherent in the process of growth.

There are constantly risks involved in change and the counselor should review what the potential risks are. If a counselor has not reviewed the potential for harm with the clients she is seeing, the awareness of possible harm could come in the form of observing it after the fact, when the client may develop great anger or distrust of counseling as a result of being at risk without a warning that it may come.

Confidentiality

Confidentiality is a very difficult subject for group counselors. When providing individual counseling, a counselor can by and large assure confidentiality because only two people are involved: If a confidence is broken, the client has only himself to blame. In a group setting, however, there are additional risks involved. Therefore, the counselor should be aware that there can be no absolute guarantee of confidentiality—and this should be shared with the group. On the other hand, the group can agree to maintain a confidential relationship and can discuss what will happen if there are breaches. The counselor, though, should explain to participants that what happens is beyond the control of the counselor and that clients each have to be responsible for the amount of information they are willing to share.

Case Example. In an adolescent correctional facility where one of the authors (Horne) conducted groups, the issue of confidentiality had three different caveats: First, the counselor was obligated to report any threats against another inmate, against a correctional officer or teacher, or any suicidal threats. Second, the counselor had to report any incidents or threats of setting fires, very dangerous activity in the facility. Third, any indications one of the members would attempt to break out had to be reported. All group members knew this and agreed to the information. Interestingly, a number of the members shared the information anyway, and the topic was dealt with in the group prior to having to report the information to guards. In this situation, the counselor worked to be certain there was a limit on the amount of disclosure that occurred since it was important to remember that confidentiality is very difficult to maintain in a correctional facility.

What we learned was that issues that dealt with group members or with personal issues were kept confidential but issues related to others in the facility who were not in the group spread very quickly throughout the correctional center. For example, one adolescent in the group indicated he was going to get even with another person who was not in the group. In less than an hour after the group ended, most people in the facility knew what had been said and were prepared to follow the two protagonists around to watch the fight begin.

It is the counselor's responsibility to set the stage for confidentiality; it is the members' responsibility to carry it out.

SUMMARY

The professional preparation of counselors requires that selection procedures be developed which identify only those with the highest potential to be admitted into the training program. This is professionally responsible both for the program and for the student: programs should not put students through training for which they are not suited, and students not suited for the training should not be allowed to go out and practice in a manner that is less than excellent. Programs are obligated to develop screening programs which are fair and predictive of successful learning of therapeutic skills.

The skills to be learned by students have been identified by professional organizations, and it is the responsibility of training programs to ensure that the components necessary for effective cognitive and skill development are included. In particular, ASGW's *Professional Standards for Training Group Counselors* should comprise the framework for training in group work. Knowledge areas as well as clinical practice is essential for effective group counselor training. Experiential components, in which students are able to experience various types of groups, are necessary, as well as the opportunity for students to attend to their own personal adjustment and growth.

While it is the responsibility of the program to be familiar with and to adopt the ASGW standards for training and for evaluating students, it is the responsibility of students to evaluate programs to which they are applying and to be certain that the program they select in fact provides quality training. Programs which fail to attract quality students will either improve standards and teaching/training performance or will continue to decline.

Once students have completed their training, they should seek certification and professional recognition by one or more of the organizations which recognize counselors for their accomplishments. Membership in professional organizations indicates counselors take pride in their work and professional identity, and it provides the opportunity to work with other professionals, as well as to participate in continuing education experiences.

Counselors also need to recognize that the completion of their degree does not mark the completion of their learning needs. In addition to learning through workshops and training at professional conferences and in-service experiences, counselors need to identify within their school, agency, or community a respected counselor with whom they may establish on-going peer consultation. It is through regular peer supervision that counselors are able to identify counter-transference issues, recognize the development of ineffective patterns of counseling, and receive professional advice for improving counseling or checking out areas of concern.

Within the community it is the responsibility of the counselor to remain current and aware of ethical guidelines, state laws and regulations, and standards of professional practice. These areas are in a period of great change, and in order to provide quality services, maintain professional skills, and serve the employing institution or practice, it is essential that the counselor remain current. The professional standards for group counseling are continually being upgraded, and practitioners are expected to remain familiar with current practice standards.

REFERENCES

Association for Specialists in Group Work. (1983). *Professional standards for training of group counselors.* Alexandria, VA: Author.

Capuzzi, D., & Muffett, L. (1980). An overview of ethical standards for group facilitators. *Journal of Specialists in Group Work, 5,* 98–106.

Carkhuff, R. R. (1969). *Helping and human relations: A primer for lay and professional helpers* (Vol. 1). New York: Holt, Rinehart and Winston.

Carkhuff, R. R. (1972). New directions in training for the helping professions: Toward a technology for human and community resource development. *The Counseling Psychologist, 3,* 12–30.

Carr, E.; Merz, D.; Peterson, J. V.; & Thayer, L. (1972). Development of a critical incident tape. *Journal of Counseling Psychology, 19,* 188–191.

Corey, G.; Corey, M.; & Callanan, P. (1984). *Issues and ethics in the helping professions* (2nd ed.). Monterey, CA: Brooks/Cole.

Dies, R. R. (1974). Attitudes toward the training of group psychotherapists. *Small Group Behavior, 5,* 55–78.

Hopkins, B. R., & Anderson, B. S. (1985). *The counselor and the law.* Alexandria, VA: AACD Press.

Huber, C., & Baruth, L. (1987). *Ethical, legal and professional issues in the practice of marriage and family therapy.* Columbus, OH: Merrill.

Huhn, R.; Zimpfer, D.; Waltman, D.; & Williamson, S. (1985). A survey of professional preparation for group counseling. *Journal for Specialists in Group Work, 10,* 124–133.

Hummel, D.; Talbutt, L.; & Alexander, D. (1985). *Law and ethics in counseling.* New York: Van Nostrand.

Jacobs, E.; Brown, D.; & Randolph, A. (1974). Educating group counselors: A tentative model. *Counselor Education and Supervision, 13,* 307–309.

Kottler, J. A. (1981). The development of guidelines for training group leaders: A synergistic model. *Journal for Specialists in Group Work, 6,* 125–129.

Keith-Spiegel, P., & Koocher, G. (1985). *Ethics in psychology.* New York: Random House.

Lechowicz, J. S., & Gazda, G. M. (1975) Group counseling instruction: Objectives established by experts. *Counselor Education and Supervision, 15,* 21–27.

Ohlsen, M. M. (1975). Group leader preparation. *Counselor Education and Supervision, 14,* 215–220.

Smith, E. (1976). Issues and problems in group supervision of beginning group problems. *Counselor Education and Supervision, 16,* 13–24.

Stockton, R. (1980). The education of group leaders: A review of the literature with suggestions for the future. *Journal for Specialists in Group Work, 5,* 55–62.

Van Hoose, W. H., & Kottler, J. A. (1977). *Ethical and legal issues in counseling and psychotherapy.* San Francisco: Jossey Bass.

Woody, R. H. (1984). *The law and the practice of human services.* San Francisco: Jossey-Bass.

Yalom, I. (1985). *The theory and practice of group psychotherapy* (3rd. ed.). New York: Basic Books.

Zimpfer, D. G.; Waltman, D. E.; Williamson, S. K.; & Huhn, R. P. (1985). Professional training standards in group counseling: Idealistic or realistic? *Journal for Specialists in Group Work, 10,* 134–143.

Appendix A

ASGW PROFESSIONAL STANDARDS FOR GROUP COUNSELING

PREAMBLE

Whereas counselors may be able to function effectively with individual clients, they are also required to possess specialized knowledge and skills that render them effective in group counseling. The Association for Specialists in Group Work supports the preparation of group practitioners as part of and in addition to counselor education. The *Professional Standards for Group Counseling* represent the minimum core of group leader (cognitive and applied) competencies that have been identified by the Association for Specialists in Group Work.

DEFINITION OF GROUP COUNSELING

Consists of the interpersonal processes and activities focused on conscious thoughts and behavior performed by individuals who have the professional credentials to work with and counsel groups of individuals regarding career, educational, personal, social and developmentally related concerns, issues, tasks or problems.

Approved by the ASGW Executive Board, March 20, 1983.
Source: Association for Specialists in Group Work, Alexandria Va.: Author, 1983. Reproduced by permission.

398

DESIGNATED GROUP COUNSELING AREAS

In order to work as a professional in group counseling, an individual must meet and demonstrate minimum competencies in the generic core of group counseling standards. These are applicable to all training programs regardless of level of work or specialty area. In addition to the generic core competencies, (and in order to practice in a specific area of expertise) the individual will be required to meet one or more specialty area standards (school counseling and guidance, student personnel services in high education, or community/mental health agency counseling).

GROUP COUNSELOR KNOWLEDGE COMPETENCIES

The qualified group leader has *demonstrated specialized knowledge* in the following aspects of group work:

1. Be able to state for at least three major theoretical approaches to group counseling the distinguishing characteristics of each and the commonalities shared by all.
2. Basic principles of group dynamics and the therapeutic ingredients of groups.
3. Personal characteristics of group leaders that have an impact on members; knowledge of personal strengths, weaknesses, biases, values and their impact on others.
4. Specific ethical problems and considerations unique to group counseling.
5. Body of research on group counseling in one's specialty area (school counseling, college students personnel, or community/mental health agency).
6. Major modes of group work, differentiation among the modes, and the appropriate instances in which each is used (such as group guidance, group counseling, group therapy, human relations training, etc.)
7. Process components involved in typical stages of a group's development (i.e., characteristics of group interaction and counselor roles).
8. Major facilitative and debilitative roles that group members may take.
9. Advantages and disadvantages of group counseling and the circumstances for which it is indicated or contraindicated.

GROUP COUNSELOR COMPETENCIES

The qualified group leader has shown the following abilities:

1. To screen and assess readiness levels of prospective clients.
2. To deliver a clear, concise, and complete definition of group counseling.
3. To recognize self-defeating behaviors of group members.

4. To describe and conduct a personally selected group counseling model appropriate to the age and clientele of group leader's specialty area(s).
5. To identify accurately nonverbal behavior among group members.
6. To exhibit appropriate pacing skills involved in stages of a group's development.
7. To identify and intervene effectively at critical incidents in the group process.
8. To work appropriately with disruptive group members.
9. To make use of the major strategies, techniques, and procedures of group counseling.
10. To provide and use procedures to assist transfer and support of changes by group members in the natural environment.
11. To use adjunct group structures such as psychological homework (i.e., self-monitoring, contracting).
12. To use basic group leader interventions such as process comments, empathic responses, self-disclosures, confrontations, etc.
13. To facilitate therapeutic conditions and forces in group counseling.
14. To work cooperatively and effectively with a co-leader.
15. To open and close sessions, and terminate the group process.
16. To provide follow-up procedures to assist maintenance and support of group members.
17. To utilize assessment procedures in evaluating effects and contributions of group counseling.

Table 1   Training in Clinical Practice

Type of Supervised Experience	*Minimum Number of [clock] Hours Required: Master's or Entry Level Program*
1. Critique of group tapes (by self or others)	5
2. Observing group counseling (live or media presentation)	5
3. Participating as a member in a group	15
4. Leading a group with a partner and receiving critical feedback from a supervisor	15
5. Practicum: Leading a group alone, with critical self-analysis of performance; supervisor feedback on tape; and self-analysis	15
6. Fieldwork of Internship: Practice as a group leader with on-the-job supervision	25

Appendix B

ETHICAL GUIDELINES FOR GROUP LEADERS[1]

PREAMBLE

One characteristic of any professional group is the possession of a body of knowledge and skills and mutually acceptable ethical standards for putting them into practice. Ethical standards consist of those principles which have been formally and publicly acknowledged by the membership of a profession to serve as guidelines governing professional conduct, discharge of duties, and resolution or moral dilemmas. In this document, the Association of Specialists in Group Work has identified the standards of conduct necessary to maintain and regulate the high standards of integrity and leadership among its members.

The Association for Specialists in Group Work recognizes the basic commitment of its members to the Ethical Standards of its parent organization, the American Association for Counseling and Development, and nothing in this document shall be construed to supplant that code. These standards are intended to complement the AACD standards in the area of group work by clarifying the nature of ethical responsibility of the counselor in the group setting and by stimulating a greater concern for competent group leadership.

The following ethical guidelines have been organized under three categories: the leader's responsibility for providing information about group work to clients, the group leader's responsibility for providing group counseling services to clients, and the group leader's responsibility for safeguarding the standards of ethical practice.

[1]Approved by the ASGW Executive Board, November 11, 1980.

A. Responsibility for Providing Information about Group Work and Group Services

    A–1. Group leaders shall fully inform group members, in advance and preferably in writing, of the goals in the group, qualifications of the leader, and procedures to be employed.

    A–2. The group leader shall conduct a pre-group interview with each prospective member for purposes of screening, orientation, and, in so far as possible, shall select group members whose needs and goals are compatible with the established goals of the group; who will not impede the group process; and whose well-being will not be jeopardized by the group experience.

    A–3. Group leaders shall protect members by defining clearly what confidentiality means, why it is important, and the difficulties involved in enforcement.

    A–4. Group leaders shall explain, as realistically as possible, exactly what services can and cannot be provided within the particular group structure offered.

    A–5. Group leaders shall provide prospective clients with specific information about any specialized or experimental activities in which they may be expected to participate.

    A–6. Group leaders shall stress the personal risks involved in any group, especially regarding potential life-changes, and help group members explore their readiness to face these risks.

    A–7. Group leaders shall inform members that participation is voluntary and that they may exit from the group at any time.

    A–8. Group leaders shall inform members about recording of sessions and how tapes will be used.

B. Responsibility for Providing Group Services to Clients

    B–1. Group leaders shall protect member rights against physical threats, intimidation, coercion, and undue peer pressure insofar as is reasonably possible.

    B–2. Group leaders shall refrain from imposing their own agendas, needs, and values on group members.

    B–3. Group leaders shall insure to the extent that it is reasonably possible that each member has the opportunity to utilize group resources and interact within the group by minimizing barriers such as rambling and monopolizing time.

    B–4. Group leaders shall make every reasonable effort to treat each member individually and equally.

    B–5. Group leaders shall abstain from inappropriate personal relationships with members throughout the duration of the group and any subsequent professional involvement.

    B–6. Group leaders shall help promote independence of members from the group in the most efficient period of time.

B–7. Group leaders shall not attempt any technique unless thoroughly trained in its use or under supervision by an expert familiar with the intervention.

B–8. Group leaders shall not condone the use of alcohol or drugs directly prior to or during group sessions.

B–9. Group leaders shall make every effort to assist clients in developing their personal goals.

B–10. Group leaders shall provide between-session consultation to group members and follow-up after termination of the group, as needed or requested.

C. Responsibility for Safeguarding Ethical Practice

C–1. Group leaders shall display these standards or make them available to group members.

C–2. Group leaders have the right to expect ethical behavior from colleagues and are obligated to rectify or disclose incompetent, unethical behavior demonstrated by a colleague by taking the following actions:

(a) To confront the individual with the apparent violation of ethical guidelines for the purposes of protecting the safety of any clients and to help the group leader correct any inappropriate behaviors.

(b) Such a complaint should be made in writing and include the specific facts and dates of the alleged violation and all relevant supporting data. The complaint should be forwarded to:

The Ethics Committee
c/o The President
Association of Specialists in Group Work
599 Stevenson Avenue
Alexandria, Virginia 22304

The envelope must be marked "CONFIDENTIAL" in order to assure confidentiality for both the accuser(s) and the alleged violator(s). Upon receipt, the President shall (a) check on membership status of the charged member(s), (b) confer with legal counsel, and (c) send the case with all pertinent documents to the chairperson of the ASGW Ethics Committee within ten (10) working days after the receipt of the complaint.

(c) If it is determined by the Ethics and Professional Standards Committee that the alleged breach of ethical conduct constitutes a violation of the "Ethical Guidelines," then an investigation will be started within ten (10) days by at least one member of the Committee plus two additional ASGW members in the locality of the alleged violation. The investigating committee chairperson shall: (a) acknowledge receipt of the complaint, (b) review the complaint and supporting data, (c) send a letter of acknowledgement to the member(s) of the complaint regarding alleged violations along with a request for a response and relevant information related to the complaint and (e) inform member of the Ethics Committee by letter of the case and present a plan of action for investigation.

(d) All information, correspondence, and activities of the Ethics Committee will remain confidential. It shall be determined that no person serving as an investigator on a case have any disqualifying relationship with the alleged violator(s).

(e) This charged party(ies) will have not more than 30 days in which to answer the charges in writing. The charged party(ies) will have free access to all cited evidence from which to make a defense, including the right to legal counsel and a formal hearing before the ASGW Ethics Committee.

(f) Based upon the investigation of the Committee and any designated local ASGW members one of the following recommendations may be made to the Executive Board for appropriate action:

1. Advise that the charges be dropped.
2. Reprimand and admonishment against repetition of the charged conduct.
3. Notify the charged member(s) of his/her right to a formal hearing before the ASGW Ethics Committee, and request a response be made to the Ethics Chairperson as to his/her decision on the matter. Such hearing would be conducted in accordance with the AACD Policy and Procedures for Processing Complaints of Ethical Violations, "Procedures for Hearings," and would be scheduled for a time coinciding with the annual AACD convention. Conditions for such hearing shall also be in accordance with the AACD Policy and Procedures document, "Options Available to the Ethics Committee, item 3."
4. Suspension of membership for a specified period from ASGW.
5. Dismissal from membership in ASGW.

Source: Association for Specialists in Group Work. Alexandria, Va.: Author, 1980. Reproduced by permission. Copyright AACD. No further reproduction approved without further permission of AACD.

Name Index

Subject Index